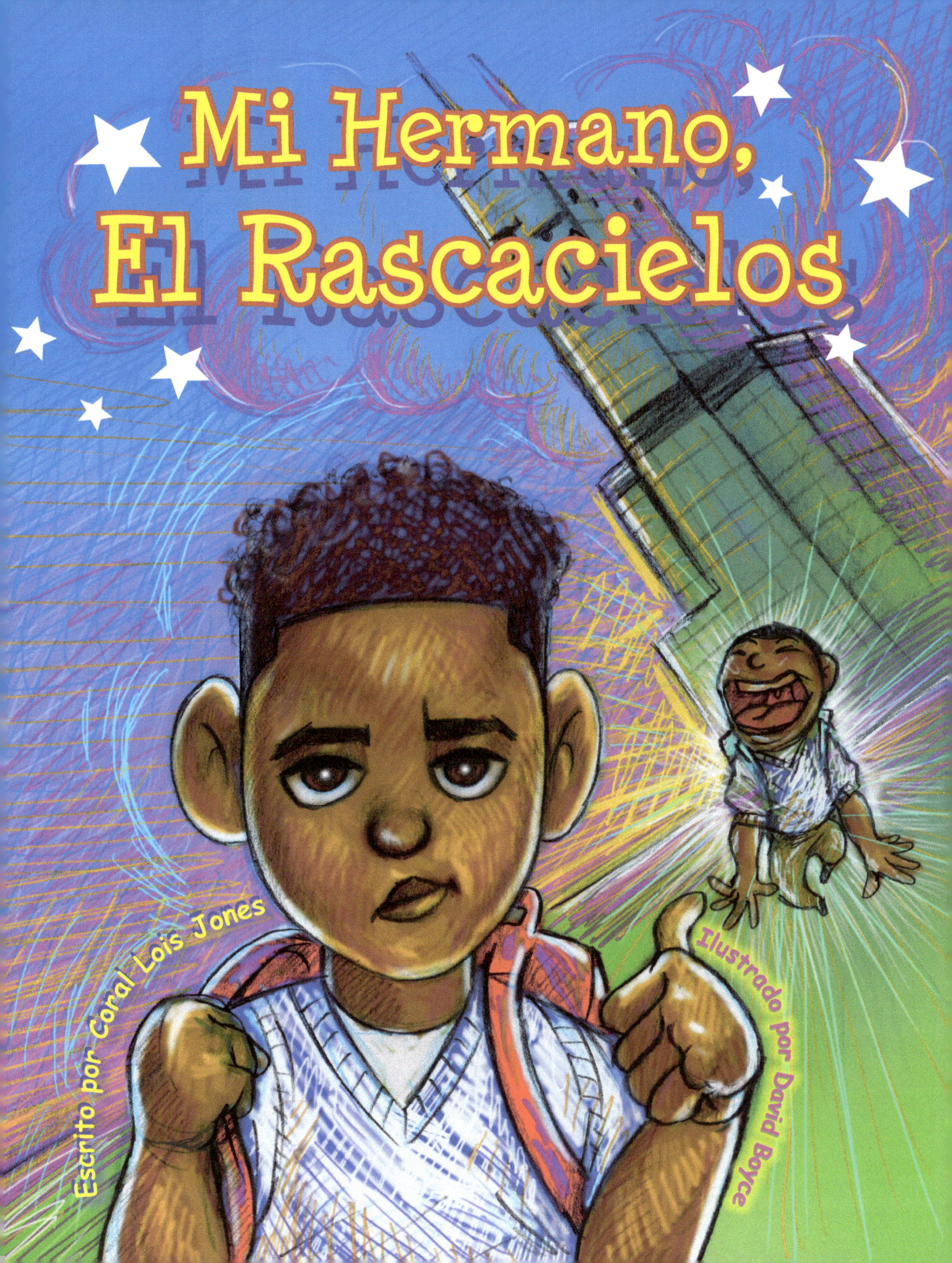

Este libro está dedicado
a Frank y Thelma Jones.

Escrito por Coral Lois Jones
Ilustrado y diseño por David Boyce
Editado por Eric Fannin
Traducción por Michelle Cacho Gómez

Derechos de Autor del Texto e Ilustración © 2021-2022 por Coral Lois Jones
Todos los derechos reservados, excepto aquellos permitidos bajo el Acta
De Derechos de Autor de 1976.
Ninguna parte de esta publicación deberá ser reproducida, distribuida o,
Transmitida de ninguna forma o por ningún medio, o almacenado en una
Base de datos o sistema de recuperación, sin el previo
Consentimiento escrito del editor.

Contenido

Estatua de la Libertad, Isla Libertad de Manhattan, Ciudad de Nueva York, Nueva York. River House, Grand Rapids, Michigan. Fifth Third Center, Toledo, Ohio. Torre Transamerica, Baltimore, Maryland. PNC Plaza, Raleigh, Carolina del Norte. Plaza Burnett, Fort Worth, Texas. Plaza del Banco de América, Atlanta, Georgia. Torre Eiffel, Paris, Francia. Torre Willis, Chicago, Illinois. Edificio Empire State, Manhattan Ciudad de Nueva York. Un Mundo Trade Center, Nueva York, Nueva York. Burj Khalifa, Dubai, Khalifa localizado en el parque Burj por Emaar.

Lyniell caminaba rápidamente con su hermano Cordaee a la Biblioteca Pública FranThel cuando tropezó con Luis. Boca abierta. Luis preguntó, "Cordaee, tu hermano es un rascacielos?"

Cardaee dijo, "No, Luis, recuerda que nuestro maestro nos dijo que un rascacielos es un edificio alto con varios pisos, y la mayoría de los rascacielos se encuentran en las ciudades. ¡No son seres humanos!

Luis preguntó, "¿Tu hermano es más alto que la Estatua de la Libertad, la estatua que se encuentra en la Isla Libertad?"

Cordaee dijo, "Bro, en el libro de historia de mi hermano, Vi una fotografía de la Estatua de la Libertad! Este rascacielos simboliza la libertad para los inmigrantes llegando a través del mar! ¡El grillete roto y la cadena en sus pies significa el fin de la esclavitud! ¡No! Mi hermano no es un rascacielos, pero es alto como uno."

Libertad Libertad
Libertad Libertad
Libertad Libertad
Libertad Libertad
Libertad Libertad
Libertad Libertad

Luis preguntó, "¿Tu hermano es más alto que River House? El edificio más alto de Grand Rapids, Michigan. ¡Ese edificio es alto! ¡El último piso es 121 metros (397 pies), y su techo es 124 metros (406 pies) con 34 pisos!"

Cordaee contestó, "¡No, él solo es alto como un rascacielos, pero es mi hermano!

Luis continuó preguntando, "¿Tu hermano es más alto que el Fifth Third Center en One Seagate en Toledo, Ohio? ¡Este rascacielos tiene 125 metros (411 pies) de altura y consiste de 29 pisos!"

Cordaee contestó, "¡No, pero sabías que mi mamá habló sobre las Toledo Mud Hens, un equipo de béisbol de ligas menores que juega dentro del Fifth Third Field! Cordaee contestó, "¡No, él es alto como un rascacielos, pero es mi hermano!

Luis preguntó, "¿Tu hermano es más alto que la Torre Transamerica en Baltimore, Maryland? ¡Ese rascacielos mide 161 metros (529 pies) y tiene 40 pisos!"

Cordaee contestó, "¡No, él solo es alto como un rascacielos, pero es mi hermano!

Luis tenía curiosidad y preguntó: "¿Tu hermano es más alto que la Plaza PNC en Raleigh, Carolina del Norte? ¡Ese rascacielos mide 164 metros (538 pies) con 33 pisos, y es el productor #1 de camotes de la nación!"

Cordaee contestó, "¡Oh! ¡No, él solamente es alto como un rascacielos, pero es mi hermano!

la Plaza PNC la plaza PNC la Plaza PNC la Plaza PNC

Luis pensó por un momento, luego preguntó, "¿Tu hermano es más alto que la Plaza Burnett en Fort Worth, Texas? ¡Ese rascacielos mide 173 metros (567 pies) de altura y tiene 40 pisos!"

Cordaee sacudió su cabeza y dijo, ¡No, él solamente es alto como un rascacielos! Oye, ¿sabías que a Fort Worth también se le conoce como Cow Town (Pueblo de Vacas)?"

La Plaza Burnett La Plaza Burnett

La Plaza Burnett La Plaza Burnett La Plaza Burnett La Plaza

Luis continuó preguntando, "¿Tu hermano es más alto que el rascacielos de La Plaza Banco de America en Atlanta, Georgia? ¡Este rascacielos tiene unos impresionantes 311 metros (1,023 pies) de altura, y tiene 55 pisos!"

Cordaee contestó, "Hablando de Atlanta, Hmmm... ¡No, él es solamente alto como un rascacielos, pero es mi hermano!"

Luis continuó con su cuestionamiento, "¿Tu hermano es más alto que la Torre Eiffel en París, Francia? ¡Ese rascacielos mide 324 metros (1,063 pies) a pesar de que solo tiene tres pisos!"

Cordaee contestó, "¡Oh! ¡No, él solamente es alto como un rascacielos, pero es mi hermano!"

Luis golpeó su pie y rascó su barbilla mientras trataba de pensar acerca de más edificios. Eventualmente, él dijo, "¿Tu hermano es más alto que la Torre Willis en Chicago, Illinois? ¡Ese rascacielos es de 442 metros (1,451 pies), 110 pisos!"

Cordaee contesto, "Chicago es el estado con el hot air politician, así es como la ciudad de los vientos recibió su nombre! ¡Oh, no, él solamente es alto como un rascacielos!

Torre Willis Torre Willis
Torre Willis Torre Willis
Torre Willis Torre Willis

Luis planteó otra pregunta diciendo, "¿Tu hermano es más alto que el Edificio Empire State en Manhattan, Ciudad de Nueva York? ¡Ese rascacielos mide 443.2 metros (1,454 pies) de alto, y tiene 102 pisos!

Cordaee dijo, "¡No, él es alto como un rascacielos, pero es mi hermano!"

Luis luego preguntó, "Tu hermano es más alto que el One World Trade Center en Nueva York, Nueva York? Ese rascacielos mide unos increíbles 541 metros (1,776 pies) con 104 pisos! ¿Sabías que es el edificio más alto en los Estados Unidos?"

Cordaee dijo, ¡No, él es solamente alto como un rascacielos, pero es mi hermano!"

One World Trade Center

Luis luego preguntó, "¿Tu hermano es más alto que el Burj Khalifa? Este rascacielos mide 828 metros (2,717 pies) de altura y tiene unos fascinantes 163 pisos! Es el rascacielos más alto del mundo!"

Cordaee dijo, ¡No, él es solamente alto como un rascacielos, pero es mi hermano!"

Burj Khalifa

Burj Khalifa

Eventualmente, Lyniell vino a recoger a Cordaee de la Biblioteca Publica Franthel. Hel dijo, "¿Estás listo? ¿Qué tal tu día?"

Luis saltaba hacia arriba y hacia abajo.

"¡Wow, tu hermanos es un rascacielos! ¡Yo quiero un hermano torre, también! ¡Uno que yo pueda aplaudir!" Cordaee se rió. "Mi mamá dijo que si él continúa comiendo y creciendo alto, ¡él va a comernos fuera de nuestra casa! Cordaee exclamó, "Un día, ¡yo voy a ser alto exactamente como él y tendré una gran carrera! ¡Solo espera y ya verás! ¡Te veo mañana, Luis!"

Rascacielos Rascacielos Rascacielos Rascacielos Rascacielos

Clave de Medidas

Metrico
1 kilometro (km) = 1,000 metros (m)
1 metro (m) = 100 centimetros (cm)
1 centimetro (cm) = 10 milímetros (mm)

Imperial
1 milla (mi) = 1,760 yardas (yd)
1 yarda (yd) = 3 pies (ft)
1 pie (ft) = 12 pulgadas (in.)

www.ingramcontent.com/pod-product-compliance
Lightning Source LLC
Chambersburg PA
CBHW050806220426
43209CB00088BA/1659

BEYOND TOURIST BRITAIN

One Hundred Scenes of Modest Grandeur

James R Warren

First Published in the United Kingdom in 2022 by Midland Tutorial Productions

First Edition: 15 June 2022

Text copyright: © James R Warren, 2008, 2022
Photographs: © James R Warren, 2008, 2022
Cover Design: © James R Warren, 2022

The right of James R Warren to be identified as the author of this work has been asserted in accordance with the Copyright, Designs and Patents Act 1988

All rights reserved.

No part of this publication may be reproduced, stored or transmitted in any form or by any means (including photocopying or storing it in any medium by electronic means and whether or not transiently or incidentally to some other use of this publication) without the written permission of the copyright owner, except in accordance with the provisions of the Copyright, Designs and Patents Act 1988.

This book may not be lent, resold, hired out or otherwise disposed of by way of trade in any form of binding or cover other than that in which it is published, without the prior consent of the Publishers.

File Prefix Code: BTB

ISBN 978 1 7396296 1 8

Midland Tutorial Productions Publishers
31 Victoria Avenue
Bloxwich
Walsall
WS3 3HS
United Kingdom

BEYOND TOURIST BRITAIN

One Hundred Scenes of
Modest Grandeur

James R Warren

MIDLAND TUTORIAL PRODUCTIONS
BLOXWICH

Wherefore by their fruits ye shall know them

The Words of Jesus Christ
Matthew 7:20

TABLE OF CONTENTS

		Page
Publication Information		V1
Title Page		R2
Epigraph		5
Table of Contents		7
Preface		9
Introduction		11
Chapter 1	The Life of the Spirit	15
Chapter 2	Residents of Grace	39
Chapter 3	The Living Rocks	59
Chapter 4	Crossing the Waters	73
Chapter 5	Saving the Sailors	95
Chapter 6	The Old Ways	115
Chapter 7	Little Towns	139
Chapter 8	Strivers in the Dawn	161
Chapter 9	Winning the Earth	197
Chapter 10	Providing the Power	229
Chapter 11	Production for Prosperity	241
Chapter 12	Making the Modern World	273
Chapter 13	Changing Trade	311
Chapter 14	Art and Landscape	337
Chapter 15	Defence and Decline	363
Conclusion		383
Understanding Picture Co-ordinates		385
British Units of Measurement		389
List of Website References		391
List of Book References		403
List of Journal References		409

Preface

To the Archaics of The Bronze Age and the Early Iron Age these Fortunate Islands were a possibly mythical and certainly barbarous adjunct to the periphery of things. Frigid and storm-swept they were an exile mitigated only by their inaccessibility. Not even the most prescient could have forecast that the isles would become the mother of empires and the midwife of our modern world.

Through a chance conjunction of circumstances Britain has become through its language, its society and its technical traditions the most influential nation on Earth.

Britain and Ireland's contribution to Civilisation is at least the equal of France and almost stands comparison with the contributions of Italy and China, though those truly great nations are very different to each other, and to Britain.

Should these words offend you then I apologise for that hurt. You have a right and duty to favour your country and to celebrate its many virtues. I suppose that I am a romantic nationalist of sorts, painfully alive to the old dictum that a patriot loves his country whereas a nationalist hates others, for I hope to present the face of my homeland with malice to none.

In a limited and eclectic way I can only present to you some of the images and words that evince the character of my country, knowing that you can and will form your own view, since if you could not you would not have read beyond my first twenty-eight words.

If you wish to read of castles and kings, or to inspect their splendors, then you will find little of interest in these pages, for I know little of these things, but know much of the common people and the little creatures who share their homesteads, and something of the works of the humble.

Do not mistake my meaning: I am very critical of Britain's current condition and even of its history. Mature love recognises the faults of its object and lives despite them.

Modern Britain has many serious problems, not least of which is its failure to integrate several minority communities, some of which are indigenous cultures of considerable size. We are possibly living through the last days of The United Kingdom, as a sovereign federation of states. The concept is probably as obsolete as its name implies but Britain and Ireland shall strive on as the living genius of the land and the people, moving forward into the fogs of history as uncertain and indescriable as any of the shifting mists that cloaked the coasts of ancient Albion.

Bloxwich
9 October 2007

Introduction

I heard some time ago that the UK has 191 ghosts on the square mile.

You may wonder how on Earth (or anywhere else) such a statistic was arrived at.

If this is so then the ambulant dead outnumber the sentient living in 6239 of the Union's 94526 square miles.

Perhaps this is why the Kingdoms are so static, for it seems that the British are as loath to win the deprecations of posterity as the reproaches of revenants.

They inhabit a zone of shades and shadows in which the very diversity of the land and the light seems to yield a heap of disparate clutter that relates to nothing rational and little coherent.

And yet the atoms and elements of the British Scene appear, suggestive here and allusive there, to record and perpetuate a few grand themes.

Throughout this series of pictures it seemed to me that three big motifs developed: Migration, the Sea, and Industrialism.

Of course you will object that these are trite characteristics of The Island Nations taken for granted by any schoolchild who does Geography. And so they are.

But it is striking how a random selection of photographs taken over thirty-five years collectively develop this impression. As I formulated the first few chapters it struck me how many of the creatures most familiar to my garden were immigrants to my land: Delilah, my Korean Wife's intelligent gray squirrel friend; the Oxford ragwort that took home in my herbaceous border to the great satisfaction of a city of little hornets, and whose fellow I chanced to capture on film atop a Highland hill; even the humble but delightful *Helix aspersa*.

The migratory theme also pops up in the least expected places: The antecedence of Holloway Prison, the necessity of Oxwich Castle, even the genesis of Stonehaven.

The pictures and their textual accompaniments have little to tell us about the social, cultural or ecological implications of all this to-ing and fro-ing. All they show is the naked fact of it, the ancient and persisting act of it, for to the Canada Goose and whole squadrons of smaller creatures Amber One is always clear for landing.

Migration is related more than tangentially to the two other great British themes, the Sea and Industrialism, that appear together in lockstep, like the obverse and reverse of an old Britannia penny.

To launch a fleet and keep it at sea requires heavy industries, not all obviously maritime or even coastal. Both our maritime trade and industries had a genesis sometime around the signing of The Treaty of Utrecht which swept Spanish and Dutch power from the seas; reached an apogee sometime around The Great Exhibition; and persisted into the last half of the last century. The Thatcher Reforms of the early 1980's destroyed the bulk of the British industrial base, and the Merchant Navy withered. Further culls of mining and manufacturing in 1992 and 2005 have left little of either British shipping or landward industry.

That review makes maritime and industrial strength seem entirely politically-dependent, but neither is principally so. Maritime trade was indispensable to an island. The organic bearing capacity of the British land is eleven million humans, but even when the population was that Britain had to import food, because much of the land was waste. Mining and manufacture were often foisted upon an unwilling populace by the realities of geology and demography. On the Exposed Coal Measures, a significant part of total area, the land was and is too poor viably to support arable agriculture, whilst many metalliferous areas were overlain by toxic gossans where even pasture was impracticable. Such wastelands were often the resort of squatters too poor to purchase land, or debarred for religious reasons from its possession. Such cruel exigency compelled the hewing of coal, the smelting of metals, and the raising of steam. For sure, science as well as seals lubricated the wheels of progress. But it is difficult to see how Davy and Faraday could have performed their great feats without the copper and vitriol provided by what in their day was already the greatest source of both. And of course both France and Italy have older traditions in mathematics and the sciences, but in those lands the Sun shines kindly, the wind blows balmily, and fruits ripen untended.

The marine-industrial nexus is obvious enough in the sailorly sections about lighthouses and ferries and the like but also pops up in the very sealess center of England in South Staffordshire where The Horseley Coal and Iron Company built the first iron steamer, or Chance Brothers cast lighthouse lanterns. Neither firm is with us today, but both were thirty years ago.

A consequence of naval power projection is that since The Treaty of Utrecht only two small campaigns have waged over the home islands, and the last of those was in 1746. Therefore, there are happily only a limited number of articles about war fixtures. Research of the few pictures I have about this was hampered by the extreme secrecy of The British Government and in particular the operation of the 1911 Official Secrets Act. This also frustrated the finding of production statistics regarding Geevor and certain other metal mines. In 1913 The Mining Records Office was disbanded and itemisations of UK metal mine production were no longer publicly available. Such statistics continued, however, to be logged because annual totals by long tons of reduced element continued to be divulged. (That might seem rather to defeat the object of secrecy, but you know what governments are like). Problems are even greater with overtly military affairs. Events at Chartley were occluded by both time and design, and for my commentary upon that I have relied totally upon some magnificent forensic work by historians. In the case of the Fauld Disaster my controversial interpretation has depended upon contemporary newspaper reports that quoted eyewitnesses, and my own geological inspection of the site.

Some sections concern sculptures or other art works "found" in public places, some very remote. Most are representational and several explore religious themes or the electric tension between man and woman, a topic not foreign to Holy Scripture. Two of these scenes are pub signs and one of those celebrates the Irish mendicant lady St Melangell who emigrated to a Welsh fastness some fourteen centuries ago.

Melangell's rescue of her hare would have had even deeper levels of delighted resonance to the Pagan Celts who cherished her than it does today, but it leads us to a cluster of images that are the first in this book and the last in this introduction.

The Life of the Spirit interpenetrates everything else in the British and Irish landscape, only sometimes overtly. And it is with this Life that our brief conspectus ends. Although much is lost to time enough survives to see our themes of land, sea and movement come full circle in the stories of Melangell, Medoc and even the Buddhists of Ladywood as the existential story of Britain roils and churns without close.

Enjoy.

Bloxwich
1 January 2008

CHAPTER ONE

The Life of the Spirit

In the beginning the land was vacant.

They say that Mesolithic adventurers first trespassed the coastal fastnesses of our West by wading a marsh form Picardy, unless such were anticipated by Swanscombe Man or someone.

No one knows why they came and it is now too late to ask.

Perhaps they were led by the clouded shadows of the shifting light or intrigued by the purpose of the retreating skeins of Spring who surely would not flee, free in flight as they were, to a foodless waste?

Today men come to escape hopeless poverty, or to evade the attentions of police in the own countries. Strangely, it is this latter cause that most identifies with the motives of The Holy Saints of The Dark Ages. We know that Columba came to escape a murder charge and Patrick to desert a slavemaster, whilst their colleagues and contemporaries often, or usually, had similar bleak tales to tell.

But Faith, like art, is born of suffering. And if Columba or Patrick preached the Word of Christ then to them it surely was a Promise, and to their heathen auditors a Welcome.

Some years ago I was at the tiny hamlet of Ilam on the empty hem of The White Peak. On a sunlit winter's morning you savor the peace of the dry lawn, and the ancient pines nursing the simple stone church before the cool green hills. You know that if you fancy it you can have a cappuccino and a chocolate cake in the tearoom, or hire a room nearby, or if you do not you can motor in air-conditioned comfort to somewhere more appealing.

Bertram did not arrive in a Volvo. For many months he and his wife struggled over the Cambrian Mountains after alighting from Ireland, presumably not from aboard a millstone. Somewhere along their eastward way his wife fell pregnant. As they entered a thick forest on a hillside the snows began to fall and the starving wife could walk no further. Bertram found a cave. Settling her therein he walked down the valley of the Dove to find food. When he returned he found that his wife had given birth, but that wolves had devoured both she and their newborn. Bertram returned to the valley village and never left, certainly in body and perhaps in spirit, for his tomb is in the tiny church that bears his name forever.

If you know Staffordshire or any part of England you may find it difficult to associate with man-eating wolves or indeed with Christianity, but though the wolves are long gone, the Faith has taken root and clung, like a gnarled and blasted thorn in the seemingly parched and barren soil of The Peak.

At a sublime level sex is a theme common to many tales of the Northern spirit. In the warmer climes of Italy or of Asia Minor the warmth of the flesh was not as vital and men and women could more readily consider the metaphysical.

Irish Madoc's story is closely alike to that of Saxon Winifred who died at the hand of a suitor less chivalrous that he who demanded of Melangel her Eostral hare. But where Winifred's head fell, also in Wales, a copious spring of pure water arose reminiscent of that which Christ, who thirsted at the Well of Sychar, promised of the Spirit to the flirtatious Woman of Samaria (John 4:5-26). And typical too of the many wellsprings of Celtic Britain, blessed of the Saints and more ancient cranial cults.

These wells refresh body and spirit today as any who have drunk at Winifred's or any other Welsh or Cornish fount can testify. But why visit a well when the Immanence of God is omnipresent pervading the cool pellucid air of a Northern dawn, as indispensable as water, and as vital as the oxygen it conceals?

Oxygen a preacher revealed but knew not.

Occasionally, when walking or driving across the British landscape you cross some clouded dell where a ruined nunnery or monastery may come to view. These too remember misbegotten trysts. For the guilt and despair of a clever king and his attempts to rid himself of sonless liaisons led to their ruin and desertion, and to the birth of a modern nation.

Everywhere the landscape and its coasts are bathed in the Love of God, swept by sunbeams the kiss of cool wet winds and the soft aspersions of the rains. For even the rampant storms of a Boreal equinox are no more than the passing bluster of a Father, or the silent fogs his sulks.

Love is as ubiquitous as it is indispensable, arising with unheralded spontaneity, as unlikely as a golden Buddhist fane on a litter-strewn demolition site, or a telephone in a display case. For like the sunny ragwort and the snowy snowdrop it spreads rankly but in secret, awaiting its season.

The Love of God tends the garden and without the fruit of the garden the snail and the squirrel starve and the works of man are as insupportable as the thoughts of man, though not His thoughts, are unthinkable.

COLESCH
The Chancel of St Peter and St Paul at Coleshill in Warwickshire

Location:	Coleshill, Warwickshire, England, UK
Date of Photograph:	am 2 January 2005
OS Grid Reference:	SP201890
Co-ordinates:	52:29:36N 1:42:16W
Elevation:	101.5 meters

The parish church of St Peter and St Paul dates from about 1200, but the nave was comprehensively rebuilt in 1868-9. This magnificent fifteenth century chancel did, however, survive albeit with some twentieth century restoration of the East wall.

The chancel measures 39 by 24 feet and has three five-light tracery windows on each side. As the picture also makes clear, the walls of the chancel are of red sandstone ashlar.

Internally, the floor level has been raised and there are remains of two sedilia. The chancel arch may incorporate fourteenth century capitals from the preceding chancel, which was otherwise almost entirely removed for construction of the present structure one hundred years later.

The church contains a twelfth century font, the oldest object within. It is of Caen stone. Richly carved stone panels depict the Crucifixion of Our Holy Savior; Our Lady and a weeping St John the Evangelist. Other richly carved and foliage-decorated panels show St Peter with his key, a bearded Paul, and The Magdalene holding an ointment jar. The font was plastered over during The Civil War to save it from iconoclasts. Enigmatic drilled holes may have contained precious stones during pre-Reformation times.

The church hosts many funereal effigies and brasses amongst which a curious engraving of its first Anglican vicar, Sir John Fenton shows him holding a Bible in a right hand that has an almost invisible sixth digit. The brass dates from his death in 1555 and may have a lost iconographical significance.

COMEGOOD
The Quaker Meeting House at Come-to-Good

Location: Come-to-Good, Feock, Cornwall, England, UK
Date of Photograph: pm 4 April 1996
OS Grid Reference: SW812403
Co-ordinates: 50:13:20N 5:04:02W
Elevation: 45.4 meters

Come-to-Good is an Anglicisation of the Cornish phrase Cwm-Ti-Coit meaning "house in the wooded valley", a name that remains apt. The Meeting House was built in 1709 of cob and thatch and the loft (gallery) added in 1717.

FORTINGA
The Fortingall Yew in Scotland

Location:	Fortingall, near Aberfeldy, Perthshire, Scotland, UK
Date of Photograph:	pm 24 July 2006
OS Grid Reference:	NN741470
Co-ordinates:	56:35:53N 4:03:02W
Elevation:	124.4 meters

This is the great yew tree in Fortingall Churchyard.

The placename "Fortingall" means the "defensive encampment of the foreigners" and is cognate with placenames such as Gaul, Galicia, Walsall, and Wales.

The yew tree is at least two thousand years old and modern research suggests that it may be as old as five thousand years. Were this true, then the Fortingall Yew would qualify as the oldest thing alive. In any event, it is the oldest living thing in Europe.

The yew (Taxus Baccata) is a notably long-lived species and maybe it is for this reason that all cultures ever held it sacred. It was included in the holy precincts of the British Iron Age, and when Christianity succeeded, the existing yews were allowed to remain in sanctuary, and new ones encouraged. It is said that the word "yew", perhaps as old as any tree, is cognate with the Hebraic term "Jehovah", and in the Buddhist East the yew is called the deodar, or "Tree of God".

It is alleged that local lad Pontius Pilate played in the shade of the Fortingall Yew, and other traditions say that our Holy Savior was crucified on one, to certify its status as a token of Everlasting Life. Some yew trees bleed a red sap when injured as if to advertise their sacred avocation.

When the Scottish Church reformed, less respect was accorded the old yew and boys lit Beltane fires within its hollow trunk whilst travellers and souvenir-hunters vandalised it for their collections.

The naturalist Thomas Pennant visited the tree in 1771 and measured its girth at fifty-six and a half feet. Shortly thereafter the great scientists Decandolle and Von Humboldt also paid their respects.

By 1825 the tree was in a bad way and shortly after a protective wall was built about it. The central trunk died but subsoil outgrowths have emerged to continue the life of the organism. Cuttings have been taken from the surviving limbs to be cloned at Roslin, and saplings have been given to Glastonbury Abbey and the Sange Ling Monastery at Eskdalemuir.

KIRKMAID
St Medoc's Chapel at Kirkmaiden near Monreith

Location:	Kirkmaiden-in-Ferness, near Monreith, Wigtownshire, Scotland, UK
Date of Photograph:	am 2 April 1999
OS Grid Reference:	NX365399
Co-ordinates:	54:43:41N: 4:32:21W
Elevation:	37 meters

This lovely sanctuary is the second landfall of the Irish missionary nun St Medoc (variously Medana, Madoc, Madin, etc.)

This is at Kirkmaiden-in-Ferness in The Machar of Wigtownshire on the **Eastern** side of Luce Bay. There is a larger Kirkmaiden: Kirkmaiden-in-Rhinns or Kirkmaiden of Drummore ten miles West on the **Western** side of Luce Bay, and in the South Rhinns region of The Mull of Galloway. The two places are intimately associated with the same woman, as shall become apparent.

The literal meaning of "Kirkmaiden" in Scots English is "Church of the Virgin".

In a legend typical for Dark Age foundations by females, and little varied, the beautiful seventh-century princess and Christian convert sailed from her native land, pursued by an ardent but noble-born soldier, who wished her to wed. The pious lady settled her handmaidens in a cave near East Tarbet Bay in the South Rhinns, the nearest

British landfall. Her suitor, however, soon reappeared, and the alarmed saint stepped on a stone that floated her and her party across Luce Bay to the desolate spot that shall ever bear her cell.

Not to be discouraged, her gentleman took himself to her refuge on the Ferness cliffs. Exasperated, Medoc asked him what he found so attractive about her. He replied "Your Eyes" whereupon the holy woman plucked them out and threw them at his feet. He fled in horror.

Nearby, overflowing the cliff, Medoc felt a small spring that shall now bear her name forever, and washing her bleeding sockets in its waters her sight was miraculously restored. She then traveled all over Scotland founding churches and bringing the Light of Christ to its benighted peoples.

The seaward ruin is of unknown date and sometimes described as "Norman" but may have been built during the Canmore era of Scottish kingship, say about nine hundred years ago. At any event, the church is first written of in 1386. It is of course dedicated to St Medana. Celto-Catholic fabrics were ill suited to the Presbyterian Reformed religion of Scotland, and in 1638 the little cliff-top chapel was abandoned in favor of a new church at NX12453692: The so-called "Old Church of Kirkmaiden" at that other Kirkmaiden in the Rhinns. Readers should note that at these times, ordinary travel was by sea, and locals would not have thought twice about commuting the ten miles across the misty bay to a place otherwise intervisible from the settlement they were at.

Victorian archaeologists identified a number of further anchoritic cells, including a St Catherine's Chapel, in the near vicinity of St Medoc's. (St Catherine, who was of course Alexandrian, was a favorite choice for chapels that could be used as seamarks by mariners). The dimensions of the Medieval St Medoc's church ruin are 14.5 meters East to West by six meters by 0.3 meters high.

The Early Christian cross slab IB33 may have come from St Medoc's Chapel and may now be found in The Royal Museum of Scotland at Edinburgh.

The slate-roofed mausoleum at the Eastern end of the structure, with its fine reproduction Norman archway of ferruginous sandstone, was erected in Late Victorian times. It accommodates the dead of the local lordly family, the Maxwells of Monreith. The last immuration was of the naturalist Sir Herbert Maxwell in 1937. Sir Herbert used to delight in pointing-out a large flat rock on the shore below the chapel, which, he said conveyed the holy company of Medoc across the briny bay. Perhaps the most famous Maxwell scion was the author, adventurer, anthropologist and naturalist Gavin Maxwell (1914-1968) whose books include "Ring of Bright Water" (1960), "People of the Reeds" and "The Rocks Remain". Gavin is buried at Sandaig in Invernesshire, but a bronze otter gazes over the chapel from the knoll above in her master's memory. There are two cross slabs in the chancel.

The graveyard is of considerable antiquarian interest in its own right. Archaeologists have detected the foundations of three further structures, one at least as big as the Medieval chapel. Amongst the graves may be found that of the French sailor Francois Thurot (1727-1760), sometime privateer and smuggler, who became a major hero of the Seven Years War (called in the US The French and Indian Wars). His body was washed ashore here after a local skirmish with elements of The Royal Navy under Elliott. He was buried honorably by the contemporary Maxwell laird, and in 1960 the Swedish Order of Coldin installed a wall plaque on the chapel in memory of their French founder. A French naval delegation paid their respects in 1967, and it is good to note that the freemasons of Carrickfergus are on the best of terms with their Swedish brethren, after Thurot famously raided their Antrim port!

The Machar of Wigtownshire is alive with the Abiding Spirits of the men and women who came to convert Scotland to Christ during the Dark Ages. Nine miles along the coast to the North, on a spectacular raised beach, lie the chapel and well of St Finbar, whilst four and a half miles South behind the beach is St Ninian's Cave where he first settled to pray before founding his cathedral and monastery at Whithorn, five and a half miles East of St Medoc's. This bridgehead of evangelism in Scotland survived the Reformation to remain, 1500 years after inception, a magnet to Christian pilgrims Worldwide.

Perhaps Burns should have the final words, today too apt:-

" Hear, Land o' Cakes, an' brither Scots,
 Frae Maidenkirk to Jonnie Groat's,
 If there's a hole in a' your coats,
 Indeed you tent it,
 A chield's amang you takin notes,
 And faith he'll prent it "

MELCHURH
The Church of St Melangell at Pennant Melangell

Location:	Pennant Melangell, near Llangynog, Montgomeryshire, Wales, UK
Date of Photograph:	4 November 2003
OS Grid Reference:	SJ024265 (SJ0241926549)
Co-ordinates:	52:49:39N 3:27:00W
Elevation:	198.4 meters

This is the church of St Melangell. Its CPAT Number is 19470.

This austere little church is thought to be the site of a late eighth century AD nunnery dedicated to the seventh century Irish anchoress St Melangell, celebrated for her rescue of a hunted hare.

The main fabric is probably twelfth century but there have been many alterations and repairs, some as late as 1992. A major restoration of 1876-77 included the construction of a new tower.

The church contains an impressive pilgrimage shrine to St Melangell who may be buried under the apse. The shrine is the earliest Romanesque shrine in Britain. It was probably contemporary with the twelfth century build but was destroyed during the

Reformation and its parts dispersed within the sanctuary. The shrine was re-assembled from these fragments sometime in the seventeenth century.

Notwithstanding this, the apse became a schoolroom and vestry and remained in these uses until 1876, whilst the largely windowless North wall was used for ball games.

The church remains a remote but active pilgrimage destination and the whole sanctuary is an exceedingly complex archaeological monument. The graveyard, which includes Bronze Age inhumations, clearly pre-dates the church, which is built over burials. Pennant Melangell is certainly the most important Christian site in Montgomeryshire and possibly the most significant archaeological remnant there.

MELINNA
The Tanat Valley Free House Pub Sign at Llangynog

Location:	The Tanat Valley Free House at Llangynog, Montgomeryshire, Wales, UK
Date of Photograph:	4 November 2003
OS Grid Reference:	SJ053262
Co-ordinates:	52:49:26N 3:24:22W
Elevation:	162.5 meters

This is the artwork of the inn sign of The Tanat Valley Free House.
The European Hare (Lepus Europaeus) is a lagomorph mammal similar to a large rabbit but does not burrow. It scrapes a nest upon the pasture surface in which it rears its young. The animal is very secretive and seldom seen except during its vernal courtship dances. It can achieve speeds of forty-five miles per hour in flight from predators, and has been credited with supernatural attributes since the dawn of time.

Notwithstanding this ancient veneration, the animal has been hunted, usually with sighthounds, at least since Roman times. Arrian was the first to mention hare-coursing as "cynegeticus" in his treatise of 180AD. He describes its practice by the Iberian Celts to whom the Welsh are related, and from whom they may have derived the practice, together with any ritual implications it may have carried.

Saint Melangell left Ireland in about 600AD to find a place where she could worship Our Holy Savior in seclusion. She found a suitable spot at the head of The Tanat Valley in Central Wales not far short of the Mercian border. This place is now called Pennant Melangell: "Melangell's glen head".

In 604AD Prince Brychwel Ysgithrog of Pengwern Powis entered this valley with his retinue and his hounds in hot pursuit of a hare. Melangell was praying in a bramble thicket and the hare ran under the hem of her habit and hid. Brychwel dismounted and demanded that the woman surrender the hare to his dogs. She refused.

Impressed by the saint's courage and compassion the prince granted her the valley as a "perpetual asylum, refuge and defence" with the dedication:-

"O most worthy Melangell, I perceive that thou art the handmaiden of the true God. Because it hath pleased Him for thy merits to give protection to this little wild hare from the attack and pursuit of the ravening hounds, I give and present to thee with willing mind these my lands for the service of God, to be a perpetual asylum and refuge. If any men or women flee hither to seek thy protection, provided they do not pollute thy sanctuary, let no prince or chieftain be so rash towards God as to attempt to drag them forth."

(Translated from a 17th Century manuscript by Professor Oliver Davies of Saint David's College, Lampeter and cited at http://www.greatorme.org.uk/melangell.html)

Melangell returned to sleep upon her riverside rock and from that day forth this sacred valley has been a sanctuary to man and beast, and to this hour hares are never shot in Cwm Pennant.

Today, Pennant Melangell is a silent hill-girt hamlet with an ancient church and a distant waterfall at its ice-carved head. The atmosphere is tangibly spiritual. The church is managed by a devotional sorority, who also keep a retreat for cancer sufferers nearby. The valley abounds with otters and other wild creatures.

In 1969 and again in 1975 Harold Wilson attempted to prohibit hare-coursing but was vetoed by The Lords. In 2002, Scotland abolished this barbaric relic of our cruel past. Then on 18 February 2005 all hunting with dogs was outlawed in England and Wales.

PEACEPAG
The Dhamma-Talaka Peace Pagoda in Ladywood

Location:	Osler Street, Ladywood, Birmingham, Warwickshire, England, UK
Date of Photograph:	12 February 2000
OS Grid Reference:	SP046867
Co-ordinates:	52:28:45N 1:55:58W
Elevation:	152.1 meters

     A peace pagoda is a Buddhist stupa open to all in quest of world peace. They exist worldwide and were pioneered by the Japanese monk Nichidatsu Fujii who, after meeting Mahatma Gandhi in 1931, dedicated himself to the end of wars.

     The first peace pagodas were dedicated at Hiroshima and Nagasaki.

     The pagoda form is a sacred tower that exemplifies the peace and compassion of the Buddha, and is appropriate for residential, meditational and educational functions. Monks are ordained at a pagoda and clearly it is available for individuals of any faith who wish to enter and pray.

     Dhamma-Talaka means "Reservoir of Truth", a reference to the Edgbaston (formerly Rotton Park) Reservoir immediately to its West. The Birmingham Buddhist Vihara was founded in 1978 by The Venerable Dr Rewata Dhamma who invited his trustees to approach Birmingham City Council for the gift of a site in Osler Street.

Burmese devotees have been prominent in collaborating with British Buddhists in bringing the new sanctuary to fruition.

The design is by David Jones and work started on the foundations in 1993. The concrete footing needed to be a meter deep and a meter wide on the disturbed land of this former industrial site. The perimeter of the pagoda at base is 153 feet and its octagonal plan represents the Eight Directions of Buddhist thought: Rectitude of View, Intent, Speech, Action, Livelihood, Effort, Mindfulness and Concentration.

Fitments of marble, crystal and teak were imported from Burma. The spire is of gold-plated steel crowned with crystal. It supports a brass flag incorporating gold and semi-precious stones. Beneath this cover lie enshrined relics of The Buddha together with items dedicated by votaries.

The Reservoir of Truth is the only traditional Burmese-type pagoda in the West.

Building completed in 1997 and the pagoda was opened on 26-28 June 1998 in the presence of one hundred monks, government representatives and visitors from all over the World.

My Late Mother was a pupil at Osler Street Primary School which once existed on the opposite (Eastern) side of Osler Street.

VARAH
MANsion house 9000

Location:	St Stephen Walbrook, Walbrook (Street), Bank, The City Of London,
Date of Photograph:	pm 14 September 2004
OS Grid Reference:	TQ326810
Co-ordinates:	51:30:45N 0:05:23E
Elevation:	12 meters

      This is the telephone that Chad Varah used to console intending suicides when they rang him in despair at St Stephen's crypt.
      It is the first of those used at the inception of The Samaritans charity in 1953.
      Amongst his many greater and lesser accomplishments, the reverend gentleman was Scientific and Technical Advisor to the "Eagle" and "Girl" children's comics, which he was instrumental in founding, and a contributing advisor to the former's long-running "Dan Dare" presentation, which eponymously starred a muscular and heroic British cosmonaut of the future.

St Stephens Walbrook is a major Baroque church across the street from the Mansion House, and just South of The Bank of England and the Royal Exchange. It was built to replace a church burnt in The Great Fire of 1666 and was itself damaged by the Luftwaffe in The Second World War. It is notable for the extreme geometrical austerity of its stunning interior: A cube for a nave surmounted by a perfect hemisphere of a dome, with a clerestory of circular and other elliptical windows. The exterior is very bland and easily missed by those who search for the church, despite an imposing and ornate tower that was intended to mark the church above tightly-clustered eaves. The designer was the seventeenth-century scientist and administrator Sir Christopher Wren, architect of St Paul's Cathedral, about eighty City churches, and one in the provinces, at Ingestre.

On Monday 12th November 2007, Lumpen Heap of Gloucestershire very kindly told me that The Reverend Chad Varah had died on Wednesday 7th November 2007 at the age of ninety-five.

WERBURGH
St Werburgh Effigy at Hanbury Church

Location:	Hanbury, Staffordshire, England, UK
Date of Photograph:	pm 26 October 2004
OS Grid Reference:	SK170279
Co-ordinates:	52:50:54N 1:44:52W
Elevation:	148.7 meters

     This statue of St Werburgh on the South Wall of Hanbury Church tower commemorates the seventh-century Saxon princess who played a key role in the Christianisation of Mercia.

     She was the daughter of the Christian Mercian King Wulfhere and granddaughter of the pagan Mercian King Penda.

     Sometime around 660AD Werburgh established a nunnery at Hanbury in Staffordshire. The site is one of the most strategic in England: It commands the limit of navigation (to Dark Age shipping) on the River Dove and controlled access from Scandinavia and Germany to The Cheshire Plain and North-West England.

     On her death, approximately at the end of the century, Werburgh was buried at Hanbury and her shrine became an object of pilgrimage. Around 873, however, Viking incursions penetrated the Trent and the Mercian capital at Repton was sacked. Werburgh's body was moved to Chester to prevent desecration, and monastic houses gathered about her new shrine. Werburgh became the Patron Saint of Chester.

At the Dissolution, Werburgh's shrine was smashed and her remains scattered. The Chester cathedral of St Werburgh and St Oswald was re-dedicated to Christ and the Blessed Virgin. The Chester shrine was restored in 1876.

WHITPRIO
Whithorn Priory

Location:	Whithorn Priory, Whithorn, Wigtownshire, Scotland, UK
Date of Photograph:	30 March 1999
OS Grid Reference:	NX444402
Co-ordinates:	54:44:01N 4:25:00W
Elevation:	56.7 meters

This is the ruin of the nave of the church of Whithorn Priory.

Whithorn is the oldest Christian foundation in Scotland and was established in about 390AD by the obscure British saint Ninian who was educated at Rome. It may be recalled that at that date Hadrian's Wall was still manned and England still Roman though it is likely that Roman writ extended no further West than Durisdeer in Dumfriesshire.

Ninian's first church, the "Candida Casa" ("Whithorn" derives from the Anglo-Saxon for "White House") was dedicated to the Roman soldier-saint, St Martin of Tours, though since Martin died on 11th November 397 it is likely that the dedication was made at the turn of the new century. Whithorn became a cathedral, to be understood merely as a church administrative center, and a missionary college from which men departed to convert the rest of Scotland.

In the later Dark Ages it passed to Northumbrian and Christian Norse hands.

The pictured fabric probably dates from the immediate pre-monastic phase between 1128 and 1177, when the priory was the seat of The Bishops of Whithorn.

From then until 1560 the priory accommodated Premonstratensian monks (White Canons), but after the Reformation the fabric entered a gradual decline until in 1822 the existing nave was abandoned as the town congregation moved to the adjacent newly-built Parish Church.

The surviving ruins were stabilised in the late nineteenth century by The Marquis of Bute who undertook archaeological excavations, extended by further digs in the 1980's.

The medieval crypt and its superstructure also survives on the Eastern side of the church path and contains a collection of local preaching crosses and other ancient carved stones.

Ever since the death of Ninian, Whithorn has been and remains a significant objective of Christian pilgrimage.

WIGTOWCH
Wigtown Church in Wigtownshire

Location: Wigtown, Wigtownshire, Galloway, Scotland, UK
Date of Photograph: pm 30 March 1999
OS Grid Reference: NX436555
Co-ordinates: 54:52:08N 4:26:21W
Elevation: 28.3 meters

The view is Northeastwards over the silted estuary of the River Cree.

The original church was founded in The Dark Ages by the Welsh saint Machute who died in 554AD. It was given by Edward Bruce to the monks of Whithorn, and passed through secular hands before becoming a Church of Scotland (Presbyterian) place of worship. The Gothic ruin in the middle distance incorporates vestiges of a medieval structure of unknown build date, but was repaired in 1730, and again in 1770 and 1831. Finally, in 1853 it was abandoned on completion of the adjacent 660-sitting edifice by Henry Roberts. Some stained glass was furnished by James Ballantine and Son in 1867. Both the Victorian structure and the ruin contain important Celtic carvings dating from The Dark Ages.

In the lovely churchyard may be found the graves of the Covenanting Martyrs, Margaret MacLachlan, an elderly woman, and teenager Margaret Wilson. In 1685 they were murdered for their Presbyterian faith by Sir Robert Grierson acting for

The King. They were tied to stakes in the estuary before the church and drowned by the rising tide. The martyrs are commemorated by three memorials in Wigtown and several more in Scotland and worldwide.

CHAPTER TWO

Residents of Grace

What can I say of the squirrel and the snail? Unalike they seem yet to share great beauty, each creature inscrutable and opinionated.

The snails love to bask on the sunlit Southern wall of my house. Like the squirrel they are immigrants from sunnier climes, but lack the rodent's winter coat.

For extra purchase and a better seal the snails cling to the paint of my garden door and when I pass thorough I sometimes dislodge them. On an occasion I noticed that one had parked six feet above the threshold and inclined himself fifteen degrees to East of top center. I thought nothing of it but the door slammed in the wind and this individual and several others detached and fell to the tarmacadam. I did some work and returned an hour or two later. The particular snail had returned to his exact resting-place: And inclined himself at fifteen degrees East of the vertical.

But this is small work for an animal of undemonstrative but unrelenting tenacity.

The gray squirrel was probably surprised when he arrived in 1874. Like the snail he did not ask to come, but was obliged to grace the gardens rather than the tables of lords. We had throughout our islands a delicate and decorous red creature who had tufted ears and diffident manners, but like his human counterparts he soon had to defer to the American newcomers, brash and big, but fit for purpose, though our purpose for him was only vanity.

Just after I lost my job I went for a walk on Cannock Chase, and naughtily trespassed into the secret glades of the forest where only the authorised are permitted to wander. On the high bough of a great pine I saw a giant black squirrel as big as a cat, and as couchant. I greeted him, but he ignored me. Passing on I walked down a track to leave The Forbidden Zone. To my great surprise a normal-sized gray squirrel stood on a branch on my flank and scolded me vehemently. Fascinated, I stood on the trackside berm to view him better. This standoff continued for some minutes. Eventually I tired of his chattering and tail-flicking and stepped backwards off the bank. Instantly, the little proprietor ceased his protests and climbed down from his perch.

Whilst various species of hares seem to be aboriginal a related lagomorph species, the European Rabbit (*Oryctolagus cuniculus*) is probably another immigrant. I recently read a piece by a historical novelist on some literary blog. He related how a helpful reader had written in to correct his claim that rabbits graced an Arthurian scene, pointing out that they were introduced by the Normans after 1066. Others plausibly claim that they came with the Romans. Whatever, like the snails they came for the table; and like the snails, it is they who have had the best of the provision.

One day in 1982 my Wife and I were on an express train that passed a large field near Lawford, above the infant Avon in Warwickshire. The low sun flecked the long grass gold amidst the deep green of the lowland pasture in the calm of a summer's sundown. A great rabbit calmly sat on a hummock holding court as twenty other delighted rabbits gambolled and danced around, as if playing tag. He did not stir a muscle as the carriages thundered behind his head, and I told my Wife that he was The King of the Rabbits. A few months later on a gloomy day we looked out for him at the same place. He was there, enthroned as before, as his gleeful subjects sported. Then a year later the same. Then he and his court vanished for us never to see again. I hope they are playing before their king in Paradise.

The birds have little heed of leave. Some geese may have been imported but for sure they are capable of intercontinental migration and practice it. Even those intended for the table may turn renegade, join a wild troupe, and live at liberty. Some years ago my Wife and I walked beside the Trent and Mersey Canal at Burston. We saw on the opposite bank a small group of about a dozen wild Canada Geese. With them was a perfectly white English farmyard goose, far from any farm and clearly a recruit to their number.

These communities live in flux, seeing bondage, liberation, assimilation and patrimony in vicissitudes as complex and as interactive as any vagaries of human society.

As the skies turned to ice and fell upon the Age of Rome the snails, like the Britons, and perhaps the rabbits and the dormice, watched and wondered. The humans thought it the end of the World for they and theirs. The other creatures were probably more stoical if no more sanguine. I like to think that as the crepuscule deepened, they ran to the silent cellars to attack the abandoned wine-barrels, and threw a party.

DELILAH
Delilah

Location: Bloxwich, Staffordshire, England, UK
Date of Photograph: pm 23 October 2004
OS Grid Reference: SK000020 (400000, 302200)
Co-ordinates: 52:37:03N: 2:00:02W
Elevation: 166.7 meters

      I do not know when we first met Delilah. I suppose it was sometime in 2001, around the time that I lost my job. She was by far the boldest of several wild squirrels, and if I were not in the kitchen she would flounce through the dining room, the vestibule and the lounge looking for me.

      For some reason I do not know, and have never had the presence to enquire, my Wife Jana assigned her this name of the Philistine anti-heroine of The Book of Judges, but we never knew her real name, for that she could not confide.

      Delilah quickly ascertained my preference to lunch early and would come and sit beside me on the kitchen bench, and gaze at me with feminine quizzicality like the prim lady she was, though not too proud to pee on my doorstep.

      Often, she would leap on to the table-top, glance at the television news and break nuts before me as I dined. The meal completed she would return home.

For years, Delilah came and went, like a waitress from The Waste Land, sharing our meals and conversing with her eyes. One morning Jana was in the kitchen when a clearly angry Delilah appeared on the floor tiles and mouthed gruff complaints in my Wife's direction. When Jana investigated she found a cat lurking around the patio, which predator fled at sight of my Wife. Delilah departed consoled.

Sometime, maybe in 2004, I was working on the patio whilst Delilah leaped around, sniffing this and that flowerpot and making herself busy. On the lawn, five meters hence, the new neighbors' Persian crouched to pounce. It was an ugly, fat animal that visited my garden to defecate. Delilah sauntered about the flagstones, nearing the cat but seemingly unaware, as I watched fascinated. Then a meter from the crouching cat, Delilah turned and confronted it in a pose of such ineffectual delicacy I thought her fate sealed. The cat fled in terror.

Shortly after this incident, Jana was weeding one of her vegetable patches at the end of the garden. The other patch was still covered by its anti-bird net, except for a chink under the Western end, where a silly blackbird had entered, but could not re-locate the gap to leave. As Jana tried to lift the net, the bird only compounded its capture by fluttering to the opposite end. Suddenly, Delilah appeared, and used her back to lift the hem of the net near the bird. The blackbird hopped free, and our friend leaped away to her trees.

Some weeks passed without our seeing Delilah. When next she called she was in a bad way. One leg was lame and one eye damaged and closed. She took her nuts and limped away. The weeks turned to months and the months turned to years, and our friend did not return.

FROG
Rana temporaria

Location: Bloxwich, Staffordshire, England, UK
Date of Photograph: pm 2 August 2007
OS Grid Reference: SK000020 (400000, 302200)
Co-ordinates: 52:37:03N: 2:00:02W
Elevation: 166.7 meters

      The Common Frog, *Rana temporaria*, is endemic to Europe, except Iberia, Southern Italy and the Southern Balkans. It was introduced to Ireland. It is a quiet and gentle anurid amphibian that starts life as a soft egg laid in fresh water, swims in the water column as a larval tadpole, and when it literally emerges as an adult seldom hops far from standing water.. Usually a somber green or yellow hue, its adult body length varies between one and five centimeters. Some of the frogs in Scotland are black or red (and not just on Clydeside!) whilst albinos are not unknown and during their courtship they can, quite understandably, turn blue.
      I first made familiar acquaintance with these creatures when my Wife and I moved to rural Staffordshire and installed a little goldfish pond in our new garden. An individual soon took residence and spent the summer calling very gently to whomsoever

might respond. One evening I sat on the patio enjoying a sundowner whilst the frog sat in his accustomed place on the opposite edge of the pond, facing the fence. My Wife entered the garden from the kitchen door and to my abiding surprise the animal turned to face her and croaked. She and he formed a special friendship, but a lady frog must have found him, for the next summer a host of tiny froglets emerged and hopped through the lawn toward the larger pond of a neighboring farmer.

When we went back to the suburbs we dug a larger pond and a solitary frog moved in and lived contentedly for many years amidst the water lilies. Sometimes she shared her home with a mate. Earlier this year we found her rotting carcass on our pavement, but rejoiced that she had had a long and happy life in the sanctuary we had provided and had died at peace.

Tadpoles feed mainly upon algae and vegetable detritus, but adults are carnivorous, eating insects, snails, slugs and worms. As I sat one evening watching my Wife's Staffordshire friend, he basked in the sun with his legs and feet dangling in the water. A curious goldfish approached and touched one of the frog's toes with his nose. The fish darted backwards reflexively and made me wonder if the frog was defensively electrified, or galvanized as they would have said in the eighteenth century.

British frogs sometimes become torpid between November and January.

In March 1995 my Wife and I motored over the Burnhope Pass in the English Pennines. We parked at an elevation of 1955 feet (596 meters) with patches of snow melting into bright rills of freezing water that passed through ice-girt gutters beside the road. We were astonished to see frogs leaping along the streams in such a cold and barren place.

The fellow in the above picture was disclosed above a drain on the Southern, sunlit, face of our house when we pruned back some lavender.

GEESE
Branta canadensis

Location:	The Wyrley and Essington Canal, Pelsall North Common, Pelsall, Staffordshire, Mercia, England, UK
Date of Photograph:	am 8 February 2006
OS Grid Reference:	SK017043
Co-ordinates:	52:38:14N 1:58:27W
Elevation:	145.4 meters

This picture shows Canada Geese on a stretch of water they share with rats, coots, moorhens and, at a respectful distance, with swans.

Canada geese first made a recorded appearance in the UK when they were imported to grace King James II's waterfowl collection in St James's Park, Westminster. It is likely, however, that the preponderance of Canada geese in Britain made their own way from Canada, and some of them may migrate seasonally.

It is certainly the case that there are both seasonal and secular variations in the assembly of geese at Pelsall, with only a few old couples usually in summer residence.

Though essentially Canadian, the species is numerous throughout temperate North America and girdles the Northern Hemisphere from British Columbia to Kamchatka:- The long way round.

British geese inhabit England, Wales, Southern and Central Scotland and Ulster.

Goslings sport a fluffy yellow plumage but adults have mixed brown and white wing and body feathers with a black head and neck and a distinctive white chin stripe.

Adult males are 3.2 to 6.5 Kilograms and females 2.5 to 5.5 kilograms. Their length is 76-110 centimeters and their wing span 127-180 centimeters. Canada geese live between 10 and 24 years.

The Canada goose eats wheat, barley, rice and maize as well as seaweed and freshwater weed. But its staple, at least at Pelsall, is grass. It grazes with a bovine tearing action, consuming as much as a sheep and defecating every four minutes, enough to unbalance the ecology of enclosed ornamental waters.

I sometimes walk along the canal to Pelsall Junction and feed whatever I find there. One fine autumn morning I was feeding the Canada geese when an unpleasant old man with an unleashed lapdog approached me. He said "Stop feeding the geese. They are vermin. They shit all over the common". My first instinct was to remind him of his outrageous hypocrisy but I smiled and continued to dispense bread. I did not want to fight him. I am getting selective in my old age.

Like many wild animals in developing Europe and North America, the Canada geese suffered and by 1900 they were nearly extinct. But the decline of subsistence shooting, and, in Britain, agriculture gave them relief and their population gradually recovered during the twentieth century. In 1966 there were only ten thousand Canada geese in Britain, and certainly as a boy I never saw any though swans, coots and moorhens were everywhere there was fresh water. By 1996 there were forty thousand and by 2000, sixty-one thousand. Writing in 2008, there are thought to be 82550 Canada geese in the UK.

Like swans, Canada geese mate for life, though widows may take new mates. Between four and eight eggs are laid in a clutch and male and female share the incubation. Incubation lasts about a month during which the parents loose their flight feathers and so are unable to fly. Predators of eggs and goslings include foxes, gulls and corvines, but the geese are fiercely protective of their chicks and rarely lose one. After six to nine weeks the goslings fledge and accompany their parents on the first spring migration, after which they return to their birthplace.

GOATS
Craigdews Hill Wild Goat Park in Galloway

Location:	Craigdews Hill, near Clatteringshaws, Kirkcudbrightshire, Scotland, UK
Date of Photograph:	pm 31 March 1999
OS Grid Reference:	NX495719
Co-ordinates:	55:01:08N 4:21:20W
Elevation:	110 meters

These are Scottish feral goats at the Craigdews Hill Goat Park near Clatteringshaws in The Southern Uplands of Scotland. They are endangered members of a strain of British goat that has run wild since time immemorial, possibly prehistory, and are racially distinct from domestic goats with whom they are, however, interfertile.

An unwise cull of Galloway feral goats in recent years reduced the surviving British population by 1,200 to 1,500.

Although goats are said to damage trees and rare Alpine forbs, it is difficult to understand the motivation for that mass killing, especially in light of the traditional Scottish shepherds' love for the wild goat. Both sheep and goats relish the sweet grasses of the most vertiginous precipices, but the sheep are less agile and often lose their footing and their lives. When present, however, goats will invariably fight sheep for command of the high places: And equally inevitably the goats win, thereby conserving the sheep.

Since 1970 locally-captured feral goats have been released into the Craigdews Hill enclosure, where there is a tarmacadamed road and a car park for viewers.

As implied above, goats favor mountains and coastal cliffs. In the British Isles they are found in isolated pockets: Rhum, Mull of Kintyre, the Moffat area of Dumfriesshire, Galloway, Loch Lomondside, Snowdonia, Lundy Island and the remoter parts of County Kerry.

British feral goats have been introduced to Australia and New Zealand, and, by Captain Cook, to Hawaii.

Feral goats are about half the weight of domestic, the billies being around thirty kilograms and the nannies around twenty-five. Both sexes sport continuously-growing horns, and those of the males can reach 76 centimeters in length.

The rut takes place in August. The nannies birth in Winter and hide their kids, returning two or three times daily. The little black fellow with the white crown at (0.75,0.3) stood stock still for the entire duration of our presence, maybe half-an-hour, but kept his eyes fixed upon us. Few predators will venture to the inaccessible ledges were kids lie, but many kids die of exposure.

Within a few hundred meters of Craigdews Hill my Wife and I saw families of large white goats grazing freely in the scrub and bracken above the road. It has since occurred to me that these may have been modern domestic goats released during the nineteenth-century abandonment of local hill farms.

I vividly remember the mutual alarm, when, descending from Ben Lomond, an enormous male with vast horns emerged from the bracken above my path. I said "Hello" and he returned to his browsing.

Many years later, my Wife and I motored beside Lough Caragh in County Kerry. We were surprised to encounter an insouciant flock of thirty feral goats sauntering the road ahead. Some Highland bullocks on a field wanted to challenge them and as the curious goats moved aside to inspect them we paused to picture the goats.

Later that day we reached the road summit of Moll's Gap Pass and there wraith-like in the dusk a big white billy patiently stood waiting for whichever traveler might kindly pause to give him a biscuit. Unfortunately we had to hurry on.

RAGWORT
Senecio Squalidus

Location:	Cairn-mon-Earn, Kincardineshire, Scotland, UK
Date of Photograph:	pm 14 August 1990
OS Grid Reference:	NO785920
Co-ordinates:	57:01:09N 2:21:19W
Elevation:	350 meters

The Oxford Ragwort (*Senecio Squalidus*) is actually a Sicilian flower, though many would call it a weed. To little bees it is as golden as its bloom.

It is a hybrid of two plants that grew upon the free-draining flanks of Etna, *Senecio Aethnensis* and *Senecio Chrysanthemifolius*.

In 1690, Horti Praefectus Jacob Bobart brought it to Oxford University, where he planted it in The Botanic Garden. Gradually, the hybrid exfiltrated and by 1794 the Professor of Botany, Sibthorp, was able to remark that it was "very plentiful on almost every wall in and about Oxford".

In 1844 the railway arrived at Oxford. The clinker beds that formed the permanent way in Britain were designed to drain, to preserve alike the wooden ties and the iron rails. The clinker was the ideal substrate for the Etna ragwort, simulating its volcanic homeland. The Victorian botanist Druce remarked of the tiny achenes of this plant, "I have seen them enter the railway-carriage window near Oxford and remain suspended in the air in the compartment until they found an exit at Tilehurst". Within fifty years, Oxford ragwort had spread along the metals to every part of the UK, and colonised other dry disturbed ground such as building sites and roadsides.

Because *Senecio* is such a promiscuous genus it has interacted with the native British groundsel (*Senecio vulgaris*) to produce a complex array of hybrids, some of which are infertile mule-like variants, but others of which are self-sustaining new species, not interfertile with their parents. There is a Scottish derived species; a Welsh species that arose in the late twentieth-century, *Senecio cambrensis*; and a species so far confined to the City of York, *Senecio eboracensis*.

A magnificent specimen, a tree of a forb some four feet high, took root as a lone guest in the Eastern border of my garden. On the Western margin, thirty meters away, a clan of tiny hornets built a perfectly spherical nest of paper in a sand pile. It was a delight to sit and watch them that summer as they plied to and fro across the garden in the declining sunlight, winging home the ragwort pollen.

The picture shows another magnificent bush that grew in a sheltered spot at around a thousand feet of altitude on the mountain Cairn-mon-Earn near Aberdeen.

SEAL
Halichoerus grypus

Location:	Fionnphort Harbor, The Isle of Mull, Argyllshire, Scotland, UK
Date of Photograph:	pm 27 July 2006
OS Grid Reference:	NM299234
Co-ordinates:	56:19:35N 6:22:09W
Elevation:	0 meters

This is the Atlantic or Gray Seal, the larger and darker of the two British pinnipeds. The pups are woolly and white but adults have mottled gray to black fur that is noticeably darker when wet. When born, the average weight of the pups is 14 kilograms, and they gain 2 kilograms per day on a diet of milk that is 60% fat. Bulls average around 2.5 to 3.3 meters and 360 kilograms, whilst cows range from 1.6 to 2.0 meters and around 125 kilograms. Males live for about ten years and females up to thirty-five years. Atlantic seals consume each day five kilograms of available fish and crustaceans, collectively accounting for less than one percent of fish stocks.

The Atlantic Seal ranges for Virginia, through New Jersey and Maritime Canada, over to Iceland, The British Isles and Norway. There is a small Baltic population. Eighty percent of Atlantic seals are in European waters; Britain and Ireland share between forty and fifty percent of the World population. The North-East Atlantic population totals about 102,000 animals.

Within the UK, the major centers of population are North Rona, The Inner Hebrides, The Farne Islands and the Pembrokeshire Coast. There are about three to four thousand Atlantic Gray Seals on The Farne Islands, amidst a total population of some hundred thousand in British waters, where the population doubled between 1960 and 2000. There are isolated groups in North Cornwall and Norfolk.

European Atlantic seals birth on nursery beaches during autumn. The pups spend only a few weeks abeach before they are weaned and go to sea. During this littoral phase they are very vulnerable to death by storm, or, on crowded beaches, accidental crushing by adults. When they wean they go to sea, where they may remain for years. Older seals tend to haul out upon sexually segregated beaches in remote coves, inaccessible to landward predators. Birthing or courting animals may, however, crawl uphill onto grass up to 150 feet above sea level and several hundred meters inland, where that is possible. Accordingly, Atlantic seals qualify as Britain's largest-by-far land predator and are capable of inflicting serious injury if approached when nursing. Under other circumstances they prefer to escape man by lolloping seaward, amid load protest.

When happily in their element, these seals will playfully inspect swimmers or sailors without serious challenge.

The fellow in the picture spent several minutes studying our manoeuvres as we docked our open-decked ferry at Fionnphort in the Inner Hebrides. He floated calmly with his head emerged within meters of our boat whilst my sister-in-law Oct-Ja threw him some dried anchovies which he ignored. His head at (0.77,0.35) appears as if it will imminently be run down by the Iona car ferry "Loch Buidhe" seen approaching at (0.25,0.6).

A little girl with us said "I hope he is not run over by the ferry". Her mother emolliently echoed her wish. Of course, the seal was an even better mariner than a Hebridean ship's master, and took well-timed evasive action.

In the Autumn of 1986 I returned to Aberdeen for a job interview. My train crossed the Tay Bridge at dusk and upon the My Lord's Bank sandbank below the bridge's Northern end I was astonished in that very urban environment to see about six large seals basking, one of whom lolloped clumsily across the wet surface as the train passed above him.

Atlantic seals feature prominently in the lore of the British seas, whether as the maids who court and win human sailors, or as the vessels of their drowned souls. Such reverences did not, however, spare the poor creatures our predation. By the close of the nineteenth century the British seal had been hunted to near extinction for its oil and pelt. Happily however, the development of petroleum gave the species a respite reinforced by war at sea and, in the mid twentieth century, protective legislation.

The seals have made a fighting comeback.

SNAIL
Helix Aspersa

Location:	Bloxwich, Staffordshire, England, UK
Date of Photograph:	pm 4 June 2006
OS Grid Reference:	SK000020 (400000, 302200)
Co-ordinates:	52:37:03N: 2:00:02W
Elevation:	166.7 meters

Helix aspersa, the English Garden Snail, is actually a creature of the Mediterranean world, from Iberia to Asia Minor via North Africa. It is said that he (or she, for *Helix* can change his sex at will) was introduced to Britain by the Romans to grace their tables. Whether that is true or not, this resilient snail is by far the most familiar UK species, if not the commonest. The modern French escargot is of a different species.

Helix has a yellowish calcareous shell of 25 to 40 millimeters diameter and three or four whorls when fully formed. There are characteristic brown or black circumferential bands of decayed (and of course ferruginous) haemoglobin that the animal excretes seasonally. The mucilaginous flesh is usually gray, but varies from white to black. *Helix* walks when hard surfaces, including brick or asphalt, are wet, but can progress across grass, earth and bark. I have seen scores in Derbyshire, decorating birch trees like fruit. When it is dry, *Helix* retracts into his shell, closing the entrance with a moisture-proof epiphragm.

Helix grazes algae, even on glass; relishes my Wife's hosta plants; and will spurn few vegetative offerings. He scrapes surfaces with a radula of hard protein called chitin. On his head are four retractable sensory antennae. The two longer forward antennae support eyes. The creature has three brains and is a superb navigator. If removed many meters from his chosen spot he will unerringly return, not merely to the exact location, but the same bodily orientation, before resuming his slumbers. During winter, individuals assemble in crevices or beneath stones, perhaps twenty or thirty strong, and become torpid. Snails who happen to fall asleep on your wheel hubs can survive the immense inertial forces of protracted high-speed journeys and subsequently walk away, apparently unaffected. But when stressed or simply out-grown, they can abandon their shells to seek another.

Besides man, the obvious garden predators include the English blackbird and throstle (known generically by the unexciting appellation of turdiforms). *Helix* has many other enemies. These include other bird species, lizards, frogs, insects and centipedes as well as the predatory snail *Rumina decollata*. Besides retraction, *Helix* resists with the charming defense of blowing bubbles. *Helix* infestation can be deterred by using concentrated garlic or wormwood solutions, and a copper band around a trunk will stop them climbing a tree to eat its leaves and fruit, for they detest the cankerous taste of that metal.

Beside its consumption as the French delicacy *petit gris*, the flesh of *Helix* is used as an inspissative in skin creams and gels used for the treatment of wrinkles, dry skin and acne. This gentle if troublesome creature has been introduced worldwide, for the sake of his flesh, but has enjoyed the last laugh, and the greatest feast.

SPIDER
Tegenaria gigantica

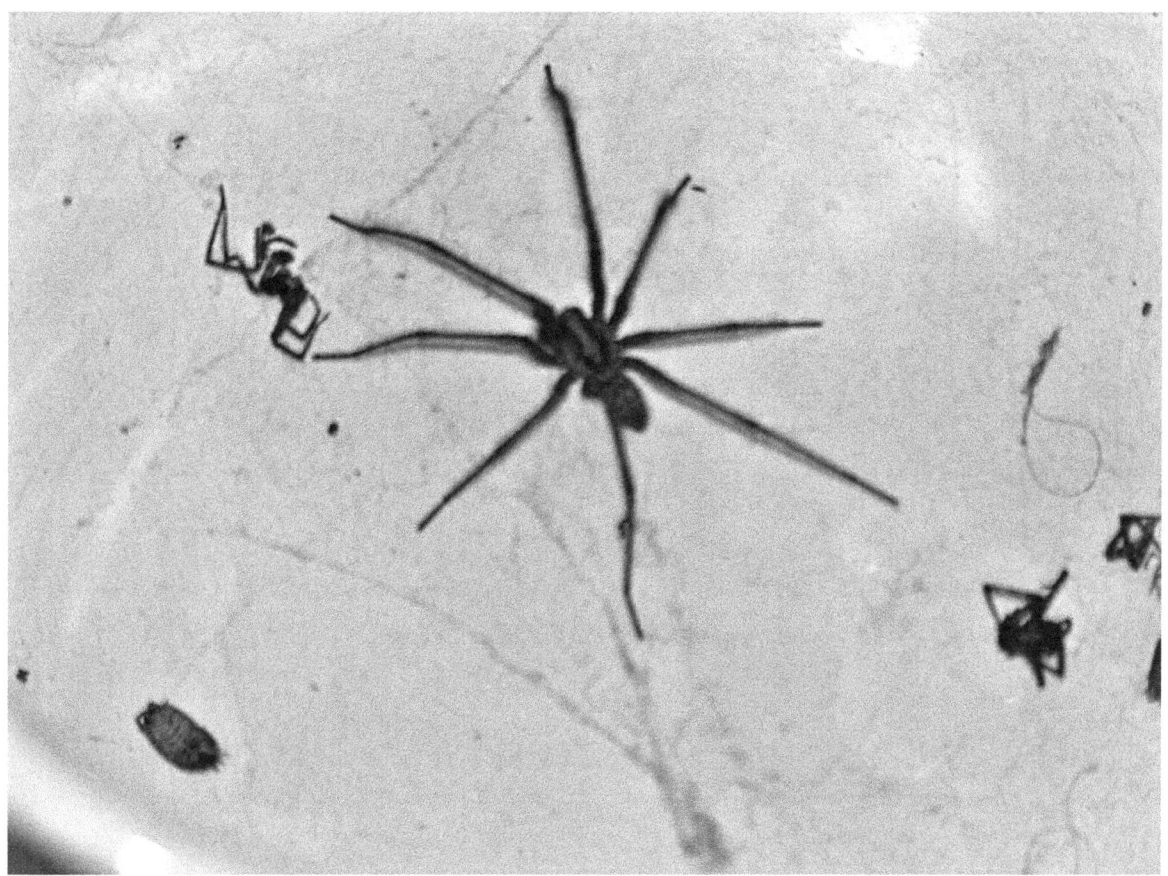

Location: Bloxwich, Staffordshire, England, UK
Date of Photograph: pm 26 September 2007
OS Grid Reference: SK000020 (400000, 302200)
Co-ordinates: 52:37:03N: 2:00:02W
Elevation: 166.7 meters

This is a small specimen (leg span about five centimeters) of *Tegenaria duellica*, more commonly known as *Tegenaria gigantica*. Popular names include the Giant House Spider, English House Spider and (the Greater) European House Spider. He also enjoys less printable appellations. As I returned to type this, one ran across the carpet of my study, a mere two days after I thought I had thoroughly vacuumed it!

A literal translation of the latter Latin binomial is "enormous tent-builder". Mature males can grow to a leg span of ten or twelve centimeters and a body length of 18 millimeters. This is to say they are eight times the size of the pictured specimen in weight and volume.

It is the fastest of the true spiders, having clocked a laboratory sprint of 1.17 miles per hour. Excited males have, however, managed more like three or four mph over my parquet floors, resting completely for minutes or hours after the first four or five meters.

Although technically funnel-web spiders, *gigantica* females and immature males lay an apparently random pattern of single strands of sticky gossamer across floors or other extended surfaces. Adult males cruise floors at speed looking for mates. *Gigantica* is such a fast and efficient predator that no other invertebrate vermin will be found (by a casual lay-observer) in a building they infest. *Gigantica* lives for around six years and lives alone except that mature males explore for females during September and early October. If they find one they will remain with her for days whilst they mate. After mating the male resumes his solitary odysseys, unless he dies of exhaustion, whereupon the female may devour his corpse.

Gigantica is endemic to France, Iberia and the British Isles, and whilst it can of course subsist in dry caves or other dry concealed natural environments, it thrives only in buildings. Accidental imports have established it in the nearly identical climes of urban British Columbia and Alberta. Isolated pioneers have been photographed in Seattle where it is hoped that they might control a similar but more troublesome British import, the Hobo Spider, *Tegenaria agrestis*.

The bite of any tegenarid is painless, due to an analgesic component in the venom. Therefore any injury inflicted by one is almost invariably blamed on an insect or even dermatitis, the culprit having run away long before it is seen. *Gigantica* produces a superficial necrotic spot about five millimeters in diameter, surmounting a hard conical weal. Both the weal and the lesion subside after forty-eight hours, but if the epidermis separates an indistinct scar may remain. There is no pain or itch. There are no systemic effects.

In the arable lands of East Mercia and in the urban English Midlands, the European Field Spider *Tegenaria agrestis* is sometimes seen. It has been detected as far North as Falkirk and Edinburgh. It is smaller than its relative *Tegenaria gigantica* and has a very similar bite effect except that its venom induces a brain stem neuritis involving visual disturbances, nausea and dizziness which can also last as long as forty-eight hours.

The poisonous *Tegenaria agrestis* never infests British buildings because *gigantica* immediately kills any example who enters. Therefore *agrestis* bites are unknown in England and virtually any Briton will swear, with misplaced pride, that there are no poisonous spiders in his country. It is a different story in Oregon and Washington State where *Tegenaria agrestis*, known to Americans as the Hobo Spider, infests homes and has occasioned at least one human fatality.

I live in a large brick-built pre-war bungalow with suspended wooden floors. It is on the outskirts of a city of two-and-a-half million in the English Midlands. *Tegenaria gigantica* share the house with my Wife and I and must easily outnumber us ten to one. In the Autumn they charge madly across the floors, especially at night. An enormous male lives under the television in the drawing-room. The other night he dashed through the semi-dark between the music center and the rowing machine, doubtless under the expectation that a lady spider awaited him. I think this was the fellow who, as I sat watching the box a couple of years ago suddenly charged me across the Indian carpet. For a second I gazed fascinated and then raised my legs as he careered under the sofa beneath me. I gingerly looked under the chair but the spider was nowhere to be seen.

For their speed, size, secrecy and gracility, *Tegenaria gigantica* are by far the most terrifying thing an English arachnophobe ever has to deal with, and yet like many weird things they prevent a plague of evils.

CHAPTER THREE

The Living Rocks

There is mystery and allure in the bones of Britain and in the weathered old complexion they support. Like a bleached and furrowed piece of driftwood stranded on the storm-swept shores of Europe, this land has a striated grain.

Lines of color trend from South-West to North-East in the lowland Heptarchy that became England. These denote the consolidated sediments of the Later Phanerozoic, various cycles of sandstones, limestones, ironstones and coals. Where shales or other softer rocks lie, the land is worn and low vales and basins sag between the hills.

In the West and the North the geology is more complex. On a map bright red or purple pustules seem to plague these Celtic lands but in reality these are cool hard eminences of granite or volcanic rocks set within a contorted matrix of altered sediments, or of peripheral sandstones and shales of Earlier Phanerozoic rocks of the Cambrian, Ordovician, Silurian or Devonian ages.

Here and there, but extensively in the extreme North-West of Scotland, the nearly lifeless gneisses and schists, or else the sterile granites and pegmatites, of the Palaeoproterozoic remain as pegs and bosses in the younger landscape.

These very ancient rocks have contributed some of the oldest lifeforms known such as the graceful sea-pen *Charnia*, discovered in 1957 by a 17-year-old Roger Mason in the not very wild wolds of Leicestershire.

Nearly two hundred years ago another gifted amateur, Hugh Miller, a stonemason of Cromarty, sought to celebrate the Works of God by disclosing the wonders within his local rocks. He lovingly described the strange oared creatures "like little boatmen" who awaited Judgment within what he called The Old Red Sandstone. In these Devonian rocks he discovered other marvels such as sea-scorpions and our earliest fishes. Many of his contemporaries also found many shellfish within the sediments of Palaeozoic rocks. The subtle gradations in the morphology of these creatures correlated with the age and lithology of their matrices. These host rocks could be tracked as horizons across country, and re-identified when displaced by fractures of the Earth's crust. In 1856 a brain tumor developed horrific hallucinations that made Miller fear for his sanity and the safety of his loved ones. He continued his work and worship but in 1858 he checked the printer's proofs of his final masterwork "The Testimony of the Rocks" and then killed himself. The following year a leisured Old Salopian published his "On the Origin of Species by Natural Selection" and men began to contemplate life without God.

Upper (and Later) Palaeozoic rocks of Carboniferous age formed thick cycles of sandstone, limestone, ironstone and coal that became of crucial economic importance to Britain when simultaneously the nation lost its American colonies, and its agricultural improvements failed to compensate its population expansion.

It was discovered that the concordance of fossil creatures extended to these economic strata and could be used successfully to predict the position of major deposits, even when fractured and shifted by massive breaks or folds. Such techniques of palaeontological stratigraphy were used right up until the end of coal and oil exploration in Britain. Latterly they were supplemented by geophysical techniques that detected tiny variations in the gravitational attraction of rocks, or of their reflectivity of sound.

To walk in Northern England or Southern Wales is to crest a rise and behold a panorama of serried escarpments lying like a shelf of books knocked down. Their steep scarp slopes are often tawny cliffs of naked sandstone or else limestone partly covered by scrub and grass. On the limestone the gently canting dip slope top is likely to be dry but sparse sheep pasture scarred with treacherous zones of riven rock or concealed caves. Here and there the "old man", the ancient hillocks and hummocks of long gone lead miners may been seen. On the sandstones the sloping plateaus are covered with sodden peat moors and this may bear heather that is burnt in due season. Often in Spring or Autumn the Sun retreats behind veils of virga that slant perpendicularly to the moorland's slope, as though softly limned with pencil. The escarpment seems to don a black cap and lour in backlit judgment upon the town-strewn vales below. Fifty years ago these impasti of urbanisation were black with soot and forested with smokestacks. Now they are gray with concrete, or the oblong aluminum roofs of huge sheds that seem to shine when wet.

To walk in Southern England is to follow a muddy but swiftly silent stream as it meanders over a loamy plain between round green hills of chalk or oolite. The rock is never unclothed except where men have riven quarries or dug great pits for brick clay, ironstone, or, in Mercia, for coal. These pits always fill, however, whether with water or with rubbish. Very locally ancient bosses of volcanic stone obtrude and may be quarried for roadmetal, but these are rare and serve only to emphasise the undistinguished undularity of the land. Occasionally you drive over a tree-dotted hilltop that you would not have noticed except that suddenly disclosed ahead an immense city carpets a plain, its margins lost in the mist of the hills beyond. The hills of Southern Scotland are also green and round, but much higher, older and emptier than the Mesozoic and Cainozoic ones of England.

To walk in a Celtic country like Cornwall, North Wales or Northern Scotland is to pick your way up a ravine beside a rocky stream prattling in vital infancy. Hard left and right bare screes rise to crags and ledges where some lichen-covered ancient rock, probably a regionally-metamorphosed schist, rises to land unseen. Heather, tussock and Boreal birch or pine scrub covers the upper slopes, but oak and hawthorn may impede your valley. You may happen to find tumbled walls and broken chimneys where miners tried to win copper, tin, lead, even gold or tungsten. As you gain height older ruins and walls may betray a deserted clachan and the rude subsistence its dwellers extorted from a sour soil. Rounding the stony shoulder of a hill you behold distant daunting ranks of black igneous peaks and ridges stabbing a gloomy sky or maybe a doubtful sea scintillating in the haze. Despite your lonely eyrie, from the valley below the unmistakable harl of high-speed traffic rises through the blustered air. Turning away you enter another, unexpected, glen of naked precipices, at whose bottom a lovely lake is riffled by unfelt zephyrs whose ripples glint and fade in fitful sunshafts.

Inevitably I pen an elided caricature of an infinitely variable and varied landscape and the most superficial description of the rocks that form its face.

AMBUACH
The Sea Stack Am Buachaille at Staffa

Location:	Am Buachaille, Staffa, Inner Hebrides, Argyllshire, Scotland, UK
Date of Photograph:	pm 27 July 2006
OS Grid Reference:	NM325351
Co-ordinates:	56:25:55N 6:20:21W
Elevation:	9.1 meters

This view is of a spectacular sea-girt rock stack separated from the Eastern side of Staffa by an abrupt sea gully some four meters wide. The stack is around nine meters high, depending upon the tide and sea-state.

The stack "guards" the Southern approach to Staffa's only made-up landing at Clamshell Cave, and is thus called Am Buachaille:- The Sentinel. Its name is usually incontextually translated as "The Herdsman" or even "The Shepherd" and is approximately pronounced "Am Booshala".

Staffa itself is a cliff-girt forty-two meter high plateau about 500 by 1500 meters and with an area of 33 hectares. It rises as a great vertical comb of polygonally prismatic columns of basalt, is underlain by an unstructured tuff basement, and capped by a amorphous entablature of chemically-similar rock. That entablature is absent from the shorter Am Buachaille.

Chemically, the rock is a sub-alkaline intrusive igneous olivine tholeiite, high in iron-titanium oxides and low in silica. The principal constituents are clinopyroxene and plagioclase with some olivine. The mean density is around 1.98 grams per milliliter, high for rocks of this type.

Whilst we usually classify lava traps as extrusive rocks, much of the Tertiary Igneous Province lavas of Ireland and Scotland are technically intrusive as there is evidence that they solidified under light overburden.

Stratigraphically, these intrusives belong to the "Staffa Group" of Tertiary Igneous Province rocks that were volcanically laid-down between 55-58 million years ago. They are geographically and stratigraphically continuous with the neighboring facies of Antrim (e.g. The Giant's Causeway), Ulva and Ardnamurchan. The total thickness of the TIP intrusions is six thousand feet. The dip at Staffa is nine degrees East.

These rocks are of major petrogenetic interest and have been the subject of scientific controversy for over two hundred years.

The most striking feature of the Staffa rocks is the columnarity of the central horizon that comprises highly-angular perfect vertical close-packed pentagonal, hexagonal and occasionally triangular or heptagonal prisms. The mean face counts of the prism sides is six, which is suggestive of a Configuration of Least Energy.

The columns are about 0.7 meters wide and 16.5 meters in the vertical. It is suggested that they solidified gradually from an extended lava sheet. This sheet had a light overburden and solidified on land. Therefore, height-wise contraction was possible without cracking as it was assisted by gravity. Lateral contraction was however complicated by three-rayed star-fractures that eventually coalesced. The resulting rock fabric was microcrystalline and Antrim exposures suggest a finer crystalline texture near the cracks that seems to substantiate more rapid cooling at the column interfaces. Such cooling along the cracks may have been accelerated by rainwater or river water penetration.

Locally, and dramatically at Am Buachaille, you can see a large-scale decumbent warping of the basalt columns along their length. Similar curving can be seen elsewhere, notably at The Devil's Tower in Wyoming. It is thought that this is due to inclined, and indeed curving, isotherms within the cooling lava sheet, perhaps due to local upwellings or other hotspots.

Since the columns always form perpendicularly to local isotherms, should the latter warp, so would the columns: Only in a geometrically-normal direction.

The profile of the island has been refreshed by isostatic emergence.

Whatever the truth about the genesis of this rockscape, it has been a source of fascination to scientists and inspiration to artists since Staffa was first "discovered" by the great naturalist Sir Joseph Banks in August 1772. Banks was on an expedition to Iceland with the painter Johann Zoffany, The Bishop of Linkoeping (Sweden), and Dr Solander.

Staffa immediately became one of the principle objects of Rational and Romantic pilgrimage. The roll of eminent visitors includes Johnson, Boswell, Robert Adam, Sir Walter Scott (1810), John Keats (1818), JMW Turner (1830), William Wordsworth (1833), Queen Victoria (1836), Jules Verne (1839), David Livingstone (1864), Robert Louis Stevenson (1870) and Alfred, Lord Tennyson.

Amongst the many votaries of the sublime who suffered privation to reach this place was the 20-year-old Berlin composer Felix Mendelssohn-Bartholdy who made a violently sick landfall in August 1829. He was not impressed by the "odious" Musical Cave to which he was led. This 69.2-meter long cathedral-like rock gallery, lined with basalt columns as if a gigantic organ, echoes to the lapping of wavelets in its floor producing a more-or-less minor-key melodic effect. From time immemorial called by the Gaels An Uamh Bhin or "The Melodious Cave" it was re-christened The Cave of Fingal by over-imaginative eighteenth century Romantics and after a few years gestation would inspire Mendelssohn's unforgettable orchestral *Overture: The Hebrides*.

Staffa is a National Nature Reserve and is in the care of The National Trust for Scotland. There is no charge for access beyond any ferry fare. It is a major seabird roost and center for cetacean spotting. It attracts many thousands of boat-borne tourists every year and scientific and aesthetic studies continue.

BRIDESTN
The Low Bridestones near Levisham

Location:	The Low Bridestones natural rock tor formation, Grime Moor, near Pickering, Yorkshire North Riding, England, UK
Date of Photograph:	pm 28 March 1997
OS Grid Reference:	SE873909
Co-ordinates:	54:18:23N 0:39:33W
Elevation:	201.5 meters

The picture shows a remarkable tor, a member of The Low Bridestones natural rock outcrops on the North York Moors near Levisham. This place is a Site of Special Scientific Interest within the meaning of Section 28 of the 1981 Wildlife and Countryside Act.

The Low Bridestones should not be confused with the nearby megalithic avenue of the same name, nor with the Bridestones standing stones at Congleton Edge.

Together with the High Bridestones, the Low are large, weathered outcrops of calcareous Jurassic sandstone on the Grime Moor Nature Reserve.

Bride was a premier goddess of Britain's Iron Age peoples cognate with the Classical deities Athene and Minerva. Some authorities maintain that her name influenced the (Roman) name of the Brigantes tribe who inhabited what is now Northern England, and that the word Bride diverged etymologically to form the modern terms

Britain, Briton, Britannic and British. If such scholarship is correct, then it is likely that Britannia, emblem of Albion, is a debased romanisation of Bride herself. The Brigantes tribe dominated pre-Roman North Yorkshire, with their capital at Aldborough. Bride was Christianised as Bridget. Grim was a god of the ancient Norse and may be cognate with the Saxon Wotan. Numerous English places are named for these old gods.

The rocks that constitute the Low Bridestones are strata of The Passage Beds, a phase of deposition between the Lower Calcareous Grit, which are older underlying sandstones, and the superincumbent Lower Limestone. They are rocks of The Corallian Series of The Middle Oolite. Their cross-bedded, flaggy character betrays the low-energy marine deltaic depositionary regime that existed at this place some 180 million years ago. They are on the "Tabular Hills" and dip South from a scarp.

The dramatic undercutting of this and some other of the tors was achieved much later, after the last glacial retreat, when eroded grit was blasted across an unvegetated surface by high winds. Wind-suspended sand is concentrated in the first few centimeters above the ground surface where its grains bounce along or saltate. The direct mechanical abrasion was minor but impacts weakened the intergranular cohesion in the weakly-indurated calcareous sandstone. Thermal cycles, such as diurnal variation, then caused the surface grains to break away.

This progressive effect is similar to the wear seen on old sandstone stairs. The mechanical abrasion of footfall is negligible, but the disruption of the constituent grains' brittle cohesion is not, and the shattered particles crumble away as dust.

BROADH
Fractured Overthrust Fold at Broad Haven

Location: North of Broad Haven, Pembrokeshire, Wales, UK
Date of Photograph: am 17 April 1992
OS Grid Reference: SM860144
Co-ordinates: 51:47:10N 5:06:16W
Elevation: 0.3 meters

      This text book example is indeed seen in several old geological books, especially those from Great Britain.

      It is exposed by littoral erosion about 1500 meters North of Broad Haven.

      As can be seen, it results from the brittle fracture (horizontal or thrust faulting) of a tectonically-induced fold already existing in intercalated sandstones and carbonaceous shales. The hade of the fault is about one and a half meters.

      The rocks are of Coal Measures (Upper Carboniferous) age and represent the most Westerly terrestrial outcropping of the South Wales Coalfield. Coal mining persisted here well into the twentieth-century despite adverse geological and logistical conditions, because of the high-value of the smoke-free anthracite coal, which found a ready market for steamships and continental stoves.

HARBORO
The Harboro Rocks in Derbyshire

Location:	Harboro Rocks, near Brassington, Derbyshire, England, UK
Date of Photograph:	am 9 November 2006
OS Grid Reference:	SK242553
Co-ordinates:	53°5'40"N:1°38'20"W
Elevation:	379 meters

      This small but rugged summit of Dinantian limestone is a favorite with rock climbers. It is classic White Peak geology. About two miles North of Carsington, it is possible on a clear day to see the Malvern Hills 75 miles to the South.

      These weathered tors are set amidst sheep pasture and numerous disused lead mines. Small silica brick factories maintain a somnolent trade nearby. Daniel Defoe visited the rocks in 1731, when he found a family in residence in the cave below the summit. The lady of the house showed Defoe and his friends around the abode where her husband had been born. Defoe found that she had shelves-full of earthenware, pewter and brass and that a hole in the roof served as a chimney. She kept pigs and a cow outside and worked as an ore-washer. Defoe gave her half-a-crown with which she was "highly delighted".

IMACHAR
Contorted Argillites at Imachar Point on Arran

Location: Imachar Point, The Isle of Arran, Buteshire, Scotland, UK
Date of Photograph: pm 9 April 1993
OS Grid Reference: NR867398
Co-ordinates: 55:36:19N 5:23:12W
Elevation: 4 meters

These dramatically deformed Dalradian metamorphic rocks inhabit the raised beach on the West Coast of Arran around Imachar Point. They were deposited in Cambrian times. They stand between the orbital road and the sea and their outcrop may have been modified by blasting.

Contorted by the Caledonian orogeny they show laminar chevron folding on the decimeter scale and are overturned seaward. The strike is North-South and the dip about forty-five degrees Eastward. These rocks sometimes exhibit inverted relict graded-bedding. Concordancy of bedding and schistosity is evident.

The rocks are low-grade chloritic schists regionally metamorphosed at 400°C and 500 Kilobars. They are derived from greywackes, more descriptively known as turbidites. Turbidites are re-deposited terrestrially-derived graded silts and muds that are formed by the settlement of debris after large submarine landslides. Turbidites are often, but not invariably, associated with subduction trenches: One of the most active turbidite-formation locales today is the Newfoundland Grand Banks area of the North Atlantic which is currently quiescent tectonically.

      At Imachar the turbidites are relatively muddy and the cleavage planes are rich in concordantly-aligned chlorite and muscovite, which are silicate minerals of the mica family.

THIRST
Thirst House Cave near Buxton

Location:	Thirst House Cave, Deep Dale of King Sterndale, King Sterndale, near Buxton, Derbyshire, England, UK
Date of Photograph:	pm 17 August 2000
OS Grid Reference:	SK097713
Co-ordinates:	53:14:20N 1:51:22W
Elevation:	288 meters

This is Thirst House Cave on the Eastern flank of King Sterndale Deep Dale, not far from Buxton in Derbyshire. It is a natural solution tunnel formed along the bedding plane of Dinantian Limestone, the country rock of the White Peak district.

Dinantian Limestone, which is virtually pure calcium carbonate, was laid down in the Lower Carboniferous. Locally it contains abundant fossils of shellfish (especially brachiopods), as well as the silicious pedicle disks of crinoids (sea-lilies). The rock was laid down three hundred million years ago within five to ten degrees South of the Equator. The environment of deposition was a tectonically-stable subtropical shallow sea not unlike the Bahama Banks. There was low rainfall and very low terrigenous sediment input. Accordingly, the stone is a dense, finely-bedded competent sedimentary rock, except where interrupted by reef knolls or later hydrothermal fissures. The limestone is gradually dissolved by nitrous and carbonic acids in rain or groundwater.

This Dinantian or Carboniferous limestone is hard and white to gray in color. It is easily workable to ashlar but is usually crushed for aggregate. Historically, it was employed as furnace flux or for alkalising soil.

The caves and other karstic features are Cenozoic and probably influenced by glacial meltwater. Indeed, the principal expressions of White Peak cave development have occurred since the Lower Pleistocene.

The White Peak covers five hundred square kilometers and is the largest British fluviokarst region. There are two hundred documented White Peak caves including Titan, Britain's deepest, and also some of the country's most extensive systems. In this, one of the most well-explored places on Earth, new caves come to light almost annually, and Titan itself was discovered within the last twenty years. White Peak caves are especially well-developed where the gravitation of groundwater is checked by tuff wayboards or by the underlying Namurian grit and shale facies.

Old reports claim that Thirst House Cave comprised eight chambers and included a waterfall and a small stream. Today there are two large chambers and a small ephemeral spring outside the entrance. Folklore avers that the spring was struck by the elf Hob (presumably the chap who hammers nails into miners' boots). The little man did so in gratitude for his liberation by a miner who had abducted him. The cave's full traditional name is Hob's Thirst House. An alternate etymology associates the name with Thor, the Norse smith and thunder god, tutelary deity of Thursday, and numerous English places including other caves.

The cave is a rough scramble from the valley way, through some thirty near-vertical meters of scree and scrub. Despite its limited extent it is currently fashionable in speleological circles.

Between 1884 and 1899 Micah Salt excavated Romano-British pottery and great brown bear bones from within the cave. Outside he found two Neolithic inhumations at a depth of four feet.

Immediately across the gorge, obscured by trees, is the sister cave, the eighty feet deep Deepdale Cavern. This may have been continuous with Thirst House before Deep Dale itself was cut by outwash. Deep Dale is now a dry valley.

CHAPTER FOUR

Crossing the Waters

Britain is an island. So is Ireland.

On several occasions, very recent in geologic time, these islands were half covered by ice that encroached from the Arctic. Where it lay this ice would gouge deep valleys with either its own ponderous fluid mass, or else its meltwater.

Britain is an island that floats on the plastic substratum of the Earth's mantle. The ice-loaded North was depressed hydrostatically into the mantle, whilst the South rose. When the ice melted the North bounced upward bringing its sea cliffs and beaches to dry land, whilst the South tipped downward drowning its valleys to deep inland.

The result of all this toing and froing and carving and flushing was a deeply-serrated shoreline attended by a flock of a thousand smaller islands. The far North became a land of fiords, and the South of rias and estuaries whilst the middle bit added great gulfs of tidal sand to its many wide river mouths.

Access between islands demanded a ferry, as did the crossing of the many long rivers and estuaries. As engineering advanced many of the narrower breeches were spanned by bridges, and the stories of these bridges and of the labors that built them are among the most interesting and inspirational of the Industrial Revolution.

We do not know when the first ferry plied in Britain but certainly the first Britons who were beyond being naked animals used them. Late in the nineteenth century and early in the last riparian development disclosed dugout boats of the Stone Age, on the banks of the Humber estuary at Ferryby and the Thames river at Southwark. Clearly these were ferries and were superseded in prehistory by larger, engineered craft of planks bound with sinew.

The Roman occupation saw the construction of long and complex wooden bridges, crucial amongst their number that between Southwark and London that may have superseded Bronze and Iron Age examples slightly further upstream. Further wooden military bridges existed in Britannia (roughly coterminous with modern England), and locally smaller engineered bridges of mortared ashlar were constructed.

During the Dark Ages the allied arts of logical organisation and engineering languished and torrents and tides took care of boats and bridges.

The Norman Conquest of 1066 and its associated innovations in Scotland re-established centralised authorities and the crossing of straits and streams again became thinkable. Monastic and other charitable foundations constructed stone arch bridges wherever stream depth and discharge would permit piers to be raised, or where narrow ravines could be spanned at a spring.

Margaret established her Queen's Ferry across the Firth of Forth and elsewhere advances in the size and construction of ships rendered ferries practicable except where, as at Menai, the energy of the flow made boat crossings intermittent or dangerous.

Notwithstanding the high-maintenance Roman structures, wooden bridges are unsuited to the humid British climate, Britain's frequent floods and its usual stream energies. All permanent British bridges of any size were compressive arch structures of mortared ashlar until the mass production of wrought iron, and later steel, made estuarine spans possible.

The eighteenth century saw a number of small cast-iron arch bridges erected in Shropshire and elsewhere and local experiments with small suspension formats. The erection of The Iron Bridge by Pritchard and Darby in 1779 marked the beginning of the use of industrial materials for vaunting spans (perhaps definable as those you can sail a masted ketch beneath?). It was, however, the Railway Boom of the next century that led to the evolution of quasi-tensional great iron bridges that culminated in Fowler and Baker's magnificent steel cantilever bridge across the Forth at Queensferry. That structure opened to rail traffic in 1890.

Meanwhile, improvements in ship construction and marine engine design made ferries both capacious and independent of wind conditions. Crucially on a coastline with the World's second highest tidal range, these developments also made ferries partly independent of the action and timing of tides. The Menai Bridge not only replaced but serviced ferries and the Albion was typical of a generation of long-range Irish ferries that fed the burgeoning ports and industries of the British West in Corn Law days that preceded The Irish Potato Famine. After that date (about 1848) the importation of colonial produce and the prostration of the Irish agrarian economy removed much of their raison d'être.

The final development of bridge technology in the last half of the twentieth century saw estuarine road suspension bridges of immense span constructed of spun high-tensile steel cables. A belated descendent of Menai, the first of these in Britain was the 1964 Forth Road Bridge, also at Queensferry. Two further estuarine suspension bridges were installed over the Severn. The culminating achievement of this type was The Humber Bridge of 1981, at the time of its opening the longest span in the World. Much smaller but nevertheless significant steel bridges were built to other patterns were conditions permitted. A box girder road bridge spanned the Cleddau by 1975 and cable-stayed designs were built over the Thames, the Clyde and the Boyne.

At a less grandiose but regionally very important level the last years of the twentieth century witnessed a campaign to bridge several of the Highland fiords and straits, or where possible to lay additional causeways. A cable-stayed design was installed at Kessock Ferry in 1982 followed by a reinforced concrete portal bridge at Kylesku in 1984. In 1995 the Skye Bridge from Kyle of Lochalsh to Kyleakin was opened. It is a reinforced concrete arch bridge of hollow-box balanced cantilever design.

During the nineteenth century a number of tunnels were built under the necks of busy estuaries. The earliest of these were in London under the Thames and further relatively short examples followed beneath rivers like the Clyde, the Tyne and the

Mersey. These essentially urban tunnels supplemented existing ferries or bridges and constructions extended throughout the last century. A remarkable and very difficult achievement of this type was The Severn Railway Tunnel of 1886 between Portskewett and Redwick. The structure is nearly four and a half miles long. Inundations hampered construction and seepage continues to be an expensive feature of this tunnel.

Attempts to drive a tunnel across the 23-mile Strait of Dover commenced in Victorian times. The project was hampered by inadequate finance, geological uncertainties and strategic misgivings on the British side: The latter were ill-assuaged by the occurrence of two World Wars. In 1984 the United Kingdom and France agreed to drive three parallel tunnels, two for running railway track, from their respective shores at Folkestone and Sangatte. The tunnel opened to traffic in 1994. It is possible to cross by through train, or by vehicle-carrier trains between the two shores. A situation has arisen whereby it is possible from London by land to reach Brussels more swiftly than Cardiff, and Paris in virtually half the time that Edinburgh can be accessed. Furthermore, the center-to-center journey between Paris and London is as swift by rail as by air and a lot less troublesome. Political impediments notwithstanding, it would theoretically be possible to board a train at Thurso and not alight until you had reached Pusan.

ALBION
The Wreck of the Albion at Albion Sands

Location: Albion Sands, Marloes, Pembrokeshire, Wales, UK
Date of Photograph: am 15 April 1992
OS Grid Reference: SM770075
Co-ordinates: 51:43:19N 5:13:44W
Elevation: 0.3 meters

This is the wreck of the Bristol General Steam Navigation Company paddle steamer Albion at Albion Sands.

The Albion was a two-masted two-decker schooner-rigged wooden paddle steamer of 270 tons burthen built at Hotwells Dockyard in Pembroke Place, Bristol and launched on Tuesday 5th July 1831. Her engines, almost certainly dual-cylinder sidelever single-expansion engines developed around two hundred horsepower and gave the ship a cruising speed of 11 statute miles per hour, equal to a fresh four on a good turnpike. The engine maker was probably Winwood and Company of Cheese Lane, Bristol and the machine is forged of hand-beaten fibrous iron, material that, unpainted and neglected, takes several centuries to rot away in the British climate, even in salt water. The Albion could steam from North Quay, Dublin to The Cumberland Basin, Hotwells in twenty-one and a half hours. At her launch "she went of the stocks in magnificent style, amidst the firing of cannon, and the exultations of the surrounding spectators; the band of the 3rd Regiment of light dragoons … playing several delightful airs".

American practice was to lever sidewheels with a "walking beam" superstructure similar to a standard beam engine but with the bob of wrought-iron lattice to keep the ship's center-of-gravity as low as possible. Around Britain, exposed to the full fetch of the Atlantic waves, and played by sudden squalls and storms at all seasons, such an arrangement would have been unseaworthy. Instead, the "sidelever" mechanism was developed, with a heavy cast-iron beam placed well below the waterline in order to maintain metacentric stability in heavy seas. The paddle format offered great manoeuvrability at slow speeds in calm waters; but, combined with the ponderous sidelever engine, was unhandy and inefficient in heavy seas, or where tide races and whirlpools were at play. Paddle steamers cost three times as much to cover the mile as did sailing packets, so the fact that they could work against normal winds and tides was a distinct market advantage, as was their ability to cut the corners of sea room by sailing through narrow channels…….

At around four o'clock on the afternoon of the 18th April 1837 George Bailey, commanding twenty crew, steamed south towards the 300 meter wide Jack Sound, a strongly tidal defile between Skomer Island and Great Britain. Aboard were five Army officers, three clergymen, Mr Sergeant Jackson, the MP for Bandon, five horses, numerous women and children and four hundred pigs, not to mention enough whiskey and porter to keep all in high spirits for a season or two.

With all his skill, Bailey navigated the chicane formed by the Tusker Rock to port and The Bitch to starboard. Suddenly, a rowing boat with four men appeared ahead and the helmsman made hard to starboard. The ship of course veered left, missing the small boat and the wheel was put hard to port but the Albion answered too slowly and struck The Crab rock off Midland Isle. Immediately the ship turned on its beam ends and then suddenly righted as it slid off into deep water.

Using all speed, Bailey powered the vessel toward a sandy cove visible a mile South-Eastwards, under the shelter of the tidal islet of Gateholm. The broken timber shipped water very quickly and the fires flooded just as the Albion reached the beach that was to bear its name.

The smoke and steam caused some suffering, but the women and children were placed in a boat and rowed ashore whilst some men chose to swim or wade there also. Others embarked in a sloop that had hove-to to render assistance.

All were saved, but after a few days the wooden hull had completely fragmented, and though there was orderly salvage of the cargo, including the drink and the Ship's Plate, the £20000 steamer itself was an uninsured total loss.

BRIGBALG
The Brig o' Balgownie at Old Aberdeen

Location:	Seaton, near Old Aberdeen, Aberdeenshire, Scotland, UK
Date of Photograph:	Summer 1972
OS Grid Reference:	NJ941096
Co-ordinates:	57°10'38.203"N: 2°5'54.972"W
Elevation:	3.7 meters

The Brig o' Balgownie is built on a constriction of the River Don on a stable geological feature immediately downstream of a meander loop and upstream of the river's final reach to the North Sea. The Don is tidal at its crossing.

The bridge has a span of 67 feet and stands 34 feet above a salmon pool mentioned by Byron in the poem "Don Juan". The bridge was called The Bridge of Don until it was superseded in 1830 by a larger bridge about five hundred meters downstream. That new bridge assumed the appellation.

The Brig o' Balgownie is a single and elegant Gothic arch of mortared granite and sandstone. Construction began around 1290 when Bishop Henry Cheyne commissioned Richard Cementarius to provide a design. It appears that the building was interrupted by The Scottish War of Independence because the bridge was completed in 1320 under the direct command and expense of Robert the Bruce, using the banished bishop's emoluments.

The original purpose of the crossing may have been to assist English military consolidations in Moray and Buchan, which occupations were of course voided at The Battle of Bannochburn. The Bruce may have had his own, but similar, strategic aims in view.

I took the picture using a Boot's Bierette manufactured by Waldemar Bier in East Germany; cost £5. But to put it in perspective I was paid £18 a week at the time. Exposure and focusing were both "guess and hope". It is by far the lightest camera I have ever carried, and with a following wind you could get a nice sharp shot.

Since the picture was taken de-industrialisation of the Don Valley has led to improvements in river water quality and the planted saplings have of course matured. A third road bridge has been built to the Brig's West, and the old bridge is now restricted to cyclists and pedestrians only.

Maybe Byron's salmon will return.

CALMAC
Aboard the "Isle of Mull" in The Firth of Lorn

Location:	The Firth of Lorn Craignure to Oban sea lane, Argyllshire, Scotland
Date of Photograph:	pm 27 July 2006
OS Grid Reference:	NM800337
Co-ordinates:	56:26:33N 5:34:19W
Elevation:	7 meters

      This view shows some happy little American girls feeding bread to seagulls as they returned from the Hebrides to Oban. The picture was taken looking Westwards from a point approximately in the middle of The Firth of Lorn, but about a couple of miles East of Eilean Musdile light at the Southern extremity of Lismore island.

      The "Isle of Mull" is a Caledonian MacBrayne roll-on roll-off steel DSMV car ferry of 4719 gross tons built in 1987 by Appledore Ferguson Limited at Port Glasgow. The 8MB275T diesel engines are by Mirrlees Blackstone of Stockport, and she can convey 990 passengers and crew plus seventy cars at a speed of fifteen knots.

In the first part of the nineteenth century West of Scotland steamship services were largely a G&J Burns monopoly, but in 1851 Burns was bought out by a partnership including their nephew, 37-year-old David MacBrayne.

The firm continued to link Glasgow and the Clyde Ports with the Hebrides and the Highland West Coast. Before the railway reached Inverness that East Coast city was also served by passenger steamers via The Caledonian Canal and the lochs of The Great Glen.

When the Hutcheson brothers retired in 1879 the steamer firm was renamed David MacBrayne and in 1906 it became a limited company. By the 1890's the railways had penetrated The Highlands, but railway companies were not legally entitled to run steamers and therefore could not offer through tickets to islands. In 1889, however, The Caledonian Railway Company sidestepped the law by creating a "separate" Caledonian Steam Packet Company (CSP), and in 1891 the Glasgow and South-Western Railway obtained a parliamentary licence to run steamers.

During the first half of the twentieth century Caledonian and MacBrayne competed to carry passengers and cargo to the Hebrides. Any cars or lorries were clumsily hoisted across the gunwales or precariously driven across planks, tidal levels permitting. In 1931 MacBrayne purchased their first diesel-electric ship, the "Loch Fyne", but trading conditions remained depressed and further innovation had to await the end of The Second World War.

In 1948, transport was nationalised, but Caledonian and MacBrayne were still administered separately. Railway use declined for both cargos and passengers and various drive-on configurations for road vehicles were evolved though tidal fluctuations and deck organisation remained difficult technical issues.

With continuing decline in the now-nationalised rail body, Scottish state non-rail services were in 1969 re-organised as The Scottish (Motor) Transport Group (SMT) and in 1973 the Caledonian and MacBrayne coastal shipping arms were consolidated as Caledonian MacBrayne Ltd.

Despite the appellation, Caledonian MacBrayne (Calmac) is a 100% state-owned organisation, the only remaining nationalised UK industrial firm.

Other than light aircraft services, Calmac is the monopoly provider of physical communications with the islands of The Inner and Outer Hebrides, except that Skye is now linked to the Mainland by a bridge. Between April 2005 and March 2006 Calmac conveyed 5.3 million passengers, 1.1 million cars, 94000 lorries and 14000 coaches.

Despite Calmac's state ownership it perversely receives few and decreasing subsides, so the majority economic cost of carriage devolves upon fare payers, a fact that inevitably leads to criticism of its exorbitant prices.

Nevertheless, Caledonian MacBrayne serves 24 ports of call using 29 ships on 26 routes in all weathers and usually at least once a week, and in dramatic contrast to English steamer outfits it has not lost a single passenger to shipwreck in 156 years of steaming through some of the World's most turbulent and tide-ripped waters.

CONNEL
Connel Bridge at Sunset

Location: Connel Ferry, Argyllshire, Scotland, UK
Date of Photograph: pm 27 July 2006
OS Grid Reference: NM911344
Co-ordinates: 56:27:21N 5:23:29W
Elevation: 0.3 meters

       This lovely steel cantilever bridge was completed on 9 May 1903 to convey the railway from Connel across The Falls of Lora at the mouth of Loch Etive.
       Loch Etive is a small fiord in Argyllshire on the West Coast of Scotland.
       The Connel Bridge's span is 500 feet (152.4 meters) and its height above the water some 50 feet (15.24 meters), though this depends radically upon tidal and meteorological conditions. Each approach is of three masonry arches.
       The railway connected the Ballachulish slate quarries to the UK standard gage network. Until 1914 road vehicles were carried across the bridge on flat wagons, and since 1966 the bridge has been a road-only crossing.
       The bridge was built by Sir William Arrol and Company of the Dalmarnock Iron Works that was East of Glasgow. It is possible that Arrol's was

responsible for the World's most beautiful, as well as long-lasting and famous, steel structures.

Arrol's built the reconstructed Tay Bridge (1887) after the first one blew down in a storm in 1879; the Forth Rail Bridge of 1890; London's Tower Bridge; the Nile Bridge in Egypt and Australia's Hawkesbury Bridge.

The firm also built the Bankside Power Station at Southwark in London, which is now the World-famous Tate Modern art gallery; and also the Arrol Gantry at Belfast, that Harland and Wolff commissioned so that they could build the ill-fated White Star liners Titanic, Britannic and Olympic, all of which sank in notorious and controversial circumstances.

HORSELEY
The Pelsall Works Bridge

Location:	Pelsall Works Bridge, Pelsall North Common, Wood Lane, Pelsall, Staffordshire, Mercia, England, UK
Date of Photograph:	pm 2 November 2007
OS Grid Reference:	SK014043
Co-ordinates:	52:38:13N 1:58:44W
Elevation:	142.0 meters

      This tiny structure supports a load-bearing arch of cast-iron, though it now carries only a footpath in a Nature Reserve.
      The castings bear the legend "Horseley Coal and Iron Company 1824".
      The (highly contagious) Black Country convention is to pronounce the word "Horseley" as "Horzli": A fact that leads to some confusion in the literature, especially in the tendency to write the placename as "Horsley".
      The small bridge was already in existence when Fryer founded his Pelsall Iron Works immediately North of the bridge in 1832. North and South of the canal were collieries and ironstone mines that intercommunicated by tramlines laid across the little bridge.

Accordingly, this little regarded monument is the World's first metal railway bridge and the lineal ancestor of The Forth Bridge, The Tay Bridge, The Bridge on the River Kwai, and a million and one other steel railway bridges, many of them of unspeakable beauty.

Pelsall Works Bridge was Listed Grade II on 31st July 1986.

The iron of which the bridge was made was cast a few miles away in Tipton near Dudley.

Its manufacturer had an interesting tale to tell.

In 1712 the World's first powered engine was employed to drain the coalmines of Tipton. By the time the canal reached Tipton in October 1793 the land was already badly affected by subsidence, and this complicated canal finance and engineering. To the North of the village a decrepit manor house, Horseley Hall, was set amongst horse leasowes (pastures) for animals who would find ready employment on and beneath land useless for agriculture, for the coal seam was eighteen feet thick and outcropped at the surface. To service local collieries rich also in ironstone the canal company built six short spurs including the Toll End and Dixon branches.

On 18th July 1792 Edward Dixon and Joseph Amphlett met with William Bedford and agreed with each other to spend £10000 buying the Horseley Estate and whatever might or might not be beneath it. They sank mines immediately.

The coal was underlain by a seatearth suitable for brick making, and limestone capable of being pressed into service as flux was available from mines at Dudley a mile to the South.

In 1809 the partnership sold its interest in the canal that served its Horseley Colliery Company and diversified into ironworking. In October of that year they purchased a 43-inch blowing engine from Boulton and Watt and erected two blast furnaces beside the Toll End Branch near Horseley Hall. The partners added a puddling furnace and a finery and three cupolas to their site so that they could make wrought as well as cast iron. A gas works for workshop illumination was erected by 1812.

In 1813 the controversial Isle of Wight entrepreneur Aaron Manby leased a house nearby and took out Patent 3705 for making hard engineering bricks from waste iron furnace slag: "Staffordshire Blues". On 29th August 1815 he joined the Company as Managing Director.

By the end of the Napoleonic War, iron casting was in full swing and eminent visitors came from as far afield as Germany to study the methods at Horseley. Patterns were made for a diversity of cast goods and by the 1820's hundreds of beautiful cast roving bridges in lattice iron had been set across Mercia's many canals. Plenty survive.

The acme of these was, and is, the Galton Bridge in Smethwick that at 151 feet was the longest span in the World when erected in 1829. It was commissioned by Thomas Telford to carry Roebuck Lane across the deep cutting of his New Main Line canal. I crossed the bridge on foot in November 2007, but it was retired from vehicular use in 1970, when I remember this canalside as still a fog-bound congeries of moribund forges.

Other Horseley innovations graced the 1820's. On 9th July 1821, Manby took Patent 4558 for an oscillating marine engine convenient for paddle steamers and by April 1822 the Horseley Coal and Iron Company had fabricated the World's first iron steamer, the "Manby", and tested it on the cut before dis-assembling it and shipping the pieces to Rotherhythe for rebuilding.

The "Manby" became known as "The Aaron Manby" and was a joint design by Aaron, his son Charles, and the eminent Naval officer Captain Charles Napier, who, fifty years ahead of his time, hoped to prefigure a class of iron battleships. The ship had a flat bottom of quarter-inch iron plate fitted on angle iron. She had a single wooden deck, a single mast and a 47-foot high funnel. The engine was by Henry Bell, the designer of the Scottish steamer "Comet". The paddles' width was limited to one and a half feet so that the total beam could be 23 feet, the maximum possible on the Seine Navigation. The "Manby" made nine knots and drew a mere foot of water.

The ship was 106'10" by 17'2" by 7'2", making 115 and twenty-three ninety-fourths effective cargo tons. On her way to Paris the "Manby" shipped a cargo of linseed and iron castings. She steamed from Rotherhythe to Rouen and thence up the Seine to Paris. As "The Aaron Manby" she plied the Seine under French ownership until 1855.

Until 1825 it was a criminal offence for an industrial artisan to emigrate, or, worse, to "entice workmen" abroad. It was also against the law to export a steam engine, though as will be seen this was more honored in the breach than the observance.

Lest magistrates mistook his meaning, Manby compounded the offence by establishing a great ironworks at Charenton and using English workers to teach the French the latest steam technology.

In 1824 Richard Harrison and John Yorke of the Horseley Coal and Iron Company testified to The Commission on Artisans and Machinery in these terms:-

"Before the establishment of the one particular concern at Charenton, the party conducting it had great opportunities of knowing our best men, in fact he was a partner in our concern; and from that circumstance he has been of course able to seduce and entice, in a very improper and most dishonorable way, our men to a greater extent than from other works, of which he had not the same knowledge; we have lost, I should think about 50 men, or thereabout. Before this establishment at Charenton was formed we had orders to a very considerable extent for steam engines for France, … since they have been in a state capable of manufacturing steam engines themselves, we have not had an order for one."

Neither Manby nor anyone else was punished.

In 1825 the embargos were rescinded.

Throughout the Twenties, The Horseley Coal and Iron Company continued to fabricate iron barges and paddle steamers but in the next decade they had an unhappy flirtation with railway locomotive manufacture. These products proved unreliable despite the active encouragement of Robert Stephenson who had a very high opinion of Horseley's boilermaker, Isaac Horton. In 1833, however, Horseley built the magnificent Swannington Incline Engine that labored until 1948 and is now exhibited in The York Railway Museum.

Iron bridge making, both fixed and swing, continued for docks and waterways and during the 1860's the manufacture of gas works equipment, including gasholders, became a staple. Also, iron lattice roofs and overcrofts became important as the Company entered a hundred years of iron and steel girder and structural fabrication.

An early such contract was to build the roof of Beckton (Becton) Gas Works in the East End of London, which remained throughout its existence the largest gasworks in the World.

In 1865 the old Toll End site was vacated and The Horseley Company moved half-a-mile South-East to the confusingly, and pleonastically, named Horseley Fields also within Tipton. At this new site they were adjacent to the railway that had replaced the canal as their essential avenue of transport.

Horseley Coal and Iron constructed metal bridges for all the railway companies in England, including, in 1885, Charing Cross Bridge in London. It also provided many of the rail bridges in India and South America including, in Bolivia, the 800 feet long and 310 feet high steel girder Antofagasta Viaduct.

Swing bridges were provided at Littlehampton, Hawarden and elsewhere and a 4000-ton steel girder roof constructed at Huddersfield (1884), as well as another Beckton roof in 1890, this time for the gasworks Purifier House.

Numerous train sheds were roofed worldwide and in 1889, three hundred and fifty tons of steel were used by Horseley to make the roof of London's Palace Theater.

In 1879, the Harwich Railway Pier absorbed eight thousand tons of iron. Numerous other heavy wharves were built worldwide.

The London Gas, Light and Coke Company continued to be a valuable customer for plant, and Horseley also outfitted the Buenos Ayres and Belgrano gas companies and built oil storage tanks for the Argentine Navy.

Sadly, in July and August 1890, the patterns for the old cast-iron bridges were broken up, but steam engines were partially replaced by gas engines and electrification.

By 1900 Horseley Coal and Iron was building all types of heavy steel lattice structures, metal lighthouses, cranes and water mains around the World.

After World War One, power station equipment became an important output and Horseley was commissioned to make many of the six-armed standard British electricity pylons. Lattice railway shed roofs evolved into aircraft hanger lattice girder spans of the patent Lamella pattern in steel or aluminum.

Horseley arranged with the German patentees to build Klonne type gas holders for steel mills and gas works across Britain, and in 1938 Horseley Bridge merged with Thomas Piggott and Sons, makers of heavy steel tubes and pressure vessels for oil refining and other industries.

It was sometime during this Interwar Era that Horseley exploited another major line in the manufacture of steel-paneled water tanks, the sort that you used to see mounted on steel-lattice towers around factories and farms. For a time this was sufficiently iconic a product to feature upon the Company's Long Service Certificates.

During World War Two, Horseley-Piggott concentrated upon making landing craft, disposable boats used for transferring tanks and troops ashore. These were made in their thousands by various firms in diverse parts of the World.

In 1945, the new combine constructed a cyclotron, an enormous atom-smashing machine, for Birmingham University, an institution that Horseley had a long tradition of supporting financially. The next year the construction of Walsall Power Station brought £409,296 worth of work and in February 1947 Horseley-Piggott merged with Wolverhampton pressure-vessel maker Thompson Brothers.

Under conditions of extreme secrecy, the UK Government determined to expand its civil and military nuclear capabilities. The new combine was ordered to design and fabricate massive stainless steel pressure vessels capable of containing fugacious gasses under high pressure as well as hot chemically-reactive melts. These vessels were shipped out on flatbed rail trucks.

By way of light relief, literal as well as otherwise, Horseley-Piggott roofed The Dome of Discovery at The Festival of Britain and erected the BBC's 785-feet 80-ton Sutton Coldfield television mast. The Dome consumed 232 tons of aluminum and 133 tons of steel.

On a smaller scale, a revolutionary welded steel portal bridge was constructed across the Walsall Canal within three boat miles of Pelsall Works Bridge, but some 125 years later.

Bread-and-butter boilers and more exotic pressure vessels continued to leave the factory gates as the civils division Carter-Horseley unveiled the first welded tensile steel bridge, a road bridge, over the Thames at Maidenhead, and in 1961 Horseley provided the 630-feet high pylons that carried electric cables skyborne across the Rivers Severn and Thames.

In 1964, Horseley-Piggott made three 60-foot diameter radio telescopes for Cambridge University. They were said to provide the same exploratory power as would have been yielded by one metal dish one mile across.

A campaign of modernization in 1965 to 1968 made what was now called Horseley Bridge Limited the most modern constructional fabricator concern outside the US. Completed projects included, in 1968, a complex pneumatic system for the Mach 1.2 Wind Tunnel at Bedford, and The Great Ouse Flood Protection Barrier.

By 1969, however, Horseley, in common with all British manufacturers was facing problems, especially from targeted foreign competition and its own failure to price bids realistically. Horseley Bridge formed a defensive ring with sector rivals Clarke Chapman and International Combustion Limited. The Government sought to nationalize the pipe fabrication sector but that fell through. In the 1970's the Clarke Chapman Group was subsumed within Northern Engineering Industries Limited, a Newcastle-centered agglomeration of the traditional UK heavy engineering sector.

In September 1968 Horseley-Piggott was commissioned to provide the steelwork for the Cleddau Bridge, a box-girder road bridge to be built across Milford Haven in Pembrokeshire. The bridge was designed by Sir Alexander Gibb and Partners and my old employer, Freeman Fox and Partners, bridge and transportation engineers. Once again Horseley was at the cutting edge of civil engineering technology and the innovative box girder construction was bedeviled with problems and delays. On 2nd June 1970 a cantilever collapse killed four men. The bridge opened to traffic in 1975, and has vindicated itself by forty-seven years of faithful service,…and counting.

During the 1970's the British Government came under irresistible pressure to abandon its independent civil and military nuclear programs. Between 1956 and 1990 Britain built various types and kinds of home-grown gas-cooled reactors and applied most of them to power generation. When the Conservative Government of Mrs Margaret Thatcher took power in May 1979 they immediately abandoned British civil nuclear development and decided to purchase American power systems on a turnkey basis. UK-made military delivery systems had already been discontinued though Britain was still obliged, under the terms of the Nuclear Non-Proliferation Treaty, to make warheads using its own resources.

These changes spelled doom for Britain's nuclear equipment makers and Horseley-Piggott now had to fall back upon its traditional Horseley rôle as a civil engineering steel fabricator.

Some years later, NEI was itself devoured by Rolls-Royce Limited, the only surviving UK engineering concern of World class.

Then in 1991, a decade after The Thatcher Reforms decimated British manufacturing and its associated services, a new purge struck. Within fifteen months, 190 of Britain's surviving fabrication firms closed.

On 15th May 1992, Rolls-Royce terminated operations at Horseley Fields, even though Horseley Bridge had a full order book at the time. A caretaker team was on site on 18th July 1992, but no champagne was popped to celebrate two centuries of The Horseley Coal and Iron Company.

Two hundred years of proud British innovation were at an end. Three men who might have known The King of France met in a pub. They thought they had bought a coal prospect. They spanned the Earth with steel.

I have a postscript, or you might call it an anticlimax. During my 2007 researches I detected a small firm in Gloucester. It makes large steel water storage tanks and calls itself Horseley Bridge Tanks. I do not know whether it is a true relic of the grand old firm, or merely a newcomer who purchased the trademark. We wish it well.

MENAI
The Menai Bridge

Location:	The Menai Strait, Anglesey-Caernarvonshire, Wales, UK
Date of Photograph:	pm 12 August 1996
OS Grid Reference:	SH556716
Co-ordinates:	53:13:18N 4:09:39W
Elevation:	2.1 meters

   This is The Menai Suspension Road Bridge as viewed from its North-Eastern flank on the Anglesey shore looking Southward towards Caernarvonshire on Great Britain.
   The minimal sea crossing to Dublin from England and Wales was achieved from Holyhead, a port on Holy Island, a patch of land separated from the larger island of Anglesey by sheltered shallows spanned by a causeway. To access Anglesey, however, travelers had to negotiate the dangerous tide race of The Menai Strait, a deep quarter-mile wide marine channel between Bodland and the Anglesey village of Porthaethwy. They crossed in small ferryboats. The race was only passable at slack water.
   British weather is very fickle and the tidal currents complex. The action of natural forces moves hidden sandbanks that can capture shipping. Many misfortunes and misjudgments occur.

In 1785 a boat with 55 passengers stranded on a sandbar in the strait. The boat swamped and help was summoned from Caernarvon, about eight miles distant. When the would-be rescuers arrived, high winds, tidal conditions and nightfall prevented an approach to the stricken ferry. The tide rose and those marooned on the sandbank were swept away. One survived.

In 1800 Ireland joined The United Kingdom by an Act of Union. Travel and trade between Ireland and Britain increased dramatically, but the treacherous little strait still accounted for nine of the thirty-six hours it took to journey from London to Dublin.

Thomas Telford was born in Eskdale, just within Scotland, on 9th August 1757. His shepherd father, John, died when Thomas was still a baby and the family was destitute. To help keep bread on the table young Thomas did odd jobs around the district, but thanks to Scotland's system of free State education he learned to read and write. As he matured he developed a talent for the new, or rather revived, profession of civil engineering, a mystery that had slumbered since The Fall of Rome.

In due course Telford became the chief surveyor and engineer of the County of Shropshire, designing numerous roads, canals and small arch bridges in Shropshire and elsewhere.

By the end of The Napoleonic Wars in 1815 Telford was one of the most eminent engineers of his generation and was approached by The Government to project a bridge over The Menai Strait. Several cast-iron arch designs had already been considered but these literally fell short of The Admiralty's stipulation that any span must be at least one hundred feet above high water so that the masts of sailing warships could pass beneath.

Telford's genius was to use the Chinese concept of the tensional iron bridge to span a chasm in The Occident.

The design involved the suspension of a carriageway spanning 579 feet of free space from two tapering 153-feet high limestone ashlar towers. Through each of those towers, two road arches were to be 9 feet wide and 15 feet high, whilst massive support arches on each shore would bring the total length of the structure to 1710 feet, nearly a third of a mile.

Constructional work started in 1819 with the limestone for the piers and arches being hewn from the Penmon Quarries at the Eastern extremity of Anglesey about nine miles East. The stone was carried to the site by boat. The towers are hollow with reinforcing cross walls inside. The ashlar is braced internally with iron struts.

Telford carried out a series of experiments to determine the optimal size and shape of the wrought iron links that he proposed to employ as tensional support. This was an area of enquiry previously unexplored in The West.

In 1820, Thomas Telford commissioned the Shrewsbury ironmaster William Hazeldine (1763-1840) to forge the metal. Due to the extremely high quality of iron required it is thought that the cast-iron feedstock was smelted with wood charcoal rather than the much cheaper coal coke. The massive links were forged at Upton Forge on the River Tern. 10476 wrought-iron links, 9 feet eye-to-eye were produced, and 4% of them were discarded as inadequate. These bars were finished and proved at Upton, under the supervision of Telford's site engineer, John Provis. The iron links were then soaked in warm linseed oil to protect them from rust. The links were either carted to Menai by road, or sent along a canal from Upton Forge to Chester, and thence by sea.

In the next year, 1821, timber centering for the arches on the Caernarvonshire shore were erected. This phase employed up to four hundred men and seven boats.

The iron links assigned to The Menai Bridge (some were used at Conway) were formed into sixteen cables each of 935 iron bars to support the 176 meter span. The total weight of iron employed was 2187 tons in 33265 pieces.

By 1824 the stonework was complete and raising the chains commenced. A first section end was hauled to the top of the Southern tower, fixed, and allowed to dangle into the sea. An identical chain was fixed to the Northern tower and left to dangle. Then a third, central, section weighing twenty-three and a half tons was rafted into place and attached to the chains hanging from Anglesey and Great Britain. To timing music, 150 men used block and tackle to raise the central chain into a span. The parting stress along the catenary was nearly fifty tons force.

The other fifteen chains were raised in a similar way, their shore ends being anchored into huge cavities carved into the living rock. Iron rods were then depended from the catenaries and a wooden roadway suspended from these, one hundred feet clear of high water slack.

Telford costed the project at £127,331. It came in at £231,500, complete with toll houses on each shore.

The Menai Bridge was ceremonially opened on 30th January 1826. The poor but brave ferrymen were unemployed. But theirs and hundreds of other lives would be saved by the splendid work astride the strait.

Fortunately, the structure was too massy and laterally-rigid to gallop, but nevertheless high winds tore away part of the wooden road in 1839 and of course it had to be repaired. In 1893 the wooden deck was replaced by steel.

As vehicles grew heavier the four and a half ton weight limit became restrictive and various load-split stratagems had to be resorted to, even the dismounting of bus passengers who were sometimes requested to walk the span: An unnerving experience on a wet and windy night as I can testify!

On 12th November 1918 Air Marshall Sir Thomas Elmhirst celebrated the silence of the guns by flying his airship SSZ73 under the span.

Between 1938 and 1940 the old iron links were progressively replaced by steel ones laminated from flame-cut high-tensile plates. The toll was removed in about 1940.

In the Autumn of 1999 the bridge was closed for road deck resurfacing.

Even together, the Menai Bridge and the road decks of The Britannia Railway Bridge across the strait about a mile to the West are barely able to cope with modern traffic. A submarine tunnel has been considered but shelved due to its need to intersect an active geological fault line.

Methods of improving the road access to Anglesey and Ireland remain under consideration.

On 28th February 2005 The Menai Bridge became a UNESCO World Heritage Site.

The Site of the Vanished Upton Forge in November 2002

CHAPTER FIVE

Saving the Sailors

The reality of British geography is that seas must be crossed to sustain the nation, and to defend it this was always so.

In a Christian land the concept of rescue and restitution keeps an abiding fascination, beyond but additional to the selfish imperatives of salvage.

The seas around Britain and Ireland are stormy but squally. Unpredictable little fits of tempest visibly form and approach but are essentially inevadable, even under power. Sailors had their own ways of dealing with these squalls, sometimes successfully. The wind can and does blow wherever it listeth but there is a statistically "prevailing" wind from the Atlantic South-West. These winds could of course assist the return of seafarers, but equally they could drive ships helplessly ashore. In a single day's storm it often happened that hundreds of ships would vanish about these shores, and thousands of lives be lost. On the Cornish and Devonish cliffs heavy wooden ships could be driven with such force that they would be splintered to matchwood and packed into pulp within caves, where today sport divers may happen upon old cannon or scattered coin: Everything else has long since been devoured by marine organisms or winnowed by currents.

Clearly some kind of shore light could mitigate loses during hours of darkness if it were powerful enough, high enough and not attenuated by mist or spray.

There is evidence that coastal church towers were sited with regard to the needs of navigation and certainly mariners practiced techniques of alignment and subtense with various degrees of sophistication. Such were of course mainly of use in daylight.

A Roman lighthouse survives at Dover and this was reinstated in the sixteenth century. Medieval religious houses built and maintained coastal lights at St Catherine's Point on The Isle of Wight, in Dorset and possibly elsewhere. In 1635 James Maxwell built a coal-burning light on the Isle of May at the entrance to The Firth of Forth, and an obvious virtue of such island or reef lights is that not only do they mark a hazard of itself, but they also provide a positive marker to navigation.

The first lighthouse built at the force of the sea was the Eddystone light tower erected by Henry Winstanley in 1698. It was built upon a dangerous sea-washed Channel rock about twelve miles South of Devon. The lighthouse was a right octagonal tower of iron-reinforced wood gorgeously decorated in the Baroque fashion and surmounted by an oil lantern within lead-latticed windows. The light tower and Winstanley vanished from the rock during a stormy night in 1703.

Two problems besides fog bedevilled the construction of effective lights. One was the lack of a technology to form a tower strong enough to resist the force of storm-driven waves. The second was the feeble and diffuse character of the illuminants available.

In 1759 John Smeaton did much to address the structural issues when he placed a fourth tower on the Eddystone that was made out of pre-cut dovetailed ashlar. This tower had a broad base tapering by a curved batter to the top so as to deflect and dissipate the wave energy gradually. This light tower served well until it was replaced with a larger stone light in 1882. It did not fail: It was the rock beneath Smeaton's tower that cracked, rendering its basis unsafe.

Light quality was improved by the general introduction of oil lamps, parabolic mirrors, and, after 1822, by the gradual introduction of the light-concentrating Fresnel lens. Later the introduction of turntables enabled coded light sequences to identify particular towers to mariners.

In 1807 Henry Trengrouse of Helston witnessed the death of the crew of HMS Anson after it drove onto the nearby Loe Bar. The men were within meters of a safe sandy beach, but could not cross the swell. 270 of the 330 aboard died. Trengrouse invented a cable-strewing rocket that could be used for inshore rescue. If a ship drove against cliffs or a beach, onshore rescuers could fire the rocket into the rigging of the wreck. It would bring a pilot cord behind it that those aboard could secure and use to drag a stronger rope aboard. This could then be used to clamber ashore, or form the cable for a breeches buoy.

Another active succor of the era was the oar-powered inshore lifeboat promoted by the Manx Quaker William Hillary. In 1824 Hillary founded The Royal National Lifeboat Institution, a charity which has rescued thousands from the sea. It currently has sixty-five plus boats at stations around Britain and Ireland. All the crew are, and always were, courageous unpaid volunteers. Primitive lifeboats led to a proliferation of improved designs. The first enhancements were buoyancy chambers to right capsized boats or to render them "unsinkable". As oar and sail gave way to steam, petrol and diesel, the boats were enclosed, made faster and more independent of sea conditions.

Fog remained a problem. Cannon, bells and firecrackers had been tried but a reliable and acoustically-consistent signal was required. The advent of rapid-start engines, and especially the internal combustion engine, made possible pneumatic horns adequate to being heard for miles. In 1859 Scottish engineer Robert Foulis installed steam horns at Partridge Island in Canada, and air horns with coded tones and durations spread to every suitable UK light station by the First World War.

Light quality and reliability problems persisted and became pressing in the case of smaller unmanned beacons in busy waterways or remote seas. In 1904 the Swedish engineer Gustaf Dalén helped found Aktiebolag Gasaccumulator (AGA), a factory and laboratory at Saltsjö Järla. He specialised in the design and production of high-intensity, long-endurance automatic light beacons lit by acetylene or petroleum, and more recently by electricity. Dalén lost his sight during a laboratory accident in 1912, but continued to work and was awarded the contract to install the navigation beacons of the Panama Canal, as well as, in that year, the Nobel Prize for Physics. Thousands of AGA automatic lights have been installed worldwide. Their modern electric beacons are often powered by solar energy or wave action and are capable of operating unattended for years.

Electrification also improved the quality and reliability of traditional lanterns to a degree at which today manning has been dispensed with, as have turntables and Fresnel lenses. Some modernised lighthouses and horns are partly powered by renewable energy and virtually all offshore lighthouses are now serviced by helicopter.

During the last half of the twentieth century coastal navigation gradually transited from visual seamark acquisition to radio goniometry, and lights and horns became secondary. Many less relevant lights, especially in Scotland, were abandoned and by the 1980's UK foghorns had ceased to blast.

The drama of the Cornish horns and the sweep of their attendant spokes of light through the night cloud is now a cherished memory of aging folk like me.

Today, routine navigation depends upon the computer triangulation of satellite microwave transmissions that can fix a position on the Earth's surface to within centimetres. Let us hope that sailors remember how to use a chart and sextant and keep such with them.

CHANCE
The Former Chance Brothers Glass Works at Smethwick

Location:	Chance Glass Works, Spon Lane, Smethwick, Staffordshire, Mercia, England, UK
Date of Photograph:	am 23 November 2007
OS Grid Reference:	SP004897
Co-ordinates:	52:30:21N 1:59:38W
Elevation:	147.2 meters

In 1814 Thomas Shutt built a glass works on part of the Blakeley Hall Farm estate to the West of Spon Lane. There was enormous contemporary expansion of domestic and industrial building with a commensurate demand for window-glass. Shutt manufactured crown glass: A gob of red-hot viscous "metal" was picked up on the end of a hollow blowpipe, blown to a balloon and spun rapidly so that centrifugal force produced a disk of glass. When the disk solidified it was cut into little glazing panes for shop or house windows. Shutt went into partnership with Joseph Stock and the Palmer Brothers, and between 1816 and 1822 the firm traded as The British Crown Glass Company.

Robert Lucas Chance was a scion of a family of farmers and craftsmen from Bromsgrove. His brothers William and George were, however, already prosperous ironmongers in Central Birmingham and would later take partnerships in Robert's firm when it faltered. Robert purchased the ailing British Crown Glass Company in 1824 and built a second glass house straight away, to be followed by a third in 1828.

A financial crisis of 1833 was resolved when new partners, including William and George, joined the firm. Improvements had been made in crown glass manufacture with the help of French craftsmen, but it was clear that the technology was physically and economically unviable. In 1832 Georges Bontemps came from Chossy-le-Roi to show Chance how to make cylinder, or sheet, glass, which was phased-in during the 1830's. This process involved stretching the gob between a pontil and a blowpipe, inflating the red-hot metal into a hollow prolate ellipsoid and slitting it lengthwise whilst still plastic. The balloon of cooling glass was then spread upon a smooth iron surface and allowed to solidify before being cut into panes. This innovation enabled Chance Brothers to become the largest maker of window, plate and optical glass at that time.

By 1845 there were seven glasshouses at Spon Lane, four producing sheet glass.

The factory expanded rapidly. By 1851 the firm had 1,200 employees and glazed the Crystal Palace. It diversified onto glass tubing, an entrée into laboratory equipment specialities. Around that time, Chance made the ornamental windows of The White House, and because it was the only company that could make opaque white glass it was commissioned to make the clock faces of The Westminster Clock Tower (now the Elizabeth Tower), usually called "Big Ben" after the name of one of its bells.

Further diversification included stained glass windows, ornamental lampshades, microscope slides, painted glassware and other specialist glass products.

During the 1960's when I was an amateur microscopist and professional laboratory technician I was in possession of several cases of Chance blank slides and cover slips. I neither knew nor cared where they were made but remember the distinctive "Chance" script logo on the boxes. They would be museum pieces now.

In 1812, the Scottish optical physicist Sir David Brewster described a theoretical geometry for focusing light using a quasi-planar compound structure and in 1822 the French physicist Augustin-Jean Fresnel had made this reality by inventing a compound glass lens structure and demonstrating its utility at the magnificent Cardovan lighthouse near the mouth of the Gironde. This new lens was of a more or less discoidal overall form compounded of concentric annuli of glass elements whose radial curvature emulated that of a continuous lenticular dioptric at their respective angular displacements from the focus. The virtues of this structure were that it consumed a fraction of the weight of glass that would be required for a conventional lens of the same power, and because the glass was thinner, the transmitted light was much less attenuated by the medium. The drawback was that the lens was useless for imaging. Both virtues suggested the Fresnel lens as an amplifier of the rays produced by feeble lighthouse lamps, in that it could husband the light into a concentrated beam visible for miles.

The Chance Works was the only British source of optical glass and during the 1850's James Timmins Chance set up as a maker of lighthouse optics for installation across The British Empire.

The English electrical physicist and engineer John Hopkinson invented a low-friction turntable system upon which a cagework of Fresnel lenses could be rotated by clockwork about a central lantern. The advantage of this system was that it could be programmed to sweep light beams of various colors, groupings and durations across a horizon to identify a particular lighthouse. Such a light would occult: Pulse rapidly in its intensity without ever actually disappearing altogether, like a police-car beacon but unlike a simple flashing light that extinguishes completely between illuminations.

James Chance built an 80-feet high tower for testing his lighthouse optic assemblies and in 1859 purchased extra land to extend his lighthouse factory. Additional land was bought in 1867 when he required an erecting shop for further lighthouse lens assemblies. Chance diversified beyond the glasswork to provide the necessary burners, as well as the cast-iron plinths and revolving carriages that supported the optics.

In 1872 John Hopkinson joined the staff at Spon Lane as Engineering Manager. In 1889 Chance Brothers became a private limited company, and in 1898 Government contracts further expanded the lighthouse production.

During the turn of the nineteenth century, Chance developed a larger and more powerful lighthouse optic called the hyperradiant, based upon a Hopkinson concept. These lens systems were up to twelve feet tall and were installed at major landfalls such as Cabo de Sao Vicente, Bishop Rock, Cape Race and Manora Point.

In 1938 the British Government became concerned about the vulnerability of its only source of optical glass to The Luftwaffe. It ordered Chance Brothers Limited to construct a shadow factory at the site of Pilkington's Limited, the plate glass makers at St Helen's, an extra hundred miles from Germany. Upon the return of peace in 1945, Chance and Pilkington's merged and the next year Chance Brothers established its Malvern factory to manufacture scientific, medical and metrological glassware.

In 1957 optical glass production at both Smethwick and St Helen's was terminated. An entirely new Chance-Pilkington Optical Works was constructed at St Asaph and is now called Pilkington Special Glass. Chance continued to make glass tableware at Smethwick in a variety of innovative designs but flat glass production ceased in 1976 with all such manufactures being transferred to The Ravenhead Works, the Pilkington complex at St Helen's. In 1981 the Spon Lane works closed and the remaining glass tube production transferred to Malvern. In 1992, the Malvern establishment demerged from Pilkington and became Chance Glass Limited, consolidating its scientific and lighting glass specialisms, concentrating upon bespoke industrial and architectural commissions.

After closure most of the Spon Lane complex was cleared but a central seven-story building of 1845 and a range of 1850's warehouses beside the New Line Canal are Grade Two Listed structures and have survived in a derelict state.

In November 2007 I found the 1845 building was being renovated, very probably as residential accommodation. The place has a very eerie atmosphere, especially along the canal towpath.

From a distance of some half-mile, my Nikon telephoto lens picked out the unmistakable sunlit shimmer of rolled glass in the upper stories of the central building.

On the face of it this should date to between 1848 and about 1925, but of course the panes might have been rolled on site at virtually no cost well into the Postwar era.

The Chance Premises at Malvern as seen on the Afternoon of 8 April 2008

HARVESTR
The Solway Harvester at Kirkcudbright

Location:	The Scallop Dredger BA794 "Solway Harvester", Kirkcudbright Harbor, Kirkcudbrightshire, Scotland, UK
Date of Photograph:	am 31 March 1999
OS Grid Reference:	NX683511
Co-ordinates:	54:50:16N 4:03:08W
Elevation:	3 meters

This picture shows the steel scallop dredger BA794 "Solway Harvester" in her home port of Kirkcudbright on the North shore of the Solway Firth. She was of registered length 19.43 meters and was built by Hepworth's of Paull in 1992. Her UK Fishing Vessel Certificate was renewed on 18th September 1997 and was good until 15th November 2000.

Her port of registry was Ballantrae and her owners were Jack Robinson (Trawlers) Limited of Grimsby.

She had seven crew: The Mills family; skipper Andrew "Craig", 29, Robin, 35, and David, 17; Martin Milligan, 26; John Murphy, 22; David Lyons, 18; and Wesley Jolly, 17.

It is thought that the Solway Harvester put out from Kirkcudbright sometime on the 9th or 10th of January 2000 and motored to Isle of Whithorn some twenty-five kilometers across Wigtown Bay. Several of her crew lived in this latter village.

In any event, by 1530 on the 11th January 2000, the Harvester found herself at a point in the Irish Sea halfway between the Isle of Man and the Lancashire coast in the midst of a worsening storm. She was in the act of running for shelter in the lee of the big island and hauled in her gear as she continued at speed on an approximate bearing of 330°.

By 1730, however, Force Eight winds were running over 4.1 meter waves from the South-West, against a countervailing current of 1.3 knots.

At 1745 the dredger hove to and broached the seas. As she rolled heavily, the bagged scallops and shipped water in her hold shifted and she capsized and sank at about that time.

Her position was 54°05.85'N 4°04.87'W, about ten miles ESE of Douglas Harbor. The wreck lay in 38 meters of water.

All seven men were missing, presumed dead.

The Manx Government announced its intention to dive the site and recover any bodies for burial, and, if possible, to raise the boat for inquest.

Within days the salvage vessel CSO Wellservicer was on station. Divers descended and recovered four bodies from the sleeping quarters and three from the gutting deck. It was reported that a hatch had been left open and that life rafts were missing. Otherwise the vessel was upright and intact, except for some crumpling to the bow which was consistent with the vessel hitting the benthos nose-first, but not suggestive of a ships' collision.

The bodies were placed in a metal capsule and transferred to the supply vessel Scotian Shore.

Relatives, officials and the press attended Douglas Docks as a crane lifted the capsule ashore. The capsule was draped in the Saltire and the Manx flag. A lone piper played "Flower of Scotland" and "Amazing Grace" as the onlookers wept. Police officers saluted as the bodies were driven to Noble's Hospital for autopsy.

On the Wednesday morning the people of Whithorn went to the church to lay 17-year-old Wesley Jolly to rest. The Priory Church could not accommodate the crowds. The Reverend Alexander Currie wept as he officiated. Then the mourners processed to the Catholic Church to remember 18-year-old Assistant Coastguard David Lyons.

That afternoon, in the tiny pilgrims' landfall church on The Isle of Whithorn, the Mills family was laid to rest amidst the coastguards and fishermen of the little community and mourners from far afield.

Recovery of the actual vessel was hampered by bad weather but the hulk was eventually hauled by crane onto the deck of the salvage vessel MV Norma. The wreck was taken to Ramsey Harbor and floated for inspection by The Marine Accident Investigation Branch.

In addition to the compromised flotation that was the immediate cause of the foundering, the MAIB drew attention to the weak attachments of the dredger's life-saving apparatus.

They recommended that servicing and securement of life rafts be vigilantly maintained, that inexperienced crewmen be certified to have completed mandatory safety training, and that other aspects of safety inspection and education be kept current.

They further stated that the protective covers of fish room slush wells be operational and their use understood; that portable diesel salvage pumps be shipped; and that bilge alarms and strainers be properly maintained.

A further set of recommendations counselled the proper stowage and securement of catch and gear to pre-empt shifts in metacentric stability at sea, and that company logistical and managerial procedures be tightened to ensure the availability and serviceability of safety-critical equipment.

On 6th March 2000, Karen Mills of Whithorn, wife of Robin, gave birth to Robbie Andrew, a brother for Sarah. Robin had agreed with his brother Craig to stand in for a sick crewman when he joined the Solway Harvester on her final voyage.

The "Solway Harvester" as retrieved from the sea bed and photographed
By the Author at 1529 14 September 2010

HELVETIA
The Wreck of the Helvetia at Rhossili

Location:	Rhossili Bay, The Gower Peninsula, Glamorgan, Wales, UK
Date of Photograph:	pm 30 April 2002
OS Grid Reference:	SS414890
Co-ordinates:	51:34:40N 4:17:25W
Elevation:	0 meters

On 1st November 1887, after a month of storms that occasioned many losses, the Norwegian oak-built barque "Helvetia" grounded upon the Helwick Bank near Mumbles off the coast of South Wales.

Registered at Horten, it was inbound to Swansea with five hundred tons of timber from Campbelton, New Brunswick.

Inevitably, the particulars of the ship's distress are confused and confusing. But the following is what seems to have happened.

By the night of Monday 31st October 1887, the Helvetia had reached Mumbles Head, at the outskirts of its port of destination. The master, Stevenson, ordered signals to be fired to summon a pilot from The Port of Swansea, five miles to the North-East.

At that juncture, a "fresh breeze" arose from the South-East preventing further progress and the Helvetia hove to.

By eight am on Tuesday the ship had been blown back five miles to The Helwick Sands. Now a gale blew up from the North-East sending the ship back to sea. But then the ship drifted shoreward and struck the bank, losing part of its deck cargo. She grounded again past Worms Head, and anchored in Rhossili Bay, where she was embayed.

The master was taken ashore by the Coastguard, using a breeches buoy. The crew stayed aboard to deter looters. Unfortunately, the wind changed direction dislodging the anchor and the ship drifted shoreward. The captain appeared and ordered the crew to abandon ship. They left in the ship's boats. The "Helvetia" drove ashore with no casualties.

The Helvetia's cargo scattered across the sands of Rhossili Bay but much was recovered and auctioned, and some found its way into the floors and structures of Rhossili houses, where it remains to this day.

A local man purchased the hulk intending to recover its valuable copper sheathing that protected the hull from attack by shipworm, the Toredo mollusk. Misfortune again intervened, however, when the wreck settled into the sand so quickly that he was unable to salvage the metal.

A tragic sequel to the wrecking of the Helvetia was occasioned by attempts to salvage the anchor of its salvage vessel. On Sunday 18th March 1888 Captain John Hopkins of the Llanelli screw steamer "Cambria" was completing the timber salvage. Previously, his own vessel had been driven ashore beside the Helvetia, and one of the Cambria's anchors was lost in shallow water during the Cambria's refloating. Hopkins commissioned five stevedores to retrieve it by boat, and bring it to Kitchen Corner (SS401876) where it would be buoyed, and finally recovered, with its chain, when conditions permitted.

The six men dragged the anchor and chain to Kitchen Corner and adjourned to "The Ship Inn" at the village above. Later that Sabbath, they rowed back to the buoy and hauled the chain into a coil in the bottom of the boat. The weight brought the boat so low that the sea was almost spilling over its gunwales. The men began to recover the actual anchor but Hopkins realised too late that the sudden Archimedean weight-gain as the mass of iron emerged would be enough to overset and sink their small vessel; chain, anchor and all. Hopkins ordered the anchor to be released. The anchor was now effectively weightless, and the sudden recoil of their boat was enough to swamp and sink it. All six men drowned.

I visited the windswept sands of Rhossili on a cold and largely sunless April day. The ribs of the Helvetia stood in defiance of more than a century of wild Welsh storms, as delicate little ripples chased and played around the timbers' sand scours. I approached the stem and was alarmed to find myself suddenly sinking through the sand. Clearly it was quick where water draining seaward from both tide and land met the still-intact copper sheathing, and, taking the line of least pressure, rose skyward.

KILCOBBN
The Lizard-Cadgwith Lifeboat Station in Cornwall

Location: Kilcobben Cove, near Lizard Town, Cornwall, England, UK
Date of Photograph: 8 April 1990
OS Grid Reference: SW715125
Co-ordinates: 49:58:10N 5:11:14W
Elevation: 20.4 meters

This is the RNLI Lizard Lifeboat Station (formerly called the Lizard-Cadgwith Lifeboat Station) at Kilcobben Cove.

On 21st February 1800 that rare bird, a Quaker rake, called William Hillary eloped with a rich Essex girl and married her. He spent the £20000 she brought raising an army to fight Napoleon. A grateful George III bestowed a baronetcy, but not withstanding that Sir William was soon in difficulties.

Then as now, the Isle of Man was beyond English Law and in 1808 Sir William repaired hence to evade his creditors. Three years later he married a local girl whilst the mother of his son was still alive!

Hillary grew concerned about the immense loss of life amongst seamen around Man and formulated a proposal for a Manx and British maritime lifesaving service. In 1823 he offered the concept to The Admiralty, who predictably proved uninterested.

Undeterred, Hillary contacted a group of philanthropic London merchants and met them in The Tavern at Bishopsgate. On 4th March 1824, they founded "The National Institution for the Preservation of Life from Shipwreck".

Since that time The Royal National Lifeboat Institution has saved over 137000 lives and now supports 230 stations with 330 boats around the coasts of the UK and Eire.

The boats are manned wholly by volunteers and the RNLI is financed entirely by private contributions and bequests.

In 1859 a lifeboat station was established at the waveswept Polpeor Cove on Lizard Point, the Southernmost extremity of Great Britain. Eight years later another was set up at the sheltered fishing village of Cadgwith about three miles to the North-East.

In 1885 a secondary Lizard boat was stationed at Church Cove, approximately equidistant between Cadgwith and The Lizard and immediately North of Kilcobben Cove. This outpost, however, closed in 1899.

In 1907 six men of both the Lizard and Cadgwith boats earned Silver Medals for their gallantry in rescuing 394 from the White Star liner "Suevic" when it foundered in fog upon the Marnheere Reef, otherwise in plain view of Polpeor.

In 1958, concerned at the continuing hazards that storm and rock presented at the exposed Polpeor Cove, the RNLI determined to consolidate both The Lizard and Cadgwith into a new super-station between the two villages.

The Kilcobben Cove station was opened by HRH The Duke of Edinburgh on 7th July 1961.

It was an unforgettable and deeply-affecting ceremony on that cloudless and calm Summer afternoon in a different England. I sat with my Late Mother and the women of the villages on a rock ledge high above the sea to the South of the slip. We studied Phillip's distant profile as he said something indistinct into a tannoy system. Suddenly, the boat dived into a nappe of sparkling water and seemed momentarily to disappear before roaring seaward. The gentle voices of the women struck up into "Eternal Father Strong to Save", the British naval hymn. The presence was indescribable, but doubtless they and I shall remember it through this life and the Next.

Sinful Quaker renegade Sir William Hillary, soldier, rescuer of sailors, and Founder of The Royal National Lifeboat Institution scowls at the seas that Christ once stilled. An impressive striding bronze by Amanda Barton, installed at Douglas Head on the Isle of Man.
Photograph by the Author at 1622 13 September 2010.

MULLHORN
The Foghorn at The Mull of Galloway

Location:	The Mull of Galloway, near Portpatrick, Wigtownshire, Scotland, UK
Date of Photograph:	pm 29 March 1999
OS Grid Reference:	NX159306
Co-ordinates:	54°38'13"N:4°51'10"W
Elevation:	24.7 meters

This is the foghorn associated with the lighthouse at The Mull of Galloway, a promontory that is the most Southerly part of Scotland.

The lighthouse at the Mull of Galloway was erected in 1828 by Robert Stevenson but it was not until 1896 that a foghorn was installed. It gave two blasts: One high and one low, each of five seconds, every three minutes. On 25th October 1918, DA Stevenson advised the Commissioners of Northern Lights to change this to two blasts each of two and a half seconds every ninety seconds.

This improved discrimination from the other local horns and enabled the Kelvin compressor diesels to run at 180 rpm rather than 235 rpm.

In 1925 the current horn installation was built using concrete and ashlar and a new Engine House with improved clock arrangements added.

It is thought the horn last blasted sometime in the 1980's when it was superseded by radar fog warnings.

MUSDILE
Eilean Musdile Lighthouse near Oban

Location:	Eilean Musdile island, Southern tip of Lismore island, Argyllshire, Scotland, UK
Date of Photograph:	pm 27 July 2006
OS Grid Reference:	NM778351
Co-ordinates:	56:27:25N 5:36:15W
Elevation:	6.7 meters

Eilean Musdile is a ten-acre islet in The Firth of Lorn.

It is owned by The Commissioners for Northern Lights who purchased it in 1830 for £500.

In 1833 James Smith built the facility for £4260, using a design by Robert Stevenson. The first Principal Lightkeeper, Robert Selkirk, was a descendant of Alexander Selkirk, Defoe's model for Robinson Crusoe.

After 1910, Musdile and Fidra were the sole remaining catoptric Northern lights. Musdile was automated in June 1965.

PORTBILL
Portland Bill Lighthouse

Location:	The Bill of Portland, Dorset, England, UK
Date of Photograph:	pm 1 April 1994
OS Grid Reference:	SY677683
Co-ordinates:	50:30:51N 2:27:23W
Elevation:	43 meters

In former times Weymouth was an important port, one of the busiest in England. Its ancient function is possibly best remembered for the facts that The Black Death made its British landfall there on 25th June 1348, and that in February 1805 William Wordsworth's brother John, Captain of "The Earl of Abergavenny", an East Indiaman, lost his life when his ship foundered in Weymouth Bay.

Weymouth is in the lee of Portland Bill, a windswept limestone promontory that juts miles into the Channel between England and France.

A fierce tidal current called The Portland Race arises from the opposition of tides confined between Portland Bill and The Shambles sandbank some three miles to the South-East.

The function of the light is to guide traffic entering Portland and Weymouth; mark the bank with a red sector; and act as a waymark for Channel through-shipping.

In 1669 Sir John Clayton took an abortive patent to erect a light at the Bill, but it was not until 26th May 1716 that the people of Weymouth were successful in petitioning Trinity House to erect a light. Two coal-fired lights were set up but very ill-run by the lessees. After sixty-one years the lease reverted to Trinity House.

In 1789, the brethren commissioned William Johns of Weymouth to demolish one of the existing pillars and replace it with another tower. In that year Argand lamps were installed, Portland being the first light in England so equipped. There were two banks of seven oil-fired Argand lamps with highly-polished reflectors. Further improvements were made shortly after when Thomas Rogers installed a separate low light with a catoptric system housing six Argand lamps to improve visibility at sea.

In 1869, the high and low lights were replaced with the current single tower. The low lighthouse survives as a bird observatory.

The present optic is arranged to transition from one flash to four between bearings 221° and 224°; and from four flashes to one between 117° and 141°. The lamp is an electric 1 Kw Mbi with a four-panel first-order catadioptric fixed lens, giving a white group flashing four times every twenty seconds. The power is 635,000 candela. The tower is sited 43 meters above Mean High Water, and has a height of 41 meters: The effective elevation of the lantern is therefore 84 meters yielding a visible range of about twenty-five nautical miles. There is an obsolete fog signal capable of blasting for three and a half seconds every thirty seconds.

The facility was demanned on 18th March 1996. Monitoring and control is now managed remotely from The Trinity House Operations Control Centre in Harwich.

CHAPTER SIX

The Old Ways

You may object that literally and figuratively Britain and Ireland are permeated so ubiquitously with "old ways" that any attempt to segregate such vague but omnipresent things to a chapter of their own is doomed to failure.

But my thesis is that the British Isles form a society in which certain revolutionary changes broke with a past that in parts has gone and in parts persists and may have had and still has subtle influences upon the national future: A future that promises revolutions to come.

Therefore I have abstracted essential traditions like the sea, science and industry, even wildlife, and given them treatments of their own almost on a basis of equality with religion.

When we remove the well-known and well-described features of the British landscape what are we left with?

Of course, thoughts of the "old ways" stand us in great danger of trespassing within the curtilage of "Tourist Britain" and exposing ourselves to the horrors of Hollywood and the Tussauds-Towers vision of commercial fakery and fantasy well beyond the broad but crooked path of critical antiquarianism.

And our problems do not cease there, because we have to example an apparently disparate congeries of seemingly mutually-irrelevant items, the more so since on the whole we will stick to public outdoors photographable finds, spurning museums and the premises of trusts, and denying ourselves the luxury of the "interpretations" of professional experts and archivists.

So here goes:-

1. Prehistoric monuments and earth disturbances (a handful fake or more usually misidentified).

2. Deserted settlements or their relict features (e.g. church towers).

3. Hydraulic Features: Aqueducts, fish ponds, moats, leats, cisterns, wells, spas, hydraulic rams, wind pumps, etc.

4. Road Features: Aggers, toll houses, milestones, "take on" and "take off" stones, pavement, notices and advertisements , signage.

5. Public houses and theaters.

6. Mausolea, tombs, gravestones, cenotaphs, including martyrs' memorials, slave graves and plague pits, together with any epigraphy.

7. Penal Paraphernalia: Prisons, lockups, gibbets, stocks, whipping-posts, etc. (mostly fake).

8. Former or present places of secular assembly including guild halls, old trees, battlefields, market places, wayside crosses and alleged moots.

9. Follies and venatic vantages.

10. Folk dances and customs (almost all post 1880).

11. Obsolete Technology: Hydraulic accumulator towers, semaphore telegraphy stations, abandoned railway paraphernalia, cranes.

12. Obsolete Technology in Use: Gas lighting, vapor lamps

This list is of course quite arbitrary and inexhaustive, but may exemplify some developing themes: Several of the point relics we have listed have to do with public demonstrations or literal or metaphorical "theater"; and much appears to relate back to communication, especially by road.

Another commonality will have struck you forcefully: Many of these landscape components are classic venues of alleged nocturnal activity on the part of Britain's tireless legion of hard-working ghosts and ghouls! Something guaranteed of itself to spook our almost as numerous army of archaeologists and "respectable" academics.

Further features of the "old ways" monuments that militate against professional analysis is their plebeian aura; their frequent poverty of primary documentation; their often sanguinary qualities; and frequent doubts in regard to functional authenticity.

The Abbots Bromley Horn Dance includes some very suspect Robin Hoodery but something involving antlers at Abbots Bromley is authentically Dark Age, as proven by the radiocarbon datings of the artefacts themselves. In contrast a raft of English morris dances, Northern "cloggy" events and their Celtic equivalents are of very recent origin, even twentieth century.

None of which diminishes the fact that folk customs and fixed artefacts of any age can, and usually do, have important stories to contribute to rational social and cultural narrative, whatever the sneers of the cognoscenti.

Mock castles and other prominent follies were often conceived to relieve local unemployment, encourage craft skills or even serve as test-beds for concrete technology or other important scientific work. This was quite beyond aristocratic pretensions or vanities, however glorious the results, in the field of landscape design.

Almost none of the wooden gibbets or penal instruments are original to purpose, unsurprisingly since they were last (illegally) used in the 1830's. Those visible almost anywhere in Mercia and the South are Late Victorian or Edwardian replicas, and at Coleshill in Warwickshire there is even a mass-produced American "Red Hannah" pillory. At nearby Bilstone there is a decayed stump of what may be an actual gibbet of 1801. A 1951 photograph of this exists showing it much taller and apparently with rusted chain and other ironwork fixtures, which latter were later stolen, as was its explanatory plaque. Like many gibbets this was erected to expose a specific individual at the scene of his crime.

In remote places, especially Northern hill country, you can sometimes find vestiges of Roman or Georgian road pavement with flanking milestones, memorials, crosses or other imperishable stonework that frequently offers legible epigraphy, some of it of great antiquarian interest.

At various places the elegant remains of medicinal spas include pump rooms and baths as well as atmospheric urban landscapes. Buxton, one of only four or five UK warm wells, offers an opera house, baths, conservatories, The Royal Devonshire Hospital (which for a hundred years supported the World's largest dome) as well as still-drinkable fountains. All is set amidst elegant streets and churches. Fetid waters and chalybeate can still freely be sampled further afield at such delightful places as Llandrindod Wells and Strathpeffer.

When I was a boy working windpumps were common in the South and as late as 1985 you could hear the steady cardiac thump of a hydraulic ram at Lilleshall Abbey. Both were visible or audible enough to merit inclusion on large-scale Ordnance Survey maps. Now almost all have vanished.

A handful of old theaters in ports or resorts such as Richmond and Harwich have survived, but as with taverns and inns this only happens after a period of use in other employment, the usual fate of redundant places of entertainment being summary demolition.

Funereal monuments are very widespread. There is a twentieth century War Memorial in at least every village and suburb. Slave graves survive in eighteenth century ports like Sunderland Point and Bristol and there is a complex of famous plague graves at Eyam in Derbyshire. Martyr's memorials are always on the exact site where the Holy victims suffered and accordingly can be literally anywhere: Salt flats at Wigtown, a street called St Gile's in the center of Oxford, and many obscure field corners in Southern England.

Several Victorian ports such as Liverpool and London preserve hydraulic power accumulators. The towers are usually decorated to look architectural. The most splendid is the 309 feet high tower at Grimsby Docks, for about an hour the only visible part of England on the old ferry route from Gothenburg. It was completed in 1852 as a simple elevated cistern. Its aesthetic is a conscious imitation of the tower of the Palazzo Publico at Sienna, from which, however, it differs in detail.

Cranes and other transhipment equipment are sometimes preserved, or just left to rot in the landscape, along with other redundant transport kit, much of which survived upon patrolled railway land protected by statute and only recently being turned to other purposes.

During the first half of the nineteenth century, semaphore telegraphy systems were laid out along intervisible hilltops to communicate The Admiralty in Westminster with naval bases in Kent, and at Great Yarmouth, Portsmouth and Devonport. A fifth major line was constructed from Holyhead to Liverpool for commercial notices. Nearly all remains disappeared when electric telegraph was introduced by 1845, but a remote station survives upon the intertidal Hilbre Island in the Dee Estuary, and ruins are possibly extant upon Puffin Island at the Eastern extremity of Anglesey.

Also widespread in my childhood were streets lit by town gas or by electric mercury vapor lamps. The former produced a ghostly green glow and the latter a cold and ghostly blue one. Already in the 1950's gas was on its way out and the ornate Victorian standards were unceremoniously uprooted and dumped in public parks ready for the scrap merchant. Gas lighting persists today only in conservation areas at Malvern or Nottingham, or sparsely in Westminster were a handful of continuously-burning Welsbach lamps are fed with methane from underlying sewers.

Vernacular antiquities are ill-studied and not usually missed until they are gone but they collectively populate a picture of the past that, with proper analysis, could help explain the present and predict the future, for it is the instruments of a community which change, rather than its functions. Computerised telegraphy is now removing much of the raison d'etre of roads and railways, even flight, but the concept of communication persists, as do the needs of law enforcement, the care of the sick, and the disposal of the dead.

ABHD
The Abbots Bromley Horn Dance

Location:	Abbots Bromley, Staffordshire, England, UK
Date of Photograph:	am 6 September 1993
OS Grid Reference:	SK076246
Co-ordinates:	52:49:09N 1:53:18W
Elevation:	111.3 meters

Most of Britain's "ancient ceremonies and traditions" date as far back as Late Victorian or Edwardian (I mean twentieth century) times. They echo an empty and rootless nostalgia for a factitious, Wagnerian age that never was, for the men of those days had thoughts too urgent for dalliance.

Except, that is, for The Abbots Bromley Horn Dance.

The eponymous "horns" are, in fact, reindeer antlers, the weapons and ornaments of a creature extinct in Staffordshire for ten thousand years. The Horn Dance is first adverted to in an order of Henry III dated 1226 that permitted the dance to be presented to the Abbots of Burton during the Barthelmy fair. That revel celebrated St Bartholomew's Day, 24th August, old style.

One of the antlers broke and a splinter was radiocarbon dated in 1976. The apparent age of the antler was 920 years.

There are six antlers for the twelve dancers. There are three "white" horns and three "blue" horns. The patina of the latter makes them seem brown or black rather than blue. The horns reside in the vestry of St Nicholas Church and have never left the parish. Their weight ranges from 16.5 pounds to 25.25 pounds, but there is a set of lighter modern red deer antlers used when the dancers tour.

The six horn dancers take down their horns on the first Monday after the first Sunday after 4th September (according to our Julian calendar). Or more succinctly, Wakes Monday. They are accompanied by six other dancers: The Fiddler (now using an accordion); The Jester; The Hobbyhorse; Maid Marion; a Bow Boy (with a toy bow and arrow); and a Beat Boy (today using a triangle to keep rhythm). All twelve are male except that in the last ten years the Bow and Beat Boys have sometimes been girls. The Jester is a fool complete with foolscap and motley, The Hobbyhorse a gowned man astride a broom handle with a wooden horse head, and Maid Marion a necessarily fit middle-aged man draped in the dirty blue woollen gown of a Medieval lady.

The name of the village reflects the division of The Bromleys between the Crown and the Church. The latter may have taken the interest in what is now Abbots Bromley on the grounds that it was a hotbed of aboriginal religion that needed close supervision. "Bromley" means "the pasture of Brom", an obscure but ubiquitous figment of ancient Mercia, and whose name is celebrated in very numerous place and personal names in the old Kingdom today: Indeed, the name of Birmingham is based upon Brom. The exact relationship between Brom and *Cytisus scoparius* the legume shrub is equally obscure and we do not know whether broom was sacred by association or place consecrated by the vegetable. Such things are lost to time and to Christ. Their ways were not our ways and their thoughts not our thoughts.

The dance and its participants clearly reflect elements of Celtic animism colored by possible Wiccan traditions and "Robin Hood" lore. The dance is a complex interweaving line dance to an unforgettable and unique rhythm. Its route around the streets and taverns of Abbots Bromley and out to Bagot Park and back measures fourteen road miles, but inclusive of local circumvolutions the procession unpaces about forty-nine miles. Technically, it is a six-figure walking step line dance inclusive of AMR and CO elements. The dance lasts from 08:00 with a (Christian) Service of Blessing in St Nicholas Church and finishes at 20:00 hours with Compline, also celebrated at St Nicholas.

The ceremony is the hereditary preserve of the Bentley and the Fowell families, but competent guests have recently been allowed to "dance in" and "dance out" with prior arrangement.

It would appear that the dance evolved as part of harvest-home celebrations, and may relate additionally to religious imprecations for the rutting success of the Needwood deer in the immanent Autumn.

Onlookers are welcome but parking is very limited and of course the light and weather are very variable

BONCROSS
Bonsall Cross in Derbyshire

Location:	Bonsall, near Matlock, Derbyshire, England, UK
Date of Photograph:	pm 21 June 2004
OS Grid Reference:	SK279583
Co-ordinates:	53:07:16N 1:35:03W
Elevation:	204.5 meters

Bonsall Cross is in the center of Bonsall Village and appears to be made of gritstone.

It is the tallest cross in Derbyshire and is of unknown date, but is presumed to be medieval. The earliest dated repair is 1620, but further dates: 1678, 1769 and 1800 are incised.

It is a market cross, specifically a feeing cross (a sort of early labor exchange). Farm laborers were hired here at annual wakes, and during the Napoleonic Wars, French prisoners were allocated to local farms at this muster point.

The circular base has thirteen steps, which may have borne a numerological significance lost to history. The surmounting ball is dated 1671.

Within Bonsall village the traditional industry was stocking manufacture though the dominant industry in its immediate hinterland was lead mining and smelting. The Via Gellia and Cromford cotton mills were also major employers and it was in the former that the blended fabric Viyella, fashionable in the last century, was developed.

Bonsall villagers are said to be the most long-lived in England. This may relate to the facts that the law decrees, specifically in regard to Bonsall, that should snow fall and a resident salt the snow before his house, then he must subsequently shovel away the resultant slush; and at no time must he keep a pig, or pig excrement, within fifty feet of a dwelling.

GREATGAT
The "Whipping Post" at Great Gate in Staffordshire

Location:	The "Whipping Post", Great Gate, Staffordshire, England, UK
Date of Photograph:	pm 18 October 2007
OS Grid Reference:	SK055400
Co-ordinates:	52:57:30N 1:55:06W
Elevation:	140.2 meters

English Criminal Law used to differentiate between Felonies, serious crimes like murder or arson that attracted transportation or capital sentences; and Misdemeanors, less serious property thefts or adulteries that invoked fines or corporal punishment. The latter was intended to be painful and humiliating but was not allowed to "endanger life or limb" and usually involved flogging the back with a cat to produce superficial laceration.

Whipping, specifically flogging, was abolished in England in 1964, but had been in decline for two hundred years and widely deprecated as a barbarous archaism, even in the 1780's. All whipping of females was illegalised in 1820 and it is difficult to find evidence of the public flogging of males beyond the 1830's.

Accordingly, the ubiquitous stocks and whipping posts of English villages are mostly fraudulent: The results of a baleful Victorian fashion for things Gothick and Olde-Worlde. Authentic punishments were usually extempore and so were their instruments. Regarded as shameful for both perpetrator and victim, English corporal punishment was usually unrecorded and never awarded the symbolic value it possessed in the German-speaking lands.

Nineteenth-century Ordnance Survey maps fail to show this expensive-looking "whipping post" at the dozy hamlet of Great Gate, publess and with a population of about fifty. Modern OS maps mark it as "whipping post" in Blackletter.

It is a sturdy sandstone obelisk that shows some signs of vertical fluting and tentative borings as if it is an old plague stone, an interpretation that could be substantiated by its liminal position, but its true origin is probably more prosaic.

Close inspection discloses an iron shackle whose hinge is actually at ground level above a kind of ashlar plinth concealed below windfall leaves. When I touched this restraint it fell open with a hyaline chime and I thought "low-grade puddled iron". This substance was manufactured between 1784 and 1974. The upper shackle had broken away with a brittle fracture and it had been fastened into its socket in the stone with a grout of barely-corroded molten lead, typical of local gate-hangers' work circa 1880 to 1930. None of this puts the post definitely into the fraud category, but equally none is suggestive of the hand-wrought fibrous iron workmanship using easily available local wood and ironstone, that you would expect of a pre-1850 date.

But the big problem is the position of the shackles: Either the victim would have to lie prone with his ankles manacled, or crouched on the plinth with his shoulder to the pillar. Whichever, it would be impossible to strike him an effective stripe, even if you groveled on the ground with him.

Notable is the little barn across the road on the right of the picture. It has one of the finest roofs I have seen anywhere. The walling is very good too though showing its age and some fine iron straps have redundantly reinforced it from inception. The roadward oaken door with iron hanger bolts is very costly and the whole ensemble is much too high-class for a small Staffordshire barn.

Adjacent to these features, but out of view, is a sandstone ashlar integrated school and master's house of 1853. Were the barn and "whipping post" fashioned of its surplus materials, at the expense of some national charity or local aristocrat?

HOLOPRIS
The Entrance to Holloway Prison

Location:	Parkhurst Road, Holloway, London N7, England
Date of Photograph:	pm 17 September 2007
OS Grid Reference:	TQ301855
Co-ordinates:	51:33:13N: 0:07:27W
Elevation:	40 meters

   Until the middle of the Nineteenth-Century the usual British punishment for serious offenders was transportation, a process that for much of history was considered more condign than death. Transportation involved shipping the miscreant to a remote colony, where they would be enslaved for between seven years and life. In wilderness destinations prisoners were usually simply abandoned to try conclusions with savages, wild animals or the weather: Some became millionaires, the vast majority promptly died.
   By the 1870's, the Australian Colonies had already been largely successful in stopping British forced migrations. Furthermore, British suffragists, mostly female, started a campaign of arson and public disorder in their quest for votes for women.

Thirdly, in 1903, the ancient gaol of The City of London, Newgate, was demolished to make way for The Central Criminal Court, the almost equally notorious "Old Bailey".

A need was established for a new gaol for the City, and by 1849 work had commenced on a mixed City of London House of Correction at Holloway, a mock-medieval castellated structure to the design of James Bunstone Bunning. This edifice inevitably became known as "Camden Castle".

This first phase, completed in 1852, had three male wings and one for females and juveniles. It provided 436 cells at a cost of £91,547:10s:8d. During the 1880's 340 new cells were added including a hospital wing.

Oscar Wilde was a celebrated Victorian inmate, but by 1903 Holloway was a female-only prison, the only secure penal institution for females in the UK. The British custom is to accommodate criminal women and girls in mental hospitals, but for the few hundred who pose a violent escape risk, or whose personal safety from outsiders is problematic, Holloway is the preferred receptacle.

Local suffragettes often found themselves in Holloway, rubbing shoulders with prostitutes who could often walk back to their beats within minutes of release.

But Holloway, which hanged five of the fifteen British women executed in the Twentieth-Century, soon developed a lurid reputation for some truly dangerous females, many of them minor European aristocrats.

It accommodated World War One IRA women Constance Markeivicz and Hanna Sheehy-Skeffington; Pro-German spies Eva de Bournonville and Dorothy O'Grady (both narrowly avoided the gallows); prominent fascists Diana Mitford and her husband Sir Oswald Mosley, personal friends of Adolf Hitler; and the Nazi synagogue arsonist Francoise Dior, niece of couturier Christian Dior and sometime wife of British Nazi leader Colin Jordan. (Even after the passage of nigh on sixty years I remember clearly how this Dior woman scandalised London by attending her wedding naked except for a diaphanous gauze shift and indulging in a barbaric blood-mingling ritual with the groom).

Until her death in 2002, Holloway was home to Manchester child-torturer and murderess Myra Hindley.

Forty-seven women waited in Holloway's condemned cell. Forty, including 27 infanticides, were reprieved, one freed on appeal, and one sent to Broadmoor, a secure hospital for the criminally insane. The five others were hanged.

Curiously, the last two to hang, within two years of each other, committed their murders in Hampstead, a wealthy suburb an easy hour's stroll from the prison.

The last British woman to hang was 28-year-old nightclub hostess Ruth Ellis who died on the gallows at Holloway on Wednesday 13 July 1955. She shot her boyfriend dead outside The Magdala tavern in nearly Gospel Oak. He had refused to keep her company over the Bank Holiday. Albert Pierrepoint, the last hangman, officiated. Sometime in 1967 the long drop apparatus was dismantled and its housing converted into a sewing room.

When the prison was rebuilt in 1970 the five bodies were exhumed and sent to unmarked graves at Brookwood Cemetery in Surrey, except for Ellis who was re-interred at St Mary's, Amersham. It each case surviving relatives refused the remains.

LETOCETM
Letocetum Roman Settlement at Wall

Location: Wall, Staffordshire, England, UK
Date of Photograph: 4 July 2004
OS Grid Reference: SK098066
Co-ordinates: 52:39:25N 1:51:23W
Elevation: 109.4 meters

These are the remains of a small Roman village called Letocetum (Celtic for "Gray Woods").

The hamlet functioned as a staging post on the main itinerary between Hadrian's Wall and the channel port of Richborough. It was also strategically-sited where the Watling Street from London to Wroxeter intercepted Ryknild Street from Metchley (in modern Birmingham) to Derby, and thence York. At Pennocrucium near modern Gailey a major road diverged through Northern Shropshire to Chester.

It is thought that Ryknild Street marked the border between the tribal lands of the Cornovii centered upon Viroconium Cornoviorum (Wroxeter) and the Coritani with their capital at Ratae Coritanorum (Leicester). Subaerial Roman remains persist at both sites, whilst at Letocetum the excavated foundations of a bathhouse and a mansio (posthouse) may be seen.

It is inferred that Letocetum functioned as a market between the Cornovii and the Coritani, and this trade possibly involved the Roman Army: Two Imperial pigs of lead with first-century Clwydian markings were found at nearby Hints in 1771 and 1883 and one is now in the British Museum.

Besides the definite bathhouse and hostel remains experts believe they have detected vestiges of temples and a small ampitheater. Eighteen extramural cemetery burials have been excavated.

Letocetum was almost certainly a pre-existing Iron Age hamlet but the earliest Roman interest can be dated to the campaigns of Ostorius Scapula in AD47. The village was burned in c200AD, possibly by the Ordovices (North Welsh). Subsequently the hill adjacent to the North was fortified and crowned with a military temple to Minerva now occupied by Wall church. It is perhaps from this vantage that a layman gets the best conspectus of the site, and saves the absurd admission charge when it is being levied!

Accordingly it is from the churchyard that I took the photograph, looking South.

PENTRICH
The Gate House of The Butterley Works at Ripley

Location: The Gate House, The Butterley Company, Butterley Hill, Butterley, Derbyshire, England, UK
Date of Photograph: am 18 October 2007
OS Grid Reference: SK401516
Co-ordinates: 53:03:39N 1:24:11W
Elevation: 107.3 meters

In 1815 The Napoleonic War ended, and with it the Government demand for arms and textiles that drove the first industrialisation. The workers of Derbyshire were laid-off and their subsistence was charged to their fellows, who also were thus pauperised. The landowner, Private Eye's famous "unemployed Derbyshire man" gazed on from Chatsworth.

Also in that fateful year, very far from Europe, the volcano Tambora exploded. The dust it sent into the stratosphere circled the Earth bringing blue moons and wet summers, with snow in the English June of 1817.

The harvest failed. The people convened.

Meetings of more than fifty were outlawed and Habeas Corpus suspended.

Thomas Bacon, a Pentrich frame-work knitter, visited various reform meetings throughout the industrial North and Midlands and reported to his village that a national army of the poor was about to march on London to unseat the government and declare a free republic.

Government spies frightened Bacon and, fearing arrest, he went to ground, but an unemployed stockinger Jeremiah Brandreth took over as the Pentrich peoples' leader.

At 10pm on 9th June 1817, Brandreth led two parties of largely unarmed men from Hunt's Barn in nearby South Wingfield. They hoped to gather further men and arms on the way as they marched toward Nottingham. There was poor discipline and many taverns were raided during their rain-sodden night. One resistor was shot dead.

The two parties re-grouped at Pentrich Lane End and, following the red glow of the furnaces reflected like a way-beacon upon the spilling cloud, marched the three miles to the great iron works of The Butterley Company in its eponymous hamlet.

At the iron works they hoped to commandeer cannon shot and other armaments. As they approached the octagonal gatehouse seen in the picture above, the Works Manager and a handful of other men closed the barrier. They asked the marchers to go away. Shots were exchanged and the rebels walked on.

The skirmish at Butterley was decisive.

Faint-hearts sloped off into the night, and by dawn the remaining revolutionaries reached the Nottinghamshire border where they were dispersed by The King's Hussars. Some were arrested there and then, and the remaining rebels rounded-up during the next few weeks.

In October 1817, the three leaders Jeremiah Brandreth, Isaac Ludlam and William Turner were tried at Derby and sentenced to be hanged, drawn and quartered upon Nun Green. The terror of the men and their loved ones as the judge rehearsed the dreadful details may readily be imagined, but is nevertheless described by witnesses and visitors. This is thought to have been the only occasion upon which a cruel and unusual punishment was awarded for an attack upon an industrial premises in peacetime. By order of the Prince Regent, the three men were allowed to die in the noose and only their heads removed at the scaffold after death. Fourteen others were transported and six jailed. Twelve others were acquitted. None of the rebels who survived ever returned to Pentrich.

The British Revolution was strangled at birth.

In a ghastly prefigurement of twentieth-century atrocities, and of Clearances of hill folk, the Duke of Devonshire's estate agents turned the revolutionaries' families out into the weather and demolished their houses, together with The White Horse Inn where they had met. Economic development of Pentrich ceased and the nearby town of Ripley, even more convenient for the Butterley works, grew in its stead.

A Pentrich March heritage trail is now marked out with blue plaques at critical junctures, and one of these graces the Butterley Works gatehouse. This gatehouse may have been built as late as 1807, when the Ripley to Alfreston turnpike was completed. It may have functioned as a post house (in the sense of a depot for light correspondence). It is Listed Grade Two.

It is only in the last thirty years that the history of the Pentrich Rebellion has seeped into the public domain, because the British Government is usually very sensitive to any record or rumor of armed dissent at home. When I attended an Anglican school in the Sixties of last century whole areas of knowledge were systematically ignored. The Soviet Union and the United States were never referred to, even in World geography lessons, in case students caught strange democratic ideas, and although much time was spent upon teaching us the history of trades' unions and The Co-operative Movement, not a word of Pentrich or other unpleasantness was breathed.

Postscript: 26 May 2022

The Butterley Company (Benjamin Outram and Company) (1790-2009) deserves a library to itself. It rooved St Pancras Railway Terminus in Central London with a strong but delicate iron-and-glass canopy, one of the largest structures of its type in the World. Well within my lifetime it also constructed The Falkirk Wheel, and the Spinnaker Tower (Portsmouth), as well as the giant crane used to install the nuclear containment apparatus of Sizewell B Power Station. Over the preceding two hundred years it provided numerous heavy cranes, bridges and stationary steam engines world-wide, many of which products survive in situ.

Alas, the resignation of the UK from heavy engineering markets has led even this venerable company to cease, and since I took the photograph, the buildings have been demolished, except I think for the previously-protected Gatehouse. The 1790 blast furnaces, The Butterley Tunnel and some other static antiquities survive as Scheduled Ancient Monuments.

RHMEARS
The RH Mears Riding Jacket Factory

Location: 10 Harrison Street, Bloxwich, Staffordshire, England, UK
Date of Photograph: am 4 October 2007
OS Grid Reference: SJ999020
Co-ordinates: 52:37:00N 2:00:10W
Elevation: 164 meters

This is the works of RH Mears and Company, makers of tailored shooting, riding and fox-hunting jackets for men, women and children. Their wares are marketed worldwide under the "Mears" and "Pytchley" brands, but there is no trace of garment-trade waste around their factory, nor anything else visibly to suggest the nature of their activity.

The only auditory clue is the rhythmic and monotonous grind of their electric shears.

In 2004, the Blair government outlawed fox-hunting in England. The shears fell silent. Although I do not approve of hunting for pleasure, I thought how inevitable that this little factory should now fall idle and join the long file of Staffordshire luxury goods makers marching to oblivion.

A few months later the shrill sweeping sound of the shears restarted.

SHOTDAWN
The Shot at Dawn Memorial

Location:	The (British) National Memorial Arboretum, near Alrewas, Staffordshire, England, UK
Date of Photograph:	am 4 May 2006
OS Grid Reference:	SK186142
Co-ordinates:	52:43:30N 1:43:30W
Elevation:	51.5 meters

This is the Shot at Dawn Memorial in The (British) National Memorial Arboretum.

It commemorates the 307 British and Empire soldiers shot by their own comrades for alleged "cowardice" in World War One. Many of the victims were actually mentally-disturbed or even neurologically-damaged by the effects of war, and deserved medical assistance at home in their own countries. Only one victim was a commissioned officer: A Sub-lieutenant.

The practice was to tie the victim to a stake at sunrise and make a detachment of his own comrades shoot him dead. Many reluctant executioners were too drunk to make a clean kill. The penalty for refusal to participate was, however, yourself to be shot at dawn. Some victims were murdered by other methods in local (French) slaughterhouses.

Australia refused to let any of its men, all volunteers, die in this way. Twenty-three New Zealanders and Twenty-five Canadians were shot at dawn. One black and one Arab were not charged with cowardice or desertion (because these are acts of will, and supposedly-inferior racial types were presumed incapable) so they were killed respectively for "threatening violence" and "prejudicial conduct". Civilian drivers could not be charged with either cowardice or desertion, so they were shot for "striking". All Irish fighters (on all four sides) were volunteers: Twenty-four, however, were shot by British comrades, four times the pro-rata figure for other nationalities.

In a country-full of sad and haunted places it is impossible not to be moved here, even on a sunlit Spring morning. The ten-foot marble statue by Birmingham sculptor Andrew DeComyn models 17-year-old Private Herbert Burden, who left the trench to visit the transport column where a friend of his had just lost a brother and Burden thought to console him. The work was unveiled on 21 June 2001 by 87-year-old Gertie Harris, daughter of Private Harry Farr, also shot at dawn. Present and representing The World War One Veterans Association were Jack Davis, 106, and Fred Bunday, 101. The statue is backed by a hemi-circle of 307 dedicated stakes. The statue and many stakes embower fresh flowers. The whole is set in a glade amidst a grove of saplings beside the tranquil but urgent waters of the River Tame.

On 8th November 2006 the British Government pardoned all men shot at dawn and, by implication, apologised for the murders. There are moves belatedly to engrave their names on the relative War Memorials up and down Britain.

Now several elderly daughters can die content.

WROXETER
The Hadrianic Palaestra Wall at Wroxeter

Location:	Wroxeter, Shropshire, England, UK
Date of Photograph:	3 July 2004
OS Grid Reference:	SJ565086
Co-ordinates:	52:43:30N 1:43:30W
Elevation:	51.5 meters

This is the "Old Work", a fragment of the Roman wall of a massive basilica-like structure.

It is made of mortared rubble faced with brick and has three distinct courses of square apertures that may have accommodated timbers. It is one of the largest Subaerial pieces of Roman ruin to survive in Britain, and predates those of the Saxon Shore by about two hundred years. It is the tallest free-standing Roman structure in Britain.

It is part of the South wall of a Forum Basilica of Flavian age (c80AD). A basilica was a large covered space in which civic and financial affairs could be conducted in all weathers. The size and arrangement of basilicas facilitated conversion to Christian cathedral churches and the Wroxeter structure may have fulfilled such a function until well after Roman military withdrawal in 410AD. Whatever the case, the basilica became a palaestra in Hadrianic times (c110AD). A palaestra is a bathhouse exercise yard. In Southern Europe, palaestras were usually garths but the Wroxeter palaestra presumably continued to be covered in deference to the British climate. The original building was 245 by 66 feet in plan.

This Roman city was called Viroconium Cornoviorum and under the Romans became the tribal capital of the Cornovii. It eventually became the fourth largest Roman city in Britain with an area of 180 acres, and probably became capital of Britannia Secunda during the devolutions of the fourth century. In the South-West the circumvallation is interrupted by the River Severn though some shift of the river course during the last two millennia is likely.

The original citadel of the Cornovii was atop The Wrekin, a prominent volcanic plug about 4.3 miles to the East. This point was sacked by the Roman advance, when its defenders, led by Virico, were immolated. Viroconium was named in honor of Virico, an arrangement not offensive to Roman sensibilities.

Numerous relics of an opulent trading town have been unearthed including extensive bath hypocausts and temple structures, many stabilised for exhibition. Small artefacts are displayed in the excellent on-site museum.

In the Dark Ages some obviously subaerial vestiges were taken to build the Saxon village of Wroxeter on the riverside about half a mile South-West of the wall fragment. Wroxeter churchyard entrance is flanked by two weathered but elegant Roman columns whilst the capital of a massive column has been inverted to make the church font.

The sparse church interior has a chilly and unwelcoming aura and is, predictably, haunted.

CHAPTER SEVEN

Little Towns

Like the Old Ways Britain's Little Towns present a complex and heterogeneous picture. Like the poor they are always with us, but also like the poor they prosper, transform, decline and continually redefine themselves.

To understand the Little Towns (and I offer no definition) we first have to understand the Big Towns: What has happened to them, and the threats and opportunities that de-industrialisation, migration and changes in communication brought to all settlements.

Every community in the British Isles is dominated by London, officially a mere ten and half million strong its contiguous built-up area sprawls over nearly seven hundred square miles. At the hub of air transport it lays claim to be the leading cultural and financial center, the largest city of Europe, and the focus of occasional congress from worldwide.

Until fifty years ago London was also the World's principal industrial and shipping center, and at the end of the First World War it seemed that London, and the larger provincial cities, were set to expand indefinitely. Policy makers tried to constrain uncontrolled sprawl and encourage tourism and agriculture by prohibiting building in peripheral "green belts", yet relieving intraurban pressures with both permissive and planned satellite towns around the major conurbations. For thirty years a kind of national fossilisation ensued, intensified by impoverishments caused by major warfare and chronic non-investment.

Disastrously, government sought to ameliorate the plight of the poorest by demolishing vast tracts of Victorian housing in the city centers and replacing them with tower flats.

An unstable stasis persisted until, around 1980, central government removed support for industry, infrastructure, and for State services that mainly benefited the lower classes. Despite this labor costs continued to rise and in an effort to prevent inflation the Government removed all wage and price controls, outlawed the construction of further public housing and outlawed trades union activity except under strict legal supervision.

The provincial heavy industrial base suddenly collapsed and within five years it became clear that irreversible revolutionary change was again afoot. As in the computer simulation games unemployment, crime and substance abuse rose persistently to be followed later by mass illiteracy and disaffection.

It seemed that whole sectors of public and private service provision would become unmanned unless Government allowed free ingress of cheap foreign labor and encouraged female economic participation. But the result of the former was to exacerbate housing shortages long guaranteed by the planning restrictions and the demolitions.

The price of domestic property toppled upward.

Industrial revenues fell as did the value of industrial land, and residential property, or land with permission to build that, consistently showed significantly higher growth than stocks or their derivatives.

An Outer London three-bed semi (duplex) house built in 1935 for £600 sold in 1967 for £4400 and then in 1995 for £340000, whilst a provincial suburban bungalow purchased for £85000 in 1994 became worth £300000 in 2006. By 1991 an Inner London house at the unfashionable end of a street was worth £1.5million and in 2006 a two-bed Highgate flat £525000 whilst a four-bedroomed Victorian terraced house was £1million. In the good-class dormitory town of Harpenden, about thirty miles North of the City but within half-an-hour by train, a six-bedroomed house was priced at £2million.

As the old century turned to a new millennium no policy or enforcement could control so that London, and indeed Britain, became the passive substratum of global demographic evolutions, like a pollen grain trembling amidst the swift buffeting of invisible molecules a million times smaller.

The collapse of industry and shipping made available extensive "brownfield" interstices within cities to which the full rigor of planning restrictions did not apply and speculators were permitted to construct high-density housing on these.

Prices rose inexorably, and it dawned on many established city dwellers, especially in London, that they could sell their houses and retire to the coast or countryside, or indeed foreign resorts, as millionaires aged forty.

Capital migrated and production fell further.

Native Britons exited the Big Towns en masse. When East European countries acceded to the EU around 2004, 683000 registered worker migrants entered the UK from that region, together with an unknown number of casual travellers. These entrants were relatively educated or well-skilled young men and women who often brought spouses and young families with them.

Property prices rose again and began to emerge as an actual engine of national capital formation in their own right. Investment was written against property, and although contagious inflation spread to the rural provinces it made economic sense to shift your base and your business to a Little Town, if you could.

London resumed its traditional rôle as the Global brokerage-place and foreign capital and workers continued to funnel in. The management of scrip became the most important source of national wealth after borrowing.

Whilst these shifts in capital and population were taking place, the accessibility of the rural hinterlands was transformed. For over a hundred years railway companies had been protected by the Government, but in 1964 the then nationalised railway was made to withdraw passenger services from virtually all villages, smaller towns and industrial suburbs. A dramatic campaign of rural road improvement and motorway construction ensued. Most outside a large city had to run a car. The population of cars toppled upward, and city dwellers soon discovered they must have one too.

Advances in electrical switching technology were progressively miniaturising computer components and expediting telephonic communication and it seemed that parallel developments in digital multiplexing promised to cheapen computerised mass communication to a degree at which it would become the preferred medium of business. If this happened then trade could conceivably base itself anywhere without financial penalty. By 2000, the integration of computing and telephony, or to be exact telegraphy, had brought this to pass.

The converged effect is the commercial renaissance of Little Towns asleep since they were eclipsed by eighteenth century industrialisation.

The first effects of this revolution may have been felt in the hinterland towns of Oxfordshire and Cambridgeshire where "science-based" manufacturing sprang up in places like Gaydon, Bicester, Newbury and Melbourne. I remember visiting The Late Mr Don Braggins and the young men of the zone refining and crystal growth firm Metals Research Limited in 1964 when they worked from a Victorian flat above Percival's Garage in the center of Cambridge. By the seventies they had moved to no doubt custom-built premises a few miles South in Melbourne, and they are typical of the many technical companies that the two great universities spawned in the last half of the twentieth century. Other more familiar products include automatic hypodermic syringes at Chipping Norton, luxury cars at Gaydon and Goodwood, liquid crystal at Poole, and countless other petty industries whose high-added values compensate expensive transport access.

More prettily-sited Little Towns like Hay-on-Wye could specialise in well-canvassed services for the well-healed car tourist. In the case of Hay, Wigtown and Atherstone second-hand book selling has rescued local economies that had lost previous bases of trade.

National Parks and "green belts" still inhibit the growth of Little Towns but there are moves to relax restrictions, especially to assist depressed agriculture.

The Solent Conurbation of Southern England is hardly a Little Town, but, alone in Britain, became a major center of manufacturing expansion during the last half of the twentieth century. Maritime and arms industries are there dominant, and the Little Towns of the Isle of Wight have grown in their shadow.

The Internet has transformed the outlook of other offshore islands, previously reliant upon oil or agriculture, and though logistical costs constrain secondary industries to only the highest added values, it is becoming ever more feasible to base creative and consultancy work in such places. Anglesey island off the Northwest coast of Wales is the UK's most poverty-stricken county district especially hard hit by access costs and the decline of the aluminum and dairy industries. It contains a scatter of moribund Little Towns. But it is a mere 100-minute commute to Dublin by hydrofoil, and that city has long been the natural shopping destination for the people of Anglesey. If cultural and psychological issues could be overcome the Anglesey towns might become natural economic ancillaries of the prospering Irish capital.

Publishing has long dispersed to Little Towns from central London, were property costs became prohibitive during the mid 1980's. Elsewhere, especially in Wales, population and economic activity has migrated to the coasts.

Craft industries like glass-blowing and brewing have also migrated from the old industrial conurbations to little towns like Tutbury, Langham and Torrington whilst a handful of major postwar industrial start-ups have stubbornly remained in their semi-rural settings such as backhoe maker JCB at Rocester and perfumer Bodyshop at Littlehampton.

Scotland, as in so many regards, is a special case. It too enjoyed a "science-based" boom in small towns between Glasgow and Edinburgh but this has not ultimately proven successful. But in the 1970's and 1980's Scotland found itself in a position of negative strength with the UK's only two non-industrial large cities, and these financial centers of Aberdeen and Edinburgh have prospered, not only by largely evading the evils of dereliction, but by very active participation in the turn-of-the-century market booms in which Little Towns have fully participated as dormitories. Stonehaven, Inverurie and Queensferry are typical of these.

The happy picture is of a widespread regeneration of Little Towns across the UK based upon the immigration of secondary and quaternary industries and family units equipped with cash and skill. Perhaps the most languishing, though picturesque of the Little Towns are marcher communities like Bishop's Castle or the townlets of Cumberland, Northumberland and Roxburghshire which are however increasingly commending themselves as retirement areas or touring centers.

Another class of Little Towns, exemplified by Repton, Sedburgh, Lampeter, Glastonbury, Iona island's Baile Mor and others continue modestly to prosper as religious and educational centers, complementing the genteel attractions of the old spa resorts like Strathpeffer, Woodhall and Llanwrtyd.

Perhaps this type of community represents in extreme relief the cultural and material gulf that is rapidly widening between the Little Town and the great cities, especially in England: Another incipient source of crisis as yet not merely unresolved, but largely unforeseen.

BISHOPSC
Bishops Castle in Shropshire

Location: Bishops Castle, Shropshire, England, UK
Date of Photograph: pm 6 March 2003
OS Grid Reference: SO323888
Co-ordinates: 52:29:37N 2:59:53W
Elevation: 196.0 meters

This tiny town of about 1500 inhabitants was founded in 792AD, by the Bishop of Hereford, who built a castle, presumably to deter Welsh incursions. The castle was abandoned in 1559 and its stone reused before the Civil War.

Bishops Castle returned two MPs until 1832. In 1802 the two hundred electors enjoyed £6515:3s:4d worth of alcoholic entertainment by parliamentary candidates but incurred them an expenditure of £31:10s on bouncers who had to be brought in from Bridgnorth!

The lovely Town Hall, built in 1765, is home to two famous silver maces wrought in 1698.

The Nesbitesque railway closed in 1935 and borough status was withdrawn by Elizabeth II in 1967, but the little metropolis still supports a secondary (high) school, a 34-bed hospital, a dentist, doctors, two banks, two breweries, a post office, four grocers and a deli:- not to mention numerous "new age" shops, a hand-cart to carry coffins to burial and a flock of geese who go to church!

IONA
The Post Office at Baile Mor on Iona

Location: Baile Mor, Iona, Argyllshire, Scotland, UK
Date of Photograph: pm 27 July 2006
OS Grid Reference: NM285241
Co-ordinates: 56:19:59N 6:23:23W
Elevation: 4.0 meters

      Baile Mor is the ferry port and only settlement on Iona. It comprises 45 separate properties and is home to the vast majority of the island's 85 inhabitants. In the Southwest of the hamlet are the Clinic, Primary School, Hall and Library, whilst North of that little civic precinct is a Heritage Centre. This Heritage Centre is in a nineteenth century manse built by Thomas Telford. The other urban element is a range of houses behind the silver-sanded beach. That street includes the Argyle Hotel, one of two on the island. Here and elsewhere, there are additionally a youth hostel, religious residential retreats and a clutch of guesthouses.
      The Post Office is also immediately behind the beach, at an elevation of less than 5.8 meters, immediately North East of the ferry jetty.

The hamlet encircles the remains of a Medieval Augustinian nunnery, the only such in Scotland, but Baile Mor's development was wholly Victorian. It arose to service steamer-borne pilgrims and tourists, and to a limited extent housed and supplied the men who quarried green marble.

The Gaelic village name means "big town": A dignity conferred with no irony, since by Hebridean standards it is truly metropolitan.

The little Calmac car ferry, MV Loch Buidhe, has limited duties during its constant daylight shuttling half a mile across the Sound of Iona to Fionnphort, because only Iona residents are allowed to embark vehicles. During my July 2006 crossing to Iona, I gazed idly at the sunlit sandy bottom below our keel and my geological curiosity was stimulated by tawny elliptical outcrops regularly deployed across the benthos. A young lady asked a man what they were. He replied "Sharks". And so they were.

Almost everyone who uses the ferry arrives to visit the restored Abbey five hundred meters North of the jetty. At that site St Columba, who introduced Christianity to The Highlands, settled. He close this spot because it was the first at which he could not see his native Ireland, from which he was banished for murder. It is the last resting place of a good score of Scottish, Irish and Norwegian kings. The Abbey and its devotional community were rebuilt by Glasgow Christians during the 1930's, and I was privileged to attend there the ecumenical service that is held daily.

In March 2006, The Mull and Iona Chamber of Commerce spearheaded a campaign to save Iona Post Office from closure. Post Offices Limited, successor to The Royal Mail, had launched a public consultation regarding their plan to axe 2500 Scottish post offices and replace some rural facilities with five hundred mobile post offices. Some of the tiny Hebridean post offices are tourist draws in their own right, especially if they still offer the hand-franking of postcards and covers.

The Iona post office occupies a twentieth-century hut, but sporting an already obsolete illuminated sign and stoves, and keeping the worst of the storm spray from a magnificent, and very rare, Victorian pillar box.

The MICC were, however, especially exercised by the potential loss of the national standard parcel post to their islands. Chamber enquiries established that of 23 typical online shops, only 5 offered mainland delivery terms to Mull. Of the 18 majority, 3 levied a delivery surcharge of over £35 (more than US$70). One of the companies charged £13 to deliver to Mull, part of the UK, but only £12 to deliver to France, parts of which are in North America. The maximum surcharge amidst this sample was £38 and the mean £12.42.

Meanwhile, a BBC poll established that 91% of the British claimed that the Post Office "play an important rôle in their community" whilst 59% aid it was "essential to their way of life". And over 80% of the British live in large towns.

In February 2008 the newly and aptly named Post Offices Limited published their Network Change Programme for the area of what used to be the Strathclyde Region. Many little post offices were earmarked for closure, especially in suburban Glasgow.

Happily, Iona Post Office was not among them.

QUEENSF
Lovers at South Queensferry

Location:	High Street, South Queensferry, West Lothian, Scotland, UK
Date of Photograph:	pm 25 July 2006
OS Grid Reference:	NT133783
Co-ordinates:	55:59:24N 3:23:22W
Elevation:	3.0 meters

South Queensferry, or simply Queensferry, is the old ferry port for crossing the Firth of Forth. It is matched on the Northern, Fife, side by North Queensferry, about a mile away across the river's narrowest estuarine point. South Queensferry is about eight and a half miles West of Central Edinburgh.

The place has an older Gaelic name "Cas Chaolais": The cliff-flanked narrows.

Today, both North and South Queensferry are dominated by the immensity of Fowler and Baker's 1890 Forth Rail Bridge, a world-famous steel cantilever structure that features on Scottish banknotes. The Forth Rail Bridge was for many years the largest and longest bridge on Earth, striding in three bold steps across a mile of sea.

South Queensferry is further bracketed at its Eastern end by the great 1964 steel-cable suspension bridge, The Forth Road Bridge, part of whose Southern stays can be seen in the photograph about (0.9,0.4).

The road ferry that plied the straight was discontinued in 1964 when the road bridge opened, but South Queensferry still accommodates ferries. The small passenger boats that ply to Inchcolm, a beautiful abbey-graced island, dock in the shadow of the rail bridge.

During 2007, an archaeological due-diligence dig unearthed evidence of Bronze Age settlement at South Queensferry.

In 1070 the sainted Queen Margaret, English wife of King Malcolm III (he who vanquished MacBeth), established a great abbey at Dunfermline in Fife, a few miles North of the Firth of Forth. It immediately became a center of pilgrimage and the traffic over the estuary became so considerable that Margaret paid to have the monks operate a Queen's Ferry at this straight. Amongst Margaret's many cultural and religious innovations were her institution of Sunday as a Christian day of worship.

At first the Queen's Ferry beached wherever tide and weather permitted, but a little port evolved, servicing also the pilgrimage route to St Andrews, on the Eastern edge of Fife. In 1071, Malcolm granted free passage to pilgrims bound for St Andrews. Quite how that concession was policed is unknown, as indeed is the status of returnees at the Northern bank.

When Margaret died in 1093, the ferry carried her to her tomb in Dunfermline Abbey, and her son, David I, granted ferry rights to the monastery.

In 1441, another monastery and hospice, now St Mary's Episcopal Church, were founded at South Queensferry.

South Queensferry was created a Burgh of Regality in the thirteenth century and in 1636 a Royal Burgh. It was in the early seventeenth century that the Small Forth Ports including Queensferry enjoyed their heyday. Their prosperity was based upon coal, salt, fish and silver production, and vigorous trade with the North Sea and Baltic seaboards. The Forth was also the home of Scotland's small but magnificent navy. English colonies were not yet open to Scotland and Clydeside trade was unimportant.

Many of the solid, crow-stepped merchants' houses and civic buildings that line the High Street date from that time. They include Laburnum House, The Hawes Inn, the Tolbooth, Black Castle (really a large sea captain's house), the Old Parish Church and Plewlands House. The Tolbooth Tower, added in 1720, demonstrates clear Continental influences. Because of the slope the High Street has a raised inland pavement that intensifies the town's old-fashioned Brigadoon appearance. When I drove the street in 2006 it was partially pedestrianised and subject to a Westbound one-way system.

After Union the Forth declined as a trading avenue, but during the mid-nineteenth century a need for swift and economical access to the fish, shipbuilding and textile industries of the Scottish North East was felt.

In 1878, Thomas Bouch's Tay Bridge was opened and the next year he commenced construction of a rail suspension bridge across the Queensferry Narrows. On 28th December 1879 the two-mile-long Tay Bridge collapsed during a snowstorm and a passenger train that steamed into the night from Wormit vanished into the river below. All aboard were killed. Work on the Forth link ceased for four years.

Then, between 1883 and 1890, Sir John Fowler and Benjamin Baker constructed the wonderful steel cantilever bridge that spans the river still. It is made of a complex three-dimensional web of riveted steel tubes and iron struts. Like many cantilever bridges it is strikingly beautiful, although today it is often partially hidden beneath plastic sheeting.

The road ferry continued and by the 1950's four ferries made forty thousand crossings a year carrying 1.5 million passengers, 600000 cars and 200000 goods vehicles. In 1956 it cost between 2/6d and 7/6d to convey a car (£0.125 to £ 0.375) or 4/6d to 54/- for a lorry (£0.225 to £2.70). Foot passengers paid 5d (£ 0.02083').

In 1958 work began on spanning the narrows with a great steel-cable suspension bridge. This was opened on 4th September 1964 and on that foggy day I was one of the last to use the ferry, Southbound from Fife. Later that day the Queen's ferry ceased to ply after 894 years of service.

When I made my first visit to Scotland as a six-year-old in 1958 I did not notice the work on the new bridge. I remember road works in South Queensferry but did not relate them to any grander undertaking. One fine October dawn my Late Mother and I left Littlehampton, and boarding The Flying Scotsman at King's Cross reached Edinburgh by nightfall. My smiling Father was sitting upon a green steam-wreathed bench as the train hove to a standstill. My Father had been drafted to The Fisheries Protection Squadron that had that year been transferred from the Humber to Port Edgar, a small minesweepers' harbor, now a yacht marina in the shadow of the Forth Road Bridge, immediately West of South Queensferry.

We stayed in what was then The Seal's Craig Hotel, visible in the photograph, and enjoyed breakfasts overlooking the great rail bridge and the busy river from the dining-room at (0.8,0.4). One morning my Late Father pointed to a submarine moving up river and I saw a black shape but did not associate it with anything in particular. More memorable was the day my Mother and I boarded a small warship, a Motor Fishing Vessel used as a ferry, in Port Edgar. We went below and sat in the hold before some neatly-coiled hempen ropes and two smiling, friendly young sailors. The ship steamed to the much larger Naval base of Rosyth on the Northern bank. Here we disembarked and my Father showed me his ship, HMS Russell, at its berth. I was especially fascinated by a portable dockside donkey boiler that supplied the frigate with service-steam, as its own boilers were cold, but electric power still had to be raised for lighting. On one of our Queensferry days my Mother took me to the back of the town and bought me a Topper annual. This colorful book depicted the adventures of Beryl the Peril, who wreaked havoc in local libraries, and all of her shaky mates. It also contained the more realistically-drawn adventures of two hale and beplaided clansmen, a burly laughing fighter with a red beard and his younger comrade. They cheerfully sledged and strode through snowbound Highland landscapes, unassistedly overpowering whole garrisons of effete and frequently bespectacled English soldiers, gaily escaping with their provisions before the Redcoats could regroup. As I happily hopped downhill with this new toy I splashed in the pavement puddles, and as we drew abreast of a gray ashlar school building, this earned me a set of smacked legs.

On another occasion we must have used the ferry for its original purpose, since we boarded a bus and my Father purchased three stiff green Single cardboard tickets to Dunfermline. I do not remember Dunfermline, to which I have never returned, neither our method of return to Seal's Craig.

A few days later my Father steamed to the Arctic Ocean and into its gathering Winter.

My complex love affair with Scotland began.

The little town of South Queensferry has a number of "traditions" of uncertain or intermittent antiquity. The August Ferry Fair, first celebrated in the twelfth century is a May queen ceremony (Summer comes late in Scotland) with band processions and fun races. Queensferry has two major brass bands. A similar modern jape is The Loony Dook, a New Year's Day dip in the frigid waters of The Firth of Forth, and a certain hangover cure.

But by far the most famous Queensferry custom is the bedecking of The Burry Man, a volunteer almost entirely covered in burdock burrs and supported by two suitably beflagged and bannered attendants. Only the Burry Man's shoes, hands and eyes remain uncovered. He also wears a floral hat and sash as the trio process from tavern to pub, collecting money. Naturally, the Burry Man cannot quaff, but considerately he is drip-feed whisky through a straw. The etymology of "Burry" is controversial, especially after a couple of drams, but may either refer to the man's burr-covered situation, or else to his "Burgh" provenance.

REPTON
Repton in Derbyshire

Location:	Repton, Derbyshire, Mercia, England, UK
Date of Photograph:	am 31 May 2001
OS Grid Reference:	SK304270
Co-ordinates:	52:50:23N 1:33:01W
Elevation:	49.4 meters

      The picture shows a village that was once the capital of The Kingdom of Mercia, England's cultural heartland. The borders of Mercia are and always were ill-defined but include most of the territory bounded by Wales and the Rivers Ribble, Humber, Bristol Avon, Kennet, and Great Ouse; and in the South-East by the Chiltern Hills.

      Mercia is the only country in post-Roman Europe (note that Lithuania was never Roman) where Christianisation met significant resistance, and many aspects of the old Wiccan religion have survived there, usually at covert or subliminal levels. Quakerism, Methodism and several other Christian heterodoxies took birth in Mercia and the people embrace a life-philosophy best described as Deterministic Fatalism. Women and their intellectual contributions have always been central. From this deviant soil, the Mercian Kingdom has furnished most of Western Europe's greatest poets and prosaists, and many key scientific thinkers such as Newton and Darwin. In many regards,

Shakespeare and the great scientists, not to mention more political sons such as the Churchills and De Montfort, have set the tone of contemporary civilisation worldwide.

The Trent is by far England's largest river in terms of water discharge and Repton sits upon a gravel terrace underlain by impermeable marls about seventy miles SSW of the Trent's exit into the Humber Estuary. Until the Medieval period the settlement was actually beside the river, but avulsion of the watercourse has relocated the channel a few hundred meters to the North.

To early settlers the river did of course provide both fish and transport but it was not the only source of drinking water, because a family of springs issued from the alluvium about Repton.

There is evidence of Mesolithic and Neolithic settlement on the terrace. There are later Bronze Age ring ditches around the village that may suggest a prehistoric metropolitan rôle. Romans farmed the area intensively though the only evidence of high-status occupation is a column base found in the churchyard in 1968.

The real history of Repton begins in the sixth century AD after The Fall of Rome. In the area occupied by modern England a loose and shifting alliance of Saxon kingdoms since known as The Heptarchy was formed by Germanic immigrant elites. Geographically central was Mercia though the literal meaning of that word is "borderland" (of Wales). Mercia was visited by Christian missionaries in 597AD and whilst there is no evidence that they were ill-used their Message received little acclamation. It is likely that the Mercian kings shortly thereafter selected Repton as a base, because in 653AD four priests were dispatched there from Northumbria to convert the Mercian royal family so that a royal wedding involving the two kingdoms could be progressed. A double abbey was established at Repton under the supremacy of an abbess.

Sometime in that century there was a period of apostacy under the expansionist King Penda, and there persist confused traditions of the young King Kenelm who was murdered by his pagan sister, and later canonised.

Nominal Christianity probably returned to the Court within fifty years because in the early eighth century the surviving Royal Crypt of Repton was commenced, initially beneath a wooden roof. King Ethelbald was entombed inside in 757 and King Wiglaf in 840. Shortly afterward the existing stone vault was built supported upon four helical columns and a stone chancel erected above. The Kenelm of history reigned between these two kings, and is thought to have died peacefully in 786AD.

Wystan, Wiglaf's grandson was murdered by an uncle in 850 and was soon canonised so that Repton became a center of Saxon pilgrimage. It is possible that Mercian royal infighting and the little capital's ready accessibility by ship had a direct bearing upon succeeding events.

Vikings arrived via the Humber in 873AD and sacked the capital and its monastery. They made a winter encampment and defended it with a large D-shaped ditch that enclosed three-and-a-half acres based upon the river. The Vikings dug an impressive canal from the Trent into the heart of this encampment in order safely to dock their ships. Mercian resistance was organised and there is evidence of a fighting massacre of Viking warriors in a forest clearing outside the settlement.

Excavations within the village were conducted in the last quarter of the twentieth century. Above the remains of a stone chapel of eighth century date Taylor and the Biddles unearthed the bones of 200 males and 49 women. As an inhumation this was probably a burial by Mercian Christians. This mass grave consisted primarily of disarticulated remains but showed few signs of violence and is thought to have resulted from a disease epidemic, though a possible massacre of monks and nuns has not been ruled out, as has neither that the males were Vikings and the females their local wives or women friends. Other Christian and Viking warrior inhumations were detected and also a broken Christian preaching cross depicting what is thought to be King Ethelbald. If this is right, then it is the earliest picture of an English monarch. A (pagan) Viking burial of cremated remains was found at nearby Ingleby (that word signifies "English town" in the Norse language). This Ingleby burial is the only Viking cremation known in the UK.

By 879 Alfred the Great of Wessex had advanced sufficiently to clear Scandinavian invaders from Mercia South of Watling Street, and in 897 the last of the Danes left England. In 927 the Saxon kingdoms of the Heptarchy united under the leadership of Wessex and the capital of the new English state was established at Winchester.

Repton entered a period of political obscurity but remained an important ecclesiastical center with its monastery and nunnery, and a parish church that unusually was served by two priests. It may have been due to the earlier preferences of St Chad that the cathedral city was established at Lichfield. Alternatively, or in addition, it may have been because Lichfield was easily accessible from London, Winchester and the South along old Roman roads.

Change resumed when Henry VIII dissolved the monasteries in 1538. Old monastic premises were often sold to courtiers or other rich bidders as housing, or parishioners might purchase all or part of the great priory churches where there was a history of their sharing such with local monks. If clerics disputed the will of the King in these matters they were often ritually disemboweled, but on the other hand if they proposed to convert their accommodation to other, non-Papal, functions they were often sympathetically heard. Since a natural proposal was to exploit their literacy, or even an existing teaching tradition, many monastic houses canvassed and were granted the translation of their facilities to charity schools. Thus were some of the most ancient of England's public schools born.

The genesis of Repton School was, however, indirect.

The monastery complex was appropriated by Thomas Thaker, steward of Vicegerent (effective Prime Minister) Thomas Cromwell. Later, Thaker's son Gilbert was worried that Bloody Mary would restore the foundation so he had most of the old monastery demolished. Only the Prior's Lodging, a guest house, a small tower and a tithe barn were retained. In 1559 the executors of the Late Sir John Port purchased the grounds of the old monastery, complete with remaining buildings, for £37:10s.

It was these executors who set up a free school for boys in the old priory, on condition that the scholars chanted prayers for the souls of Sir John and his family. The staff may have been, at least in part, former monks of Repton. Sir John's endowment paid for the education of local boys whereas those from outwith the district were allowed to attend upon payment of fees. Upon the restoration of Protestantism, chantry was outlawed, but Repton School continued its educative functions.

Repton's development was hampered by its relative inaccessibility and in particular there was no bridge over the Trent between Burton and Swarkstone. The school went through many vicissitudes and under William Stevens the roll fell to one boy.

But Repton School survived to participate in the great Arnoldian boarding-school boom of 1850-1880 when under the headmastership of Steuart Adophus Pears the roll doubled in three years and five additional boarding houses were opened.

Today the school has 450 students and a variable number of staff of both sexes, and is a leading UK and Dubai public school with a cheerful rather than an intellectual ethos. It is a noted source of proficiency on the stage, and in comedy and letters. During the twentieth century it gave us two Archbishops of Canterbury, Jeremy Clarkson, Christopher Isherwood, Basil Rathbone, Roald Dahl, and Graeme Garden amongst countless less well-known exponents of the arts.

The village was further assisted by the opening of a bridge over the Trent in 1839 and a gasworks in 1855, both very late for the UK. Alarmingly, the gasworks was built next door to its thatched manager's house! In due course the works gained a second gasholder and the tiny town settled into a complacent obscurity, with some peripheral expansion after The Second World War.

In 1969 Repton village was designated a Conservation Area and this was extended in 1982.

When I visited in 2001 it was a sunny but silent village, except in the atmospheric Saxon crypt at the great church's Eastern end. Ancient openings at the top of this basement gave out onto the schoolyard and disconcertingly I could follow the weirdly amplified and clarified conversations of masters as they smoked and drank coffee above me. It was an unforgettable if mundane experience, that could possibly be emulated nowhere else. In the empty chamber I wondered where the old kings had gone. Perhaps the scholarly chatter had long since interrupted their slumbers, and they had risen from their catafalques to wonder off in disgust?

STONHVN
Stonehaven in Kincardineshire

Location:	The Bervie Braes, Stonehaven, Kincardineshire, Scotland, UK
Date of Photograph:	pm 14 August 1990
OS Grid Reference:	NO877852
Co-ordinates:	56:57:32N 2:12:18W
Elevation:	31.1 meters

   The Highland Boundary Fault is an ancient fracture in the Earth's crust that strikes in a roughly South-West to North-East direction between Helensburgh and Stonehaven. A westward extension can be traced into the Isle of Arran. You can see it in the picture as an almost perfectly horizontal straight bluff across the whole width six-tenths of the height from the bottom. Where it reaches the sea you can discern a line of low red cliffs.

   In 2003, within the siltstone of the Cowie foreshore around (0.75,0.6), the Kemnay bus-driver Mike Newman discovered the 428-million-year-old fossil millipede *Pneumodesmus newmani*, the oldest air-breathing creature known.

   North and West of the fault are Dalradian schists, phyllites and slates formed during the Caledonian Orogeny, whilst South and East these are unconformably overlain by Devonian sandstones and conglomerates. At the interface is a thin ophiolitic facies, the Highland Border Complex.

So geologically speaking those background hills are in The Highlands, whilst the little town and our vantage are in The Lowlands. Indeed, to take the picture I stood on The Bervie Braes, a crumbling cliff of Old Red Sandstone.

It is thought that somewhere on those distant hills in AD 83 or 84 Agricola's twenty-thousand Roman legionaries confronted the Caledonian Confederation of King Calgacus, whose opinion of Rome Tacitus immortalised by placing in his mouth the words: "They Create a Desert and Call it Peace". The Romans fought uphill to defeat the Pictish thirty-thousand, but the men of Rome soon tired of their frigid conquest and returned South, for whilst the land of the Pict is not exactly a desert it is a poor and reluctant land where neither wheat nor wine will grow.

The splendid Stonehaven Bay depicted was populated haltingly and much later than in the more yielding climes of the South, indeed the development of this territory postdates the development of Massachusetts. Scotland was desperately poor.

Unsurprisingly, the capital of The Mearns or Kincardineshire county was at Kincardine, an inland "town" about fifteen miles WSW of Stonehaven. When Kincardine ruled a contemporary described it as "a miserable hamlet of no more than two or three thatched cottages with neither food for man nor beast". But there was a castle.

The site of the future Stonehaven was a semi-wilderness between the Northern unnavigable River Cowie and its sister stream, the Carron, that entered the bay at its Southern end. Beside the gorge of the Lower Carron slept the villages of Dunnottar and Fetteresso, both with castles and on the North shore above the Cowie was some kind of fishing hamlet overlooked by its little church of St Mary of the Storms.

In Scottish Feudal terms, Stonehaven was a Burgh of Barony with restricted legal rights and indemnities as compared with Royal Burghs.

An ember of maritime trade must have been kindling on the near shore for sometime in the sixteenth century the Earl Marischal of Scotland, a local potentate, built a red sandstone warehouse on a quayside. You can see the Western part of it on the edge of the photograph at (0.98, 0.5).

In 1600 the ancient capital of Kincardine was abandoned and the seat of government moved to the Earl's warehouse, this red sandstone building, which was converted into a Court House and torture chamber:- The Tolbooth.

Like some Continental monarchies, Scotland preserved a strict Feudal System. The vast majority of inhabitants were bound to the soil as vassals of local lairds who could use them as they saw fit, but there were minority classes of "free" men of several types who had to be referred to official authorities for civil or criminal justice. In the latter case, after a more or less brutal examination, these persons would be acquitted or subjected to either torturous mutilation or a death sentence. Even the hangman of Steenhive or Stanehyve as they styled the new capital was indentured to "severest corporal punishment" if the Earl Marischal found him less than rigorous in his duties, but on the plus side he was entitled to a rent-free cottage, or failing that an extra daily bowl of porridge. As late as 1715, when the Old Pretender landed at Stonehaven to commence the First Jacobite Rebellion, he was accorded the special honor of being invited to supervise the torture of a woman and her baby child in The Tolbooth, which he did.

This cruel and puerile form of governance prevented land improvement and put a severe break upon scientific and theological enquiry, upon migration, and upon industrial development. Accordingly, Scottish towns, including Stonehaven, failed to prosper.

As years turned to decades and decades to centuries English and enlightened Scottish opinion grew progressively intolerant of such custom. As far as the British Government five hundred miles South at Westminster was concerned the most annoying thing about Highland feudalism was its military brigandage. Local lords could compel the unpaid fighting service of male vassals and use their cohorts to terrorise the Scottish countryside or even make brief incursions into England.

Finally, in 1745 the Highlands rose in a Second Jacobite Rebellion and marched a tidy four hundred miles to Derby in England's Mercian heart. The British put the revolt down brutally and destroyed the Scottish Feudal System and all its trappings, both the picturesque and the ugly.

Notwithstanding all of that, the Scots insisted upon retaining their own legal system and over the years evolved a corpus of rather liberal law that they retain to this day.

Remarkably, despite or perhaps because of its dark past, Scotland responded with a sudden and brilliant Enlightenment of scientific, democratic and industrial development and within fifty years the stormswept statelet became one of the most prosperous and respected nations on Earth.

Stonehaven was not a coal belt community but responded in its own way.

By 1711, the hamlet capital already had a sailors' hostelry, The Ship Inn, on the harbor wall. After 1746 the town burgeoned. The Tolbooth was vacated and in 1767 a new Court House built. The pretty lead-spired Town House at (0.6, 0.55) was erected in 1790, by which time the town had reached the Carron some quarter-mile West, and in the final years of the eighteenth century the local landowner Robert Barclay of Ury laid out a New Town in the fashionable Hippodamian plan. This development between the mouths of the Cowie and the Carron doubled the size of the town, shifting its center of trade North of the Carron that Barclay bridged in 1781.

In the center of the New Town a Market Place with Market Buildings was laid out in 1826, and the copper spire at (0.25, 0.7) added in 1856. It was in the Market Square in 1822 that the rubber technologist Robert Thompson was born, inventor of the pneumatic tire, the hydraulic dry dock, and several designs of sugar press, crane and road tractor. Another famous Stonehaven invention, sadly not due to Thompson, is the deep-fried Mars Bar.

The gas works at the site of the gasholder visible at (0.2, 0.5) in this 1990 photograph was erected by the joint stock Stonehaven Gas Company in 1837. The retorts were removed before my time and the gasholder itself has vanished. The land was too contaminated for residential development and in October 2007 plans were announced to lay a car park on the site.

To the South of Barclay's Carron Bridge an imposing neo-classical County Buildings was erected in 1863 beside a large elementary school, a police station and other civic buildings. Fifteen years later a Town Hall was built upon Allardice Street, the main street, behind the Market Square.

The railway from London reached the hillside a mile West of the town in 1847, on its way North to the industrial port of Aberdeen fifteen miles ahead. But attempts at industry were made nearer the harbor. A local linen industry briefly flourished with flax fields in the Mearns hinterland, but a net factory supported by linen manufacture and local fishing that was established beside the Carron flourished well into the last half of the twentieth century. Brewing, distilling and tanning also depended upon the agriculture of the hinterland and set up at the other end of the New Town.

Fishing evolved in two separate zones. The Northern rock beach at Cowie was long a center for fishing with inshore skiffs. This zone at (0.7, 0.6) can be discerned with the aid of the low white wall of the Swimming Pool some mile North of the vantage. The near harbor was, and is, hard South against the lee of Downie Point. The South Pier of the harbor was built in 1825 to supplement an existing North Pier. During the nineteenth century herring boom both herring and whitefish fishing expanded in Stonehaven culminating in 199 boats employing over 400 in 1883, but the trade then declined precipitately to 64 boats in 1889 and 19 in 1909. In terms specifically of herring the climax was reached in 1884 when 102 boats landed 13700 cran. At this point Stonehaven also berthed four small coasters, some of which plied Baltic trade exporting herring. (A cran is 37.5 Imperial gallons or 170.5 liters: Notionally 1200 fish).

During the twentieth century Stonehaven tried to redefine itself as a little seaside resort for Glasgow holidaymakers but the beach was rock and boulders and the North Sea cold and wild. The town was at a great disadvantage even vis-à-vis Ayr and the other sheltered Firth of Clyde resorts. Also Aberdeen offered a sandy beach miles long.

By the end of The First World War expansion had ceased and Stonehaven reverted to being a sleepy, sandstone Scottish town, with an indescribable sentimental charm recognisable to those who have read AJ Cronin or JM Barrie, or who have recollections of the Old Scotland.

When I arrived in 1968 there were no double yellow lines or paid-for parking spaces anywhere in Kincardineshire, or in my recollection anywhere in Northern Scotland except the city of Aberdeen. The sole set of traffic lights in Kincardineshire, erected at the intersection of Evan and Allardice Streets in the county town were maintained as a status symbol. You could park where you liked and drive how you saw fit, for the latter would only be interrupted in the event of gross and repeated inebriation.

I took my motorcycle test around the empty streets of the New Town later in the Autumn of that year. As we walked up Cameron Street the examiner said "Tell me the number on that standard over there". I looked desperately along the line of lamp posts at the tiny tin bands eight feet above the pavement and tried to descry the nearest half-inch high characters. As we walked slowly forward I almost realised too late that he meant the four-inch high characters on the number plate of a parked Standard car, a Coventry marque long deceased. I told him and got a certificate that I redeemed for a full licence in the county offices, which had moved into an old house up the hill. I rode back down Evan Street, passed the Co-op, the tobacconists, and David Waldie's newsagents with its mahogany facade, turned round the beveled glass Art Nouveau magnificence of

Ramsey's ladies' drapers, without which any wee town was naked, and rode back up the beech-flanked brae onto The Highlands and the five miles to my Father's smallholding. In 1975, Kincardineshire and its administrative apparatus were officially abolished.

The population was about five thousand, approximately the same as it had been for fifty years. In 1973, the Aberdeen Oil Boom commenced. Some new residential development and an industrial estate were built to the West of the railway and the population crept up to 6,500 by the mid-1980s. As cars became commonplace development gathered pace as Stonehaven became an Aberdonian commuter town, a rôle greatly assisted by the fact that it had the only remaining railway station in the county. Stonehaven was inhibited a little by the massive expansion of Portlethan, about ten miles nearer Aberdeen and the reopening of Portlethan station. But by 2001 the census population of Stonehaven was 9,577 and as of December 2007 the estimated population of the town is 14,000 souls.

Stonehaven may not reach parity with New York or Tokyo, at least not in our lifetimes, but it has more than doubled its size in thirty years during which most British towns have shrunk.

The Earl Marischal's torture chamber is now a tearoom.

WIGTOWN
Wigtown in Scotland

Location:	Wigtown, Wigtownshire, Galloway, Scotland, UK
Date of Photograph:	pm 30 March 1999
OS Grid Reference:	NX434553
Co-ordinates:	54:52:04N 4:26:40W
Elevation:	42.7 meters

Wigtownshire is the remote and sparsely-populated Western end of the region of Galloway. For administrative purposes, the County of Wigtownshire was officially abolished in 1974, aggravating Wigtown's centuries-old economic depression.

Wigtown is a former Royal Burgh and County Town of high antiquarian interest. It shares with many Scottish and Irish small towns a quiet and quaint, even romantic, atmosphere, set off by a backdrop of horrific history. And as with elsewhere in Ireland and Scotland, whatever the religion, the look and feel is distinctly French.

Wigtown is a village that has struggled with negligible resources to be a provincial capital. It is dominated by an enormous, redundant County Hall of 1862 in an imposing, Gallic style that would not look out of place in Manchester, Birmingham or even Lille. For centuries it struggled as a port, often assessed by the King's tax collectors as having "No ships and No boats". Its Bladnoch Distillery is the only source of Lowland Malt whisky and has had a rocky history, closing for a time in the 1990's, during which decade the town's other employer, the creamery, closed for good. Like similar townlets,

Wigtown is attempting to revive around the book trade, but is inevitably challenged by the global computerisation of the business, in addition to its geographical remoteness. There is no airport and the motorway system's closest useful approach is 78 miles away at Gretna. There is a railway from Stranraer to Glasgow, 85 miles away and a short sea crossing to Larne in Northern Ireland. Over the turn of the century, twenty second-hand bookshops, publishers and related enterprises have established in the burgh.

In reverse of the usual arrangements, the church and town were planted upon an eminence; and Wigtown Castle lower down beside the River Bladnoch. This castle, which may have been a Saxon foundation, was reinforced by the Edwards but slighted upon Scottish Independence, probably by the Bruce's themselves.

The town has been Christian since 554AD, became a medieval monastic center and the scene of major Covenanter dissent after The Act of Uniformity. It is world-famous as the site of the martyrdom of two Presbyterian women in 1685.

On the Southern outskirts is Baldoon Castle. It is associated with the disputed seventeenth-century heiress Janet Dalrymple and a confused story of murder and madness in the bridal chamber. The tale is said to have inspired Sir Walter Scott's novel "The Bride of Lammermoor" and the Donizetti opera "Lucia di Lammermoor". Needless to add, a white lady patrols the somber ruins, being especially reliable on the anniversary of Janet's death, which took place on September 12th 1669.

Postscript 26 May 2022

I hope you will forgive both the digression and the language, but I failed to mention in the 2008 script several interesting facts about the etymology of the placename prefix "Wig-" in British and indeed European place-names.

"Wig-" occurs in many British place names, especially in the Northern half of the island, as in Wigton, Wigtown, Wigtownshire, Wigan, etcetera. The literal meaning of "Wig" refers to Danes, Vikings, or other Nordic settlers, objects of contempt to the Anglo-Saxons of more than a thousand years ago. The English Liberal Party was derisively described as "Whigs" until the early twentieth century. The word-element is cognate with the offensive English term "wog", an insult unknown in North America. Inevitably, like the Quakers and the Tories, the Whigs arrogated the insult and adopted it as a self-referential badge of pride.

Very similar is the Southern and Continental syllable "Wal-" as in Walsall, Wallachia, Walworth, Wallonia, Walsham, Wales, Cornwall, and its variant "Gal-" as in Galicia, Galton, Galston, Galgate, Galway, Galloway, and an hundred and one similar variations. "Wal-" and "Gal-" mean "foreigner" in a more or less neutral tone.

CHAPTER EIGHT

Strivers in the Dawn

The remarkable thing about heroes is the often accidental character of their achievements. Other commonalities include the rôle of luck, of friendship, and the indispensable influence of personal aptitudes.

We may smile at the simplicity of old-fashioned Marxist analyses of the social determinism of achievement, and yet there is something of "cometh the hour, cometh the man" when we find that the "Watt" governor was devised simultaneously by three mutual strangers, or that Evolution was discerned thirty years before its publication, and by a very differently-favored naturalist than Darwin.

Few of us today have heard of Sir Richard Grenville or Sir Cloudesley Shovell, yet both contributed significantly to our maritime strength, and their queens wept at the news of their deaths. Similarly, few of us have heard of William Oughtred who devised an unsharp tool that was a boon to shipwrights, or of John Harrison who invented a machine that cannot float, but saved sailors.

Some did not perceive themselves as heroes, and did not set out to innovate. And yet they changed history in unforeseeable ways. John Howard and Elizabeth Fry sought only to serve Christ, who enjoined us to comfort the captive, by mitigating the suffering of prisoners. But in encouraging more humane treatment they provided a motive for the establishment of rich colonies, without which Britain may well have lost to Germany. William Wilberforce and Thomas Clarkson set out only to manumit slaves, because slavery involved cruelty, and yet the freeing of slaves gifts paid work to the free poor and prompts the capitalist to look to machines, and the industries the poor can build.

To many of the great scientists it was enough to worship God and to tempt the godless to Faith by exposing God's wonders before them. Such may have been good enough for a Michael Faraday or a Hugh Miller, but for a misogynist introvert such as Henry Cavendish the laboratory was a capital place to evade society, as was a mountainside for Nevil Maskelyne. Or to John Napier and Isaac Newton the laws of numbers might lead along a sparkling path to hermetic knowledge or inconfutable Proofs in an uncertain and evanescent world.

Bondage and release come in many forms.

Another kind of unfree man made good was the Scot, especially if he could quit his native land. Freedom is found in some unlikely places. James Watt and William Murdoch each found everlasting fame at Smethwick. They were very different to each other and different again to their colleague Matthew Boulton, whom we may never have heard of, but without whom Watt and Murdoch, geniuses both, would have died unknown.

Speaking of disparate Scots William Wallace and Jane Haining were of indescribable heroic courage quailless in life as in the horror of their final hours, and yet theirs was a conservative sort of valor, validated by the restoration of old conditions that they made persist in the face of history.

As such is usual of the heroism of the upholders, the honor of the peace goes often to the innovator. Like our own Dorothy Pattison who consoled the injured poor and founded a hospital, small things but sorely needed and still here.

She was the first female to stand in stone upon a pedestal, but pedestals and plinths across this land bear ever the weight of courage and endeavor of a thousand British heroes.

In the center of London a tall Corinthian composite column commemorates Horatio Nelson, an admiral who led the defeats of Napoleon's fleets at Aboukir Bay and at Cape Trafalgar. Nelson's statue surmounts the column and about it a fountain-graced piazza contains four much lower plinths. One of these bears a statue of King George IV, a man of heroic diet who by dint of dauntless devouring achieved a mass of 111 kilograms by his thirty-fifth year, but not before he had secretly married a twice-widowed Catholic, gallantly denied it, and, using a proxy, fearlessly stepped-in to prevent Parliament granting civil rights to persons of her persuasion. Two of the other plinths accommodate statues of the mid nineteenth century British Indian Army generals Sir Henry Havelock and Sir Charles James Napier.

Havelock occupied Kabul in 1839 and during the 1857 Indian Mutiny he led the recapture of Cawnpore. Later he helped to relieve the Siege of Lucknow, where he died of dysentery.

Napier was a veteran of the Peninsula War. In 1842 The East India Company commissioned Napier to move against Sindh, a Muslim province in what is now South-Eastern Pakistan. Napier's opinion was that the campaign would prove a "useful and humane piece of rascality". At the subsequent Battle of Mlani, Napier defeated 22000 Sindhis with 2200 fighting troops, 500 of whom were white. He went on to occupy the then capital of Hyderabad and by 1843 the whole province. Napier famously notified his victory with one word of telegraphic economy: "Peccavi". The Directors of the honourable company voted the general £60000 in silver rupees. Napier went on to conquer the Sikhs in 1849, but more usefully he suppressed the Hindu custom of suttee, which was the ritual burning of widows upon their husband's pyre.

More stately and more ominous than any of these are the cool clean lines of the fourth pedestal, the famous Empty Plinth.

The Empty Plinth has never suffered a burden to remain. Inevitably, this is a great embarrassment to modern planners, arts pundits and politicians. There it sits, as it has for more than one hundred and fifty years in passive provocation. For a season, heavily-pregnant marble ladies, German pigeon hotels of colored glass or even resin casts of the plinth's own hollow interior have graced its surface but always the jealous genius of British Glory seizes the usurper and strikes it down, for like the empty Sanctuary that Titus defiled, the plinth bears whatever transcendent you can conceive, and so can never disappoint.

Before we turn to the pictures let us spare a word for the great mathematicians whose lonely and often incomprehensible labors made the tools that a modern world requires. We mentioned John Napier, Isaac Newton and William Oughtred but there was also a legion of country clergymen and half-forgotten strivers, who, knowing that the French would make them look small and silly, and the English not even that, strove on to limn the new language and logic of science and trade. Such as Bradwardine, Bayes, Briggs, Pell, Gregory, Taylor, MacLaurin, Horner, Russell, Simpson, Stirling, Coates, Hamilton, Clark-Maxwell, Gompertz, Pearson, Spearman, Turing; and in our own day Sir Tim Berners-Lee, devisor of the World Wide Web, and Dr Sir Andrew Wiles, who, notwithstanding my previous remark, has proven Fermat's Last Theorem.

BMW
The Golden Boys of Birmingham

Location:	The Boulton and Watt Memorial Sculpture, Broad Street, Birmingham, Warwickshire, Mercia, England
Date of Photograph:	pm 30 January 2008
OS Grid Reference:	SP063867
Co-ordinates:	52:28:43N 1:54:30W
Elevation:	138.1 meters

This group of gilt bronze statues in Broad Street, Birmingham shows three colleagues who played key rôles in World industrialisation. They are (from left to right), Matthew Boulton, a Birmingham inventor and businessman; James Watt, a Scottish instrument maker who designed the first economically-viable artificial power source (a type of steam engine); and William Murdoch, a Scottish chemist and inventor active in Cornwall.

Together these men established The Soho Works, a large stamping mill and erecting shop in Smethwick on the North-West edge of Birmingham. This was the World's first powered metal fabrications factory. Their principal years of activity at Birmingham were between 1770 and 1800.

The group, sculpted by William Bloye, stands on a Portland stone plinth outside the old Registry Office, south of Centenary Square and the central War Memorial. The figures appear to be discussing the plan of a steam engine. Boulton holds a slide rule, a tool for rapid but approximate computation, whilst Murdoch gestures with a pair of dividers. One of the dividers is missing. The principal and central figure of Watt is untooled.

William Bloye was Head of Sculpture at Birmingham School of Art and drew up preliminary designs in 1938. The next year the project benefited from an £8000 bequest by Richard Wheatley, but war intervened. Later, Birmingham City Council contributed an additional £7500 and the group was commissioned.

Let the epigraph behind the pedestal complete the story:-

"This memorial unveiled by Sir Percy H Mills Bt KBE
September 14 1956
Commemorates the immense contribution made by Boulton Watt
and Murdoch to the industry of Birmingham and of the World
The Conception of Richard Wheatley a leather goods manufactur-
er of this city coupled with his generosity and a contribution
by the City Council enabled these statues to be erected
BY W BLOYE
SCULPTOR"

James Watt, the most important of these three great genii, was born on 19th January 1736 at Greenock, the son of a Covenanting shipwright. Scotland was still feudal, but Greenock its principal port faced the American trade.

At seventeen Watt went to London to study instrument-making and a year later returned North to Glasgow to set up shop as Scotland's only mathematical instrument maker. The Incorporation of Glasgow Hammermen prohibited him from craftwork of any kind in their city.

In 1758, Watt was however invited to set up a small workshop in Glasgow University where he was befriended by scientist Joseph Black, author of the concept of latent heat, a key to effective heat engine design.

Four years later, though Watt had heard of steam (Newcomen) engines, he had never actually seen one, but attempted to construct a model. He soon learned that the University already had a model Newcomen engine, but that it was in London for repairs. Watt had it returned immediately and his experiments on it determined that the little machine wasted four-fifths of its heat on its own cylinder.

Watt arranged for the model to condense its steam in a separate heat exchanger rather than with a cold-water spray in the work cylinder. By 1765 he had perfected a separate condenser at this prototypical level, and modern industry was born.

Watt tried to build a full-sized phenotype with the help of his friend Dr Roebuck (inventor of the hot blast) at the Carron Iron Works, but the precision bore technology required did not exist and Watt was too poor to afford a patent. Roebuck purchased Watt's rights to the design, but then himself became bankrupt and so Roebuck sold Watt's design to a Matthew Boulton of Birmingham to defray his own debts.

Boulton realised that he needed Watt on site at Smethwick to help get the separately-condensing steam engine on the market, and installed him in The Soho Works as a full partner.

Meanwhile, fellow Mercian industrialist John Wilkinson evolved the necessary precision boring technology at Bersham in Wales, and by 1776 Boulton and Watt were installing the first paying steam motors. Their business model was not to make outright sales of units, but to install them and charge a percentage of the fuel savings made vis-à-vis Newcomen engines of the same duty. Such a system was simple and profitable with their first customers, the Cornish tin and copper mine proprietors.

By 1780, the Boulton and Watt engine was rapidly spreading to other applications. Despite patent issues with the simple crank, Watt was able to convert the reciprocating motion of the engine beam to the rotary motion of a flywheel using a "sun and planet" gear invented by William Murdoch, a Soho employee, and our other great triumvir.

At the other end of the beam, Watt designed a "parallel linkage" that enabled the natural arcuate travel of the beam end to translate to an all-but-rectilinear vertical motion at the power cylinder crosshead. Watt's fourth major design innovation was a centrifugal throttle governor that enabled the engine to maintain a steady pre-determined speed under fluctuations of load.

At a later date, the usability of the steam engine would be further enhanced by enclosure of the cylinder from the atmosphere and the introduction of double-acting systems, but already the four key improvements enabled the engine to be applied to a very great diversity of automatic and semi-automatic manufactures: Rolling, milling, grinding, turning, spinning and weaving key amongst them, with furnace-blasting and mine shaft winding at the supply end.

Henceforth the physical power of industries was liberated from fickle winds and rare waterfalls of variable flow to be capable of being sited almost anywhere on the great plains of Europe, but especially upon its numerous coalfields.

And rotary action and fuel economy made the application of steam power to marine and land transport thinkable.

By 1784 the Boulton and Watt engine was five times as fuel efficient as a Newcomen engine. The Newcomen engine would retain a tenuous survival only at collieries, where a convenient consumer of waste coal was useful.

In 1794 Boulton and Watt decided to focus exclusively on steam engine manufacture and rental. In the next thirty years they would install 1164 steam engines with a total design horsepower of twenty-six thousand.

Notwithstanding that, in 1800 Boulton and Watt's patents expired and the two men passed the great factory to their sons, whilst William Murdoch was established as a proper partner.

In semi-retirement Watt continued to be a prolific inventor, in fields quite unrelated to steam. He died at Handsworth on 19th August 1819.

Matthew Boulton was an eminent inventor and innovator in his own right, but it was his commercial and legal talents that eased the birth of industrialisation.

Born at Birmingham on 3rd September 1728, Boulton's father was a manufacturer of small metal goods, the speciality of the then small Mercian town. In 1755 the Boulton family bought Sarehole Mill, a watermill on the tiny River Cole about four and a half miles South-East of Birmingham. They used it to roll sheet metal.

Much later the mill would become the romping-ground of the infant JRR Tolkein and one of the inspirations for his tales of the Hobbits. It is now a scheduled industrial monument.

When Matthew Boulton Senior died in 1759, our Matthew went into partnership with John Fothergill to establish The Soho Manufactory on the borders of Handsworth and Smethwick, about two miles North-West of Birmingham. There he made a variety of trinkets and general brummagem ware including steel buttons, imitation diamonds and stained glass, probably for the Guinea trade.

The Mercian Plain is in a rain shadow and though high for Europe is relatively windless by British standards. Three large sluggish rivers drain its edges but brisk streams or falls are absent. Birmingham workshops and The Soho Manufactory in particular were power-starved though coal, whilst absent under the actual town of Birmingham, lay abundantly all about it.

In 1767 Boulton befriended the brilliant but indigent Scottish technician James Watt, and installed him at Soho with a Partnership.

Watt's former partner, the Scottish ironmaster Dr John Roebuck, owed Boulton £1200, and the latter accepted Roebuck's two-thirds share in Watt's patent steam engine in settlement.

In 1788, with Watt's power plant installed at Soho, not only did the pair make the famous separately-condensing engines, but Boulton in particular felt confident to stamp coins on an industrial scale. They minted cooper coins for Sierra Leone, The British East India Company and Russia. In 1797 Soho started to produce the celebrated "cartwheel pennies" for UK circulation, the first objects ever to be mass produced by automatic means.

Despite his patent of the same year for a type of hydraulic pump, Boulton's real contribution lay as an organiser and optimiser of production systems. In many respects he was in advance even of twenty-first century British practice in workforce husbandry. He installed labor-saving devices wherever he could see economic advantage and developed bills of interchangeable components to enhance efficiency as well as allied methods of mechanical reproduction. Boulton effected other economies and productivity improvements by vertically-integrating production on one premises, where production was harmonised with design and marketing specialisms. He employed only fit adults in clean, well-ventilated and well-lit workshops and from almost the outset deducted one-sixtieth of wages to finance 80% benefits for sick or injured employees, or to pension their widows.

Boulton died at Birmingham in 1809.

The third great Soho innovator, William Murdoch, was born near Cumnock on 21st August 1754, the son of a soldier and millwright. Like his fellow Scot,

James Watt, he was a poor boy educated by the State, and also like Watt he excelled at school in mathematics.

Murdoch assisted his father with his engineering work, including the bridging of local rivers, before, in 1777, walking the 271 miles to Birmingham to ask Watt for a job. He was taken on and for the next ten years Boulton and Watt used him as an engine erector in Cornwall, after a spell in the Soho Foundry pattern shop.

Murdoch soon showed that his talents extended beyond those of virtuoso craftsmanship to original discovery and invention.

At the Wanlockhead lead mines near his native Cumnock Murdoch improved engine valve arrangements and whilst down in Cornwall Murdock maximised the partners' profits buy effecting further technical efficiencies in their leased engines.

Shortly after this phase, and possibly around 1790, Murdoch invented the system of using piped coal gas for illumination. It is said that his Cornish lodgings were the first premises to be so lit, but The Soho Manufactory was also piped for gas about this time, and by 1805 a number of other industrial installations including cotton mills would be lit by gas. To store the gas and help govern the pressure, Murdoch invented what he described as a "gasometer", still the usual British word for a large expansible gas storage tank. Murdoch completed an exhaustive system of experiments to optimise the distillation, storage and transmission of gas, as well as capture its byproducts.

During this thirtysomething phase of prolific innovation, Murdoch also developed the sun-and-planet gear, the D-shaped steam slide valve, the pneumatic message tube and several coal-tar chemical preparations. One of these was an iron-to-iron cement and filler whilst others were aromatic precursors of the aniline dyes.

Murdoch was active in the experimental use of compressed air and pneumatic transmission generally as well as the invention of machines for boring wooden and stone pipes.

In 1784, Murdoch produced the first UK model of a steam carriage and it is speculated that this may have influenced his Cornish neighbor Richard Trevithick to work up similar contraptions.

Murdoch continued steam carriage experiments in Devon and Cornwall until at least 1794, when Trevithick is known to have visited Murdoch to view a model, and there is some evidence that a ridable vehicle was demonstrated.

During the last years of the eighteenth century, Murdoch's extramural efforts turned to chemical innovations, and besides gas and coal-tar products he developed various pigments, paints and anti-fouling preservatives. In 1795, he took out a patent for an isinglass substitute made from cod at a fraction of the price of Russian isinglass made from sturgeon. The Committee of London Brewers paid two thousand pounds to licence Murdoch's isinglass production process.

In 1807, Boulton and Watt powered Robert Fulton's Hudson River steamboat and this work led to Murdoch's involvement in the marine engine, which matured ten years later into the mechanisation of the paddle steamer "The Caledonia", the first powered vessel to cross to the Continent. During trials, Murdoch optimised the paddle depth to minimise fuel consumption and yet increase the speed from eight to twelve statute miles per hour.

After the trials "The Caledonia" crossed the North Sea from The Surrey Docks in London to Rotterdam, and thence steamed up the Rhine to Koblenz. Between 1813 and 1825, Boulton and Watt fitted about fifty vessels with a total of more than three thousand horsepower.

In 1815 William Murdoch installed the first post-Roman gravity fed hot water supply. This was at Leamington Spa Baths. Two years later he fitted a type of air duct heating system at his Handsworth home. This too may have been inspired by Classical archetypes.

Murdoch died in 1839, and like his two eminent colleagues was interred at St Mary's Church, Handsworth, "The Westminster Abbey of the Industrial Revolution".

DAVY
Statue of Sir Humphry Davy before The Market Hall Penzance

Location:	The Market Hall, Market Jew Street, Penzance, Cornwall, England, UK
Date of Photograph:	am 3 April 1996
OS Grid Reference:	SW473303
Co-ordinates:	50:07:08N 5:32:11W
Elevation:	29.3 meters

Humphry Davy was born on 17th December 1778 at Madron in Cornwall, the first-born son of a woodcarver. He quickly matured into the greatest English chemist of all time, and his brother John and cousin Edmund also became successful chemists, in a place and time pregnant of genius.

Davy's Cornubian youth was bright but not atypical. He attended Penzance and Truro Grammar Schools leaving the latter aged fourteen. As a boy Davy was interested in fishing and mineral collecting and returned to the former at the end of his life. When Davy was fifteen his father died leaving Mrs Grace Davy to raise five amidst the debt be bequeathed. To avoid jail, the widow took up millinery in Penzance and in partnership with a lady refugee from The Terror opened a boarding-house. It should be remembered that in the 1790's Cornwall had more steam engines than the rest of the World put together, and one of her first lodgers was Gregory Watt, the son of James.

Having thus set the tone, the rest of this narrative will read, like some fourth-rate historical novel, like a who-is-who of the Late Enlightenment.

Humphry was befriended by the Quaker saddler Robert Dunkin who taught the young genius the rudiments of experimental science.

With the financial help of a friend, Mrs Davy apprenticed sixteen-year-old Humphry to a surgeon-apothecary of the town, hoping to establish him in a medical career. This employer was Dr John Bingham Borlase, scion of the eminent Penwith family that included the antiquarian and early mineralogist, The Reverend William Borlase. Humphry served Borlase as a laboratory technician for about three years and in 1798, at the age of twenty, got a job in Thomas Beddoe's Pneumatic Institution at Bristol.

This outfit specialised in research into the possible application of gases to therapy. Alarmingly, one of these was chlorine, a gas discovered in 1774 by the Swedish chemist Carl Scheele, whose laboratory is now preserved at Skansen. Throughout the eighteenth century the properties of this gas remained obscure. Davy demonstrated that the bleaching properties of chlorine derived of its chemical displacement of oxygen from water, but failed to grasp the elemental nature of the halogen and sought to isolate it from oxygen feedstock.

It may have been about this time that the young Cornishman debunked the eighteenth century theory of phlogiston, a thermodynamic fluid supposed to transit between materials involved in combustion. The genius contrived a clockwork apparatus that melted ice by rubbing it against a surface and showed that no such agent could have entered or left the water produced.

Either at Bristol or in the Tradea laboratory of Davis Giddy, Humphry Davy prepared Nitrous Oxide (N_2O), a gas that Davy, through self-experimentation, showed had analgesic and hypnotic properties. These characteristics instantly commended Davy and the gas itself to a fashionable coterie of poets around Bristol. This set included Samuel Taylor Coleridge, the opium-eating author of "Kubla Khan", Robert Southey and PM Roget. The men inhaled this "laughing gas" at numerous "Hilarious Evenings" and at the writers' instance Davy, a keen Grecian and poet since boyhood, edited the second edition of Wordsworth's "Lyrical Ballads". But it was to be nearly another half-century before the gas was first employed as a surgical anesthetic, in Connecticut.

Whilst at The Pneumatic Institution, Davy continued to investigate other gasses, including ammonia which he determined as the trihydride of nitrogen, but he nearly died when he inhaled water gas, a substance prepared by passing steam through red-hot coke: It is a mixture of hydrogen and carbon monoxide.

During further experiments, Davy damaged his eyesight with Nitrogen Trichloride, an even more noxious cognate of ammonia, and whether for these or other reasons his love of gases waned. In 1800 he published an account of his work "Researches, Chemical and Philosophical" and his reputation was assured.

We should note that Davy did not "discover" either ammonia or nitrous oxide. The preparation of these gases and several others had been described by Joseph

Priestley in his book "Experiments and Observations of Different Kinds of Air" completed in 1786. A modern reader would, however, doubt Priestley's appreciation of the chemical integrity of his various gases. In fairness to Priestley, the modern concept of atomicity would not crystallise until the nineteenth century and Priestley understood his different gasses as essentially *physical* species.

In 1799, the exiled American empire loyalist Sir Benjamin Thompson, Count Rumford, founded The Royal Institution of Great Britain in Mayfair, London. This was, and remains, a fashionable laboratory and lecture hall that provided, and provides, a forum for the popularisation of science. In the first half of the nineteenth century it was also of itself a major research facility.

In 1801, Davy was invited to lecture at the RIGB, and with financial support from Sir Joseph Banks and The Honorable Henry Cavendish, the pathologically introverted discoverer of hydrogen, the young Cornishman was appointed its Professor of Chemistry.

The next year Davy determined that the tropical plant extract catechu was a cheaper and more effective alternative to oak gall in the tanning of leather, and this led in 1803 to his being admitted a Fellow of The Royal Society (of British scientists) and a Member of The Dublin Society. Another consequence was that in 1805 he was awarded The Copley Medal, but at a more mundane level the plant research led to a sequence of lucrative agricultural research and teaching contracts in both Britain and Ireland.

By 1806, Davy had developed a complex of theories concerning the relationship of electricity to matter at what we would now call the molecular level. He identified that polarised hydrogen atoms were instrumental in the formation of acidic properties and that it was hydrogen and not oxygen that defined acidity. He postulated that the use of electricity to decompose chemicals, electrolysis, was the most promising route to the isolation of new elements and set forth this manifesto in his 1806 lecture "On Some Chemical Agencies of Electricity".

In 1807 Davy assisted in the formation of The Geological Society of London when the Askesian Society was wound up, and about this time he was also instrumental in setting up The Geological Society of Cornwall and initiating the nucleation of its eminent mineral collection at Penzance.

Davy now focused his chemical attentions on the most reactive and recondite elements, mostly common constituents of everyday minerals that nevertheless cannot be isolated in any convenient way using hot reducing agents like coke, charcoal or even hydrogen.

He set about using the passage of electric currents through hot melts to achieve the pure metallic forms of The Alkali Metals (Group One Elements) and The Alkali Earth Metals (Group Two Elements). There were no generators: They would be invented by Davy's student, (Sir) Michael Faraday, another working class genius, but a man of the strictest principle who refused two knighthoods. So the necessary power was evolved symmetrically from the corrosion of copper and zinc in Voltaic piles, or as we would now say, "dry" cell batteries.

In 1807, Humphry used electrolysis to isolate the soft, silvery, easily melted metal Sodium, which combines with Chlorine to form common salt, and the very similar, but even more explosive, sister metal Potassium. Rubidium and Caesium, rarer and even more electropositive, had to await the refined technique of another era.

In the days when boys could still buy dangerous chemicals in High Street shops, I purchased a can of caustic soda, intended for use by cleaning women. In my Father's back garden at Ware I melted this and repeated Davy's experiment by applying the current from a twelve-volt telephone battery across two carbon electrodes in the noxious liquid. I watched fascinated as bright little silver globules of molten metal emerged magically from the black probe and spun their way through the water-clear melt. The experiment was then terminated and I watched as the tiny orbs disappeared into the dirty white opacity of the resolidified chemical.

Now of course, a grown man could not perform the trick without several permissions and a successful premises inspection.

Davy was more persistent. By 1808 he had struck forward to isolate Calcium, Barium, Boron and Magnesium, all key assets of our age. Cleverly, he used the highly-electropositive potassium to reduce Boron from borax by traditional reduction.

In 1812 Davy was knighted.

The previous year Bernard Courtois had isolated a strange violet substance from seaweed, and though the UK and France were at war, Napoleon invited Davy to come over and have a look at it. The little Corsican also wanted an opportunity to award Davy a medal.

Before Davy left he interviewed a young bookbinder who had applied for a Royal Institution job as a laboratory assistant. This craftsman was a native of Elephant and Castle, a working class district on the other side of the river. Davy thought he might be useful to man Davy's traveling laboratory on its Continental expeditions. The young man, a devout and abstemious Sandemanian, was called Michael Faraday.

So in 1813, Davy packed Faraday and his own wife, the loyal but volatile Jane Apreece, into the lab and set off to meet Europe's eminent men of science.

When Davy reached Paris he was treated as royalty (I mean fêted not beheaded!) and presented to The Empress of France, Marie-Louise Napoleon. The Emperor was apparently away on military duties, though of course diplomatic etiquette may have required him to snub a foreign enemy. In any event, Davy got his French medal and in addition Gay-Lussac presented him with a sample of "Substance X", which appeared to be a greasy purple solid with a distinctly marine aroma. Davy quickly established that this stuff was chemically very like Chlorine and even did some comparisons of its compounds with those of the green gas. Substance X was of course pure Iodine.

The Davy party posted on to Florence where Davy secured a diamond and isolated it in a glass chamber. He focused the rays of the Southern Sun upon the exorbitant stone whereupon it obligingly caught fire. By analysis of its products of annihilation, Davy demonstrated that the diamond was nothing more than carbon, and the same as coke or charcoal. In fact you could stoke one of the new engines with it.

The Society for Preventing Accidents in Coal Mines in Sunderland was incorporated on 1st October 1813. County Durham was a part of Britain where firedamp (methane) was a frequent explosive hazard in collieries, though both coal and methane were substances alien to Cornwall. Shortly after it was founded, the Society's chairman, Sir Alfred Milbanke wrote to Sir Humphry Davy asking how safety might be improved. Davy visited the mines and was appalled to see naked flames in use as illumination. He devised a revolutionary oil lamp where the flame was sealed behind iron gauze which allowed air in and light out but absorbed the thermal energy of a fire front, preventing the ignition of any larger mine explosion when the methane concentration reached its critical level in air. As a bonus, the Davy flame burnt blue to betray the presence of methane.

The simple Davy lamp took many years to be universally adopted but nevertheless saved many thousands their lives or their sight Worldwide.

The statue of Sir Humphry in Penzance carries in its right hand this death-defying invention, symbol of the light Davy bequeathed the Earth.

By 1813, Davy was this country's pre-eminent scientist and received of The Royal Society its Rumford Gold and Silver Medals and the Northern coal owners clubbed together to buy Davy a silver service that was later auctioned to endow The Davy Medal.

In 1818 Davy was created a Baronet and in 1820 became President of The Royal Society, a position he had to relinquish eight years later as his health worsened.

Five years later the Secretary of the Admiralty, John Croker and Davy founded the Athenaeum Club in Pall Mall. Davy became its first President and Faraday its first Secretary. At the time of writing in December 2007 the club boasts 52 Nobel laureates in every field of the prize and a modern library of 80000 books as well as important archives relating to its members and their often epochal innovations. Women have been admitted since 2002. In 1828 Sir Thomas Stamford Raffles, naturalist and founder of Singapore, asked Humphry Davy to help him set up The Zoological Society of London.

Since the 1700's The Admiralty had used copper sheathing to protect the wooden hulls of warships from the boring of the barnacle-like Toredo mollusk ("shipworm"). In the 1820's they asked Davy to do some work to improve the technique. Davy demonstrated that the attachment of a piece of a more electropositive metal such as iron or zinc to the copper sheeting would prevent corrosion of the copper itself. This is now an important maritime and industrial method called The Principle of the Sacrificial Anode.

Unfortunately, this modification of the copper's electrochemical presentation enabled the shellfish to adhere to it, the opposite of what was wanted!

At this time, Sir Humphry's health declined and he returned to the Continent, settling at Rome. He was in Geneva when he died on 29th May 1829 and is buried in Plot 208 in The Plain Palais Cemetery in that city. He was fifty.

When asked what had been his greatest discovery the Cornishman replied "Michael Faraday".

Back in Mayfair, Faraday resumed his electromagnetic experiments.

KELVIN
Lord Kelvin Statue in the Botanic Garden at Belfast

Location:	The Statue of Lord Kelvin, The Botanic Gardens Stranmill Road Entrance, Belfast, County Antrim, Northern Ireland, UK
Date of Photograph:	pm 7 June 2007
OS Grid Reference:	J335725
Co-ordinates:	54:34:59N 5:56:11W
Elevation:	21.9 meters

This very eminent and religious Victorian applied physicist took a big hand in the development of the submarine telegraph and the associated signals technology.

Although he was a convinced calorist he collaborated with Joule to promulgate The Mechanical Equivalent of Heat, and thus helped lay the foundations of physics as a modern science of energy and energetic transactions.

Kelvin is the author of The Second Law of Thermodynamics. Kelvin's gravitational model of planetary heating allowed him to posit that the Earth and the Sun must be at least some millions of years old.

Though ignorant of radioactivity Kelvin's work helped to lay the foundations for Clark-Maxwell's synthesis of light and electrical-magnetic phenomena and opened the way for twentieth-century developments in Relativity and Quantum Mechanics.

As a technician, Kelvin was superb, inventing over forty precision devices crucial in advanced research for his day, though possibly not the compensating compass.

He worked in Glasgow or on ships for over fifty years, but was born in Belfast in College Green East, less than half a mile down the hill. His father was a mathematics professor and his mother of unknown origin, possibly a landless Catholic girl. I think I am right in saying he was the second son of seven children.

PRIESTLY
The Reverend Joseph Priestley at Birmingham

Location:	Chamberlain Square, Birmingham, Warwickshire, Mercia, England, UK
Date of Photograph:	am 30 January 2008
OS Grid Reference:	SP065868
Co-ordinates:	52:28:48N 1:54:17W
Elevation:	136.9 meters

Dr Joseph Priestley is one of the most complex and in some ways one of the most inscrutable of the figures of The European Enlightenment, though often dismissed as a minor player.

Much of his continuing fascination rests upon his exemplary qualities as a thinker typical of his time, or a harbinger of what England could have become, and did not.

And I mean England, and especially Mercia, because in several respects Scotland and the anglophone countries overseas followed the paths that Priestley pursued.

Almost the most economically significant of Priestley's innovations was his invention of artificial carbonated water.

But Priestley's most famous achievement, at least amongst British nationalists, is his "discovery" of oxygen.

Even such an apparently straightforward point is however equivocal. At a captious level I suppose we could say that the gas was "discovered" by the algae of the Proterozoic who, perhaps a billion years ago, spawned it forth from its primal captivity to its persisting fugacity as a free constituent of our Earthly atmosphere. But when we ask when men became aware of "oxygen" as a distinct and self-subsistent entity the answers are no more definite.

In 1772 the Swedish chemist Carl Wilhelm Scheele described a gas he had isolated by heating various metallic nitrates and oxides, but arguably he agreed with his contemporaries in ignorance of the elemental or original status of his discovery, for the scientists of his day were wedded to a concept of fluid heat called Phlogiston Theory, which, like the relicts of Aristotle, colored all conclusions.

Priestley's "discovery" of oxygen took place on 1st August 1774 at Bowood House, the seat of Priestley's patron, The Earl of Shelburne. Here Priestley used sunlight to dissociate mercuric oxide *in vacuo*: A procedure sufficient of itself to demonstrate the uniquity of the evolved gas. Both Scheele and Priestley, however, failed to "appreciate" oxygen as a chemical element.

In that year, Priestley traveled to Paris to meet the great French chemist Antoine Lavoisier, then a twenty-nine year old who was to die on the scaffold during The Terror twenty years later. Priestley called the gas "dephlogisticated air" and seemed to imply to Lavoisier that he had happened upon it by accident. Clearly, the experimental method demanded a degree of premeditation and at some level the "accident" may have been a polite fiction.

Lavoisier performed a definitive quantitative experiment upon the combustion of tin sealed *in vacuo*, and was almost certainly the first human to appreciate the self-subsistent, quantal character of oxygen as a chemical element somewhat in the modern atomic sense of the scientific understanding of such matters. As, however, with all history we must be wary of the retroprojection of our ideas into times and places where they are alien.

Joseph Priestley was born on 13th March 1733 into a family of woollen cloth dressers at Birstall near Batley. An affluent uncle and aunt raised him and his five siblings after the early death of their mother. As English Calvinist Presbyterians, the land, the church, the universities and military commissions were all closed to them, so the young Joseph's early education was at best spasmodic.

At the age of nineteen, however, Joseph Priestley traveled to The Daventry Academy, where he spent the next three years. This was a Dissenting equivalent of a university, and as in an Anglican university of the time the curriculum was primarily theological; but unlike an Anglican university it also taught modern knowledge, and it is thought that Priestley attained a grounding in science at Daventry.

To men of Priestley's day, whatever their faith or occupation, the primary object of scientific research was the Discovery of The Great Glory of God manifest in His Creation. In the eighteenth century there was little contradiction between science and faith, at least in Protestant countries, and except for a handful of aristocrats like Cavendish and Lavoisier, scientists were almost invariably clergymen. Priestley, however, also represents the beginnings of a tenuous third force in science: The working-class empiricist. This is a tradition that would play a secondary but glorious rôle in British progress, through figures like Trevithick and Faraday to the great technicians of the twentieth century, only dying-out with the de-industrialisation of the 1980's.

Further complications: Priestley was independently wealthy (he had to be to afford books and apparatus) and certainly saw himself as a theologian and preacher, rather than a scientist or teacher. Theologically, Priestley was an Arian until 1767. Arians believed in the Trinity of The Father, The Son and The Holy Ghost, but viewed The Father as superior. If we think anything of this position it is probably "fair enough", but to the Anglicans and Catholics of that time such thinking was an obscenity. After that year Priestley moved towards a Unitarian position in which only God The Father was real; Jesus was a good but purely mortal man; and The Holy Ghost was a pleasant superstition. Again, many Christians of our time may feel such a doctrinal position basically tolerable, but in Priestley's time it was a position that, whilst it had many declared and secret disciples, placed him well beyond the pale of social acceptability.

Priestley was a very opinionated and disputatious man. He published not only his scientific discoveries and cogitations, but also and more prolifically his ideas about God and Christ. In England, Dissenters and atheists could publish with few restrictions, but Priestley alienated The Church of England and won many other privileged and not so privileged enemies.

After leaving Daventry, Priestley took a succession of preaching jobs. Presbyterian ministers have to enjoy the ongoing approval of their congregations to retain their employment. Brief work with Presbyterian congregations in Suffolk and Cheshire was followed in 1761 by appointment as a languages teacher at Warrington Academy. There Priestley developed his interest in natural philosophy (physics) and in 1767 he published his first scientific work "The History and Present State of Electricity". He was elected to The Royal Society, then and now Britain's most prestigious institution for scientists, and married Mary, sister of the great ironmasters, John and William Wilkinson. Priestley's financial independence was assured.

During the next ten years Priestley did his most important work in electrostatics and gas chemistry, and his fame spread amongst the savants of Europe.

Between 1767 and 1773, he moved back to Leeds, another town burgeoning in the dawn of industrialisation, where he ministered at Mill Hill Chapel. After this stint of preaching he became Librarian to The Earl of Shelburne on an emolument of £250 per annum, of itself the income of a lesser gentleman. Priestley, however, became ever more radical and outspoken in politics and religion, and this may have been a factor in the split with Shelburne that took place in 1780.

Consequently, it was in 1780 that Priestley made his fateful decision to travel to Mercia's principal town and take charge of The New Meeting at Birmingham.

The Mercians are seldom distinguished from other English, but have a distinctive regional culture. Though poets and writers with few equals worldwide, they have a strongly anti-intellectual tradition, and whilst working engineers and entrepreneurs are often tolerated, the Mercians have little patience with theoreticians or progressives.

In 1780, however, Birmingham was expanding dramatically as the World's first true industrial city. Five years earlier, its population at 74000 had exceeded that of every other English city, except for London and Bristol. It was enjoying its heyday as the center of metal goods manufactures: pins and buttons to cannon and steam engines in every known metal and alloy. Even in 2008 vestiges of this tradition persist, though most of Birmingham's great factories are long gone.

Birmingham had no town council and little law and order but in expansive and prosperous times there was little unrest. The Mercian working classes were, and are, notably deferential but in the eighteenth century, unlike today, Birmingham had a sizable middle class and a small but active cultural life.

Liberty, reason and enterprise were in the air. It looked as if Britain might follow America and become a free republic. Science and enlightened religion were gaining prestige and in diverse ways assisting the progress of the new Industrial Revolution.

On 14th July 1789 the Parisians revolted and declared their ancient monarchy a nation of liberty, equality and fraternity under a sovereign People. The French arrested, and later killed, their royal family, and anyone else they considered exploitative or reactionary.

The Church of England and the aristocracy of Europe watched in horror as Priestley and Jacobin sympathisers across Europe and the fledgling US crowed with excited, and sometimes imprudent, satisfaction.

Spencer Maden, rector of St Phillip's, lead the Anglican clergy and the petty magistracy of Birmingham in a counterattack upon their local radicals and libertarians.

On 14th July 1791, eighty-one of the latter, but not Joseph Priestley, convened for a celebratory dinner at Dadley's Hotel in Temple Row. It was the second anniversary of The Storming of the Bastille. Most of the town's wealthy liberals attended.

Whilst they were thus distracted, the mob was incited, for Church and King, to storm the liberals' chapels and houses, and to pillage and burn them. The New Meeting and Old Meeting Chapels were set on fire, as were two other places of worship, twenty-seven houses and several businesses. The mob was going to burn also The Quaker Meeting House in Bull Street (where the Author has worshipped on several occasions) before someone in the mob reminded the rest that the Quakers were too apathetic to take one side or the other and were thus not worth assaulting.

By the time the rioters reached Priestley's house, Fairhill, in the then salubrious Southern suburb of Sparkbrook, the reverend doctor and his wife and children were found at home. They left for London immediately. All of Priestley's life's work, his books, papers, letters and apparatus were stolen and destroyed, and the house burnt to a ruin. Much history, including Priestley's crucial correspondence with Scheele, and with Lavoisier and other leading French, has been lost forever. A friend later reported to Priestley:-

"The road for half a mile of my approach was strewn with your books, the mob were carrying others away, and there were not above twelve octavos on the shelves when I entered the room, the floor of which was totally covered, two or three inches deep with torn leaves, chiefly manuscript"

Parts of the mob moved upon houses of other intellectuals. Several more at adjacent Sparkhill were raised, but at Edgbaston Hall the Father of Pharmacology the great physician Dr William Withering, the first man to employ digitalis in scientific medicine, decided to defend his house, ironically a rented property. He and some friends confronted the mob with firearms and it slunk away. Elsewhere, Samuel Galton, the Quaker arms manufacturer, resorted to bribery of the rioters using both beer and gold, a stratagem that proved equally successful.

In the words of Dr PM Jones speaking on 28th February 2004:-

"It was a personal tragedy, a tragedy for the Birmingham Dissenter community, and more generally, a tragedy for the spirit of free enquiry all rolled into one"

On a slightly lighter note, Dr Jones added:-

"To the astonishment and irritation of the town's medical practitioners, all their nervous patients and hypochondriacs had been cured by the drama!"

Priestley received financial help from friends and his wealthy Wilkinson in-laws and tried to rebuild his life at London. But he was a pariah, and neither could his three sons find advancement for they were tarred with the sins of the father.

On 7th April 1794, the Priestleys set sail for Pennsylvania. They settled in the backwoods community of Northumberland, five days hard riding from Philadelphia. Even that, largest settlement of anglophone America, was often isolated in Winter. News from Paris had taken four days to reach Priestley at Birmingham; at Northhumberland it took eighty. Scientific apparatus was almost unsourceable, but by 1797 he had re-established his laboratory.

Ironically, the Americans found Priestley's strident republicanism at best tiresome and at worst dangerous. Similarly, his religious position was widely deprecated and he was seldom invited to preach either locally or in Philadelphia. He narrowly avoided deportation back to Britain, something that even today Americans will rarely consider. Pennsylvania was of course a Quaker state, and Quakers were and are a rather tolerant brotherhood. Perhaps I should say siblinghood, for then as now even women were permitted freely to speak in collective worship. Notwithstanding which, Quakers are not very sympathetic to Unitarianism. Priestley would probably have been better received if he were a Jew or a votary of one of the local aboriginal animisms.

Joseph Priestley is something of a transitional figure, a missing link between the old agrarian world of faith and celebration, and The Age of Mechanism.

He passed away in Pennsylvania on 6th February 1804.

The consequences for Mercia were even more serious. It ceded scientific leadership to Scotland and London. By the twentieth century the torch had passed to Germany and the United States.

RECORDE
The Memorial to Robert Recorde at Tenby

Location:	St Mary's Church, Tenby, Pembrokeshire, Wales, UK
Date of Photograph:	pm 12 April 1992
OS Grid Reference:	SN134004
Co-ordinates:	51:40:19N 4:42:00W
Elevation:	30.5 meters

"Then what you say to this equation? If I sold unto you an horse having 4 shoes, and in every shoe 6 nayles, with this condition, that you shall pay for the first nayle one ob: for the second nayle two ob: for the third nayle foure ob: and so forth, doubling untill the end of all the nayles, now I ask you, how much would the price of the horse come unto?"

The answer is of course, to use Robert Recorde's own coinage (and a pun he would have relished), one zenzizenzizenzic cubed, or as he taught us to say, $2^{24} = 16,777,216$ obs.

Robert Recorde was born in 1510 in the charming walled port of Tenby in the Englishry of South Wales. His father Thomas was probably a prosperous sea merchant and his mother tongue would have been English, though his mother, Rose Jones, was a Machynlleth woman. We know little else of Robert's childhood.

Sometime around his sixteenth year Robert entered the University of Oxford. We do not know how he managed physically to reach the Mercian town: He could have shipped to Bristol and walked over The Cotswold Hills risking the wrath of bored sheep and the cupidity of bandits: Or he may have chosen a longer but easier sail to London, and thence by river.

Whatever the accidentals, we know that by 1531 he had graduated Bachelor of Arts and was elected a Fellow of All Soul's College. His subject specialism was almost certainly medicine and he very probably took up teaching at the college, a position he could have retained whilst he remained unmarried. He became something of an expert in British history and the Anglo-Saxon language, subjects still taught at Oxford. It was probably at All Soul's that Recorde first came to Court notice by befriending John Leyland, King Henry VIII's antiquarian, but this is speculation.

It is thought that Recorde was still at Oxford when he wrote "The Grounde of Artes", a book published in 1543. It broke fresh ground in English education. The book discussed the arithmetic of fractions and whole numbers, computation (with counting boards as well as pencil-and-paper), proportion and other bread-and-butter topics of commercial mathematics. But it also introduced Arabic numerals to England, demonstrating their computational convenience, as well as adumbrating the symbolic mysteries of algebra, a science being formulated by Recorde's Continental contemporaries, especially the French mathematician Francois Vieta.

In 1548, Recorde took time out from mathematics to author "The Urinal of Physic", a medical text.

Recorde's expository style disclosed the benefits of his teaching experience. First and foremost, he wrote in the vernacular and not in Latin so that merchants and seamen, and indeed merchant seamen could follow the arguments. He divulged complex constructs after simple principles had been shown and mastered. He was not afraid to invent new words and symbols to denote nameless concepts, but made sure they were earthy enough to be remembered by the most surd student. And as we saw with the horseshoe problem he had no fear of looking silly if it would achieve the professional objective.

Lastly, but not leastly, Recorde had a felicity with book titles that most publishers would die for, and "The Grounde of Artes" flowed through three editions in as many years. In the 1552 edition Recorde introduced relatively advanced heuristic topics to England. One of these was the Italian algorithm of *regula falsi* or "false position": A process that enabled the progressive numerical solution of otherwise intractable equations.

Recorde was something else novel for the time: He was an eclectic expositor who selected convenient pearls from prior wisdom discarding all that was not wholly apt to the task at hand. In 1551 he published "Pathwaie to Knowledge", a kind of condensed Euclid in which academic proofs were ruthlessly deleted in favor of down-to-earth explanations, and applications.

In 1556 there followed "The Castle of Knowledge" in which Recorde carefully expounds the convolutions of Ptolemaic astronomy to the plain Englishman, and even discloses the new science of Copernicus, wisely omitting any comment or commitment that may have offended doctrine.

Our next certain record of Recorde relates that he entered Cambridge to read for an MD. The Cambridge archives state that Recorde already had had a BM for twelve years, so it is virtually certain that Robert picked up this medical degree at Oxford. He graduated MD in 1545 and left for London to practice medicine.

Two years later King Henry died, and The Duke of Somerset established a regency on behalf of Henry's boy successor, Edward VI. Shortly after The Privy Council asked Recorde to question someone in The Tower who had been arrested for being a "false prophet". It is conceivable that Recorde's medical training suggested he be used to control the torture of this prisoner, but this is less likely. It is more likely that Recorde's training in academic theology commended his use in what was essentially a canon examination.

Recorde's Government work must have been appreciated because shortly after he was placed in charge of the Bristol Mint. For the first time Arab numerals appeared on an English coin. It was the Bristol-minted silver crown, worth five shillings or one quarter of a pound. It may have been here that Robert refined his ideas about alligation, the mathematical theory of blending alloys of known composition to achieve a third mixture of metals in selected proportions.

Whatever the case, it was at The Bristol Mint that Recorde had his first run in with Sir William Herbert, The King's Governor. In theory Herbert was a tutor in charge of the boy king's personal education and discipline, but in practice he had an even more responsible rôle as State troubleshooter, minder and fixer at large. Herbert arrived in Bristol and asked Recorde for cash to put down a revolt. Recorde refused unless he was presented with a draft bearing the King's signature. Herbert arrested Recorde on a technical charge of treason, and Recorde was recalled to Court to cool his heels.

In 1551 Robert was eased back into favor and dispatched to control the King's silver mines and mints in Ireland. The mines failed and there were unsurprisingly industrial relations altercations with the German miners. By now, Recorde's old enemy William Herbert had been promoted to be Earl of Pembroke and he recalled Recorde ignominiously to London.

Five years later with "The Castle of Knowledge" at the printer's, the young King had died and his half-sister Bloody Mary and her absentee husband, the baleful Philip II of Spain, had ascended the English throne. Ever eager to serve, Herbert now obliged by massacring Protestants. Unwisely, Recorde charged the Earl of Pembroke with misconduct and Herbert immediately countersued for libel in the sum of a thousand pounds.

Recorde was speedily tried and the case went against him. He either could not or would not remit to Herbert his thousand pounds of winnings, and was therefore imprisoned. Ironically, Recorde was owed a thousand pounds back-salary for his Irish services, but the Government did not credit that to his estate until 1570.

It was almost certainly in prison that Robert completed his last and most original book:- " The Whetstone of Witte, which is the Second Part of Arithmetike, containing the Extraction of Rootes, the Cossike Practice, with Rules of Equation, and The Woorkes of Surde Numbers". The book is dedicated to the seamen venturers of The Muscovy Company, founded two years earlier to trade with Russia and seek The North-East Passage to the Orient.

For a couple of hundred years the Italian mathematicians had had a cumbersome habit of elaborating algorithms in words in which they had referred to the unknown quantity to be determined, "x the unknown" if you will, as "Cosa" or "thingy" as we might say. Hence, in English, this proto-algebraic system came to get called "The Cossike Arte" or just plain Cossik, Cossic or even Cos.

Now the ancient Latin word for a cutler's whetstone was "cos": And the pun becomes as clear as the metaphor is brilliant.

In "The Whetstone of Witte" Robert Recorde left us the never-to-be-forgotten comparison:-

"I will sette as I doe often in woorke use,
a paire of paralleles, or Gemowe lines of one lengthe,
thus: ======= ,
bicause noe 2. thynges, can be moare equalle"

The stage had been set for science.

The 28th June 1558 found him in The King's Bench Prison at Southwark. He willed his last pennies to his nine children and died within a few weeks.

SCHIEHAL
Schiehallion from Loch Rannoch

Location: Schiehallion from Loch Rannoch, Perthshire, Scotland, UK
Date of Photograph: pm 23 July 2006
OS Grid Reference: NN714547
Co-ordinates: 56°40'1"N:4°5'57"W
Elevation: 1083 meters

"Perthshire afforded us a remarkable hill"

Said the Reverend Nevil Maskelyne and anyone would think so if they saw its perfect Fuji-like symmetry from Rannochside.

Schiehallion is considered to be near to the center of Scotland, if that is defined in simple terms as the median of the extreme latitudes and longitudes. The hill is the only eminence of Northern Europe to have been recorded by name by the Ancient Greeks and is said to have been sacred to their contemporary Caledonians. The mountain is ascended by about 20000 people per year and is partially owned by The John Muir Trust who maintain the summit's access routes. The summit is two meters shy of the altitude of Snowdon, the highest hill in England and Wales.

The hill proper is composed entirely of the Pre-Cambrian Schiehallion Quartzite, a metamorphosed sandstone with a uniform density of 2.65 grams per cubic centimeter. This fact enabled Charles Hutton to compute the mass of the mountain after he had made a careful staff-and-level survey of its surface that yielded its volume. In the process, Hutton drafted the World's first contour map.

Maskelyne had previously set other scouts to scour the Three Kingdoms for an isolated hill with excellent symmetry; but elongated East to West; and of uniform material. To the consternation of the irascible moonraker they reported that only this frigid and stormy place would do for what he had in mind.

In September 1774, the great astronomer built (with a little help) bothies and towers for the telescope on two platforms, one each at two thousand feet on the South and North flanks of Schiehallion. In each lonely bothy, on many chilly nights, Maskelyne suspended a plumb line, and measured its inclination by reference to the fixed stars. The mass of the "remarkable hill" deflected the plumb-lead ever so little, but by a measurable amount, against the preponderant pull of our planet.

Knowing Hutton's mass of Schiehallion, Maskelyne could now compute the mass of The Earth, and by implication G, Newton's Universal Gravitational Constant. Amongst the cornucopia of scientific fallout was the fact that the Earth could not be hollow, as many Enlightenment savants had thought. The planet's volume had been known since the time of Ancient Greece, and a quick bit of slide-rule work by Hutton now showed that its density, at about 4.5 grams per cubic centimeter, was far too great to enclose any large void.

Now the size and evolution of The Universe were within grasp: And Nevil Maskelyne had weighed The Earth!

I was but dimly aware of these things when, exactly two hundred years later, I mapped the rock-relations of the Northern flank of Schiehallion as a trainee geologist.

TREVIT
The Statue of Richard Trevithick at Camborne

Location:	Camborne Public Library, Cross Street, Camborne, Cornwall, England, UK
Date of Photograph:	am 4 April 1996
OS Grid Reference:	SW647398
Co-ordinates:	50:12:41N 5:17:52W
Elevation:	104.9 meters

Richard Trevithick was born in a small cottage at Tregajorran, in the heart of the Camborne-Redruth tinfield in West Cornwall. On the day of his birth on 13th April 1771 the area was crowded with deep tin and copper mines providing the bulk of the World's supply of these metals, crucial to early industrialisation.

Cornwall was very rich in metals of all kinds but had no coal, which had to be shipped from South Wales and was consumed voraciously by the inefficient low-pressure Newcomen engines of the time. The young Trevithick delighted in watching these ponderous contraptions as they pumped water out of local mines, in one of which Richard senior was a captain.

Richard junior was the sole boy in a family of five sisters and attended a Camborne elementary school where one of the masters described him as "a disobedient, slow, obstinate, spoiled boy, frequently absent and very inattentive". The student, however, had a ready aptitude for arithmetic though he remained semi-literate throughout life.

In Trevithick's youth more efficient separately-condensing Boulton and Watt engines infiltrated the tinfield effecting some economies of fuel but they remained thermodynamically-inefficient low-pressure machines.

In 1790, Trevithick was hired as an engineer at East Stray Park Mine where he constructed and adapted Watt-pattern engines and reversed the sense of plunger pumps to invent an hydraulic engine.

In 1797, Trevithick wed Jane Harvey, daughter of John Harvey, an iron-founder in the nearby town of Hayle. Throughout the nineteenth century Harvey's of Hayle would make enormous Cornish steam beam engines (actually called Cornish Engines). These were highly fuel-efficient and typically applied to mine or waterworks pumping duties. In the twentieth century they would be superseded by electric motors or steam turbines. Trevithick invented them.

As late as 1974, I saw the majestic ruins of Harvey's foundry when I passed aboard a coach. I am told all is now cleared.

Trevithick realised that steam engines could be made much more powerful compact and economical if they could be configured to use active high-pressure steam, say at 140psi, rather than the customary low pressures around 20psi, where much of the power was derived from the passive condensation of the steam beneath atmospheric pressure.

This was already appreciated at an academic level before Trevithick, but the limitations of boiler and boring technology meant that safe and reliable deployments were impracticable.

By 1799, Richard had made some sort of high-pressure steam engine. There is evidence that he made a model steam carriage and tested it on local byways, but in 1801 he constructed a boardable steam carriage at Camborne Hill. Trevithick's early high-pressure steam engines did not use a closed steam circuit, and in particular they steered clear of Watt's jealously-defended patent separate condenser apparatus. Instead they exhausted pulses of steam direct to the atmosphere, a potential source of thermodynamic inefficiency. This lent the engines a characteristic puffing action, so he called his carriage "The Puffing Devil".

"The Puffing Devil" was the first automotive locomotive of any kind.

On 24th December 1801 "The Puffing Devil" carried Trevithick and several companions to the hamlet of Beacon about half a mile away. Three days later the heavy steam carriage broke its structure on a pothole and its passengers adjourned to a convenient hostelry to console themselves with roast goose and ale. They returned to discover that the water had all boiled away and the splendid conveyance had burnt to a crisp.

Trevithick patented his high-pressure steam engine in 1802 and at Coalbrookdale engineered a test rig to measure its duty. Its piston ran at 40 strokes per minute and the boiler pressure was 145psi. Richard sent a drawing of a locomotive to fellow Cornishman, the scientific impresario Davis Giddy, but there is no evidence this machine was actually constructed.

In 1803, Trevithick again collaborated with his cousin Andrew Vivian who had piloted "The Puffing Devil". They built an improved steam carriage that ran a bus service between Holborn and Paddington, places then on the Northern periphery of London, about three miles apart. This proved more expensive to run than a horse-drawn carriage and was withdrawn.

That year a Trevithick stationary pumping engine at Greenwich exploded killing four men and this refocused Trevithick's attention upon the need, with high-pressure steam, to incorporate safety systems that did not rely upon human skill or diligence.

Trevithick invented a weighted-lever plug valve for use atop the boiler above the water level. It could be adjusted to confine deferent limit pressures of steam by moving a weight along a horizontal bar to increase or decrease the moment on the steam plug. This helped to prevent boiler accidents but explosions could still result from defective boiler manufacture or maintenance, or "screw down" by operatives attempting to maximise engine performance.

A different issue arose when boilers were allowed to steam dry and became hot enough to start general conflagrations. To ameliorate this problem, Trevithick invented the device of a lead plug below the waterline that would melt out if it emerged into the steam head. This would release the steam pressure safely but in a manner dramatic enough to attract the attention of stokers who would then presumably douse the fire in the firebox.

In the previous year (1802) Trevithick had installed a high-pressure engine at the Pen-y-Darren Ironworks in Merthyr Tydfil. It had done service driving automatic hammers. Trevithick returned to Pen-y-Darren and in collaboration with the proprietor, Samuel Homfrey and his staff, Trevithick mounted the hammer engine on wheels to, in 1804, give the World its first railway locomotive.

Homfrey was sufficiently interested to purchase the patents on the locomotive and he wagered neighboring ironmaster Richard Crawshay 500 guineas (£525) that the loco could haul ten tons of iron along the (horse) tramroad from Pen-y-Darren to Abercynon, which was nine and three-quarter miles.

Amid crowded scenes of expectancy, on 21st February 1804, the loco was coupled to five wagons loaded with ten tons of iron and seventy men boarded, including Homfrey and Crawshay. Davis Giddy and an unnamed Government agent looked on.

The Pen-y-Darren locomotive steamed the entire route in four hours and five minutes. Crawshay's five hundred guineas was Homfrey's.

The design of the Pen-y-Darren loco was very simple, but several key features would conserve until the very end of steam locomotive manufacture in the closing years of the twentieth century.

One feature that did not was its basic four-wheeled automobile-like chassis. But the engine had a single stroke slide-bar piston configuration coupled to a flywheel. There was no condenser but some of the power of the exhaust steam puff was used to augment the fire-draught to increase the efficiency of combustion.

Crucially, at Pen-y-Darren, the rails were made of smooth cast-iron, and the locomotive maintained traction by adhesion only.

Between 1805 and 1807 Trevithick was involved in an abortive project to drive a tunnel under the Thames at Rotherhythe but was defeated by water ingress. It would be another thirty years before the project was consummated, by the Brunel family.

Trevithick returned to steam in 1808. He had a new loco, named by a friend's daughter "Catch Me Who Can", built by Hazeldine and Rastrick in Bridgnorth. He ran it along a demonstrational circular track on what is now the site of The Chadwick Building at Euston. In 1808 this was a field on the very edge of London's built-up area. He charged one shilling for a ride on his "Steam Circus", not allowing patrons to escape the realisation that his machine was faster than a horse.

But at this time the new technology was frustrated by wooden or cast-iron rails that were too weak to sustain the weight of locos. It was not until wrought iron was puddled by the thousand ton that the steam railway escaped from the laboratory and the circus.

Trevithick went on to apply his high-pressure engines to various avenues of static heavy manufactures, as well as steam dredgers and other marine ancillaries and in 1808 he brought his reluctant family from Cornwall to Limehouse. However, in 1810 Trevithick caught typhoid and though he recovered his partnership went bankrupt. By the end of the year the Trevithicks were back in Cornwall.

In 1812, Trevithick invented the Cornish boiler, a format where the major cylindrical envelope is interpenetrated by a single large fire tube. This increases the area of fire contact, more than doubling the thermal efficiency of the total system. Cornish boilers were first used with the existing Boulton and Watt low-pressure engines at Dolcoath. The Dolcoath Mine at Camborne was by 1812 and for most of its working life the largest copper mine in the World.

That same year of 1812, as Napoleon retreated ignominiously though the snows of Russia, and the British sacked Washington (the town not the soldier!), Trevithick invented a monumental high-pressure format of the beam engine called the Cornish Engine. As aforenoted, this remained the most fuel-efficient type of engine until the turbine era and became the engine of choice for reliable heavy pumping duty in mines or waterworks. Cornish engines remained at work in such sectors until the 1960's, or even later in the china clay mines of Cornwall. Most but not all were literally Cornish in nationality, made either at the Harvey foundry at Hayle, or the Sandys-Vivian works at Perran on the Fal Estuary. A handful of late examples were cast by Holman Brothers, the Camborne jackhammer makers.

It was during this phase of his career that Trevithick engaged a more checkered flirtation with the Spanish silver industry in Peru and elsewhere. Between 1811 and 1819 he made several trips to South America, fell in and out with local backers, and got caught up in Bolivarian wars of independence. But early nineteenth century steam technology was too weak to work satisfactorily on the airless and arid plains of The High Andes, and eventually he had to quit his mine at Caxatombo, abandoning £5000 of ready concentrate to The Spanish Army.

In another of those "historic novel" moments, Trevithick happened to meet Robert Stephenson as he Trevithick was trying to find a ship in the Columbian port of Cartagena. Trevithick bummed fifty pounds of the young railway engineer and shipped to Falmouth. That was as late as 1827 and marked the end of Trevithick's not very profitable American adventures.

Trevithick continued to innovate. In 1829 he designed a closed cycle engine and a vertical tube boiler, and later a storage room heater. When the Great Reform Bill was passed in 1832, the Cornishman proposed to commemorate it with a thousand-feet high cast-iron column surmounted by the statue of a horse. It was of course never erected.

In his last years Trevithick earned £1200 from a design for a new form of steam reaction turbine. It was intended as a marine engine, but the money would have been absorbed by Trevithick's many creditors. He took ill with pneumonia and retired to a bed in The Bull Inn at Dartford, where he died on 22nd April 1833.

WITHERIN
William Withering

Location:	Cairn-mon-Earn, Kincardineshire, Scotland, UK
Date of Photograph:	pm 14 August 1990
OS Grid Reference:	NO785920
Co-ordinates:	57:01:09N 2:21:19W
Elevation:	350 meters

The picture shows *Digitalis purpuria* (the Common Foxglove) blooming on a sheltered spot near the summit of Cairn-mon-Earn at the Eastern limit of The Scottish Highlands.

Digitalis is a genus of about twenty species of biannual plantaginate herbs which sport arrays of beautiful campaniform flowers of variable coloration, usually white yellow or purple. Digitalis is endemic to Europe and Western Asia. The common wild British variety, *Digitalis purpuria*, will grow spontaneously in any shaded, well-drained spot. It has beside Foxglove, various baleful folk monikers such as "Dead Man's Fingers" (also a pallid marine organism) and "Witch's Gloves".

Every part of digitalis is violently toxic.

The most poisonous parts are, however, the leaves of the upper stem of the second year's growth. A fragment of such a leaf will cause death, as will drinking the vase water in which foxglove cuttings have decoratively been displayed. The precursors of digitalis poisoning are vomiting, anorexia (appetite loss), diarrhea, stomach cramps, delirium, hallucinations and headache. Later or more severe symptoms include xanthopsia (everything seeming a green or yellow color) and blue halos around any lights in view, as well as convulsions. Cardiac arrhythmias are the proximal causes of death.

The herb is lethal to all creatures except certain specialist butterflies and their caterpillars, and such of course certifies the weed's invulnerable ubiquity.

For centuries, the foxglove, in extended dilutions, has been a herbal nostrum drunk as "tea".

William Withering was born at Wellington in Shropshire on 17th March 1741, and became a typical scientific polymath of The European Enlightenment, making major contributions to botany and mineralogy as well as medicine. Between 1762 and 1766 he trained as a physician at Edinburgh Medical School, then the best in the World, and commenced his career a year later at Stafford Royal Infirmary.

He joined an informal Mercian science club called The Lunar Society due to its members' habits of exploiting moonlight to ride to dinners in each other's homes. Many of the key scientists, technologists and industrialists of the age were members, and Withering was befriended by fellow physician and Lichfield man Erasmus Darwin, a scion of the Wedgwood ceramics millions.

In 1775 Withering was appointed to the staff of The Birmingham General Hospital at the instance of Darwin. Almost immediately, a patient presented with a congestive heart failure, called "dropsy" at the time, and that should have been fatal. The patient had, however, imbibed a traditional foxglove nostrum and made a spectacular recovery.

During the next nine years, Withering made a diversity of preparations from different parts of the foxglove collected at different seasons to test their efficacy on a total of 156 dropsy patients. This enabled him to identify both the best and the safest way to administer the infusion to heart patients.

Withering wrote up his results, and in January 1775 submitted a paper. It was called "An Account of the Successful Use of Foxglove in Some Dropsies and in Pulmonary Consumption". Later that year his friend Darwin presented the paper to The College of Physicians in London.

Scientific pharmacology was born.

We now know that the active principle of the therapy – and the poison – is a glycoside chemical colloquially known as digoxin, or its near relative, digitoxin. These drugs act by disturbing the balance of electrolytes within nerve cells, and in particular the cells of the vagus and other elements of the parasympathetic nervous system. Specifically, these glycosides cause an increase in intracellular sodium, which in turn drags up the cell's calcium concentration. This tends to steady the heartbeat, and depending upon both circumstances and the way in which the drug is administered, it either speeds up or slows down the heart.

Later in that eventful year of 1775, William Withering was elected a Fellow of The Royal Society. During the Church and King Riots of 1791, Withering successfully defended his home, Edgbaston Hall, from the Birmingham mob. He died peacefully on 6th October 1799. The exact location of his grave is not known but there is a memorial stone plaque, featuring the foxglove, within Old Edgbaston Church.

CHAPTER NINE

Winning the Earth

The complex geology of Britain has guaranteed a very wide diversity of mineral blessings, but scattered widely and seldom in quantity. Most of the nation's mines and placers lasted a year or two, except for coal or tin workings that could be active for centuries.

The minerals raised are or have been in four chief classes:-

1. Fossil Fuels: Coal, Oil Shale, Oil and Natural Gas
2. Chemical Feedstocks and Fluxes: Limestone, Salt, Fluorspar, Potash, Alum, Gypsum, Anhydrite, Barytes, Pyrite and China Clay
3. Metallic Ores and Halogens: Copper, Tin, Iron, Lead, Silver, Gold, Zinc, Arsenic and Tungsten with minor amounts of Vanadium, Cobalt, Manganese, Chromium, and Antimony. Northern Ireland has furnished Aluminium (Aluminum).
4. Constructional Materials: Stone, Sand, Gravel, Chalk and Clay

In addition to these, chemical elements have been abstracted from non-lithospheric sources at various periods and locations. Magnesium, Iodine and Bromine have been abstracted from seawater and Gallium from industrial coal-soot. For many years Oxygen, Nitrogen, Argon and Xenon have been obtained by the fractional distillation of air.

Despite their limited amounts by World standards the diverse British mineral deposits played a key rôle in the motivation of early industrialisation and in providing its physical wherewithal.

For Britain, fossil fuels and chemical feedstocks were, and to an extent remain, the most economically important of its natural resources.

Commercial gemstones are largely absent. The most important is the unique banded fluorspar called "Blue John" that is mined in The Treak Cliffs Cavern and its adjacent adits a mile or so West of Castleton in Derbyshire, at which village small jewelry items that incorporate blue john may be purchased. In the nineteenth century jet was mined at Whitby and agate at various places in Angus, or as it then was Forfarshire. Gem-quality sapphire is obtainable at Loch Roag in the far North of Scotland. Collectors' minerals, especially spectacular cubic fluorspar crystals from Teesdale, are still produced. Several other minor minerals including obsidian, flint and graphite are archaeologically important.

On remote hillsides archaeologists have detected sharp chips struck from obsidian by men of remote ages. Neolithic peoples in the Breckland of Norfolk and elsewhere undertook the first systematic mining. They dug bell pits in search of flint of sufficient quality to be knapped into sharp tools. At Brandon one of the World's oldest industrial outfits, a flint napper's workshop, survives. Today it specialises in the manufacture of gunflints for enthusiasts and theatrical producers.

It is likely that the first metal to be mined in native Britain, other than native gold, was native copper. Copper ore is very widespread but its reduction requires a complex and energetic technology that was not accessible to primitive men. Such native copper would have been more abundant in Cornwall than elsewhere and can be found in small amounts both in the killas and in the Lizard serpentine. On the imposing limestone promontory of The Great Orme in North Wales is a complex of open cast and gallery workings of the remote Bronze Age. Many shafts and galleries are only wide enough for a child to crawl through and several antler picks and other archaic artefacts have been found therein. The copper deposits of The Great Orme were worked again by the Victorians, this time from a steam-powered shaft mine in Llandudno. When it became possible to reduce copper ore the immense reserves of copper carbonates, sulfides and ferrosulfides that exist in Cornwall and West Devon became accessible, and those counties began their three millennia of mine work.

In the late eighteenth century the great porphyry copper deposit at Parys Mountain on Anglesey became the World's biggest copper mine but by the end of the Napoleonic Wars the South-West had reasserted its historical dominance and remained the World's principal source of copper until the first years of the twentieth century.

Pockets of workable copper exist throughout the UK from undersea at Land's End to Sandwick in Shetland and tiny occurrences occur throughout Wales, Scotland and in the volcanic bosses of the English Midlands. The third most important source of cooper after Cornwall and Anglesey was The Bunter Sandstone of Mercia and Yorkshire, or more especially associated pipe deposits peripheral to the sandstone. The Ecton Mines of Staffordshire enjoyed a brief period of late eighteenth century bonanza and provided the capital to finance the construction of nearby Buxton as a modern spa resort. Further significant mines of this class were at Middleton Tyas near Scotch Corner and at Alderley Edge near Stockport. The Alderley Edge deposits are thought to have been worked by the Romans.

In contrast to copper, tin is very restricted in occurrence, only having been won in Cornwall, and to a minor degree on nearby Dartmoor. Tin almost invariably occurs as its oxide cassiterite but this is easily reduced and tin was exported directly from Cornwall between the Bronze Age and 1998AD. For most of the three millennia involved, Cornwall was the Occident's only source of the metal, which was of course an essential component in the manufacture of bronze for tools, weapons or for hydraulic and architectural fitments. Production boomed in the nineteenth century for alloys, coatings and chemical manufacture, but declined dramatically in the last century due to the development of Malayan and Bolivian sources, and the rise of aluminum.

Quantitatively, iron has been by far the largest metal tonnage brought to grass in Britain. Many millions of tons of blackband ironstone were raised from collieries in The Black Country, Scotland and elsewhere in the critical years of The Industrial Revolution from 1750 to 1850 and formed the bedrock of British industrialisation. Before industrialisation the chief sources of iron were The Weald of Sussex and Kent, and The Forest of Dean. By 1650 these two areas were, however, hampered by deforestation, much of it due to competition from shipbuilding. By the mid nineteenth century the blackband iron itself began to decline but changes in technology, especially the Bessemer converter for steel production, encouraged the development of high-quality hematite reserves in West Cumberland. Further technical advances in hearth fettling permitted large reserves of low-grade sedimentary ores in Cleveland and in the East Midlands to be utilised for steel making and by the mid twentieth century drag-dug open casts in Oxfordshire and Northamptonshire were the principal UK sources of iron ore.

The fourth major British metal was lead. Historically, major deposits occurred in Lower Palaeozoic argillites in the distal killas of Cornwall, in Mid Wales, in the Shelve area of Shropshire and in the Leadhills area of the Scottish Southern Uplands. The largest and most extensive deposits occurred however in the Lower Carboniferous limestone (Dinantian Limestone) of the English Pennines, The Mendips, and The Clwydian Range of North Wales. The lead occurs mostly as its sulfide galena that is reduced with relative ease, even with crude wood furnaces blasted by hilltop winds. Later more economic smelting involved closed coke furnaces and long flues to capture significant amounts of the volatile metal lost as fumes. The Romans worked mines in the Mendips, at Carsington and Castleton in the Derbyshire Pennines, and in the Halkyn Mountain of Flintshire. They also ventured into Mid Wales and mined at Dylife and possibly elsewhere. The Mid Wales lead industry later boomed in the sixteenth and seventeenth centuries when the product was cupellated for silver, and the recovered lead was hard enough for ammunition. It was Welsh silver that financed the Royalist side in The English Civil War. In contrast the contemporary Derbyshire mines produced malleable silver-poor lead ideal for plumbing and roofing applications. During the industrial nineteenth century Mid Wales again became an important lead source but large North Pennine mines were opened up whilst the Derbyshire and Mendip fields declined. The disturbed ground or "old man" of the old lead claims is a ubiquitous feature of Northern limestone uplands. The last English lead mine was the prodigious Greenside Mine at Glenridding in The Lake District that closed in 1962.

In the latter twentieth century many Pennine lead mines enjoyed a second life as fluorspar mines for steel smelting flux, but the last of these mines, near Hucklow in The White Peak, now specialises in the supply of high-quality product to a UK hydrofluoric acid maker.

Silver was worked in the nineteenth century at Combe Martin in Devon, and locally in Cornwall and Central Scotland, but throughout history almost all British silver has been refined from lead, especially that sourced from Mid Wales or the North Pennines.

Gold has been mined by the Romans at Dolaucothi in South Wales and more extensively by the Victorians in Merionethshire. The gold for royal jewelry is sourced from the Clogau Mines in Merioneth and the Gwynfynydd Mine further East enjoyed a brief revival in the 1980's. Placers have been worked in Scotland in the Southern Uplands and in the far North at Kildonan.

Zinc blende, the metal sulfide, was frequently found in association with lead ores, and was locally important in The Mendips where, in association with Cornish copper and the local coal it formed the basis of the Bristol brass industry which flourished between 1650 and 1800.

Arsenic and tungsten were once important products of Cornwall and Devon. Borrowdale graphite formed the basis of the still extant Keswick pencil industry and during the two national emergencies of the twentieth century pockets of strategic metals were worked at scattered locations. Such included the vanadium mine at Pim Hill near Shrewsbury and manganese mines on The Lleyn Peninsula, whilst uranium was mined near Plymouth and possibly at Carrock Fell in Cumberland, where cobalt and tungsten were also available. The other British tungsten mine was at Castle-an-Dinas in Cornwall. In the first decades of the twentieth century the Shetland serpentines provided chromite, whilst bauxite associated with the Tertiary Volcanic traps was sent from Northern Ireland to Highland aluminum refineries.

Amongst the fossil fuels coal is historically by far the most important mineral produced in Britain and enabled the country to industrialise. Its association with ironstone and fireclay in cyclical deltaic deposits of Upper Palaeozoic age made the first steps of modern automatic industry possible. The age and depth of British coal has led to advanced induration and carbonisation producing a range of high qualities for different applications such as gas distillation, raising steam, coking or marine bunkerage. Coalfields are both widespread and extensive, and coal measures exposed at the surface, the traditional coalfields of The Industrial Revolution, often continue beneath younger strata as concealed coalfields. In the Middle Ages and early modern period the coal of Central Scotland was developed to fuel saltpans and heat premises, whilst the Northumberland and Durham Coalfield developed for the latter application, exporting its coal coastwise to London.

In the Industrial Revolution these coalfields fuelled local iron industries of their own whilst the Northumberland and Durham field continued to support London. They were joined by a massive development of very thick, surficial strata in The Black Country west of Birmingham that supported further major ironworks and metal manufactures; and by a second major development in the valleys of Glamorgan. This Welsh coal fed vast iron and steel mills and copper refineries as well as a specialism in marine and export coals. Elsewhere large coalfields developed in South Lancashire and South Yorkshire to support local textile industries and fine steels. Smaller coalfields supported local industrialisation; For example, The Potteries, North Wales, the Bristol and West Cumberland coalfields, and those of Leicestershire and Derbyshire, though the Derbyshire field is really part of a much larger complex.

In the twentieth century the bigger concealed field of the East, especially in Nottinghamshire and the Selby area became relatively more important and these furnished the national electrical base load for much of the twentieth century.

In a 1977 coal audit the then National Coal Board defined three classes of British coal deposit:-

(i) Coal In Place: This was defined as the total amount of coal under the land part of the UK that occurred in seams over 2 feet thick and less than 4000 feet below surface. The coal mined up to 1976 was thought to sum to 25000 million tons and was discounted from the "coal in place" total.

(ii) Recoverable Reserves: That portion of the coal in place that was in known coalfields and could be recovered using 1976 technology.

(iii) Operating Reserves: That portion of the recoverable reserves that were fully proven in regard to quality, thickness and mining conditions and which was either accessible to 1976 mines or had been proven sufficiently to locate new mines.

In terms of those definitions Coal In Place totalled 190000 million tons; Recoverable Reserves 45000 million tons (equivalent to 300 years supply); and Operating Reserves 6000 million tons.

In 1983 a detailed analysis of operating reserves identified 4,845 million tons at then operating deep mines.

As of December 2005 the Coal Authority revision for the six then operating deep mines identified that with economically-justifiable investment these mines could supply a further 352 million tons in addition to which the Margam drift could contribute 36 million tons. The previous month The Coal Authority calculated that potential opencast reserves totalled some 619.2 million tonnes. The CA declined to record an opinion about reserves at the Amble or Canonbie drifts, or at private mines.

In the 1850's the Scottish shale oil mines were developed for kerosene production, and in the next century small oilfields were based on Jurassic reserves of fluid crude in Dorset and Nottinghamshire. Petroleum production was however insignificant until advances permitted the development of vast submarine oilfields in the Northern North Sea that from 1975 gave the UK twenty-five years of self-sufficiency in oil.

Allied to the North Sea petroleum are reserves of natural gas and such gasfields also lie beneath the Southern North Sea off Norfolk, and locally elsewhere. This gas was first piped ashore in the 1960's and soon displaced coal gas from grid supplies, accelerating the eclipse of the coal industry.

Chemical feedstocks, fillers and fluxes are also of continuing major economic importance to the British economy. The Romans mined and evaporated salt from beneath The Cheshire Plain and this industry persisted and then, around 1850, boomed. The establishment of enormous alkali works firstly in Liverpool and then on the plain itself at Northwich and elsewhere has underwritten the Cheshire salt industry into the twenty-first century. Fluorspar too is a chemical feedstock and also a smelting flux, but sources in Weardale and The White Peak have recently been mothballed. China clay has been a major Cornish product for nearly two hundred years, providing a principal World source of this important ceramic component and excipient for the paper and drug industries. Potash is mined near Whitby, and locally there are a few gypsum mines.

Beneath alluvial plains and on coastal sandbanks sand and gravel are extensively dredged. Transport costs are high and the amount of activity is very dependent upon the dramatically variable demand of the road and construction industries.

Vestiges that survive to be photographed are almost always the surface works of upland metal mines, especially if a house-built Cornish engine was erected (not necessarily in Cornwall) to provide pumping. The pump houses were so strongly built they can survive as conspicuous ruins for two hundred years and are often mistaken for small castles. They can of course last even longer if they are converted into housing or barns. Collieries disappear almost immediately, leaving scrub wasteland and a tip as their only mementos. The tip is often mistaken for a natural hill. Old quarries or sand and gravel pits, are either landfilled or form deep lagoons that a layman will often mistake for natural lakes. These lagoons are often used for recreational purposes such as sport diving (much of it illegal and always highly dangerous), for bird watching or angling. Motor-accessible upland mines are sometimes the object of heritage stabilisation or the resort of speleological archaeologists or cavers.

ABEREIDD
The Blue Lagoon at Abereiddi

Location: The Blue Lagoon, Abereiddi, Pembrokeshire, Wales, UK
Date of Photograph: pm 15 April 1992
OS Grid Reference: SM794314
Co-ordinates: 51:56:16N 5:12:29W
Elevation: 17.4 meters

This is the so-called Blue Lagoon, a sea-flooded slate quarry.

On the day my Wife and I walked from Porthgain there was a vernal wind blowing violently on shore such that sea-foam blew like soapsuds across the cliff-top path!

It is interesting to compare the roughness of the sea with the halcyon riffling of the lagoon in this picture.

DOROTHEA
The Dorothea Quarry Pumping Engine House at Talysarn

Location:	Talysarn, Nantlle Valley Caernarvonshire, Wales, UK
Date of Photograph:	pm 21 April 2004
OS Grid Reference:	SH479531
Co-ordinates:	53:03:15N 4:14:37W
Elevation:	106.7 meters

This is the Pumping Engine House at Dorothea Slate Quarry.

The Dorothea Quarry specialised in the production of blue and purple slates, mostly for roofing. Slate is a metamorphosed shale and that in Snowdonia is of Ordovician age. The quarry officially opened in 1829 though illegal quarrying in and around Nantlle had been active throughout the eighteenth century. Further investment was made in 1835 but production did not really get underway until the building boom of the latter nineteenth century. The quarry closed in 1970.

The Dorothea Quarry is five hundred feet deep and the last four hundred are in water. Around 1900 the company experimented with electric pumps to keep the quarry dewatered but was dissatisfied with them. Accordingly, in 1906 they installed a Cornish engine by Holman Brothers of Camborne, said to be the last ever built.

The engine pumped ten gallons per second from five hundred feet working in a shaft of 465 feet depth. Its two coal-fired Lancashire boilers fed steam to a sixty-inch diameter single cylinder that rocked a cast-steel beam of twenty-three tons. The engine worked until 1951 when it was replaced by a sixty horse-power electric pump. It did brief duty in 1956.

The engine and its house remain intact though the pump assembly has decayed and the boilers have been vandalised by copper thieves. Demonstrational steam is now raised by what looks like a small propane steam generator in an attached shed. The structure is Grade One Listed, the same as Caernarvon Castle, but its future remains in doubt.

In recent years the deep and frigid waters of the now flooded Dorothea Quarry, just out of frame to the left, have become the locus of illegal sport diving and there have been many fatalities, perhaps amounting to three a year. The nearest decompression chamber is in Liverpool and the only thing to do with a victim of narcosis is to send him back down if there is air enough, possibly to die of hypothermia. There are one or two moving memorials around the lake.

Perhaps understandably, trespassers are not welcome.

GEEVOR
The Victory Shaft of the Geevor Tin Mine near Pendeen

Location:	Pendeen, near St Just-in-Penwith, Cornwall, England, UK
Date of Photograph:	pm 31 March 1996
OS Grid Reference:	SW374345
Co-ordinates:	50:09:08N 5:40:51W
Elevation:	97.5 meters

Cornwall is one of The Occident's few minable sources of tin. The Duchy supplied the metal continuously between the Bronze Age and 1998AD. Without Cornish tin the very Bronze Age would have been impossible, and the great bronze artifacts of Classical Antiquity would never have been cast.

The picture shows the surface complex at Geevor as it appeared in the Spring of 1996, some five years after closure. Geevor is a modern consolidation of several ancient and famous tin and copper setts along the Westernmost cliffs of Penwith.

Many mine galleries extend a mile or two under the Atlantic Ocean, and the old time miners claimed to hear the pulsing rumble of boulders above their heads as waves broke above. Occasionally there were tragedies when the sea broke through to galleries, or miners broke through to the sea. Beyond the seaward ends of those galleries there is no land until Labrador.

A working called, in the Cornish language, Carn Wheal Bal (Mine Works Crag) was mentioned in the 1690's, but the local town of Penzance was already a coinage town by 1663. Cornish coinage towns were administrative centers where locally produced tin was weighed and taxed . The word "coin" is cognate with old verbs "to know", and there is no implication that actual money was manufactured in these places.

By 1716 a Wheal an Gever (workings near the goats) was at work here and by 1766 this was called Wheal Geavor and had been joined by sister mines. One of these had a steam pump by 1815, but the mines fell on hard times and it was not until 1851 that Geevor re-opened under the moniker of East Levant. The mine expanded inland to subsume other setts but closed again in 1891, before re-opening in the next year.

In 1895 The West Australian Gold Fields Company Limited took over and shortly afterwards Geevor and the other St Just mines were electrified using power transmitted from the big coal-burning power station at Hayle about fourteen miles to the East. This power station dominated the Hayle Estuary (a pleonasm!) during my boyhood in the Sixties of last century, but has since disappeared.

Between 1892 and 1896 the Mining Records Office logged no tin production at the Geevor sett itself, but 72.5 tons of block copper ore worth some £4096 was brought to grass. Such figures would be dwarfed by the tin totals of the twentieth century.

In 1918 Geevor milled 24,956 tons of tin ore, employed 205 underground and 98 on the surface.

The Victory Shaft was sunk in 1919 and named to honor the end of The First World War.

By the 1950's the future of Geevor seemed bleak, but the discovery of the Grenfell and Simms Lodes revitalised the mine. An ingress of the sea in the old Levant galleries was successfully plugged with concrete around 1967, and in 1975 the Victory Shaft was deepened and a spur shaft driven seawards to garner new reserves. In 1980 the crushing mill was extended.

In 1985, the London Tin Fix failed and the price of tin plummeted. Geevor was mothballed. Production resumed in 1988 and limped along until 1991 when the pumps were switched off. By that time Geevor employed 400 men and extended to a depth of 350 fathoms, with workings extending far beneath the sea.

Much internal machinery was sold for scrap but the site was purchased by a coalition of local government and heritage organisations in order to set up a Mining Heritage Centre.

The Geevor Mining Heritage Centre duly opened in 1993, but is only accessible to callers in the summer months.

Forty remaining shaking tables for the hydraulico-gravitational concentration of cassiterite have been preserved together with the winding house and its electric winders.

Geevor is the UK's largest preserved mining monument and is part of The St. Just Mining District World Heritage Site.

Ingots of Geevor Tin:
The Upper Ingot was Cast from Metal Recovered from the
20 July 1885 Wreck of SS Cheerful

GOODLUCK
The Good Luck Mine near Wirksworth

Location:	Good Luck Mine, Middletondale, Cromford, Derbyshire, England, UK
Date of Photograph:	pm 9 November 2006
OS Grid Reference:	SK269566
Co-ordinates:	53:06:18N 1:35:54W
Elevation:	209.4 meters

This old lead mine, the Good Luck Mine, is situated on the Southern side of the wooded valley of Middletondale near Cromford and Wirksworth.

Driven below the Lower Matlock Lava the mine is essentially a consolidation of several early nineteenth century setts undertaken by the local entrepreneur John Alsop.

The adit was commenced on the 25 October 1830 at the end of the farmers' season, and shortly thereafter an 11-inch gage tramway was installed. This was made of the virtually indestructible hand-rolled wrought iron produced in those days, and remains essentially intact.

The adit was driven for ninety meters through barren limestone before the Silver Eye Vein was intercepted, though because this and another vein reached soon after were already in work, the Good Luck miners had to come to terms with neighboring venturers. After about a year, however, the Good Luck Vein of 5% granular galena in a barite gangue was struck, set above a clay wayboard that could represent altered extrusives. The Good Luck Vein never exceeded 50 centimeters in depth and usually averaged about 25. In the early 1830's crosscuts were made from the main drive in order to exploit several scrins.

By 1840 the Good Luck Mine was essentially exhausted but later adventurers raised a little more galena, and The Mining Record Office logged 1.2 tons brought to grass in the period 1872 to 1882. Furthermore, some barite and fluorite brought extra profit, whilst the copper minerals azurite and malachite were detected. In the 1920's spoil dumps were re-processed and some further galena was prepared for mining in the 1950's.

In 1972, the Good Luck Mine was nicked at The Barmote Court by representatives of The Peak District Mines Historical Society who maintain it as a heritage monument. By the ancient laws of The King's Field, someone else can propose to work the mine if it remains idle for two weeks: But no-one has stepped forward and now perhaps never shall.

Good Luck is now in charge of an independent charity who are tidying the site. Applications for entry should be addressed in the first instance to the PDMHS at Matlock Bath.

GWYNGOLD
The Gwynfynydd Gold Mine in Merionethshire

Location: Gwynfynydd, Merionethshire, Wales, UK
Date of Photograph: pm 12 July 2001
OS Grid Reference: SH736280
Co-ordinates: 52:50:05N 3:52:40W
Elevation: 190 meters

Intermittently worked since the nineteenth-century, until 1990 this was a source of gold for the Welsh gold jewelry makers of Dolgellau and Tregaron.

The mine also did party tours for £10 ($20) a head using minibuses from Dolgellau.

Since 1990 it has been mothballed.

Lost in the forest on the other side of the Afon (River) Mawddach is the great Glasdir copper mine where ore flotation technology was pioneered in the late nineteenth-century. In the 1960's and 1970's efforts to exploit this Coed-y-Brennin deposit in open-cast on a Chilean scale were successfully resisted by Snowdonia conservationists.

Non-British Flickrites may be amused to note that this was taken in July: Midsummer in the Northern Hemisphere.

LIONSALT
The Red Lion Salt Works at Marston

Location:	The Red Lion Salt Works, Ollerton Lane, Marston, Cheshire, England, UK
Date of Photograph:	pm 7 August 2004
OS Grid Reference:	SJ670754
Co-ordinates:	53:16:30N: 2:29:42W
Elevation:	27 meters

      This is the former pan salt works of Henry Lloyd Thompson and Sons Limited on the Cheshire Salt Field.

      In this part of England a synclinal intermontain basin of some fifty miles diameter contains a thick bed of Permo-Triassic evaporates, of which common rock salt (NaCl) is of great historical and current importance.

      Local brine springs were known to the Romans, who evaporated salt in lead tanks, and Roman and Medieval tanks have been excavated in the vicinity of Marston. One mine of solid rock salt operated until recently at Winsford, other postwar extraction being of solute.

Together with Lancashire (and local) coal, Cheshire salt was central to the development of the Mersey alkali industry under James Muspratt and others, and also the twentieth-century re-vitalisation of the British chemical industry led by Brunner-Mond; as well as the Lever and other soap interests.

After the Middle Ages iron pans superseded lead, and coal supplanted wood fuel, augmenting existing competitive advantages over sea salt.

In 1670, digging identified the local rock salt stratum and by 1781 the Bottom Bed had been reached. By then the dredging of the Weaver Navigation in 1710 and the cutting of The Trent and Mersey Canal in 1777 had facilitated the salt trade, which was prosecuted at Marston by both brine pumping and rock salt mining.

At this time, the Thompson family held integrated salt industries including boat yards and a colliery, and in 1781 The Duke of Bridgewater employed a Boulton and Watt engine both to pump brine and wind rock salt at Marston.

The Red Lion Salt Works in this picture dates from 1894 and specialised in the open pan evaporation of brine to make high-quality potable salt, in preference to vacuum evaporation. Industrial customers, however, gradually adapted their processes to utilise the cheaper vacuum grades produced elsewhere.

Even in the nineteenth century open pan working was deprecated because of the habit of male and female operatives working naked in the intense heat and humidity; the resulting over-consumption of alcohol as a rehydrative antipyretic; and because of the corrosive and carcinogenic fumes that blew from pan works.

During the twentieth century some limited concessions to modernity were made. Fuel oil supplanted coal and after The Second World War glass-fiber moulds were installed with the product manipulated using stainless steel tools.

In 1947 a second-hand steam engine was purchased, and in 1958 a submersible electric pump: Each for abstracting from separate bores.

By 1960, The Lion Works was the only remaining pan works and became increasingly dependent upon the sale of edible cake salt to Third World markets.

In 1986, perhaps fifty years after expectation, Thompson's last Nigerian customers withdrew, and the factory closed.

Vale Royal Borough Council purchased the site to pre-empt demolition and the complex was certified as an assembly of Grade Two Listed Buildings and as a Scheduled Ancient Monument. The works is an Anchor Point on The European Route of Industrial Heritage (ERIH) itineraries.

In 1993 The Lion Salt Works Trust leased the site, together with the adjacent Red Lion Hotel tavern, from which the factory took its name. The factory was decrepit and corroded in 2004, and there is some decayed asbestos cladding evident. In the Summer of that year Ptolemy Dean and Marianne Suhr canvassed financial support for heritage rehabilitation in the Channel 4 (now BBC) national television series "Restoration".

The future of the monument remains uncertain.

MAGPIE
The 1870 Watt Whim House at The Magpie Mine

Location: The 1870 Watt Whim House Ruin, The Magpie Mine, Sheldon, Derbyshire, England, UK
Date of Photograph: pm 15 November 2003
OS Grid Reference: SK171681
Co-ordinates: 53:12:37N: 1:44:41W
Elevation: 317 meters

      This late component of a complex, evolutionary site was built to house a steam winding engine, set at right angles to the main cables' azimuth further East. It sits surrounded by mine spoil heaps amidst sheep pastures South of Sheldon village.
      The Magpie Mine is the most complete, exemplary and evocative of Britain's remaining upland mining monuments outwith Cornwall. It is also the most photographed, presenting in all lights and weathers a wistful and melancholy White Peak beauty, instantly appealing to laymen as well as specialists.
      The mine was worked for lead and latterly also zinc. The lead is not commercially argentiferous and negligible spar was raised at this site. Working

commenced sometime in the seventeenth century and ceased in 1958. The Mining Records Office logged some 995.4 short tons of galena brought to grass between 1872 and 1911, together with 25 tons of blende in 1883. The Magpie Mine is on The King's Field.

A magpie is a saprophagous corvine bird, about 0.3 meters in span, with lovely black and white plumage that diffracts a bottle-green sheen in sunlight. It is endemic to Mercia and in Saxon folklore is a bird of ill omen.

The Magpie Mine, visible for miles on a deserted skyline, is the site of several murders and reputedly cursed and haunted. At any event, despite its long history, it has been one of the least prolific of Derbyshire's great mines, bankrupting all who nicked its stowes.

Romantic and quintessentially English, approached in declining light the scenic group presents a mysterious, even lurid, aspect rather reminiscent of the painted tableau on old-fashioned fairground ghost train rides, or perhaps pre-war Hollywood backdrops of the blasted heaths of Britain.

From the standpoints of the archaeologist, the field lecturer, and the landscape artist, the Magpie is veritably the mine that has everything.

The surface assemblage examples nearly every feature of Georgian and Victorian metal mining. Besides the whim house is a ruinous Cornish pumping engine house with a lean-to boiler house and Cornish chimney, erected by the innovating agent John Taylor in 1867; a further nineteenth-century winding house, roofed complete with drum and rusting cables; a corrugated-iron post-war diesel winding shed (one of three Listed metal buildings in the UK); a 1950's steel headstock complete with cable and cage; a complete Agent's House with detached privy and attached Smithy; a complete 1840 square dry-stone winder chimney with ruinous horizontal flue; a powder house; a reconstructed horse whim; a belland yard; slime pits; a crushing circle; a reservoir and numerous heaps and ancillary buildings. Attentive students, who nevertheless wander slightly away, will discern a rotting jigger, two lengths of cast-iron snore, a millstone (perhaps pressed into service for crushing), a ruined shaft coe and six cast-iron domestic baths.

Below, a major sough was driven between 1873 and 1881, where pneumatic jackhammers and dynamite were used for the first time in Derbyshire. During his agency of the 1860's, Cornishman John Taylor introduced cast-steel borers, steel cable and safety helmets.

The Founder Shaft is seventeenth-century and the currently-mounted Main Engine Shaft was sunk to 728 feet in 1823. Service was by road throughout the mine's working life. The mine, sited at the intersection of the Butts, Bole and Shuttlebark veins was last worked in 1958 by New Zealander firm Waiki Limited: They lost £80,000. In 1962 The Magpie Mine was purchased by The Peak District Mines Historical Society Limited and is a Scheduled Ancient Monument. There is unrestricted pedestrian access.

The Cornish Engine House and the Head Frame

MAWSTONE
The Mawstone Mine Entrance at Youlgreave

Location:	Mawstone Farm, Bradford-by-Youlgreave, Derbyshire, England, UK
Date of Photograph:	pm 21 July 2005
OS Grid Reference:	SK211634
Co-ordinates:	53:10:13N 1:41:12W
Elevation:	155.8 meters

The Mawstone was a lead mine that exploited mineralisation of carbonaceous shales on the edge of Dinantian Limestone in the White Peak District near to Bakewell.

This unusual leadfield geology made the mine prone to firedamp (methane gas) pollution, and methane is explosive in the wrong combination with air.

In 1932 five miners died in a methane explosion at Mawstone. Three comrades went in to rescue them and were killed by the resulting carbon monoxide, which is poisonous.

The mine closed. The men are buried in Youlgreave churchyard.

PELSALL
Knights Hill at Pelsall

Location: Allens Lane, Pelsall, Staffordshire, England, UK
Date of Photograph: am 2 November 2007
OS Grid Reference: SK015028
Co-ordinates: 52:37:22N 1:58:42W
Elevation: 134.1 meters

At about 0855 on Thursday 14th November 1872 a hundred men of Starkey and Morgan's Pelsall Hall Colliery emerged for breakfast. At 0900 there was a sudden call on the mine telegraph and the cage was brought to grass with three men clinging to its bonnet. The men reported that the mine had flooded. The cage was lowered with rescuers who retrieved nine men, but twenty-two remained below.

The days of autumn drizzle continued as the pumps were steamed to maximum capacity. Heavier storms threatened. The partners Ness, Starkey and Forrester descended, but Ness and Starkey were overcome by chokedamp (carbon dioxide gas) and had to rescue one another. Crowds gathered at the pithead and in surrounding pastures.

George Augustus Selwyn was an Anglican Missionary. In 1842 he traveled to New Zealand with his wife and little son and established the Church of

England in New Zealand and the Pacific Islands, becoming the first Bishop of The South Seas. There he traveled 2277 miles by ship, canoe and foot, converting a similar number to Christ. In 1868 he was ordered by the Lambeth Conference to assume the Bishopric of Lichfield.

Over Friday and the weekend Selwyn and the local Wesleyan Minister the Reverend William Winspear waded through the rain, mud and cinder to conduct morning and evening services at the pit head whilst students from the Theological College collected donations from the crowds.

By Monday the water level in the mine had reduced a little.

Sister Dora (Dorothy Pattison), foundress of The Walsall Hospitals (and the first common woman to be commemorated by a public statue) was invited to take over the local schoolroom to receive bodies.

The rain became heavy and as the dense Black Country smoke sank and the lurid pit bank fires illumined the wintry dusk gathering across the foggy swamps and swags of Goscote the affect upon the visiting reporters of The Times and The Illustrated London News was indelible.

Six and a half million gallons is 1429.8 tonnes of water.

By Wednesday morning the pumps had raised six and a half million gallons and a watch pocket complete with its contained watch. It was guessed that a man might be trapped against the grille at the bottom of the snore, so the pump was stopped. Rescuers descended and found the remains of 18-year-old Thomas Starkey, who was brought up to his father and brothers waiting in the pit office.

Amongst further pathetic scenes that afternoon were the retrievals of further mangled remains including that of 14-year-old Thomas Coleman whose waiting mother had just finished her prayer for "my poor little boy that I may lay out his lifeless body".

By the Friday, eight days after the breakthrough, the water was low enough for rescuers to reach the "crop of the shallow", an elevated gallery that acted as an air-lock sealed by the floodwater below.

Here they were confronted by a ghastly tableau.

Ten dead men cuddled together for the last vestige of warmth in the sodden darkness. Three men sat in a tub and four in another as one was in the act of pushing with his spare leg. When these dead entered the crop the air was obviously sweet, but meteorological changes at the surface influence the migration of subterranean gasses. The men had succumbed to chokedamp.

An inrush of water from unmapped old workings had washed away the props bringing down the gallery roofs. In the shallow space that sometimes remained emerged, chokedamp collected: As effective a drowning agent as the water itself, but nevertheless turning the linings of men's lungs to acid so that they might drown in their own phlegm.

Altogether, nineteen men and boys had been asphyxiated by "Carbonic Acid Gas" (carbon dioxide), whilst two drowned in water. The twenty-second, 14-year-old John Heyward, was never found. As indicated above, some men and boys were mechanically broken antemortem.

At the subsequent inquest the Mine Surveyor testified that as far as he knew the ground was virgin, but that he recollected that some time previously a 90-year-old had mentioned to him that he had been told of nearby "old shafts" in his youth. It was established that 19-year-old Isaac Cash had broken into an old gate road running at right angles to his heading. Later exploration of this old gallery continued beneath the church and disclosed relics of eighteenth century miners: Such were illiterate, used no dial, and kept no records.

On Monday 25th November the twenty-one found men and boys were interred in a Pelsall vault in continuing heavy rain and amidst scenes of desolate grief. Two special trains brought mourners from all over The Black Country. Others marched from Rushall behind the band of The Bloxwich Rifle Volunteers. Fifteen widows and forty-five orphans were left without sustenance: There was of course no State benefit system bar the workhouse. The local middle class raised 935 guineas from amongst each other, including more than a hundred from the Bloomer family, owners of Pelsall Iron Works.

(A guinea is twenty-one shillings; £1.05 in modern terms).

On Wednesday 25th December 1872 each of the twenty-two men who had risked their lives to save their comrades were given a Holy Bible.

Each orphan under fourteen received 2/6d per week and each widow 9/6d a week until she re-married: However, no family was permitted to get more than £1 a week.

(9/6d is £0.475, approximately US$0.99 in November 2007).

In the parish church of St Michael and All Angels an obelisk of pink and gray granite commemorates the dead. It was consecrated as late as 1974, and was said to have been financed by the accrual of the Pelsall Colliery Disaster Relief Fund.

The photograph depicts the low, wooded eminence of Knights Hill, usually called Mouse Hill today after a flanking street. It is in fact a mound of colliery waste that was the site of Pelsall Hall Colliery, the scene of the disaster. Observers noticed that wheat and blackberries grew on the heap before the colliery reopened in 1873. The mine finally closed in the 1890's, the victim of insuperable water problems.

Even in November, the Clean Air Acts and the demise of the coal industry in Europe mean that The Black Country now belies its name. It is therefore impossible to depict the sodden and soot-steeped landscape that my Late Mother described as recently as the 1950's. The scene is now one of sunny suburban somnolence.

For many years local folk rehearsed a story about each 14th November at Knights Hill. As the day declined the soft mizzle would turn to an insistent autumn rain. The playful rats would seek their beds amidst the crumbling revetments of the cut. Shroud-white kine would cough like ghosts in the gathering gloom. The darkling mists would sidle along the dells and dingles of a Staffordshire nightfall.

And then, with sudden sloth, at the moment that their shift would have ended, the lost would wearily walk again down the slope of Knights Hill.

Whilst ignorant of this history, and after, I found Mouse Hill an affecting and strangely attractive place in all weathers, and even in busy traffic conditions.

Thus is the Land consecrated by suffering.

THE PELSALL HALL COLLIERY, NEAR WALSALL, THE SCENE OF THE FLOODING.

A contemporary steelpoint engraving of the Pelsall Pithead taken from The Illustrated London News

PORTGAIN
Porthgain Harbor in Pembrokeshire

Location:	Porthgain, near Fishguard, Pembrokeshire, Wales, UK
Date of Photograph:	15 April 1992
OS Grid Reference:	SM813326
Co-ordinates:	51:56:57N 5:11:00W
Elevation:	6.1 meters

A small intrusion of Lower Ordovician dolerite (diabase) exists within Lower Silurian facies around Penclegyr on the coast about a half a mile ENW of Porthgain. Immediately South of this coastal geology is a more extensive area of Ordovician mudstones and shales that are tectonically altered to slates around Abereiddi, but constitute a useable brickearth at Porthgain itself.

Porthgain harbor was constructed in 1840. Ingress and egress was always perilous, but Porthgain is the only haven on this exposed coast, except for that at Abercastle. Harbor works continued in the 1860's and the little port was rebuilt between 1902 and 1904 to provide for the Edwardian boom in roadstone (dolerite) production for tarmacadamisation, especially of London streets. The crushed dolerite was stored in five immense quayside hoppers (now Scheduled Ancient Monuments) that fed sail and steam coasters which exported the mineral. Roadstone production commenced before 1878 and ceased in 1931. Ordovician brick clay was quarried near the harbor and brought to the quayside through a short tunnel from whence it was taken to brickworks in the village.

Porthgain Village Industries ran the extractive and brickworks industries from 1878 to 1936.

An early twentieth century light railway ran from the clifftop roadstone quarries to the harbor bins. It also brought slate from the "blue lagoon" quarry at Abereiddi. It used four second-hand steam locomotives though one proved too weighty for the way. The rigorous climate of salt-spray and high winds promoted rotting of the sleepers and other operational difficulties. In the Spring of 1992, after taking the picture, my Wife and I walked through the fields to Abereiddi, partly along the old trackbed. The storm-force wind, fortunately blowing onshore over the cliffs, bought flocks of foam suds from the sea that soaked us and settled upon the fields, a most memorable effect fifty-five meters above high tide.

TANKER
The Tankerville Mine at Stiperstones

Location:	The Tankerville Lead Mine, Stiperstones Village, Pennerley, Shropshire, Mercia, England, UK
Date of Photograph:	pm 20 May 2005
OS Grid Reference:	SO354994
Co-ordinates:	52:35:22N 2:57:17W
Elevation:	324.3 meters

The Tankerville Mine was the second most prolific of the metal mines of the Shropshire Orefield in Central England. The distant land in the blue haze is Wales. The winding house was sadly demolished in the late 1960's but its superb brick chimney of 1865 is arguably the best of its type. The Walker Shaft engine house operated pumping apparatus. The mine provided lead, silver and zinc but closed in 1893.

The Tankerville Mine is named after its owner The Earl of Tankerville, hereditary heir of The Duke Of Northumberland. The local subsurface was drained by a Boat Level in 1797.

During the existence of the Government monitoring authority, The Mining Records Office (between 1845 and 1913), the actual Tankerville Mine is logged as bringing 13056.2 tons of lead ore to grass with 23522 troy ounces of silver. 236.9 tons of zinc ore was also raised. Underground production of lead was logged between 1869 and 1895; of silver between 1872 and 1883 and of zinc between 1881 and 1891.

A contiguous sett, The Ovenpipe, was however separately recorded and this brought 809.4 tons of lead ore to grass from 1865 to 1868. By comparison, the orefield's most prolific mine at Snailbeach produced 100643.8 tons of lead ore during the life of the MRO.

The earliest records of the 1830's relate to the lessees Walker, Cross and Company who drove a crosscut called The Ovenpipe Level from the Boat Level to work a small pipe vein.

Around 1860-1862, Arthur Waters extended the crosscuts to happen upon an ore mass worth £16000 and ordered The Engine Pit to be driven down to meet it. If the ore was worth £20 per ton this ore find must have totaled about 800 tons. During the 1860's a family of surrounding mines continued to work but capital was concentrated upon the Ovenpipe bonanza.

The Ovenpipe Shaft was sunk below adit level and water ingress proved too great for horse pumps. Accordingly, Waters placed a second-hand engine thirty yards from the shaft to power both pump rods and roller crushers, and it may have been at this time that the wonderful chimney that still graces the site was raised. The old colliery engine had a 16-foot beam with a 3'6" stroke and was rated at sixteen horsepower.

The Ovenpipe Shaft was deepened to 74 fathoms (a fathom is six feet or 1.8288 meters) and was vertical to 11.6 fathoms below adit. From that depth it inclined at an angle of fifteen degrees to the vertical in order to follow the ore body: This enabled the shaft to pay for its own sinkage, but later complicated pumping and haulage operations.

Levels were driven from this shaft into the Old Lode, which was then stoped out. A Southward drive at the 42 fathom level intercepted the top of the Main Lode. This proved to be very rich and the bonanza intensified.

By 1870, fifty miners worked three shifts and the steam engine raised ore from 0600 hours to 1400, drove the crushers from 1400 to 1700 and pumped from 1700 to 0600. The ore was raised by kibble from a chain, the kibble skidding along planks up and down the inclined portion of the shaft. Men climbed ladders in the rod compartment. Ore was concentrated on site by jigger and buddle before being sent to the Pontesbury smelter by horse and cart. On the return journey the carts brought coal from the Pontesbury collieries.

From the bottom of The Ovenpipe Shaft a crosscut followed the 74 fathom level to Main Lode, and an internal shaft (a winze) delved that. This complicated ore retrieval and only fifty tons per month was possible, so Waters had a shaft sunk directly onto the Main Level from the surface. To finance this The Tankerville Mining Company was floated in 1870 with an issued capital of £72000. It was calculated that the new shaft would sextuple the rate of production. Whatever the case, the share price rose from £20 to £30 within days of issue and a dividend of £3000 was paid in the first four months.

That same extraordinary year saw the winze continued from the 52 to the 102 fathom levels and a high-pressure Fowler engine installed underground for winding. One hundred and ninety fathoms of wrought-iron chimney were installed to bring its boiler smoke to the surface: A literal oven pipe. At the surface, in 1871, three further engines of six, twenty-five and sixty horsepower were installed for haulage and crushing duties.

By 1873, the Watson's Engine Shaft from the surface was well advanced and a 25-horsepower winding engine installed. The underground Fowler engine was no longer needed and was removed. Later that year a balance bob for the new engine was installed at the shaft head and the new engine given additional pumping duties.

Because the Watson's Engine Shaft also inclined at depth, there was expensive wear and tear on both the pumping and the kibble systems so that timber maintenance cost £200 per month.

By 1875 the ore was pinching out at depth and drainage problems becoming more severe, but the installation of a 40-inch Cornish engine by Harvey's of Hayle solved the water problems.

In 1878, three problems conspired to bankrupt the Tankerville Company. Firstly, the ore decreased in both quality and quantity with depth to the extent that the cost of raising each ton exceeded the market value of the material; frost prevented concentration in the latter part of the year; and the price of lead fell. In addition, a background factor kept transport costs high around Stiperstones: The Snailbeach railway had only reached as far South as Crowsnest.

An exploratory shaft was unsuccessful, but Tankerville limped on under a new company floated in 1880. Cheaper and more efficient hewing was now possible using pneumatic jackhammers, but the price of lead continued to fall in the face of great American and Australian strikes.

A large reserve of low-grade ore remained but the mine continued to lose money and the pumps were turned off in May 1884. The mine of course flooded below adit level.

Lord Tankerville worked the remaining mine directly in 1889 and 1890, with four employees, but it was a hopeless undertaking and in 1891 some of the machinery was sold for £193:7s:6d.

Some lead and barytes was scavenged from tips in 1893 and in 1902 the remaining equipment was auctioned off. In 1921-23 there was further raking-over of the dumps for barytes and calcite and a handful of men may have been scraping a living underground but really it was all over.

In 1929 the old Boat Level was blocked internally by shaft collapse.

Sometime in the 1960's the eminently listable winding house complex was demolished and the sturdy Cornish engine house vanished into a jungle of ivy and scrub. It was said that the magnificent chimney could be glimpsed from the road but when I drove past in the Eighties of last century I did not notice it. A large plain of brilliantly white tailings was however obvious in the valley below the complex, but this has now been landscaped out of existence. By the Nineties the enthusiasm of The Late Mr George Hall and The Shropshire Caving and Mining Society led to a partial rehabilitation of the site. The engine house was tidied of vegetation and the great chimney carefully and tastefully repointed. Rustic stairs have been laid from the road and the mine is now safely and easily accessible.

Unlike many industrial ruins the ambience is not eerie but strongly suggestive of one of the boskier Cornish dells, with its spring, quietude, whitewashed hamlet, undergrowth and dairy herds. Cavers complain of subterranean lagoons of cow excrement but those who stay in the fresh air can have a very pleasant look around or stroll along the footpaths.

CHAPTER TEN

Providing the Power

In 2008 almost all the stationary power used in Britain comes from electricity. Currently, (no pun intended and I trust none taken) almost 40% is derived from burning natural gas in turbines, about 20% to 25% from nuclear steam generation and about 3.5% from direct hydropower. The balance is supplied from the remaining coal and oil steam turbine power stations (30%), with a 1.5% contribution from wind farms. These proportions are both inexact and in a state of flux.

Energy density is the amount of energy you can get from a given mass of fuel if you burn or otherwise appropriately process it to release energy. Energy density is measured in megajoules per kilogram (MJ/Kg). Near synonyms often encountered in literature include "Fuel Specific Energy", "Heating Value", "Calorific Value" and "Heat of Combustion". Energy is the product of Power and the Time through which the power is applied.

Before industrialisation the provision of power was an abiding problem. Energy for space heating or processes was provided by burning wood (6-17 MJ/Kg), or in the case of London "sea coal" (24 MJ/Kg) shipped in from Newcastle-upon-Tyne. Occasional mechanical power and textile working was provided by horse, oxen, dog or human muscle power. But animals are inherently feeble and the power they apply diminishes exponentially as waste products build up in muscle tissue. Extensive rests of recuperation are then required.

Sustained power was only available at watercourses, and even there limitations of discharge and head severely constrained the available power. The spot power of a stream is half the product of fluid density times the discharge multiplied by the square of the velocity of flow. Since the density of water is virtually constant at about 1000 kilograms per cubic meter the power obtainable from a stream or river rises arithmetically with the amount of water passing (discharge) but by the square of stream speed which is proportional to the change in water height (head). Therefore, unless you have enormous rivers like they have in Russia or Africa, it usually only makes sense to seek waterpower in mountainous districts that have a heavy rainfall, or in narrow defiles on the edge of such districts.

Waterpower installations suffer from drought, flood and freezing, and the smaller they are, the more prone to losing power through such agencies.

The Romans probably introduced waterpower to Britain, employing primitive Vitruvian wheels in lowland streams. In the far North, Norse settlers introduced horizontal click mills some six hundred years later.

Until about 1850 slow streams in the English lowlands were often used to grind wheat or gunpowder, but they were insufficiently energetic for most industries.

The earliest factories gathered beside swift little rivers like the Sheaf, Rivelin, Loxley, Porter and Don near (now in) the Yorkshire town of Sheffield where their power was used to forge iron or sharpen iron and steel products. Textile miles clustered beside the rivers Wye and Derwent in Derbyshire and their tributary streams, as well as further North in the valleys of the Goyt and Hebden Water. Similar early water powered industries developed locally in Gloucestershire and mountain Wales, as well as in the pre-industrial iron region of The Weald, though in The Weald the topography and climate was grossly unsuited to waterpower. As late as 2004 the Trefriw Woollen Mill in the Conway Valley used water from the Gwydyr Forest mountains to power their looms. Just North of this fascinating scene, at Dolgarrog, a similar installation manufactured aluminum by exploiting the fall of water through penstocks.

By far the largest development of UK hydropower is for public electricity generation in the Scottish Highlands where high rainfall and the height and steepness of the terrain makes this feasible.

The largest direct hydroelectric development in Scotland, at Mossford below Loch Glascarnoch produces 247 MW. The largest British coal-fired power station at Drax delivers 3.945 GW (i.e. 3,945 MW) whilst the Heysham nuclear complex in Lancashire provides 2.49 GW.

It is possible that the Romans also introduced primitive windmills, but there is no direct archaeological evidence of that in Britannia. Around 1100AD, early windmills began to appear in England and though largely immune to drought, flood and frost they suffered from constraints of their own: On the whole more severe than those that limited watermills. Though Britain is the windiest inhabited country and a February gale rages as I write the wind is still very fickle, in both speed and direction. To get any sort of decent blow the mills could only be sited on hilltops. I live on a hilltop in Central England and in my back garden is an enigmatic circular sulcus in the lawn. It is the robbed-out foundation of an old windmill removed circa 1840, when the first steam mills were built in Walsall, a town without viable waterpower.

The modern impellor-generator sets, sometimes misleadingly called "turbines", that populate offshore or moorland wind farms can generate up to 2 MW at a wind speed of over 6 meters per second (m/s). Unfortunately, a typical load factor of 10% reduces that to a more realistic 200 KW. New designs are being prepared to yield up to 6 MW at similar rates. At that 200 KW average five thousand wind turbines are needed to replace a single nuclear power station.

The flow of air obeys the same basic laws of physics as the flow of water but power-velocity relations are complicated by the significant compressibility of the working fluid which implies that there is a differential in mass concentration (i.e. fluid density) as well as pressure across the power abstractive engine. At a technical level, wind turbines are significantly affected by turbulence, mechanical reluctance and other practical vagaries that mean that any power yield curve is adjusted by a contoured modifier more or less individual to the machine design and the environmental circumstances.

The upshot of all this is that wind turbines only start to operate at all when the wind speed reaches anything from 2.5 to 6 m/s. After that threshold speed power increases "cubically" until a maximum at maybe 15 m/s when yield theoretically plateaus but in practice falls sharply.

Yield formulae useful in the "cubic" yield regime estimate power output as half the product of the dimensionless modifier function times the static air density (1.292 kilograms per meter cubed) times effective sail area multiplied by the cube of the wind speed.

The theoretical indication is that for unitary modifier functions and impellor areas wind speed has to be 9.1815 times water speed for equal power yields.

The advent of successful coal power in 1789 utterly transformed British viabilities. Coal was widespread and could be transferred to wherever it was required by canal, sea or later by railways. Crucially, it could be used reliably to power moving conveyances on water or land. British coal quality varies but is always better than lignite and has an energetic yield of some 24 to 32.5 MJ/Kg.

In Britain the application of coal power preceded that of electricity by a hundred years. Each factory had one or more steam plants and their rotative engines powered line-shaft transmissions that distributed motion to individual production machines. In the first decades of application the engine flywheels were coupled to rigid rotary iron rods that conveyed motion horizontally and vertically via bevel gears. From the mid nineteenth century more efficient belt-drive systems conveyed power to line-shafting on different floors by means of multiple cotton ropes running in whole-height rope races from an engine drum bedded at ground level.

From 1880, such purely mechanical arrangements were gradually replaced by in-house electricity generation with electric motors to power local line-shafting or even individual machines. Economic electrification was however hampered by the difficulty of making steam engines turn fast enough to coax reasonable returns of electricity from dynamos. Various colossal but frantic patterns of new reciprocating engine were devised such as the Willans engine and these found particular favor with Ferranti's and the other public supply companies. From 1888 the introduction of the steam turbine solved this problem and the institution of the alternating current system made the centralisation of generation and economies of scale and efficiency viable.

The primary fuel continued of course to be coal but all but the largest industrial installations began to transfer to purchased electricity and the consolidation of The National Grid in the 1920's cemented the trend. In the South, new factories were inevitably built engineless.

Meanwhile, since the turn of the century petroleum had gained ground. Since it could be used, at least in refined forms, to heat the elastic fluid directly, and because its energy density was about 42 MJ/Kg, it was much more weight-efficient than coal and steam. Therefore it was far superior for road transport and indispensable for aviation.

In 1912 a young Winston Churchill ordered that all Royal Navy capital ships must henceforth be oil-fired, using British-sourced oil from Persia. The supply of oil grew between the wars and post-war oil-fired power generation gradually began to usurp coal.

Coal came under further pressure when in 1956 the World's first commercial nuclear power station opened at Calder Hall in Cumberland, adjacent to a large plutonium refinery that it helped to service. It was followed by several generations of nuclear electricity generating stations, all sited on the coast (or in one case a large lake) to provide adequate water coolant. The nuclear fuel, Uranium 235, has an effective energy density of 88 million MJ/Kg.

Nuclear power was bedevilled with cost issues and waste disposal problems whilst in 1973 the quadrupling of oil prices made oil power uneconomic overnight. Supply-side cost problems continued to burden industry and the consumer until the 1980's. In the mid 1980's the British Government determined to close many older coal stations and the collieries that supplied them. The Coal Strike of 1984-85 accelerated the process and in 1991-92 many of the remaining coal mines closed.

At nationalisation in 1947 Britain produced 187.5 million tons from 958 deep pits, and by 1955 this had risen to 211.3 million tons from 850 mines. At the time of The Coal Strike there were 150 remaining pits. In 1994, ten years after The Coal Strike, 42.7 million tons were won from 17 mines.

By the new century six viable deep mines remained nationwide. In 2002 Scotland's last deep mine at Longannet closed and for the first time in recorded history The Northumberland and Durham Coalfield was also without a single pit. The Warwickshire and Staffordshire complex of coalfields nearly died and West Mercia found itself with a solitary coal mine.

At the height of coal production official yield from well over a thousand British deep collieries topped 287 million tons for 1913.

In 2007 five coal mines produce 15 million tons, and Britain produced less coal than on the eve of The Industrial Revolution. Two-thirds of Britain's current coal needs are imported. In 2007 the international coal price doubled but British mining was too weak to take advantage of that development: UK coal production actually declined by 1.5%.

The collapse of coal and oil was partly compensated by de-industrialisation, and partly by the introduction of gas turbine generators utilising natural gas. Until 1986 the law had restricted the use of this fuel for electricity generation but subsequently regulation was relaxed and gas-powered generating stations proliferated.

The position in 2008 is that much of the English base load is provided by natural gas supplemented by coal, oil and both home and French nuclear power. The Government is preparing to revive British nuclear generation, phase out gas, promote domestic energy conservation, and develop offshore wind power supplies.

On 18th January 2008, The Tower Colliery, the last deep coal mine in Wales, closed.

GOONWIND
Goonhilly Wind Turbines and East Earth Station

Location: Cross Lanes, Lizard Peninsula, Cornwall, England, UK
Date of Photograph: 2 April 1996
OS Grid Reference: SW707214
Co-ordinates: 50:02:41N 5:12:34W
Elevation: 90.8 meters

This is the Goonhilly Downs Wind Farm near Cross Lanes.

By the end of 2000 there were 76 UK wind farms, sited mainly upon high moorland plateaus or in shallow coastal seas. Their total of 862 turbines furnished 408 MW of electric power, about the same as a small nuclear power station.

The six Cornish wind farms yield 31 MW: When the wind is blowing sufficiently!

The 14 turbines at Goonhilly each have a rated output of 400 KW and accordingly the output of the farm is 5.6 MW. This is notionally sufficient for 3171 homes at a mean consumption of 1.76612 KW per household, or for sake of argument 7851 people. This covers about 80% of the needs of the nearby market town of Helston.

Goonhilly was developed by Cornwall Light and Power and opened in April 1993.

HEYSHAM
Heysham Nuclear Power Station in Lancashire

Location:	Half-Moon Bay, Heysham, Lancashire, England, UK
Date of Photograph:	15 April 1995
OS Grid Reference:	SD404595
Co-ordinates:	54:01:39N 2:54:46W
Elevation:	8.8 meters

This is part of the AGR nuclear power station complex at Heysham.

The UK was the first country to use nuclear power to generate electricity for sale, though from the outset such activities were always harmonised with the production of fissile materials for military use; and also from the outset, techniques of slow fission were employed that were quite different to US commercial designs.

Early UK designs for power station reactors were of the so-called Magnox type. These employed a natural uranium fuel clad in Magnox alloy, mainly magnesium with an inert coating. These fuel assemblies were arrayed in a graphite moderator interpenetrated with boron control rods and cooled with pressurised carbon dioxide.

Whilst Magnox cladding had a low neutron-capture cross-section (i.e. it was transparent to neutrons, the active atom-splitting projectiles) it also limited operating temperatures and therefore thermal efficiency. The strongly electropositive magnesium also complicated the safe containment of waste, whether in actual ponds or in damp conditions generally.

The first station at Calder Hall adjacent to the Windscale (Sellafield) plutonium refinery in Cumberland was opened on 27th August 1956. Like all nuclear power stations of any type it used its hot coolant from the reactors to raise steam that was fed to turbine-alternator sets in the traditional arrangement.

During the 1960's a further 13 Magnox stations were commissioned with a total capacity of 4.724 GW.

In the 1970's a more powerful design, called an Advanced Gas-cooled Reactor (AGR) was developed. These are fuelled with enriched uranium in a graphite moderator. The fuel elements were clad with stainless steel. The coolant is carbon dioxide under forty bars of pressure. This design led, in the eighties and nineties, to a family of 7 stations with a combined yield of 8.38 GW. Each station provided about three times as much power as the older Magnox design.

The American pressurised-water design was only employed at part of the Sizewell generating facility in Suffolk (and on submarines). It transpired that either British technology produced power more expensively than US or French PWR stations, but it is argued that the British designs are inherently safer.

In 1997 about 27% of UK generated power was nuclear but decommissioning of some of the old Magnox plants and growth in other sources has reduced the proportion to 25.4% in 2007.

Heysham is by far the biggest British nuclear power station at 2.49 GW, and compares with some of the big fossil-fuel power stations. It can notionally supply 1358911 households, maybe around 3365000 people, or a city 1.4 times the size of Greater Manchester.

There are two AGR reactors on each of two adjacent sites.

Stage One opened in 1983 and is scheduled to decommission in 2014. Stage Two opened in 1988 and is intended to continue beyond 2023. The operator, British Energy, wishes to build another nuclear power station at this convenient seaport site.

The picture was taken in a more relaxed security climate and I am told that it is now problematical to express an interest in the installations on site.

The Northern Part of Heysham Power Station

SKOMER
The Horse Mill on Skomer Island

Location:	Ruins of Old Farm, Skomer Island, Pembrokeshire, Wales, UK
Date of Photograph:	am 16 April 1992
OS Grid Reference:	SM726094
Co-ordinates:	51:44:16N 5:17:40W
Elevation:	68.9 meters

This is a horse mill for grinding cereals.

Skomer Island comprises 722.285 acres (292 hectares) and is a lozenge-shaped undulating plateau of about two hundred feet elevation rising to 260 feet in the center. It comprises Lower Silurian lavas and ashes intercalated with marls and quartzites. This geology has given rise to deep dissection of the coastline. The extrusives are thrust Northwards over Old Red Sandstones that are of course younger.

Skomer features Bronze Age relics and was densely-peopled in the Iron Age, when it is thought to have acted as an entrepot.

The soil is a thick guano-enriched loam but the windswept and almost waterless character of the island ensured long centuries of desertion. There are no trees. Herbaceous halophytes abound. The dominant vegetation is fescue and bent grasses but bluebells, red campion, thrift and the alien ragwort flourish in their seasons. Lichens are notable.

Around 1300AD rabbits were introduced and became ubiquitous, thriving on the islands rich and diverse herbiage. The only predator, the Black-Backed Gull, cannot pursue them underground. When I visited in April 1992, I found very extensive warrens full of tame rabbits at the West and South of the island. One individual had advanced myxomatosis. The burrows are shared with puffins, and, in the Summer months, with Manx Shearwater. There are mice and shrews on the island and the large, tame and unique Skomer Vole (*Clethrionomys glareolus skomerensis*). Atlantic Seals colonise the offshore rocks and cetaceans ply the surrounding seas.

A field system took shape in the seventh century, but there is little evidence of continuous agriculture until around 1800 when the farmstead was erected in the center of the island, and arable cultivation re-attempted. In 1843 the farm underwent major reconstruction and it was at this time that horse mills were installed for threshing and grinding. A limekiln was built at North Haven to burn manure for the acid soil, and though coal was readily imported for that, steam was impracticable due to the paucity of freshwater on the island. Around the time of the Second World War a Fordson tractor was landed, and its remains were still visible beside the mill in 1992. The likely crop at that time was potatoes. By 1950, the last Skomer farmer, Reuben Codd, gave up agriculture in favor of ferrying scientists and tourists to the island. He domiciled himself and his family on Great Britain. In 1954 the unoccupied farm sustained major storm damage and become ruinous.

In 1957 the island was taken over by the Nature Conservancy Council who maintained it as a National Nature Reserve with a scientific base and a Resident Warden. Limited numbers of paying visitors were permitted.

In 2005 the landing at North Haven was extended and modernised by the Heritage Lottery Fund who converted the farm ruins into a "Total Visitor Experience" and plan to entertain 20000 tourists per season.

TONGLAND
Tongland Hydroelectric Power Station

Location: Tongland, near Kirkcudbright, Kirkcudbrightshire, Galloway, Scotland
Date of Photograph: 31 March 1999
OS Grid Reference: NX694535
Co-ordinates: 54°51'36"N: 4°2'2"W
Elevation: 32.9 meters

Tongland is a small village in Glenken that formed around a medieval Premonstratensian monastery whose ruins remain. During the First World War, a factory was built at Tongland in which Galloway cars were made during 1921 and 1922.

The village saw residential expansion in 2004-2006.

Slightly downstream is Thomas Telford's 1806 single-arch stone road bridge over the River Dee.

During the 1920's plans were made to build hydroelectric power stations along the conterminous course of the rivers Ken and Dee and to draw supplementary water from the Doon catchment.

The primary strategy was not to electrify Galloway, though that was a concomitant. During the 1920's The (British) National Grid was emplaced as a strategic resource. The Grid is an interconnected network of high-tension electric cables erected, or on rare occasions buried, to cover the entire UK. It increases the nation's resilience to partial foreign occupation and supply bombing, and also enables routine power supplies to be economically optimised across the country. The especial merits of the Galloway scheme were twofold: As a hydro contribution it could be switched in and out of The Grid within minutes to absorb surge demands, unlike the highly-inertial steam stations that take hours to reach operating speed; and furthermore, whilst the Scottish winter is cold it is also wet so that the season of highest demand might coincide with that of most copious water supply.

Parliament found such ideas compelling and on 10th May 1929 passed The Galloway Water Power Act. The first phase of the scheme was to include five power stations and was designed by William McLellan of the consultancy partnership Merz and McLellan.

From the outset, special consideration was given to the environmental impact of the scheme in an important fishing resort area. The concrete arch dams were styled as unobtrusively as is possible for such things, whilst the power stations were given bold but clean Modernist profiles. An "Amenities Committee", acting under civil engineer Sir Alexander Gibb took charge of aesthetics whilst enjoying specialist advice from designer HO Tarbolton, who was also active on the later Pitlochry Dam in Perthshire. The dams were equipped with fish ladders to allow spawning salmon continuing access throughout the basin.

Construction of the five initial facilities commenced in 1932 and completed in 1936. The total installed power was 107 MW, and although this does not sound worthwhile by modern standards the build cost was £29 per installed Kilowatt, making the scheme one of the cheapest power projects in UK history.

The Tongland generating station was completed in 1935.

The operating head at Tongland is about 106 feet and feeds three turbines each with 11 MW synchronous alternators that may now readily be viewed, complete with their archaic "Flash Gordon" switchgear, from the new Visitor Center.

The site is dominated by a vast blue-painted steel drum that towers behind the turbine hall. Whilst I do not know the design purpose of this rare structure it may function as a surge tank intended to dissipate the otherwise destructive elastic energy of the water column when penstocks are too quickly closed. I was not able to gain casual access in 1999 but the environs were delightfully prewar, with original steel bus shelters and the like.

Because of its "antique futurism" Tongland Power Station is sometimes used as a television or film set. Decommissioning will not be necessary in the foreseeable future.

CHAPTER ELEVEN

Production for Prosperity

It seems that the Palaeolithic and Mesolithic peoples who entered Britain were hunter-gathers who worked flint or natural glass into sharp flakes. They attached these shards to wood to hunt wild game, which they ate or skinned for leather and sinew. The earliest men may have scoured the shore for shellfish or combed the scrub for nuts and berries, in their seasons. Certainly, ancient middens contain plentiful shellfish remains. Chickens are thought to be of Far Eastern origin but their remains have been detected in Iron Age deposits at Glastonbury. Other early exotics include such Roman introductions as the rabbit, the edible dormouse, the pheasant and the peacock, these two birds being Asian natives.

The perfection of stone tool technology in the Neolithic enabled woodland to be cleared for wheat cultivation. Clearance also enabled the pastoral rearing of cattle and sheep whose meat and leather could replace or extend that of game. A further contribution of sheep was to wool and early spinning and weaving which were of course done by hand methods.

The introduction of copper smelting and casting technologies enabled robust and easily-sharpened bronze tools to replace stone, and five or six centuries later the smelting and forging of iron superseded bronze.

By the outset of the Iron Age, about 900BC, the wheel and the sickle had been introduced.

Woodland continued to be both extensive and important providing building and boat-building resources, and wood for cooking and smelting, as well as game, tannin, nuts and pannage.

Agriculture and metal-working were already well established when the Romans arrived in AD43. It is said that they came for our freshwater pearls, but besides such fripperies we could offer such staples as copper, tin, lead, wheat and slaves in abundance. In return, the Roman brought not only the exotic game but more importantly organisation and technology. They drained the land with ditches and tiles, laid roads and increased demand for metals, cut stone and baked ceramics. The Romans increased the amount of enclosure, using ditches, hedges and wattle fences. They converted the chalk and oolite uplands of Southern England into immense wheatfields. By the fourth century AD Britannia was the most important wheat producer in Europe and eight hundred wheat ships left Britain each year to feed the garrisons of Gaul. The wheat was ground by waterpower, which increased the demand for clay and stone to build and maintain systems of leats to power the mills and water towns. In Roman times orchards, vineyards and herb gardens appeared for the first time, salt was developed, and England's only indigenous spice, mustard, was brought under cultivation. Ponds were dug for carp and tench and these ponds would be important sources of protein for the next thousand years.

The population of Britannia reached about five million, approximately half the natural land capacity of Great Britain.

When the Empire receded from this land cultivation and industry decayed. Demand for stone, ceramics and metals greatly diminished and the population fell back to one and a quarter million.

During the eleventh century AD a modest recovery occurred. The needs of a foreign occupier increased the demand for cut stone and military metals, as well as wood and food. Since the Fall of Rome much of the landscape had reverted to oak and beech wood and this was now of sufficient maturity to provide abundant constructional timber, whilst coppice wood could provide charcoal for iron reduction in such forested Southern centres as The Weald and The Forest of Dean. There was only a little enclosure, but agriculture was partly re-organised into rotated strip cultivation for arable crops together with grazing on extensive common lands. Primitive crop rotations were introduced with fields being allowed to lie fallow (uncultivated) in order to recuperate nutrients lost to cereals. Later, peas and beans were alternated with wheat and barley to enhance the richness of the soil. It is now known that bacteria live in root nodules in leguminous plants, and that these bacteria fix atmospheric nitrogen, feeding it to the legumes, and leaving some in the soil to benefit other plants. Otherwise, the soil depends for its nitrogen on lightening, animal waste and corpses. Later, the fixative legume clover was introduced from Flanders and rotated with turnips.

By 1345AD the population had grown to four million. In 1347AD a bubonic plague epidemic entered Britain at Melcombe Regis in Dorset and within eight years of this Black Death's arrival the British population had almost halved to 2.5 million. There were no longer enough men and women to work the land. The last vestiges of soil slavery disappeared form England, and, on the contrary, servile men could name their price for any labor they might design to sell.

For two hundred years raw wool had literally been the staple export of England, principally going to Flanders and Italy. Only ten percent was woven at home. King Edward III prohibited further exports of unmanufactured wool and weaving industries burgeoned in Devon, The Cotswolds, The West Riding and especially East Anglia. Where subsistence arable villages had been, sheepwalks proliferated.

During the sixteenth century, the discovery of The Americas and trade with the Orient brought spices, sprouts and the potato, but it would be two hundred years before the last would establish itself as the staple crop of Ireland and the Scottish North and West. Its resilience to high winds, high rainfall, salt and acid soil made it by far the most reliable crop in those districts. It was also the most concentrated source of carbohydrate. Also in the sixteenth century further field enclosures increased rural efficiency and disease control and rendered the selective breeding of crops and animals feasible.

By 1650 the population had again reached five million, but war and plague intervened to stabilise that number. In mid century a two hundred year campaign to drain British wetlands for agriculture commenced. In those pre-industrial times the mass production of drainage tiles had not reached England but Dutch and native engineers collaborated in the cutting of large ditches and canalisations in Eastern England and the installation of wind-driven scoop pumps. The Fens and The Somerset Levels were drained and The Wash partly reclaimed from the sea.

The habit of broadcasting seed by hand wasted most seed and seed-grain to the birds, the weather and sub-optimal concentrations. In 1701, at Crowmarsh Gifford in The Thames Valley, Jethro Tull invented a horse drawn seed drill that sewed seed in rows in holes of specific depth and then covered it. He also invented a horse hoe for weeding and comminution of the soil.

In 1730, Joseph Foljambe of Rotherham invented an iron plow with a wrought-iron covered mouldboard. This increased the speed and precision of horse plowing and the durability of the plow itself. Fifty years later, James Small of Dalkeith perfected a light, strong, all-iron design, and also in the 1780's the threshing machine was invented.

The cumulative effect of these innovations was to increase the food supply, cheapen food and make its availability more reliable. Generations left the land for the towns, the sea and for colonies. The population rose beyond its Malthusian limit of six million and headed for eleven, the ultimate natural capacity of Great Britain, where it stood on the eve of The Industrial Revolution.

The fundamental fuel of the human organism is sugar which is directly metabolised to water, carbon dioxide and energy. Cold climate starch foods like cereals and potato are indirect and inefficient sugar sources as the physiological conversion of starch to sugar is itself an energetic drain.

In hot moist climates the sugar cane, a direct source of sucrose, will grow. In 1625 the Dutch introduced sugar to the Caribbean Islands. Many of the Caribbean islands are volcanic and prodigiously fertile, all are warm and most are well watered. Cane cultivation soon proliferated trough the Spanish islands of Cuba and Puerto Rico, French Hispaniola, English Jamaica, and the arc archipelago of the Swedish, Danish, Latvian, Dutch and British Leeward and Windward Islands. Between 1680 and 1800 production boomed. Cane was harvested by slaves and crushed by windmills before being packed for Europe, which obtained ninety percent of its sugar from this source.

The first Jamaican sugar mill powered by steam was established in 1768, and soon after steam replaced direct fire in the extraction of the sugar itself. In 1815 Edward Howard invented the closed kettle for sugar refining in which cane sugar was boiled under partial vacuum. This saved fuel and reduced caramelisation by reduction of the boiling temperature.

Chocolate is a source of metabolic fat and also of the alkaloid narcotics theobromine and phenethylamine. The two drugs lower blood pressure and increase brain serotonin to have a sedative effect that accounts for the addictive properties of cocoa. This, too, is of Central American origin and like sugar was a favorite indulgence of the European wealthy, who drank it as a suspension in hot water. Like that of sugar, the price of cocoa would fall dramatically as the eighteenth century progressed and in a dry form it would become accessible to the lower classes.

All British chocolate was made by Quakers well into the 1970's. Until the 1820's most occupations were debarred to them, and Quakers had conscientious objections to alcohol, tobacco and slave products: Which is not to say there were no Quaker brewers!

Joseph Fry founded his Bristol chocolate factory in 1759. The works moved from Newgate Street to Union Street in 1777, and in 1795 installed a Watt engine to grind cocoa beans. By 1822 Fry's was Britain's largest chocolate producer. In 1847 Fry's Keynsham works produced the first moulded chocolate bar and their famous Creme Bar (still produced by Cadbury) appeared in 1866. Fry's produced the first chocolate Easter Egg in 1873 and chocolate coated Turkish Delight in 1914. After the First World War Fry's merged with Cadbury's, a Birmingham maker of excipiated milk chocolate founded in 1824, conveniently close to the Birmingham Quaker meeting house in Bull Street. As of 2008, Cadbury is thought to be one of the UK's most valuable manufacturers with a reputed capital of near to $31000 million. It is difficult to be sure about either its nationality or worth because of its very intimate integration with US food firms:- In 2010 Cadbury's was purchased outright by Mondelez International, formerly known as Kraft Foods of Illinois.

In 1981 Fry's chocolate bars were rebranded as Cadbury's and in 2007 the Fry works at Keynsham closed. The flavor of British chocolate has changed markedly in the last ten years reflecting changes to American sources of cocoa supply, and the US preference for a sourer taste.

During the seventeenth century local coal and clay led to the inception of industrial ceramic production at several centers, but mass production commenced on The North Staffordshire Coalfield. The quality of the product was initially utilitarian but increasing experience and systematic experimentation allowed higher value-added products to be made. The chief pottery towns of Burslem, Fenton, Longton and Tunstall developed their own specialisms and hundreds of small firms became dominated by the high-class tableware makers Wedgwood (1759), Minton (1793), Royal Doulton (1815 at Lambeth: 1877 at Stoke) and Spode (1776). The completion of the Trent and Mersey Canal in 1777 greatly facilitated export of the fragile product as well as imports of coal, flint, bone and china clay. By the mid twentieth century gas had replaced coal for firing kilns and a very great diversity of ceramic product was output from the Pottery towns of North Staffordshire, by that time dignified as The City of Stoke-on-Trent. The products ranged from cups and saucers to lavatory pans to heavy electrical insulators. At the end of the twentieth century cheap imports led to the rapid decline of The Potteries and Royal Doulton's Nile Street works closed in 2005.

Glass making boomed in the 1820's as Britain moved away form craft technology. Chance of Smethwick was founded in 1824 and was supplemented by various Tyneside firms. The mass market for cast sheet glass was however addressed by the Pilkington Brothers' founding at St Helens of their Ravenhead Works. Soon after it commenced production in 1826 it became the largest glassworks in the World. Between 1953 and 1957, Pilkington and Bickerstaff developed the float glass process, a method of casting optically-clear glass on a bath of molten tin, obviating the need for grinding and polishing. In 1970 the family firm was itself floated on the stock market. Pilkington went on to develop a self-cleaning coated float glass called Pilkington Activ. Photocatalysis breaks down organic dirt deposits in sunlight, and the dirt is then washed away by rain. At the time of its sale to Nippon Glass in 2006 Pilkington accounted for 19% of the World glass market.

During the nineteenth century cotton replaced wool and linen as the chief clothing fiber and became the dominant export manufacture, a status it held for more than one hundred years. The industry played a leading rôle in the inception of industrialisation between 1770 and 1820 and concentrated in South-East Lancashire, where the climate was humid enough to prevent fibers from breaking when drawn; where there was abundant soft water and coal; and where Liverpool facilitated the import of raw fiber and the export of finished cloth. The immediate trigger of cotton industrialisation was the abolition of Cotton Duty in 1774, a tax that had been levied to protect the previously all-important wool industry.

In 1733 John Kay laid the basis of a revolution in textile production. Until that year the weft shuttle had passed from hand to hand through the warp sheets of the loom. Kay developed a method of knocking the shuttle from side to side under impulse, and both the width of the cloth and the rate of weaving increased dramatically.

This increased the requirement for yarn and in 1764 James Hargreaves replicated the Nuremberg wheel into eight-fold multi-spindle formats capable of being steadily turned by mechanical power. The number of spindles per spinning frame were multiplied again as reliable designs evolved. By 1778 there were over two hundred thousand of these so-called Spinning Jenny frames in the UK, most water powered.

The weaving side developed more slowly and specialist hand weavers persisted until the 1840's. By 1785 however Edmund Cartwright had developed a power loom factory at Doncaster, and after 1805 the power loom became common.

Pure cotton fabrics were woven in Britain by 1750 and by 1790 raw cotton imports from the Americas had reached 31,447,605 pounds weight. By 1802 cotton accounted for five percent of British production by value. By 1812 this was eight percent and there were 100000 spinners and 250000 cotton weavers. By 1830 more than half the value of British exports was accounted for by cotton cloth, a position that persisted for the next hundred years. The cotton center of Manchester became, with Birmingham, the World's first industrial city, and its forest of smoking chimneys a wonder for artists and early photographers.

Across the Pennines in the West Riding of Yorkshire a parallel development occurred with wool from animals, especially sheep. Wool cloth production declined in Southern England and extinguished in East Anglia, but concentrated in water and coal powered factories around Leeds. As in East Anglia, and indeed in cotton Lancashire, individual towns of the conurbations developed sub-specialisms, for example worsted in Bradford and shoddy in Batley. The Spinning Jenny had burgeoned Yorkshire Wool as well as Lancashire Cotton, but between 1720 and 1740 Yorkshire production had already doubled. Weaving however spread relatively slowly and in 1803 only 6% of Yorkshire wool was power woven, though this had increased greatly by the 1820's. By the mid nineteenth century coal and imported wool had given Yorkshire a decisive edge and enormous mills were built.

Silk manufacture was foreign-dominated until 1685 when the revocation of The Edict of Nantes encouraged French weavers to settle in Spitalfields. In 1718 Thomas Lombe invented an integrated system for spinning, winding and twisting silk yarn. Lombe set up a water powered silk mill at Derby that employed three hundred. The Courtauld crepe factory was established at Braintree in 1793, and other high-value specialist mills appeared beside other lowland streams in the South-East. The introduction of the card-programmed Jacquard loom from France during the 1820's greatly cheapened the production of intricate woven patterns. This enabled a decorated silk shawl industry to flourish in the Scottish town of Paisley. It was, however, in the East Cheshire and North Staffordshire towns of Macclesfield, Congleton and Leek that the mechanised industry had concentrated by 1851.

The consumer metals industries concentrated beside the Severn Estuary and at Sheffield. An exception was for intricate value-added products or ornamental stampings, which were crafted at Birmingham or London. The founding of brass from local materials became a significant industry at Bristol, and throughout the eighteenth and early nineteenth century was a characteristic Bristol industry. Copper was imported by sea from Cornwall, whilst the calamine zinc ore came from the nearby Mendip Hills. Coal fuel came from the local Bristol Coalfield. The product was used in chandlery or sold for Guinea goods. Colonial interests also influenced the other Bristol specialisms: The refining of cocoa, tobacco and citrus fruit. In the 1820's brass making migrated to Birmingham but tinplate making became important at Lydney and Llanelli. Both these towns were ports where local coal and iron could be integrated with Cornish tin and tropical palm oil brought by sea. From the 1840's increasing volumes of tinplate were demanded by a burgeoning food-canning industry. Whilst industry has died at Lydney and in the Forest of Dean generally there is still an enormous tinplate mill at Llanelli. Galvanised iron, which contrary to implication is wrought iron (or later mild steel) hot coated with zinc, was developed for utilitarian sheet metal exposed to weather. Buckets, baths, water tanks and bins were fabricated at Lye in the Worcestershire Black Country by the mid nineteenth century, and in 2006 a handful of galvanised iron factories survived there. In 1743, Thomas Boulsover invented Sheffield Plate, a copper substratum covered with a rolled veneer of silver. It was used to make downmarket table flatware in substitution of solid silver, also a Sheffield speciality that continues to this day. By 1840 electrical technology had advanced to a degree where thinner coats of pure silver and other fine metals could durably be coated upon base metal, and the electroplate industry evolved at Birmingham. Most Sheffield plate ceased production around 1840 but Sheffield continued to forge and grind hard steel for cutlery until as late as the 1990's. Allied to that was the production of silver fruit knives, though these became obsolete with the introduction of stainless steel after The First World War.

After the relaxation of precious metal standards in the 1850's the mass production of gold and silver jewelry concentrated at Hockley in Birmingham. Competition from Birmingham, and the decline of local silver sources spelt the death knell of the industry in other provincial centers such as Exeter, Chester and Newcastle-upon-Tyne, though the associated industries of architectural lead products survived in Newcastle until April 2002, and in 2008 continue with a labor force of 125 at Chester.

BIRASSAY
The Birmingham Assay Office

Location: The Birmingham Assay Office, Newhall and Charlotte Streets, Birmingham, Warwickshire, Mercia, England, UK
Date of Photograph: pm 30 January 2008
OS Grid Reference: SP064873
Co-ordinates: 52:29:02N 1:54:23W
Elevation: 127.7 meters

Hallmarking is the result of the process of testing the purity of precious metal (assay). The hallmark is a set of official symbols impressed into the metal that certify its standard of purity.

Modern British hallmarking applies to objects of gold, silver or platinum to be sold for ornament or personal use, but not to bullion, coin or industrial goods.

King Edward I in 1300 instituted English assay and hallmarking. Longshanks, as he was called, was probably the first British monarch to possess the technical and administrative wherewithal for such an enforcement, and the assay law was intended to protect both the purchaser and the craftsman. It led to a dramatic growth of the English precious metals trade that is still a small but important feature of the British industrial landscape.

The Company of Goldsmiths, who impressed a leopard's head upon articles that met their standard, first applied this certification to silver wrought in London. The leopard's head is still the mark of London today.

The other surviving Town Marks of the British Isles are Birmingham (anchor), Sheffield (rose), Edinburgh (castle) and Dublin (harp). Formerly, there were assay offices at Exeter, Chester, Newcastle-upon-Tyne and elsewhere.

In 1363 a second punch impressed a Maker's Mark, and when in 1478 the London goldsmiths set up a Goldsmiths' Hall they hired a full-time assayer and added an annually changed Date Mark to the hallmark set.

The Hallmarking Act of 1773 established the Birmingham Assay Office in a rapidly-expanding town whose inhabitants had specialised for centuries in metal fabrication, and would until the first years of this millennium. By 2006 the Birmingham Assay Office was the largest in the World, processing more than twelve million items annually.

In 1762, Matthew Boulton relocated from Snow Hill in the town center to a massive new works at Handsworth. He was frustrated by the delay and expense of sending precious products for assay at Chester, a 154-mile round trip by horse and cart during which goods were often damaged or stolen. Boulton and his friend Lord Dartmouth agitated in Parliament for a Birmingham Assay, and the Sheffield cutlers asked the men to plead their case for a Sheffield test center as well. When in London, Boulton and the Yorkshiremen stayed at The Crown and Anchor Inn in the Strand. So it was decided: Sheffield would take the Crown for its mark, and Birmingham the anchor. Later the Yorkshire city would adopt a rose instead.

Pure gold is 24 carat, but is too soft for jewellery or other frequently-handled objects like pens. By Act of 1824, Birmingham was allowed to assay gold as well as silver and in 1854 the introduction of 9, 12, and 15 carat gold standards, in addition to 18 and 22, brought gold jewellery within reach of The Working Class. The Birmingham precious metal fabricators boomed. The 1973 Hallmarking Act simplified and consolidated the thirty existing Hallmark Acts and introduced compulsory platinum marks for the first time. In 1995 the Birmingham Assay was permitted to offer technical and valuation services and three years later minor amendments were made to punch configurations in the interests of EU harmonisation. Today, many of the smaller or more delicate items are marked by laser.

The current premises on the corner of Charlotte and Newhall Streets in what was then the heart of The Birmingham Jewellery Quarter opened in 1878. At an initial cost of £9448 the building rapidly expanded to cater for an exponential increase in volume throughout the next hundred years. Telephone was installed in 1885 and electricity replaced gas lighting in 1890.

In 2008 the Birmingham Assay Office is at the forefront of metal and gemstone assay technology with a complex of spectrographic laboratories for both routine and commissioned work; for diamond certification; and for the support of retail valuation practices. It also supervises and enforces the control of nickel in watchstraps and other apparel in order to minimise the metal's allergenic dangers.

The Birmingham Assay Office is a prime recourse for those requiring advanced consultancy in precious metal or gemstones, worldwide.

Until 1773 the penalty for counterfeiting a hallmark was death: In that year it was changed to 14 years transportation. It is now up to ten years imprisonment.

It is still compulsory to submit precious metal jewellery and houseware for assay if it is made in, or enters, the UK.

What happens to work that does not reach its appropriate standard? It is crushed and returned to the sender!

BRATCH
The Bratch Pumphouse

Location: The Bratch, Wombourne, Staffordshire, England, UK
Date of Photograph: pm 28 December 2005
OS Grid Reference: SO868937
Co-ordinates: 52:32:28N 2:11:46W
Elevation: 80.5 meters

      The Bratch Pumphouse is a Gothicko-Moorish fantasia designed by London architect Baldwin Latham and built in 1895. It was commissioned by Bilston Corporation and built by Willcock of Wolverhampton for £6113 all-up, including the now demolished ninety-foot smokestack.
      The facing material is Ruabon pressed brick with Hollington-stone dressings. The structure is of concrete and the roof appears to be slate. There is complementary blue banding, probably of Staffordshire Blue slag bricks, a virtually indestructible material.
      Pumping commenced on 2nd July 1896.
      Inside the house are mirrored-twin (inverted) vertical double-acting triple-expansion engines by James Watt and Company. During the currency of the

contract, James Watt unfortunately went into liquidation and the engines were completed by Thornewill and Warham at Burton-upon-Trent. They incorporate eccentric-driven Corliss valves. A Corliss valve is an American design of semi-rotary spring-loaded trip valve designed to maximise steam expansion for economy by abruptly closing the inlet valve after a small volume of high-pressure steam has entered the cylinder.

Each 404 ton engine covers 440 square feet of floor area, and has a design pressure of 150 pounds per square inch, presumably at the high-pressure end. Only one engine, Victoria, is steamed demonstrationally. The respective cylinder diameters are 16, 26 and 40 inches and there is a three-foot stroke. The fourteen ton flywheel is eleven feet in diameter and eight inches wide.

The coal-fired Lancashire boilers have been scrapped and demonstrational steam seems to be generated using mains gas.

The building and its contents are Grade Two Listed and public steamings usually coincide with the July and December holiday periods.

CHARLCOT
Charlcotte Blast Furnace for Iron in Shropshire

Location:	Charlcotte, near Bridgnorth, Shropshire, England, UK
Date of Photograph:	24 March 2003
OS Grid Reference:	SO638860
Co-ordinates:	52:28:18N 2:32:03W
Elevation:	165.2 meters

In this formerly forested area, charcoal, ironstone and limestone were simultaneously available, though cheap water transport was not. These materials were tipped into the top of the furnace in alternating layers and the molten crude iron product periodically tapped at the base of the furnace and cast into rough ingots called pigs. Any further processing, including casting, forging or cementation for steel, necessitated an expensive re-heat.

Blast furnaces were introduced to Britain in 1498, when they superseded a more primitive reduction furnace called a bloomery. A crucial feature of the blast furnace was forced ventilation with cold air through tuyeres at the base. This effected hot burning of the charcoal, chemical reduction of the ironstone, and a degree of metal refining. The power for the bellows came from a waterwheel on a small leat.

A complex pattern of leats and cinder hillocks remains beneath deciduous trees at this site and the six-meter high stone furnace is substantially intact.

The Charlcotte furnace exemplified many in the wooded marcherlands of pre-industrial Britain and was possibly erected sometime in the seventeenth century. It is first mentioned in documentation of 1712. It declined from 1770 and was blown-out in 1793, by which time the Shropshire Iron Industry had migrated to the East Shropshire Coalfield around the modern town of Telford where the modern coke-based industry and mass-industrialism generally engendered.

The capacity of charcoal furnaces was limited by the friability of charcoal (as opposed to coal coke) which necessitated the careful adding of stone in small increments. This and the accelerating inflation in the price of charcoal throughout the eighteenth century gave a powerful economic impetus to the growth of coalfield smelting, as did the frequent association of exposed coalfields with navigable waters.

Between 1733 and 1777 the Charlcotte furnace was operated by the Knight family. This family ran a complex of furnaces, forges and tinplate mills at nearby Bringewood Forge in Herefordshire where experts have identified vestigial remains of works abandoned in the first half of the nineteenth century.

CLAYMILL
Claymills Pumping Engine Linkage Apparatus

Location:	Claymills, Stretton, near Burton-upon-Trent, Staffordshire, England, UK
Date of Photograph:	pm 29 December 2002
OS Grid Reference:	SK262258
Co-ordinates:	52:49:47N 1:36:41W
Elevation:	44.8 meters

The flywheel and pump parallel linkage in the Claymills sewage pumping station.

Two mirrored-pairs (i.e. four engines) were installed by Gimsons of Leicester in 1885 for the purpose of pumping sewage in the Burton treatment works where special arrangements were needed to deal with the effluent of the local major brewing industry.

The engines were always worked in balanced pairs, with the other pair on standby.

They are Wolff double-compound jet-condensing Watt-type beam engines. Each unit has a 24-inch bore 6-foot stroke high-pressure cylinder exhausting to a 38-inch 8-foot low-pressure cylinder. The valve apparatus is of the Cornish pattern.

Each unit rocks a wrought-iron beam that powers a 24-foot diameter 24-ton flywheel via a Watt parallel linkage.

The sewage is moved by the illustrated reciprocating ram mechanism that has a 21-inch bore pump cylinder of 6-foot stroke that thus draws 0.4087 metric tonnes of wastewater per stroke. Accordingly each balanced pair shifts about three-quarters of a long ton per stroke.

GEORGIAN
Georgian Glass Limited at Tutbury

Location:	The Old Silk Mill, Silk Mill Lane, Tutbury, Staffordshire, England, UK
Date of Photograph:	am 26 October 2004
OS Grid Reference:	SK211288
Co-ordinates:	52:51:25N 1:41:13W
Elevation:	63.4 meters

One of two hand-crafted table crystal works that remain in Tutbury, a Little Town that has been making glass since 1472.

It is good to see men working with skill at something they can take a pride in after so much of British industry in the big conurbations, including almost the entirety of the once-renowned Stourbridge Glass speciality, has vanished.

The men work in a converted silk mill, hence the cast-iron stanchions to bear the weight of looms on the upper stories. I took this picture from the street, standing at the open shuttered window onto the sidewalk. Clearly, the men did not feel the nip of the late autumn.

On 26th November 2006 the owner of Georgian Glass Limited announced that he was to retire on that 25th anniversary of his founding the company, and to hand over to his son, also a glassblower.

On 1 December 2011 Georgian Glass ceased production. Tutbury crystal is now craftsman-made at Stourbridge, another ancient center of blown glass.

IMICU
The Vanished IMI Copper Refinery at James Bridge

Location:	The IMI James Bridge Copper Works, Darlaston, Walsall, Staffordshire, England, UK
Date of Photograph:	pm 20 November 1999
OS Grid Reference:	SO993976
Co-ordinates:	52:34:39N 2:00:44W
Elevation:	127 meters

This facility was owned by IMI (Imperial Metal Industries) Limited and its tall smelter chimney was a conspicuous landmark near Junction 10 (Walsall) of the adjacent M6 motorway.

It was the last UK copper refinery, and its closure on 31 December 1999 marked the end of a four-hundred year tradition of copper processing in Walsall, a city in Central England better known for its horse furniture, which it still makes.

After brief mothballing, the site was cleared in 2000.

JCB
The Product Park for the JCB Factory at Rocester in Staffordshire

Location: The JCB (Excavators) Limited Factory, Rocester, Staffordshire, England, UK
Date of Photograph: pm 18 October 2007
OS Grid Reference: SK102394
Co-ordinates: 52:57:11N 1:50:56W
Elevation: 92.0 meters

This is the Rocester headquarters of the British mechanical excavator maker Joseph Cyril Bamford (Excavators) Limited, usually known as JCB. It is the third amongst the World's four significant excavator manufacturers. The machine is habitually called a "digger" in the UK and a "backhoe" in the US, though properly a backhoe is only part of the configuration. The diggers are self-propelled and work on diesel-hydraulic principles.

The Bamfords are an old-established family of Uttoxeter agricultural implement makers. JCB, however, commenced on 23rd October 1945, when Joe Cyril used a £1 electric welding machine to make a farm trailer out of war surplus. He sold the trailer in Uttoxeter market for £45 (about $90 in 2007, or around $180 in 1945). By

1948 Joe employed six. He moved from his garage to stables at Crakemarsh and in 1950 bought the old United Dairies factory at nearby Rocester, (pronounced "roaster") also in rural Staffordshire.

JCB made the first modern hydraulic digger in 1953 and during the Sixties there was dramatic expansion on the Rocester site, which was landscaped and a lake dug by the product to the shape of Lake Lucerne. Exotic waterfowl were brought in to ornament the lake. By 1964, three thousand diggers had been made.

Today, JCB has 278 different digger models, in addition to other capital equipment products such as fork lift trucks, and also fashion accessories. The firm employs eight thousand in seventeen factories in the UK, USA, Germany, Brazil, India and China. Four of the seven UK factories are in Staffordshire. Thirteen hundred are employed at Rocester, which remains the World headquarters. JCB has 550 dealers in 150 countries. The corporation is still wholly-owned by the Bamford family.

Mechanical excavators are now habitually referred to as "JCBs": At least in Britain.

Innovative by habit and conviction, in 2004 JCB started production of the JCB444, the first diesel engine of their own design and manufacture.

In April 2006, JCB constructed a car powered by two JCB444s each with a two-stage turbocharger. One engine powers the front wheels and one the back to yield a combined 750 break horse-power. On 23rd August 2006, Andy Green drove this car at 350.092mph (563.418 km/h) to claim the Land Speed Record for a diesel-powered vehicle.

At the other end of sublimity, JCB keeps a synchronized digger dancing team to demonstrate the power and precision control of their products at show events.

KIRKPAT
The Malleable Iron Works of William Kirkpatrick Limited

Location: Frederick Street, Walsall, Staffordshire, Mercia, England, UK
Date of Photograph: pm 4 February 2008
OS Grid Reference: SP007985
Co-ordinates: 52:35:04N 1:59:24W
Elevation: 121.6 meters

This is the brass and malleable iron foundry of William Kirkpatrick and Sons Limited. It specialises in the production of architectural ironmongery.

Kirkpatrick Limited was founded in 1855 by William Kirkpatrick JP (1817-1887). It was inherited by his son Vincent but became a Limited Liability company in 1901, when selected employees became shareholders. The Kirkpatrick family and its, effectively hereditary, working shareholders still own the company.

Malleable iron is a substance that is cast in molds as a white-hot liquid, where it solidifies as ordinary (gray) cast-iron. It is further treatment that renders the malleable form. Malleable iron is much more resilient to fracture than ordinary cast-iron and has a greater tensile strength, though not as much resilience as wrought iron or mild steel. Unlike steel it does, however, share something of wrought iron's resistance to weathering and corrosion.

Accordingly, malleable iron is an ideal medium for architectural ironmongery. Kirkpatrick produces two basic patterns: A florid "Antique" style; and a "General" style with cleaner, Gothic lines. Products span the gamut of domestic ironwork, except for fencing, and include:- Letter Boxes, Bolts, Latches, Door Handles, Knockers, Hearth Furniture, Hinges, Escutcheons and 2500 other lines of ironmongery.

The raw iron is melted using an electric induction furnace. The melt is cast by hand into rough shapes within greensand molds. The solidified castings of gray cast-iron are packed into hematite powder inside iron drums and annealed in electric ovens at 980 degrees Centigrade for eighty hours. Each oven has a capacity of between six and eight tons.

This process reduces the carbon content of the iron and thus increases its strength and malleability to the extent that it can be hammered and riveted.

After this heat treatment the malleable iron item or component is shot-blasted and ground to improve finish, and if appropriate assembled into a marketable unit. After assembly, rust-proofing is applied to the product, followed by two coats of paint.

The 2003 accounts show that the 106 employees generated a turnover of £2,538,914 of which £10,097 was pre-tax profit, indicating a gross return of nearly 0.4%.

LAUNER
The Launer Handbag Factory at Walsall

Location: Holtshill Lane and Balls Hill, Walsall, Staffordshire, Mercia, England, UK
Date of Photograph: am 4 February 2008
OS Grid Reference: SP017986
Co-ordinates: 52:35:07N 1:58:31W
Elevation: 133.5 meters

This Launer of London factory specialises in the manufacture of handbags, attache cases and wallets made from high-grade calf leather, lizard or ostrich skin. Any visible parts are gold-plated. There are eighteen staff.

Launer is one of the last of the Walsall leather accessory makers. The firm was founded by Czech refugee Sam Launer in 1941 and earned a Royal Warrant for handbags in 1981, though Launer had been supplying the Royal Family with leather accessories since 1968. Until 1981 much of the Launer production was for the "Gucci" brand of expensive personal accessories, and it was in that year that Gerald Bodmer, the current Managing Director and chief designer joined the company and reinforced its own-brand production based upon the latest design trends from across fashionable Europe.

The best-textured patches are cut from selected animal skins and specially tanned. These components are skived and split so that raw edges can be concealed in the finished product. The components are then assembled by hand but machine-sewn in order to achieve a high-finish. To maintain the highest practicable output quality manufacturing tactics are discussed and refined at each stage of item fabrication.

Typical of the production handbag output is the Royale that, as of February 2008, retails at £775. This is a conservative 23-centimeter two-compartment calf bag available in one of seven colors. It has internal zip and mirror pockets. Orderable over the Internet, delivery can be expected within seven to fourteen days.

Larger men's wallets include the 22 by 14 centimeter black leather Travel Wallet that incorporates three document sections and a zip pocket. It would set you back £170.

Launer currently has three British Royal Warrants: The Queen, The Duke of Edinburgh and The Prince of Wales. Other Launer bag users included the late Princess of Wales, and currently include The Duchess of Cornwall, Crown Princess Masako of Japan, Judi Dench and (the Late) Margaret Thatcher.

Queen Elizabeth toured the Launer works on 4th March 1991.

Besides the firm's own Internet outlet of www.launer.com retail stockists include Harrod's and Fortnum and Mason.

LEEKMILL
The Earl Grey Inn and London Silk Mill at Leek

Location: Earl Grey Inn and London Silk Mill at Leek, Staffordshire, England, UK
Date of Photograph: 11 September 2002
OS Grid Reference: SJ989563
Co-ordinates: 53:06:18N 2:01:04W
Elevation: 199.3 meters

In October 1685 the King of France had a bad idea.

He decided to issue The Edict of Fontainebleau that revoked the 1598 Edict of Nantes which had granted toleration to French Protestants: The Huguenots.

These Huguenots comprised a landless class of craftsmen in silk, silver, glass and furniture. As a result of the bloody persecution that resumed, half a million Huguenots took themselves and their skills to England. Settling at first in Spitalfields (London) and the Derby area, by the early eighteenth century a number of them had infiltrated the East Cheshire and North Staffordshire area to the South of Manchester.

Meanwhile, even in England, you could not vote unless you owned land and you could not own land unless you were a Confirmed and jurant member of The Church of England. The Commonwealth and the events of the last half of the seventeenth century had begotten numerous native Presbyterians and Quakers. None of these English or French non-conformists, and of course no Jew or Catholic, could attend a university, sit in judgment, obtain a commission, or in any way participate in civic life.

But they could work, and to such men the route to wealth and respect led through the shop.

By the 1670's a silk industry had engendered in Leek.

Leek Friends' Meeting had opened a house by 1700, as had the Baptists, whilst Leek Presbyterians had a meeting house by 1715.

During the 1730's people with not-quite-English names like Myott, Lombe or Davenport set up in Leek as silk twisters or weavers, sometimes dabbling in mohair or linen as the winds of trade directed. By 1799, three thousand practiced silk manufacture in the town.

The spinners and weavers of Leek were by and large small independent craftsmen in their own premises. So they were reluctant to heed the wooing of the Right or the Left. When the Jacobite army passed by in 1745 the men of Leek greeted it with apathy and when fifty years later the Blanketeers stormed through to assault the capital our lads had little comfort for them or their Government pursuers.

Gradually the silk trade grew and in the 1820's well-lit weavers' houses were constructed around Albion Street in South-West Leek. This is now a cobbled conservation area and when in about 2004 some barmy official ordered his men to tear up the cobbles and lay tarmacadam, the residents told him to put the stones back in short order! In 1816 Badnall and Langharn had introduced steam to their mill in Mill Street and by 1835 Leek had seven steam mills with 119 power looms served by 744 operatives of whom 477 were women or girls. By 1818 there were in Leek 200 weavers on engine looms and 100 on hand looms, absorbing the output of the spinning mills. As in the Scottish silk town of Paisley, the introduction of the Jacquard loom, programmed with punched cards, introduced something of a revolution in patterned weaves. In addition to these numbers there were fifty broadloom weavers making handkerchiefs and shawls.

By 1839 over three hundred domestic looms worked full-time, either on ribbon or broad goods.

In the 1820's there were plenty of mill owners and prosperous working men around Leek as around other industrial towns of the Midlands and the North. The few who were represented voted for county seats and their interest was swamped by the country landed and nabob retirees who could purchase votes, either in the shires or in decrepit rural townlets.

Many weavers were purchasing, or already had purchased, their modest premises with mutual finance. The Leek Building Society opened its doors in 1824 and was soon joined by several more, who with other co-operative institutions were to play a major role in the future of the town and of Britain.

On 15 November 1830, the Swing Riots precipitated a vote of no confidence in the Tory government of Arthur Wellesley, Duke of Wellington, and his government fell.

Two years previously Charles Grey, the 2nd Earl Grey and leader of the Whigs had attempted to enfranchise Manchester and Birmingham, at the respective expense of rotten boroughs Penryn and East Retford. He had failed.

Now the Whigs came to power and Grey introduced The Representation of the People Act 1832 ("The Reform Act") to abolish the rotten boroughs, suppress electoral corruption and enfranchise the new industrial towns and cities. The suffrage doubled overnight from 200,000 to include all adult males who owned or rented land above a threshold rental value: Fourteen percent of males could now vote. It was not until 1867, however, that non-propertied men could vote.

And for an encore Grey and his Whigs abolished slavery in the British Empire.

Across the road the severely functional four-story structure is London Mill, built at a time when the Ashbourne Road it fronts was called London Road. It was built in 1853 for unknown silk spinners and was purchased in 1863 by Brough, Nicholson and Hall whose names are set in stone over the door. This firm moved from smaller premises in Union Street and traded at London Mill until around 1960 when they sold the mill to Job White and Sons Limited. The premises, derelict in 2002 is now (May 2007) proposed for conversion to retail, business and residential uses. The exterior is substantially as built with nineteen bays, the three central of which support an elegant pediment.

The Earl Grey bar is perhaps the smallest I have seen anywhere. Three bar stools stand opposite three pull-pumps and there is standing room for a further eight or ten customers. Its doors were open to the street as I passed but no staff or customers were in evidence.

The last silk mill at Leek ceased working silk in 1994, though vestigial processing of artificial fibers remains in the town.

The largest employer in Leek today is The Britannia Building Society whose magnificent new World headquarters grace the Southern entrance to this homely and unpretentious Staffordshire town. It is the UK's second biggest mutual building society with assets of £32.4 billion ($ 65 billion) and 4600 employees, of whom around 2400 work at Leek. The society has three million members.

Postscript 29 May 2022

On 1 August 2009, the Britannia Building Society was subsumed within the Co-operative Financial Group and many branches of the Britannia disappeared. London Mill is now fully boarded-up and still for sale. After brief conversion to a hipster restaurant, the Earl Grey tavern seems to have been restored as a bar, complete with wall signage. (Streetview: October 2021).

MAYNARD
The Old Maynard Wine Gum Factory

Location:	Vale Road, Harringay, London N42, England
Date of Photograph:	am 17 September 2007
OS Grid Reference:	TQ325879
Co-ordinates:	51:34:31N: 0:05:21W
Elevation:	20 meters

When I was a boy, Maynard's was a ubiquitous presence in the North London scene, with confectioner's shops in every high street, graced with their distinctively-scripted Art Deco "Maynard's" fascias.

Charles Riley Maynard and brother Tom started their Stamford Hill candy factory in 1880, whilst Charles's wife Sarah Ann served customers in the adjoining shop.

The company was incorporated in 1896 and in 1906 the expanding concern moved a mile or so to the Harringay site in the picture.

Also around the turn of the century, Charles Gordon, heir to the candy firm, suggested to his father that they diversify into making "wine gums", an idea that outraged Charles senior, a strictly teetotal Methodist!

Nevertheless, Charles Riley gradually came round to the idea when his son persuaded him that the projected new sweets would contain no actual alcohol.

A classic was born!

The manufacture of Maynard's Wine Gums commenced in 1909. The new factory site below an embankment of The New River, permitted clean Hertfordshire spring water to be used in production whilst the proximity of The Lea Navigation and numerous railways afforded coal and sugar to be cheaply shipped from the South and gelatin from the North. London itself provided a ready market of some ten million people, and the World's largest commercial port was within five miles.

The works grew consistently, irrespective of trade depression or war, to become a four-figure employer of local labor.

The sweets themselves came in five shapes, colors, and flavors: Kidney, crown, diamond, circle and rectangle stamped "port", "sherry", "champagne", "burgundy" and "claret".

In 1990, Maynard's combined with the Tottenham licorice mill Barrett's plus effervescent candy firm Trebor. Later in the same decade this combine merged with the Anglo-American soda pop and confectionery conglomerate Coca-Cola Corporation as part of its Cadbury chocolate and candy arm. Retail assets were divested.

In 1998, the London factory closed and Maynard's Wine Gum and associated sweet manufacture was continued at a Sheffield premises that had come on-stream in 1991. By 2002 worldwide sales of Maynard's Wine Gums alone had reached a value of forty million pounds sterling per annum.

The Stoke Newington premises is now a warehouse for The Oriental Carpet Company and its associated Turkish concerns.

The Maynard Wine Gum in Autumn 2007

POLITI
The Old Politi Turkish Delight Works

Location: 10 Manor Road, Stamford Hill, London N16, England
Date of Photograph: am 17 September 2007
OS Grid Reference: TQ335870
Co-ordinates: 51:33:58N: 0:04:30W
Elevation: 25 meters

Like Maynard's, Bassett's and others, Politi was a representative of the Stoke Newington and Lea Valley sugar candy industry.

Rahat Locoum (perfumed sweetness) is a sugary gelatinous confection suggestive of the scent of roses and white or pink in cloudy color. In the UK it is known as "Turkish Delight" and imports, from the Ottoman Lands, substantially commenced in the 1830's, when steam began to permit the rapid transit of the readily-spoiled sweetmeat through torrid climes.

In 1872 the Greek Jew, David Politi, emigrated to Britain to evade persecution but it is not clear whether he came from the actual Hellenic Kingdom or from Ottoman-occupied Aegean lands.

Like many of his race, he settled in Stamford Hill and developed his Turkish Delight specialism within the local candy industry.

Politi "British Manufacture Turkish Delight" was an up-market Christmas delicacy divided into bite-sized chunks dusted in a mixture of cornflour and castor sugar to stop them coalescing into a sticky mass. The sweet was wrapped in cover-all paper and packed into 5.25-inch diameter wooden tubs 2.25 inches deep. A complementary wooden fork was packed inside atop the wrapping. Chocolate was not involved.

The pictured premises, at 10 Manor Road, was built in 1911 and housed a 1901 Marshall of Gainsborough horizontal steam engine that was still at work at least as late as 1978, and also a 1950 standby inverted vertical made by Sisson of Gloucester.

It is thought that both engines were still in use during the first half of the nineteen-eighties, but that by 1987 Politi's had ceased to trade. It is also said that both engines were then removed to an unknown place for preservation.

Recently the premises was occupied by a Jewish manufacturing bakery and is now the Royal Furniture works. The factory next door specialises in making the distinctive black Homburg-type hats worn by conservative Orthodox Jewish males.

CHAPTER TWELVE

Making the Modern World

The Renaissance and its Mercantilist economic expression brought new problems. Gold and silver flooded into Europe, fuelling inflation, speculation, social dislocation and investment. It brought new opportunities for power, gain and crime and weakened the grip of The Church, leading to a crisis of leadership, or more exactly rulership.

Urgent new needs beset society and the State. New and exact methods of measuring metal for coinage and cannon were needed; Ways of piloting ships across featureless wastes of ocean were needed; Ways of concealing confidential information in transit were needed.

These were the sort of issues to which British mathematicians were encouraged to apply themselves for, being British, they had to solve mundane but pressing problems, leaving the luxury of theory to foreigners.

One of the morning stars of applied mathematics was the Pembrokeshire mathematician Robert Recorde, who authored numerous practical books and introduced the = equality symbol to the World. Like Newton over a hundred years later he was told to organise a mint and in 1552 he extended his book "Grounde of Arts" to include his discoveries in the computation of alligation, the mathematical art of accurately composing a specified mixture from two other mixtures mixed. This was useful mot only to minters but to founders and physicians.

Around 1602, the Scotsman John Napier devised a way of transforming numbers into other numbers that could be added to speed and simplify the multiplication of the originals; or subtracted to facilitate division. These logarithms would also help to eliminate human error in arithmetic, assist in the correlation of observational data, and form a basis of automated computation. A few years later the Englishman Henry Briggs would re-configure Napier's logarithms to the radix of ten, making them even more transparent and convenient for industry and commerce. We can get a feel for the issues of the early seventeenth century when we are reminded that Briggs was often consulted on astronomy, surveying, navigation and mining. Briggs travelled to Edinburgh to confer with Napier in 1616. On his return Briggs used logarithms to compute tables of natural trigonometric functions to ten places (sines to fifteen), forming a tool of precision for future science.

Napier had also popularised a nifty computational tool, a set of engraved repositionable engraved rods that essentially instantiated the method of jalousie multiplication. The whole set of ivory, wood or brass bars was the size and shape of a small pocket calculator and could be used as such. Napier described these rods and their use as "rabdological", or "of stick discourse" but inevitably the calculator became styled "Napier's Bones".

William Oughtred was born at Eton. (I mean the genteel little town in the shadow of Windsor Castle: Not the rough comprehensive school on the outskirts of Slough). In 1622, Oughtred went one stage further and engraved Napier's logarithms as physical scales on two wooden rods. The rods were slid beside each other to multiply or divide numbers on the scales. The slide rule was born, our first analog computer. It found immediate application in the computations of shipwrights.

Another Scottish mathematician, James Gregory of Drumoak used his geometrical skills to explore optics and in 1663 designed a reflecting telescope. He also anticipated Newton by discovering The Fundamental Theorem of Calculus and making an early statement of Taylor's Series. Another of his inspirations for which someone else is usually credited was the exceedingly versatile but simple technique of Simpson's Rule, another key tool in the experimenter's and technologist's tool kit.

Many innovations of the seventeenth century were integrated and extended by the culminating genius of Isaac Newton, a Lincolnshire man, who published his "Philosophiae Naturalis Principia Mathematica" in 1687. Building upon the kinematic laws of planetary motion formulated by the German mathematician Johannes Kepler about eighty years earlier, Newton introduced the concept of forces in equal opposition, bringing to science a dynamical structure essential to further progress. This enabled Newton predictively to explain the evolutions of the Solar System in terms of gravitation and the Conservation of Momentum. As part of his grand project, Newton formalised the rules of a differential and integral calculus, extended the tools of numerical analysis, and placed a useful and supremely powerful forecaster in the hands of astronomers and navigators.

The more explicitly to assist sailors, in 1699 Isaac Newton invented a reflecting quadrant which doubled the precision of celestial angles. This instrument was to enable navigators to measure the angular altitude of celestial bodies so that they could estimate their latitude at sea. In 1730, Londoner John Hadley invented a navigator's octant that simplified the measurement of celestial altitudes by presenting the image of the Sun or other star beside the horizon using mirrors. A practical problem remained: The wallowing of a ship at sea made it hard to tell when a heavenly body and horizon were actually matched.

In 1757, Kirkbean naval officer Captain John Campbell invented the sextant. This also measured angular altitudes but used the horizon as an actual reference point so that the movement of the ship (and the instrument) was suppressed. Also the sextant could be used with stars at night and, using protective filters, the Sun by day. To increase the precision of measurements vernier and micrometer drum technologies were developed for the sextant. Further improvements in both handiness and precision were made by using brass instead of wood in the construction of the new instrument, and the sextant was trialled in the measurement of nocturnal lunar distances as a potential navigational assist.

For a definite positional fix both latitude and longitude are required. Whilst, with knowledge of local time, the celestial altitudes could be used to establish latitudes at sea, the problem remained of determining longitude. In theory, the angles between the Moon and stars, in conjunction with a printed forecast, could provide longitude. An eighteenth century astronomer royal, Nevil Maskelyne, provided such a route to knowledge of longitude. A more direct route was, however, the comparison of local and standard (e.g. Greenwich) time, if a shipboard clock could be made robust enough and accurate enough to keep standard time for a voyage of years.

Subsequent to some serious accidents, the Admiralty offered a prize of £20000 to anyone who could provide a method accurately of determining longitude at sea.

Yorkshire clockmaker John Harrison decided to compete and by 1736 had demonstrated a prototype chronometer that successfully predicted longitude on a voyage to Lisbon.

A truly successful clock would not only have to weather the extreme dynamics of a storm-tossed ship but also continuous if more gradual changes in temperature, humidity and atmospheric pressure. Over the next twenty-five years Harrison developed the precision technology required for a sea-going chronometer. Spin-offs that propagated throughout production practice included the bimetallic strip and the caged roller bearing as well as developments of fusee technology. By 1761 Harrison had made a large watch called H4. When tried by HMS Deptford on a voyage to Jamaica, the chronometer lost five seconds of time which introduced an error of 1.25 minutes of arc or one nautical mile at those latitudes. On a second voyage, to Bridgetown, H4 was compared head-to-head with Maskelyne's Lunar Distances method. On this occasion H4 yielded an error of less than ten miles, whilst the Lunar Distances method produced a thirty mile error, and required much more skill, labor and time than the clock method.

As navigation and shipbuilding expanded to equip world trade, the forests of Britain depleted. Soon all available wood had to be conserved for building and as the price of charcoal rose new methods of smelting became ever more urgent.

As early as 1618 Dudd Dudley had baked Dudley coal in a clamp as if it were wood to produce a spongy clinker-like charcoal substitute. This coke he successfully applied to reducing ironstone, but the sulfurous Black Country coal gave a poor coke that led to a brittle and intractable iron. Nevertheless, it could be wrought good though the economics were still against coke-iron development at that time.

In the first years of the eighteenth century the Bristol Quaker brass founder Abraham Darby went to The Netherlands to study the technology involved in casting brass cooking pots. When he returned he decided to adapt these sand casting processes to making cheaper pots in iron. Darby bought an old charcoal blast furnace at Coalbrookdale in Shropshire and adapted it for coke. On 10th January 1709 he fired it loaded it with a mixture of ironstone and coke made from local coal. Fortunately this coal happened to be sulfur-poor and produced a high-quality cast iron from which thin-walled but robust pots could be made.

Though use of the correct coking coal now meant that cast iron could be mass produced, a problem still remained with wrought iron, which required the highly energy-intensive process of repeated faggoting and hot-beating to manufacture.

In 1740 the Epworth Quaker John Huntsman invented the crucible process for making fine steels for clock springs. He moved to Sheffield where he used a coke-fired furnace to heat ceramic pots to 1600 degrees Centigrade. Firstly, 15 kilograms of iron were placed in these crucibles. When they were white-hot crude blister steel and flux were added. After three hours the dross was skimmed and the steel poured into moulds to form ingots. The product was much more homogenous and reliable than cementation steel and formed the basis of Sheffield's vast production of sharp tools and weapons.

Before Huntsman's crucible method Sheffield made 200 tons of steel per year. By 1840, Sheffield made 80000 tons of steel per year, half of Europe's entire production.

In 1779 Gosport ironmaster Henry Cort received an iron hoop contract from the naval base across the harbor entrance in Portsmouth. He realised he was in no position to fulfil such a large order. To expedite wrought iron processing he installed, in 1783, a shaped rolling mill, and a year later he invented puddling furnaces in which pig iron was "boiled" to remove volatiles and produce high-quality iron for rolling to wrought. Around 1830 the recovery and quality of iron from high volatile sources was improved by fettling (lining) the furnace baths with iron oxide in the form of forge scale or red hematite.

Because of their prolonged melting, the liberal use of fettles and fluxes, and their small batch formats it is clear that crucible steel and wrought iron could be nothing but energy-intensive and expensive.

A major step forward occurred in 1855 when Sir Henry Bessemer invented his Converter to mass-produce mild steel from molten pig iron. The crude iron liquid was poured into a thirty-ton capacity clay-lined iron pot mounted on hollow trunnions and equipped with tuyeres (air ports) around its base. Compressed air was pumped through the molten iron oxidising impurities that rose to the surface as slag. Because this oxidation was exothermic the temperature of the melt actually increased during the blast. After the blast the converter could be rotated and the slag poured away. Any desirable alloy components were then added to the melt, mixing made with a little further air injection, and the steel poured to cast.

At first only an acid steel could be made using fine hematite, but in 1878 Sidney Gilchrist-Thomas lent the converter a dolomitic fettling to produce a basic steel from the much commoner and cheaper, but lower-grade, phosphoric iron ores.

Later in the century Gilchrist-Thomas' open hearth steel making techniques further cheapened steel production and increased both the range of iron ore qualities that could be used and the variety of special steels produced, as well as making continuous production feasible.

Whilst the production of iron, coal and coke burgeoned in the eighteenth century serious issues arose regarding the cost and capacity of transport. Such problems were intensified by the fact that such resources were often distant from navigable water, especially in Central England. Also some products such as pottery, glass and porter beer suffered from the violence as well as the cost of road transport.

In response in 1757 the first canal, The Sankey Navigation, was cut a few miles to link St Helen's to the River Mersey, and by 1761 The Duke of Bridgewater had commissioned Leek millwright James Brindley to engineer a canal from the Duke's coal mines at Worsley to the center of Manchester about eight and a half miles away. Potter Josiah Wedgwood agitated for a canal past his Etruria works to connect him with the sea and in 1777 The Trent and Mersey Canal satisfied his need. It connected those two navigable rivers establishing a link between the North and Irish Seas via the English Midlands.

Before the end of the eighteenth century a "Silver Cross" of canals connected the Mersey, Trent, Thames and Severn across Mercia with their crux at Birmingham.

Many further canals served the industrial North and in 1835 Scottish civil engineer Thomas Telford capped the golden age of the canal when he opened the magnificent Birmingham and Liverpool Junction Canal, usually if inaccurately known as "The Shropshire Union".

Horse-drawn canal transport was inherently slow and locks or their alternative contour loops greatly increased delays. The method was unsuited to small, perishable or valuable items or to mail or passengers. All such mainly stayed on the road. Roads had themselves been improved during the eighteenth century to improve speed and comfort and suppress the vagaries of flooding, tree-fall and crime. Nevertheless, the roads remained expensive and of limited bearing capacity.

For centuries roads had been locally improved by laying wooden planks, stone or even cast-iron to preserve the surface and lower rolling friction. Sometimes these substrata were flanged to guide the cartwheels. When around 1800 high-pressure non-condensing steam engines began to promise a mobile power source the possibility of mechanising such rail roads was considered, but wooden planks could not support the weight of engines and an economic way of producing sufficiently resilient iron needed to be evolved. As puddled iron and later steel technology developed, useful rails became available.

A breakthrough was achieved at the 1829 Rainhill Trials when experimenters identified several designs of fast and economical steam rail locomotive. The next year the World's first intercity railway opened between Manchester and Liverpool to assist the movement of both traders and cotton. A major engineering achievement involved was the successful and stable crossing of the Chat Moss morass, which complemented the cutting of the line through solid sandstone at Edge Hill.

Between 1836 and 1846 British railway construction, financed on a joint stock basis, boomed. Two hundred and seventy-two Acts of Parliament enabled railway companies to compulsorily purchase land and lay way and depots across Britain and Ireland. By the year 1830 a mere 98 route miles of railway had been built. By 1840 1485 route miles had been laid. Then the laying of track boomed, and by 1846 the mileage was 4536. By 1851 this had risen to 6800 miles actually laid out of 9375 permitted by Parliament. In 1860 there were 9074 route miles which rose to 20255 by 1920.

Tyneside engineers George and Robert Stevenson had organised most of this mileage, together with bridge and locomotive provisions. They adopted the old Tyneside coal-chaldron gage of 4 feet 8.5 inches, which became the World standard.

Between 1833 and 1854 the great engineer and naval architect Isambard Kingdom Brunel laid 3008 miles at broad gage (7 feet 0.25 inches). This Great Western Railway (GWR) covered the sector from Neyland (Pembrokeshire) to Exeter including Bristol, which was connected to London in 1841. The broad gage offered greater train capacity, stability and speed. Brunel intended that passengers should be able to purchase a through GWR ticket from Paddington in London to Manhattan in New York. To that end he designed steam ships to complete the journey form Bristol. The World's first iron screw ship, The Great Britain, was built to Brunel's design in 1842 and launched in 1843. It could convey 720 passengers. The Great Britain completed her maiden voyage to New York in fourteen days. In 1858 Brunel collaborated with London shipbuilder John Scott Russell to build The Great Eastern, a leviathan 17274 gross ton 4000 passenger combined screw and paddle iron steamer intended to travel from Britain to Australia non-stop without refuelling. It was originally intended actually to call this ship SS Leviathan but the British are superstitious about attaching Biblical names or the names of Classical gods to ships: Perhaps they should have remembered their qualm when fifty years later they decided to call a trio of Belfast liners Titanic, Olympic and Britannic. Brunel was one of the first practicing engineers to understand dimensional analysis. He successfully argued that since fuel capacity increased as the cube of length and frictional energy losses merely as the square, then range would increase arithmetically with size. Bigger was faster or further, not just safer. The Great Eastern was a passenger transport fifty years ahead of its time, but served indispensably as a telegraphic cable layer. She was scrapped in 1889, but remained the biggest ship ever built by British hands until the launch of the 31938 ton RMS Mauretania in 1907.

Brunel also built several innovative large bridges. His great elliptical brick arch span that takes the GWR over the Thames at Maidenhead remains the largest brick arch in the World. Constructed in 1838 it is also the widest and the flattest. In 1855 Brunel commenced work on The Royal Albert Bridge, an immense high-level wrought iron lenticular truss structure to convey the railway over the River Tamar from Devon to Cornwall. The towering intellect and tiny man smoked forty cigars a day and slept four hours. As Prince Albert opened the bridge in 1859 the dying 53-year-old Brunel was steamed across on his deathbed. Considered by many to be the greatest engineer of history in a history and place crowded with competition for those laurels, Brunel is certainly at the apogee of comprehensive scientific civil engineering due to a lone genius. Brunel died on the 15th September 1859.

As we leave the high noon of the mid nineteenth century the world of devout heroes and solitary geniuses gives way to the age of the salaried technician. But wonders were still achievable, and ensued.

In the transition were specialists like Wheatstone, James Young Simpson and Joseph Lister, no strangers to pathos or drama.

Charles Wheatstone first achieved notoriety with a cunning experiment. He made three spark gaps in an otherwise continuous length of copper wire and rigged high-speed revolving mirrors to time the delay, if any, between the right and left hand sparks relative to the center. The lag of the middle spark proved that electricity had a speed, and Wheatstone alleged that speed to be 288000 miles per second. To Wheatstone the result suggested that electric pulses might be exploited to send telegraphic messages of unimaginable speed. We now know that that speed ought to be the speed of light (or, say, X-rays) in copper and that this cannot exceed the speed of light *in vacuo* which the seventeenth century Danish astronomer Ole Rømer computed to be about half Wheatstone's value. Nevertheless, the value of Wheatstone's exercise is that mirror techniques would later be used by Hippolyte Fizeau to measure the speed of light in the laboratory, and then Michelson and Morley would move forward to use laboratory mirrors to confirm that the speed of light was independent of the Earth's movement, a result that led directly to Relativity in the twentieth century.

Wheatstone's big innovations were, however, considerably more workmanlike.

On a day in 1835 he revealed his invention of the spark spectrograph to a British Association meeting in Dublin. Presumably the audience would have been incredulous to know that this unassuming instrument would, within one hundred years, analyse the stars and discover helium.

In 1837 a July day found Wheatstone, in a dingy room at Euston Station, the London terminus of The London and North-Western Railway, working by the light of a stinking tallow candle, perhaps for secrecy's sake. He had had a special six-strand copper cable laid along the railway track to Camden Town, one and a half miles towards Birmingham. The pattern of electrification of these six wires actuated pointers on a lettered indicator board, a digital system of immense suggestivity for later electrical and computational developments. Wheatstone exchanged messages with Camden Town along the wires, and the experiment was deemed a success. Not all of the alphabet's letters were however represented: A fact that would later frame a black farce.

In July 1839, Brunel and the other Directors of The Great Western Railway approached Wheatstone and his business partner William Fothergill Cooke with a view to laying an experimental telegraph beside the railway from Paddington to West Drayton at a range of 13 miles. They were so impressed with the results that they ordered an extension to Slough (twenty miles) which was reached in 1841. The GWR charged a curious public a shilling a time to look into the Paddington telegraph office where they were told that fifty messages were dispatched every minute, each travelling at 280000 miles a minute.

Four years later, in another of those inexplicable metaphysical communions between a Quaker and applied science, the Paddington telegraph would earn sensational notoriety.

John Tewell had been transported to Australia for petty theft but sometime in the early 1840's he returned to England a very rich man. He married and settled down in Berkhamsted, a small town about 27 miles North of Slough but more like 53 via rail through London. On a night in 1845 Tewell travelled to Slough to visit his mistress. There he poisoned her to death with prussic acid (a solution of hydrogen cyanide in water). Within hours her body was found at her address, and, suspecting Tewell, police pursued him to Slough Station, where they learned he had just taken a train towards London.

Immediately the police attempted to telegraph Paddington with a description which commenced "He is in the garb of a Quaker...". But there being no "Q" on a Wheatstone board the Slough telegrapher attempted a phonetic rendition as "kwak...". Instantly, the diligent London respondent wired back in the telecoms jargon of the time "Repent!". Slough tried again only to get "Repent! Repent!". After a few minutes of this the post boy, who happened to be in the Paddington office at the time, suggested that Slough be allowed to drive out the full message. This was done.

The local London police were quickly summoned and waited on the platform for the Slough train to arrive. To the vast astonishment of all present, Tewell was arrested on alighting, and escorted to his fate.

In the hard life of the past, surgeons were reluctant to operate, since if the patient did not die of shock or cardiac arrest or hemorrhage, then lingering death by sepsis was more than likely. Scottish surgeons were habituated to harrowing mastectomies and other peripheral excisions. Ether had been tried as a surgical anaesthetic but caused pulmonary irritation that could make a patient drown in his own sputum.

In July 1831 American doctor Samuel Guthrie discovered trichloromethane, a simple haloalkane that came to get called chloroform. Like several other organic halides the chemical exhibited anaesthetic properties. In self-administration, Bathgate surgeon James Young Simpson discovered its powerful soporific as well as analgesic character, and by 1847 it was common in Edinburgh operations. Its use spread very rapidly after Victoria had it administered to suppress her pains in childbirth, and a great instrument of mercy graced the Earth.

Sepsis was still a danger. Working forty-five miles West in Glasgow Royal Infirmary, Essex surgeon Joseph Lister, yet another Quaker, found that by spraying a weak solution of phenol (carbolic acid), pathogenic organisms could be killed. Not only was this caustic coal derivative useful when sprayed but it could also be used to sterilise instruments and, with due caution, clean wounds. Deaths from surgical sepsis declined dramatically.

Back on the electrical front, Scottish mathematician James Clark-Maxwell busied himself trying to integrate fifty years of findings in experimental electrical and magnetic science into some sort of self-consistent theory. Pausing only to invent the color photograph, in 1861 Clark-Maxwell showed that electricity and magnetism propagate through space as mutually-complementary mathematically-orthogonal transverse waves. They travel at the speed of light, indeed *are* light, and as such can propagate indefinitely, though with attenuation. The way was open to radio, radar and interplanetary travel control.

Interest turned to the question of electric transmission through a vacuum and the larger question of vacuum versus aether. In the 1890's Manchester man Joseph John Thompson set up two metal plates opposed across a long glass tube. He evacuated the air and set up a high direct-current voltage between the plates. Rays travelled from the negative cathode. By setting a second pair of charged plates normal to the axis betwixt the first set, he found that the negatively charged member of that secondary set of plates repelled the "cathode rays". Since light was imperturbable by electric charge, and since there was no conventional matter left in the tube, Thompson concluded that the rays must consist of particles and that all these particles themselves had a negative charge. Another experiment showed that when a magnetic field was applied across the ray beam it could cancel out the deflection caused by the electric cross plates. Because the relevant electrical and magnetic field formulae were already known, Thompson could calculate the charge to mass ratio of the (identical) particles. He calculated that this charge to mass ratio was more than a thousand times that for the hydrogen anion, so either these particles were very highly charged or they were very light in mass.

JJ Thompson announced his discoveries in 1897. He had discovered the electron, the first subatomic particle, and assisted in the correct interpretation of the findings of Becquerel and The Curies. The way was open to thermionics, electronics and television. It also offered a youthful Einstein his opening to photovoltaic theory and within thirty years quantum theory was organised on this foundation.

Early in the twentieth century, New Zealander Ernest Rutherford was working at Thompson's old college, The Victoria University of Manchester, when he noticed that radioactive alpha particles either passed clean through gold foil, or, more probably, scattered from it in a systematic way. This confirmed that matter was almost wholly empty space. It earned him the Nobel Prize for Chemistry in 1908. Rutherford then found that radioactive isotopes have a characteristic decay "half-life" and this enabled actual ages in years to be pinned on individual rock formations and eventually the whole planet and any suitable meteorites that happened to land on it. In 1919 Rutherford fulfilled the old alchemists' dream when, using nuclear bombardment (a much more delicate procedure than it sounds) he managed to transmute one element into another: Nitrogen 14 became Oxygen 17. Rutherford had split the atom in Manchester.

Meanwhile the physicians and biologists had not been idle either.

In 1922 Darvel man Alexander Fleming was working in Paddington when he discovered the lovely lozenge-faceted crystals of the antibacterial enzyme lysozyme, perhaps a rare chemical whose name is as attractive as its complexion. It is a principal constituent of tears and Fleming was able to caution surgeons that the reason the phenolic irrigation of wounds sometimes actually assisted infections was because the powerful caustic phenol destroyed these more delicate but effective natural antiseptics. Fleming was an untidy worker and in 1928 he left a certain staphylococci culture on a Petrie dish whilst he went on holiday. He left the laboratory window open to the filth of Praed Street. When he returned he noticed that the bacteria had died back in circles around centers where spores of the airborne fungus *penicillium notatum* had alighted. The first miracle antibiotic penicillin was to hand, an agent that could cure gonorrhea in four hours, or septicemia in days.

Electricians continued their work.

In 1919, Birmingham physicist Francis Aston invented the mass spectrograph, a direct outcome of the JJ Thompson work that greatly assisted precision structural analysis of chemical and nuclear products, including of course natural proteins, some of which were too delicate for traditional wet chemistry. The way was open to the designer drug.

In 1932, Sir James Chadwick discovered the neutron, a neutrally-charged baryon particle of the atomic nucleus, the agent of isotope differentiation. Here was a heavy, energetic, electrically-imperturbable little cannonball that could strike neighboring nuclei to free its fellows. The way was open to the atomic chain reaction and nuclear power.

In early 1935, Robert Alexander Watson-Watt used the BBC shortwave broadcast antennae at Daventry in Northamptonshire experimentally to detect a Heyford bomber that he had fly conveniently overhead. The ultra-secret experiment was successful and radar was born. By 1937 three radar stations were ready for air defence detection and by the time of The Battle of Britain in 1940 there were twenty coastal radar ranging stations. They meant that the British did not have to waste precious gasoline on patrols or expose their few aircraft to routine wear and tear. It also meant their pilots could sleep or rest, and rise refreshed to tackle an enemy of known size and position. The Nazis did not think the British were technologically-advanced enough to have achieved radar, and deluded themselves that the pylons were for long-range naval radio communications.

In 1953, after the War had ended, English biologist Francis Crick worked with his American colleague James Watson to elucidate the replicative mechanism of the genetic vector protein deoxyribonucleic acid (DNA), a chemical of enormous complexity whose molecular weight is in the hundreds of thousands. They discovered that living cell construction always progressed from "stock" DNA to a "carrier" intermediary RNA, which then expressed as a functional protein. Crucially, they determined that DNA could replicate its contained constructional code because it had an intertwined double-helical physical structure to its molecule. This explained how genetic inheritance was possible in living organisms. The way was open to engineered methods of overcoming inherited disease.

A third separate strand of applied science developed erratically, and would come to owe much to the electricians, but was really much of a piece with the earliest endeavors of the sixteenth and seventeenth century mathematical scientists.

Beginning in 1822, mathematician Charles Babbage sought methods of eliminating human error from routine calculations. He was courted by The Admiralty with a view to the development of some pre-settable machine that would automatically and speedily compute and print error-free tide tables. Naval experience had shown that manually-produced tables took too long to calculate for practical sea use, and when presented were raddled with clerical and printing errors. Babbage proposed a steam-driven, brass, multiply geared and shifted calculating machine that he called a Difference Engine, together with a fitted printer. Plans and partial prototypes failed to win official support, and though the requisite precision production technology did exist at the time it was difficult and expensive to commission.

Undaunted, Babbage moved forward to design an even more elaborate system of mechanical computers he called an Analytical Engine. It would have included the three fundamental computer processes of sequential operations, conditional branching and recurrent looping. Furthermore, it would have been programmed using punched Jacquard cards, the same in principle as the Hollerith cards of a 1960's digital mainframe computer. In 1843 Babbage asked his mistress, the mathematician Ada, Countess of Lovelace to write some card-code lists that would test his analytical engine. She chose to program the putative computer to compute a sequence of Bernoulli numbers: Such a procedure employs loops of various, conditionally-decided sizes to compute mathematical objects that soon grow to enormous scope. It is therefore a reasonably rigorous preparatory test mechanism. Having done this job, Ada was accordingly the first computer programmer in human history. In 1991, The British Science Museum constructed a complete Babbage Difference Engine from his plans, and using the tolerances and materials of Late Georgian times. It worked.

After Babbage the digital computer went into another hundred-year hibernation. Analog computers were developed, especially to test industrial design options and for naval gun control.

Then in the 1930's the British and Germans resurrected the concept of the digital computer with a view to war applications. Around 1935 Hitler visited the German pioneer, who had built a demonstration computer in a domestic living room at his Berlin flat. The not very technical dictator was not impressed, and the German digital computer effort was side-lined. During the Second World War the British built thermionic electronic proto-computers for military signal decryption and applied them successfully to reading German field plans and other secret messages, mainly those entrusted to radio. After the War, one of the key British pioneers, Alan Turing, worked at The National Physical Laboratory on plans for an "Automatic Computing Engine" (ACE) and by 1946 had a design for a stored-program computer. In 1949 he was appointed Director of the Computing Laboratory of The Victoria University of Manchester and worked on the software for the Manchester Mark 1 digital computer. Meanwhile, on 10th May 1950, ACE executed its first program.

The way was open for mass computing, numerical control, fully-automatic telephony, and the Internet.

BELPERWR
The Horseshoe Weir at Belper

Location:	Northern arm of The Horseshoe Weir on The River Derwent at Belper, Derbyshire, England, UK
Date of Photograph:	11 July 2005
OS Grid Reference:	SK345481
Co-ordinates:	53:01:46N 1:29:11W
Elevation:	61.6 meters

The small town of Belper was founded by Norman monks who called it "Beau Repaire", which approximately means "lovely sanctuary".

The weir was installed in 1797 to provide sufficient hydraulic head for a breast-shot suspension wheel that powered the early cotton mills of Jedediah Strutt.

The structure was built to power the West Mill and by 1820 impounded some 5.8 hectares of pond on the Derwent. It was modified and increased in height in 1819 and 1843. It is now tenanted by a small hydro-electric company that has a turbine hall nearby.

The weir is Listed Grade Two Star but is currently on The Derbyshire Historic Buildings Trust "Buildings at Risk" register. A diving inspection is to be undertaken to assess the state of the structure.

By 1804 the West Mill had been joined by a North Mill on the left (Southern) bank of the Derwent. This was equipped with a large but lightly built suspension wheel that was eighteen feet in diameter and twenty feet long. It was by Thomas Hewes. The wheel engaged a spur cog that transmitted power to a shaft that in turn distributed the power to various zoned stories of the building via rigid rods and bevel gears.

The existing North Mill superseded one built in 1786 and burnt down in 1803. Subsequent to advice from Charles Bage who in 1796 built the World's first iron-framed building, a flax mill at Ditherington, Strutt built the new North Mill of brick arches over a frame of turtle-backed cast-iron beams, mounted on cast-iron columns. The beams are yoked together with wrought-iron ties and the floors lightened with clay pots. The foundations are of stone. Taken together the design is almost fireproof.

Originally, the cotton was carded on the third and fourth floors and spun in 4236 separate threads using water frames on the first and second stories. The sixth floor was a school. Later, mule spinners were installed to diversify the product.

The Strutt Family divested at Belper in the 1950's and my understanding is that English Sewing Cotton Limited has suspended operations at its Belper sites. The North Mill is open to the public at regular times and is listed Grade One. Together with the Bage flax mill it may be regarded as the ancestor of steel-framed buildings everywhere including classic American skyscrapers though not, alas, of the suspension designs favored by Old World engineers and tragically exemplified by the New York Twin Towers.

BUTTERLY
The 1790 Charge Bank and the Modern Butterley Engineering Works

Location:	Butterley Engineering Limited, Butterley Hill. Ripley, Derbyshire, England, UK
Date of Photograph:	am 18 October 2007
OS Grid Reference:	SK402516
Co-ordinates:	53:03:38N 1:24:04W
Elevation:	111.9 meters

   The image shows the steel fabrication factory of The Butterley Company at Butterley in England, now known as Butterley Engineering Limited. Founded in 1790, it is the World's oldest heavy engineering concern and played a major role in the industrialisation of Britain and the World. At various times it has manufactured steam engines, armaments, bridges, cranes, rails and water-lifts, as well as being a primary producer of coal, iron and brick.
   Benjamin Outram (1764-1805) was a major figure of The Industrial Revolution. Son of surveyor Joseph, the civil engineer Benjamin went into partnership with canal designer William Jessop in 1788.

Together they built The Cromford Canal to connect Arkwright's cotton mills in and around Cromford on the Eastern edge of The Peak with the Trent Valley system of navigable waterways, and thence with the sea.

This project occasioned the driving of a canal tunnel through a hill at Butterley, which fortuitously disclosed massive resources of coal, ironstone and brick clay.

Outram continued his local canal building which involved, in 1796, installing the World's first iron aqueduct, the 44-foot single-span Holmes Aqueduct, demolished in 1971.

It was, however, at Butterley that his lasting works commenced. Outram went into partnership with Jessop and banker John Wright to establish an iron works called Benjamin Outram and Company, based upon the tunnel-disclosed minerals. In 1790, the Butterley Hall estate fell vacant and Outram purchased it and its subsumed minerals. Benjamin Outram manufactured primitive iron rails for horse-railways ancillary to the local canals and by 1796 the Butterley furnaces were pouring almost a thousand tons of pig-iron per annum. As the demand for war iron rose, so did production and by 1810 Butterley and its sister plant at Codnor Park produced 4,500 tons of pig per annum.

When Outram died in 1805 the name of the firm was changed to The Butterley Company.

In 1812, Butterley produced the Steam Horse locomotive and two years later fabricated the ironwork for London's Vauxhall Bridge across the Thames. Besides the very local coal and iron, limestone flux was sourced from Company mines at Crich and brought along the Cromford Canal.

In 1817, Butterley Works was at the center of events in the ill-starred Pentrich Revolution, when staff repulsed a starving mob intent upon stealing arms for a march upon London.

By 1830, a second boom had arisen and Butterley became the largest industrial concern in the East Midlands. A third furnace was brought to blast and Butterley participated in the steam engineering components of the Cromford and High Peak Railway as well as the engineering of the Croydon and Godstone horse line.

A myriad of iron goods was now cast or forged at Butterley including steam dredgers, locomotives, heaters and lock gates, including those for Telford's Caledonian Canal in Scotland. By 1863 it had the most capacious rolling mill in Britain and between 1854 and 1867 engineered William Barlow's iron-and-glass rail terminal shed at St Pancras in North London. With a width of 247 feet it was the World's widest unsupported vault and still exists to shelter waiting Eurostar trains from the weather.

In 1947 The Butterley Company lost its coal mines to nationalization but by 1850 the company employed ten thousand. In 1965, however, the Codnor Park plant closed and in 1968 Lord Hanson purchased the firm for £4.7 million.

Lord Hanson devolved the enterprise into Engineering, Brick and Aggregate divisions. In the mid-1980's the foundry was demolished disclosing the long-forgotten furnace charge bank of 1790.

This 1790 charge bank is the monolithic masonry structure that dominates the left-hand side of the above picture of the contemporary works, and includes a blast furnace.

Today, Butterley Engineering specialises in the advanced end of bridge and crane fabrication together with ancillary hydraulic and electrical technologies. It also progresses turnkey infrastructural projects worldwide.

In recent years it has completed a series of literal landmark projects including massive cross-over fire-doors for the Tai Lam railway tunnel in Hong Kong; The Falkirk Wheel; and the 165-meter tall Spinnaker Tower pylon in Portsmouth Harbor.

The Falkirk Wheel is an innovative 1800-ton rotary boat-lift in Central Scotland. It connects the Forth and Clyde Canal with the Union Canal. The wheel is 35 meters high and 28 meters long and bears two 6.5-meter wide counterbalanced caissons each carrying 250 tonnes of water, besides possible payload. The rotation is actuated by the self-weight of water spilling into the upper vessel from The Union Canal. Both canals had been derelict since the mid twentieth-century but had originally communicated via a flight of locks.

April 2009: The Spinnaker Tower on The Gunwharf Quays at Portsmouth

Postscript 29 May 2022

As of August 2021 (Streetview) the Butterley works are partially cleared. The Listed portions along Butterley Hill road are standing but in very bad repair, and the charge bank and remaining buildings are severely disrupted by feral tree growth.

DITHERIN
Ditherington Flax Mill at Shrewsbury

Location: Ditherington, Shrewsbury, Shropshire, England, UK
Date of Photograph: 7 November 2002
OS Grid Reference: SJ497137
Co-ordinates: 52:43:11N 2:44:37W
Elevation: 54.9 meters

Ditherington Flax Mill proper is a Grade One Listed building whilst subsidiary buildings on the site are Grade Two Star. It was designed by Shrewsbury wine merchant and surveyor Charles Bage (1751-1822), architect of Strutt's Belper mills. Bage would own and run the mill himself, with his partners John Marshall and the brothers Thomas and Benjamin Benyon. Whilst Bage's technical abilities were universally admired, his partners and others had a poor opinion of his business skills, and Bage was not a successful individual entrepreneur.

The Ditherington mill was built between 1796 and 1797 for flax spinning, a process that generates explosively-combustible airborne fiber. Accordingly, Bage built his mill of brick on a rigid cast-iron frame.

As the first iron-framed building in the World, Ditherington Mill is the mother of all skyscrapers, and clearly a monument central to World Heritage.

From the outset, the mill used two Boulton and Watt engines made at The Soho Works and sent to Ditherington by canal in 1797. The relevant scale drawings survive in the custody of Birmingham City Archives.

The completion of the mill coincided with the opening of the Shropshire Canal between Newport and Ditherington. This enabled coal to be brought cheaply from the East Shropshire Coalfield centered upon Oakengates, even though the Shrewsbury Coalfield around Hanwood is geographically much nearer. The canal also enabled flax to be brought in from The Continent, and the finished yarn economically to be shipped out.

A then-existing Shrewsbury industry finished Welsh woollen cloth before that was passed East, and this formed the skills base for the factory production of woollen, cotton and linen textiles at Shrewsbury. That factory production flourished in the late eighteenth and early nineteenth centuries before it was eclipsed by Ulster and The North. Indeed, in 1796 thirty-three linen workers of Shrewsbury were so rich that they registered to vote!

Tow yarn, a by-product of linen production, found a ready market in the carpet weavers of Bridgnorth and Kidderminster, further down the River Severn.

Process water was drawn from the Bagley Brook. Canvas was made in addition to linen thread, but only between 1811 to 1814, probably for wartime Admiralty requirements. The Shrewsbury textile manufacture declined markedly in the 1830's, a decade when the actual town population contracted. In general, the use of mechanical weaving for linen proved difficult and Bage did not master the technology.

Flax spinning at Ditherington ceased in 1886 when a malt kiln was abutted to the building and the whole complex turned into a maltings, which it remained until 1987. Traffic on the Shropshire Canal was almost non-existent after 1930, and the canal was closed postwar.

Since 1987 the complex has been derelict and though residential conversion has been suggested it has proved difficult to finance a viable future for the building. However, pressure continues to prevent clearance of the site in view of the major curatorial implications involved, and the whole Castlefields-Ditherington corridor is beginning to engage Governmental strategy planning because of its character as a deprived area.

ECTON
The Deep Shaft Engine House at Ecton

Location: Ecton, near Warslow, Staffordshire, England, UK
Date of Photograph: am 5 April 2006
OS Grid Reference: SK098583
Co-ordinates: 53:07:21N 1:51:14W
Elevation: 302.1 meters

    This is the Deep Shaft Engine House at Ecton Copper Mine.
    Ecton Hill is a steeply-rounded eminence of low-grade sheep pasture overlooking the valley of the River Manifold on the South-Western flank of The White Peak. It is a place of great natural beauty. The hill comprises alternating shales and limestones of Lower Carboniferous age which were contorted into a complex anticline some 285 million years ago. There are superposed complex fold structures within the larger anticline. During the Triassic Period, some 180 million years ago, hydrothermal fluids were injected into vertical fissures in the existing rocks. These emplaced ore bodies as sheet-veins and quasi-cylindrical pipes. At depth the ore consisted of chalcocite, a copper sulfide, and chalcopyrite and bornite, which are forms of copper ferrosulfide. Sometimes blende, which is zinc sulfide, accompanied the copper minerals. Higher up the

pipes, rainwater percolation altered the copper ores to carbonates such as azurite and malachite, and here a fourth metal, lead, was deposited in the form of its sulfide galena.

Bronze Age antler picks have been found in the workings on Ecton Hill but serious mining did not get underway until the seventeenth century AD, when Ecton became the first British mine to use explosives.

Around 1760 His Grace The Duke of Devonshire, the freeholder, assumed direct control of the mines, and major investments were made. By 1767 the mine was 960 feet deep and 430 feet of this was below the Manifold and had to be artificially drained, principally by a four horse-power hydraulic balance beam engine installed underground. In 1772 it was noted that tubs with cast-brass wheels running on grooved rails were being run along the sough by boys in order to bring some of the ore to grass, and it was about this time that Ecton was briefly the most prolific copper source in the World, and Cavendish was able to use it to finance his construction of a new spa resort at Buxton. By the 1780's Ecton's output was equivalent to 12% of the entire output of Cornwall's many copper mines, and in 1786 yield was 4000 tons per annum and the mine was the deepest in the World. Further reserves would be inaccessible unless the Duke would take the risk of installing new technology.

In February 1788, the Birmingham-based Scottish engineer James Watt was invited to visit Ecton and propose a design for a steam engine to raise ore and possibly also water. Watt's first idea was to install a machine to raise forty tons and 7680 gallons per eight-hour shift, but this was soon re-expressed as a 95-kibble per diem duty of 4-cwt kibbles. His final design allowed for 160 6-cwt kibbles raised 120 fathoms (720 feet) per eight-hour shift. By 1795, however, the Ecton Deep Shaft would be over 1300 feet deep with 924 feet of that below adit.

The installed Boulton and Watt engine was rated at eight horse-power and was a sun-and-planet double-acting single-expansion condensing beam engine with a sixteen-inch diameter cylinder and a four-foot stroke. The flywheel was twelve feet in diameter. The cylinder and piston were supplied by John Wilkinson of Broseley for £50, whilst the pumps were cast by The Coalbrookdale Company and brought by water via Stourport and Great Heywood to Froghall, from whence they were drawn by team. Precision parts, presumably the valve gear and its attached governor, were made by Watt at his own Soho Manufactory in Handsworth. A copper boiler worth £15:8s:7d was sourced locally and everything installed in or near the pictured building for an all-up price of £750. The installation was ready for use on 27th November 1788.

Water could not be sourced by gravity and was pumped up the hill by a secondary beam. Even more startling Watt innovations appeared. The winding ropes were made of hemp tapered from seven to five inches diameter and were 1320 feet long. When wet they weighed well over a ton. The engine was too weak to haul such a dead weight of uncoiled wet hemp so Watt dug a second, shallower, balance shaft to the South of the engine and rigged a sixteen-foot diameter helical spiral fusee drum to pay out a balance cable as the payshaft cable rose with its load. The fusee was designed to even out the tensile force at each state of wind, and was essentially the same as the fusee used in eighteenth-century timepiece technology.

In practice, each kibble took 140 seconds to ascend with 40 seconds for stopping and emptying. It was difficult to find a satisfactory maker for the advanced hemp ropes and they were problematical in use, so it is likely that wrought-iron chain replaced the hempen ropes early in the nineteenth century.

Further engines were installed underground and by 1850 the Boulton and Watt machine at Deep Shaft was "idle and dilapidated". In 1855 it was scrapped and sold for £16. The next year the boiler fetched £40 and six cwt of associated brass was sold for £33.

In 1891 all mining ceased at Ecton and the Deep Shaft engine house became a field barn. About 1930, the second story was removed and the roof re-laid to form a cowshed but the internal medial partition between the boiler and engine rooms was retained.

The Deep Shaft is capped only with rotting timber baulks and should not be approached.

FROGHALL
The Froghall Copperworks near Cheadle

Location:	Froghall, near Cheadle, Staffordshire, England, UK
Date of Photograph:	pm 1 October 2004
OS Grid Reference:	SK023474
Co-ordinates:	53:01:29N 1:57:56W
Elevation:	140.5 meters

This view shows the wharfage on the Caldon Canal and the adjacent copper wire mill of Thomas Bolton and Sons Limited at Froghall.

The factory was located midway between supplies of cheap waterborne coal from the North Staffordshire Coalfield and copper from the mines of His Grace The Duke of Devonshire at Ecton near Hartington. (These mines, once the largest copper mines in the World, financed the building of the spa town of Buxton). Waterpower from the River Churnet and a local tradition of iron mining and smelting facilitated early industrialism.

The origins of the Bolton firm are obscure but by 1783 the Walsall coppersmithing family had moved their business to nearby Birmingham. In 1852 they acquired the premises of The Cheadle Brass Company at Oakamoor, about two miles downstream of Froghall, and also beside the River Churnet.

This they converted to copper wire production, using the World's first continuous wire drawing machinery to spin the first Transatlantic Telegraph Cable of 1858 and the two succeeding cables.

The first cable was destroyed by a combination of electrical overload and apparent shark attack.

Throughout its life the Churnet Valley copper wire industry has specialised in spinning ultra high-quality, oxygen-free copper wire for critical applications in the telecommunications and power industries, and supplied the cabling for the Channel Tunnel and the Petronas Towers in Kuala Lumpur.

After World War Two the Oakamoor works were closed and demolished and production concentrated at Froghall. The Bolton family sold-out in 1961 and Thomas Bolton and Sons merged with the MacKechnie Group of Walsall.

The remainder of the Froghall Copperworks is one of the last vestiges of the once-great, but largely undocumented, Staffordshire Copper Industry.

HAKIN
The Hakin Observatory at Milford Haven

Location: Hakin, Milford Haven, Pembrokeshire, Wales, UK
Date of Photograph: pm 13 April 1992
OS Grid Reference: SM892059
Co-ordinates: 51:42:45N 5:03:10W
Elevation: 47.9 meters

The Hakin Observatory is a ruined astronomical observatory and astronomical training college at Milford Haven.

This 1992 photograph shows the observatory as a collection of semi-ruinous farm outbuildings. At the turn of the century the ruins were stabilised and part of the structure rehabilitated. It is a Grade One Listed Building.

The original construction was taken in hand by Charles Francis Greville (1749-1809) at the end of the eighteenth century, the intention being to provide a mathematical, engineering and technical college, and in particular a navigational training school for Naval officers and possibly also for fee-paying students. The brick dome, which was built with eight equidistant broad slits, would have accommodated a telescope and transit apparatus, possibly intended for teaching the Maskelyne longitude methodology, though at this period that was becoming operationally-redundant due to the perfection of marine chronometers.

Greville died before the college was completed in 1811, and Thomas Firminger (1775- 1861), a former Assistant to the Astronomer Royal The Reverend Nevil Maskelyne at Greenwich, was appointed Superintendent at Hakin.

First-rate equipment was assembled for Hakin, including the Lee Transit Circle made by Edward Troughton of London in 1793, originally for Gavin Lowe of Islington. It is said that this inventory was landed at Milford Haven town, but never completed the extra overland half-mile to Hakin. In any event, much of the apparatus, including the circle, was sold to the Reverend Lewis Evans of Woolwich, and the observatory and college never opened for use.

Shortly after the Napoleonic Wars ended, the focus of Royal Naval developmental science shifted to Pembroke Dock somewhat East of Hakin on the Southern side of Milford Haven ria.

The ruin appears to be constructed of lime-mortared current-bedded Old Red Sandstone ashlar.

LONGDON
The Iron Aqueduct at Longdon-upon-Tern

Location: Longdon-upon-Tern, near Telford, Shropshire, England
Date of Photograph: 7 November 2002
OS Grid Reference: SJ617156
Co-ordinates: 52:44:13N 2:34:05W
Elevation: 50.9 meters

      The aqueduct at Longdon-upon-Tern is made of one inch thick plates of crystalline gray cast-iron supplied by William Reynolds ironworks at Ketley. The bridge was erected in 1796 to a design by Thomas Telford. It is a girder bridge reinforced with rays of lateral ribs and bolted together on stanchions. There are brick abutments and shallow masonry piers. The cost of construction was £2000.
      The two troughs conveyed The Shrewsbury Canal over the River Tern in a span of 62 yards (52 meters). The Western, narrow trough accommodated tow-horses whilst the water-filled East trough, a standard seven feet in breadth, conveyed narrowboats.
      The Shrewsbury Canal was authorized in 1793 and the original stone aqueduct at Longdon must have been operational for a matter of months before being removed by floods in February 1795.

Telford's standing iron replacement postdates Outram's 44-foot long structure on the Derby Canal (the Holmes Aqueduct) and predates Telford's own masterpiece at Pontcysyllte. Accordingly, Longdon is not really the World's first iron aqueduct as usually averred, but is nevertheless a Scheduled Ancient Monument quaintly marked on OS maps in blackletter.

The Whole of the Shrewsbury Canal was open to through traffic by 1797. The Shrewsbury Basin at Ditherington closed in 1922 and the entire Shropshire Canal closed in 1944. The Northern stretch of canal from the aqueduct has been obliterated by plowing, whilst the Southern approach persists as a broad, unfurrowed embankment.

The Longdon-upon-Tern Aqueduct from the South-West

NEWFOUND
The New Foundry at Stourbridge

Location: Lowdes Road, Stourbridge, Worcestershire, England, UK
Date of Photograph: 11 May 2005
OS Grid Reference: SO894848
Co-ordinates: 52:27:38N 2:09:22W
Elevation: 67.1 meters

The New Foundry was erected in 1820 as a railway locomotive factory and general ironworks for Foster, Rastrick and Company who ran it until 1831, when it was taken over by their sister firm John Bradley and Company who continued operations until 1982. Under Foster and Rastrick the foundry made blast furnaces, rolling mill equipment, sugar mills, structural iron beams, wrought iron rails, and four locomotives.

John Bradley and Company was a Member of The Marked Bar Association, certified as producing rolled wrought iron of the finest grades. In much of the Twentieth Century under Bradley's the premises functioned as a hand rolling mill and was thought to be the last in the UK when it ceased this work in 1982.

Since 1982 a specialist rolling mill for salvaged wrought iron has been established at Thirsk. This does bespoke work for the restoration trades.

The New Foundry site was electrified by the General Electric Company of Witton in 1927.

The New Foundry building proper has an unsupported hipped roof spanning 50 by 150 feet. The rafters are of wrought iron beams with cast-iron tie-bars. The whole roof structure is archeologically-important. The walls are of brick with dentillated eaves and other neo-classical embellishments.

The use of the New Foundry complex ceased in 2004 when Sidney Smith Castings Limited terminated operations at the site.

The most famous Foster and Rastrick product was the steam locomotive The Stourbridge Lion, which was the first to run in North America. The Lion was a 0-4-0 4-feet 3-inch gage machine built in 1828 for use on the Honedale Railway in Pennsylvania. An important railed dock survives at Stourbridge for the loading of export engines onto canal barges. The Lion had an eight and a half inch cylinder with a three-foot stroke and a four-foot diameter driver wheel. Its use ceased in 1834. The boiler survived and is owned by The Smithsonian Institution, the US equivalent of The British Museums. This and other fragments of The Stourbridge Lion are currently exhibited at Baltimore in Maryland.

By contrast, the Agenoria of 1829 spent a much longer working life in Stourbridge coal shunting operations and is now on exhibition at The (British) National Railway Centre in York. (Agenoria was an obscure Mercian goddess).

In 1829 Rastrick was a judge at the Rainhill Trails, and Foster and Rastrick supplied fish-bellied rail for the 1830 Liverpool and Manchester Railway. Shortly after Rastrick left Stourbridge to work on the London and Brighton Railway project.

The New Foundry complex consists of the main shop pictured which is Listed Grade Two Star; the Georgian manager's residence Riverside House (Grade Two); and the former Canal Dry Dock with Workshops (Grade Two). Many of the later additions to the site have been cleared. The remaining complex is on the English Heritage "Buildings at Risk" register.

The West Midlands Historic Buildings Trust is leading intensive consultations to identify a sustainable use for these monuments. It is not known whether American agencies have been approached for assistance. The dry dock is full of debris and its entrance tunnel bricked-up. The foundry and workshop are vandalised and Riverside House has been burnt to a shell by arsonists, but is restorable.

When I visited in May 2005 there was fly-tipping and evidence of illegal vehicle breaking. There were also indications of haunting by drunks and drug abusers though the place was deserted on the sunny weekday afternoon. Perfunctory security measures were unattended and in disarray.

Amongst the options for sustainable use currently under study are a sports hall or a fifteen-doctor general practice for the New Foundry itself; and various combinations of residential, business and heritage conversions for the complex in general.

Like all of Britain's historic former industrial monuments its survival is very uncertain unless continuing economic employments can be found. Regrettably, this usually implies changes of use.

ROYALCOL
The Royal College Building at Glasgow

Location:	Eastern side of the Royal College Building on Montrose Street, Glasgow, Lanarkshire, Scotland, UK
Date of Photograph:	25 July 2003
OS Grid Reference:	NS595655
Co-ordinates:	55:51:43N 4:14:42W
Elevation:	38.1 meters

The Royal College building was erected between 1903 and 1912 and is the headquarters of a major technical university.

John Anderson was a notorious radical and Jacobin sympathiser who in 1791 invented a new type of cannon and presented it to the beleaguered Directory as his "Gift of Science to Liberty".

At the age of thirty Anderson had become Professor of Oriental Languages at Glasgow University, but his real vocation was the exciting new science of Natural Philosophy, and in 1760, at the age of 34, he become Glasgow's professor of that subject. This was the same year in which he published "The Institutes of Physics", a standard textbook for a hundred years. We no longer use the word "institutes" in his sense, but this book was probably the first publication is which the word "physics" was used in ours.

On 13th January 1796 the old scientist died. He left instructions that his estate should be employed to realise a university of "useful learning" to provide practical and vocational education, and "Anderson's Institution" was duly built.

The organisation has had at least eight different (official) names. For over two hundred years it has habitually got called "The Andersonian Institution": Never an officially-sanctioned appellation.

Today the University of Strathclyde is Scotland's leading scientific and technological research and teaching facility. Its patent royalty income topped £30 million in 2003 and it supports more than forty "spin-out" companies, ranking it seventh amongst UK new firms generators, and possibly the dominant non-Russell institution.

It is one of the UK's six Fulbright Centers for US exchange students and Scotland's third biggest university.

Strathclyde University has 22000 degree students including a large cohort of postgraduate students from nearly every country. It is Britain's biggest provider of taught master's degrees and there were 2279 international MSc students at the last count, which does not include EU students or business or arts scholars. Furthermore, there are 34000 continuing education students and 3200 staff. There are 360 courses taught, 160 at postgraduate level. It is one of Glasgow's largest employers.

The campus now occupies most of the land between the Cathedral and George Square in the very center of the city.

Amongst a galaxy of illustrious alumni are: The missionary, physician and explorer Dr David Livingstone; John Logie Baird, inventor of television and rubber socks; and numerous others.

The Author undertook his first two postgraduate degrees at Strathclyde University, both in Civil Engineering Hydraulics.

UCL
Snackers at UCL

Location: The Wilkins Building, University College London, Gower Street, Bloomsbury, London, England, UK
Date of Photograph: pm 26 May 2006
OS Grid Reference: TQ295822
Co-ordinates: 51:31:29N 0:08:02W
Elevation: 29.6 meters

The grand portico of University College London.
The University College London was founded in 1826 by a committee of liberal thinkers amongst whom James Mill, Jeremy Bentham and Henry Brougham were prominent. It was intended especially for those debarred from Oxford and Cambridge by reason of non-jurancy (not being confirmed members of The Church of England), and therefore was of immediate benefit to able Scots, Quakers, Jews and Catholics and eventually to those of any faith worldwide.
Alumni include Alexander Graham Bell, Gandhi, Jonathon Ross and Ricky Gervais.

UCL, as it is usually known, although technically part of The University of London, is a vast university in its own right, with an endowment of £90 million pounds and 21,620 students of whom 9,650 are postgraduates. There are 3,800 teaching faculty many of whom are active in research. In 2004 UCL was permitted to grant its own degrees alongside University of London ones.

UCL is a member of the "G5" British universities recognised by The Times as of "international standing" (the others being Oxford, Cambridge, The London School of Economics and The Imperial College of Science and Technology). UCL accounts for 40% of the entire UK university research expenditure, and occupies much of the inner London suburb of Bloomsbury, which, however, it shares with The British Museum, a number of big hotels, and numerous hospitals and smaller colleges.

It boasts 19 Nobel Laureates and 3 Fields Medal recipients (mathematicians). Currently, 35 Fellows of the Royal Society (of scientists) are employed.

The palatial Main Building illustrated (called prosaically The Wilkins Building) was built between 1825 and 1832 to a design by William Wilkins. It is an imposing if confined domed ashlar building with a decastyle composite pronaos.

WIGGIN
The Old Hall Works of the Former J&J Wiggin Limited

Location:	The Intersection of Revival and Woodall Streets, Bloxwich, Staffordshire, England, UK
Date of Photograph:	am 4 September 2007
OS Grid Reference:	SK000019
Co-ordinates:	52:36:56N: 2:00:04W
Elevation:	164 meters

Walsall has a centuries-old tradition of forging metal lorimery for horse harness and during Victorian times became the World's near-monopoly supplier of such essential tackle. With the onset of the twentieth-century, road transport technology was revolutionized whilst most of Europe's draught horses perished in the mud of Flanders, together with the continent's key men.

Walsall went into a sudden and steep decline from which it has never recovered.

But Staffordshire at large had another ancient tradition: The manufacture of luxury consumer durables for the elite classes. Such included enameled vinegarettes, crystal glass, china, decorated jasperware, black japan, silk, dress shoes, hunting jackets, flush lavatories and a plethora of other Bond Street exotica, including proverbially if more prosaically, the kitchen sink.

Even into the twentieth century strange synergies could crystallize.

James Thomas Wiggin and his son James Enoch lived in a row of eight terraced houses next to the former Free Methodist Chapel in Revival Street, Bloxwich. For some years the chapel had functioned as the local Salvation Army Mission Hall.

In 1893 the two James's established the firm of J&J Wiggin to make hand-forged buckle tongs in their Bloxwich homes. The capital assets comprised a set of hammers, an anvil and a coke-fired hearth.

As the business grew, James Thomas's four other sons joined the firm and in 1901 it became necessary to expand next door into the now-unoccupied old Mission Hall: The premises that was to give the company a name of world renown.

J&J Wiggin diversified into curb-chain making and nickel and brass casting. By 1904 thirty people were employed. In 1913 Wiggin acquired the nearby drop-forge works of V Broadhurst and Company that made bridle bits and stirrups. The Broadhurst arm later changed to making pipe flanges and was still functional in 1960.

It was also in 1913, in the Yorkshire town of Sheffield some seventy miles North of Walsall, that the metallurgist Harry Brierley invented a remarkable chrome-iron alloy that would not rust or tarnish and was immune to much other chemical attack. He called his creation stainless steel though it was initially marketed as "Staybrite".

The First World War interrupted normal evolutions when, in common with all other British factories the works was greatly expanded and re-tooled to make arms and ammunition. It was in 1914 that the chapel and houses were quickly demolished and the current sheds and offices erected.

In 1920 normal service resumed with the manufacture of chromium-plated brass bathroom fittings. The plated brass was soon replaced with "Staybrite". For the first time the firm used the "Old Hall" trademark to market this material. The eclipse of the horse necessitated further changes in the product range. The manufacture of roller skates was entered to cater to the new craze, and windscreen frames were made for Ford and Standard cars.

In 1928 a decisive event occurred. William Wiggin was by now in charge and had just celebrated twenty-five years of marriage to Nellie. The couple had received numerous presents of silver tableware, but Nellie felt that the expense of post-war service made this (so to say) a white elephant, in view of the continuous polishing required in the sulfurous Black Country atmosphere. She suggested to her husband that they make tableware of stainless steel. Experiments were put in hand. The first such product to go on sale was a toast rack, and then in 1930 the World's first stainless steel teapot was born.

In 1934 The Daily Mail newspaper sponsored the Ideal Home Exhibition at Olympia in Kensington, West London. The Sheffield steelmakers Thomas Firth and John Brown occupied a part of the exhibition space they called "Staybrite City". Wiggins sub-let part of this area to exhibit their "Old Hall" range of stainless steel tableware which was very well received and Dr WH Hatfield, Head of Research at Firth Brown, commissioned Harold Stabler to design a range of tea and coffee services for Wiggins.

During World War Two the Wiggin works re-tooled to make chains for The Royal Navy, but in 1945 the growing range of Old Hall hollowware resumed its rapid expansion.

In the 1950's and 1960's, Robert Welch was commissioned to design a toast rack, dishes and cutlery in the modern idiom. He won several awards for his Old Hall work and the pieces are now collectors' favorites. In 1958 Wiggins won the contract to outfit the new P&O liner "Oriana" with Welch-designed hollowware. By then five hundred people crowded the small factory on the site of the old mission hall.

The stainless steel tableware seemed to last perpetually and had replaced silver as the usual form of wedding-present hollowware. J&J Wiggin was now the largest hollowware maker in the World.

Wiggins floated as a public-limited company in 1960 and its acquisition of The Cheltenham Tool Company in 1967 added "Lifespan" stainless steel cutlery to the product range. In 1968 it bought The Bridge Crystal Glass Company.

In 1970, Old Hall was itself absorbed into the Prestige Group of domestic metalware companies. But during the Seventies a decline in demand for UK hollowware, and indeed other British products, accelerated. British industrial concerns agglomerated into ever larger defensive combines in a largely futile attempt to resist foreign predatory behavior but in a shrinking world other governments were quick to assist native enterprise that promised to put an end to British competition once and for all.

By now, the American firm Oneida was the largest company in the field and sought to eliminate its World competition, by whatever means. In 1982 it purchased J&J Wiggin and on 29th June 1984, Oneida closed The Old Hall Works.

The surviving scion of the Wiggin dynasty lives in nearby Levedale and is president of a flourishing Old Hall collectors' society. Members exchange pieces, and in addition there is no difficulty in purchasing Old Hall ware on the Internet.

The semi-derelict factory now accommodates the intermittently-active Tudor pine furniture workshop and a working automobile repair shop. A small annex warehouses spares for a discontinued commercial vehicle, the Ford Transit van. And the rest is a roost for feral pigeons. In March 2009 the Old Hall showed signs of fire damage.

Postscript 29 May 2022

Shortly after the photograph was taken the entire site was cleared. The western side of Woodhall Street (pictured) was replaced with modern terrace housing. The eastern site remains derelict land.

An Old Hall Bon Bon Dish of circa 1965

CHAPTER THIRTEEN

Changing Trade

Any discussion of Britain's recent changes in trade has to be dominated by the salient facts of the nation's post-war history: The collapse of its traditional activity sectors; mining, manufacturing and shipping.

The eclipse of these great employers and export earners has set the backdrop to the socio-economic milieu of the Britain of 2009 and determined the character of many of the monuments of vernacular culture that you can now photograph and describe.

At the end of The Second World War nearly half of all Britons worked in manufacturing, and millions more in mining and the sea-related trades. Today, in 2008, mining occupies about five thousand, and with 3,527,800 jobs remaining in manufactures that secondary sector employs some 13.1% of the workforce.

The UK population is thought to be around sixty million of whom about 29.4 million are "working", but the position is confused by the presence of an unknown number of foreign transients or immigrants, many of whom are *de facto* workers. These are thought to number up to three million at a given instant. The British working age is taken to be between 18 and 65 years of age, although a person is legally permitted to leave school at 16 and may continue to work until death.

In 1875 the British Merchant Marine weighed 50 million deadweight tons spread between maybe 60000 ships. By 1982 that was only 30 million DWT.

Any figures I present for the 2007 size of the British merchant fleet are probably meaningless. This is because of the extremely promiscuous nature of globalised asset ownership and the fact that different assessors include or exclude different types and sizes of ship. One possibly realistic estimate is that the British merchant navy is around 9566275 DWT comprising 673 British-owned vessels of which 429 are British-registered.

A more pessimistic appraisal from the industry was that by 1998 there were a mere 1100000 DWT of British-owned shipping, spread between about one hundred ships. British-*registered* ships were only 200000 DWT, dominated by a handful of American-owned Cunarders. Between 1980 and 1997 the number of British Merchant Marine officers fell by 78% and ratings by 65%. Notwithstanding all of that, 95% of all British tonnage of exports and imports is still sea-borne, or 77% by value, and 7% of domestic tonnage in the archipelago is transported by water. In 2007, World shipping increased by 4%.

Meanwhile, British aviation handled 112.5 million commercial passenger tickets in 1994 that rose to 232 million in 2007, an average 6% annual compound growth.

A major spasm of de-industrialisation occurred in 1981 and especially affected the heavy engineering sector and its ancillary services, causing physical devastation of the landscape across much of Ulster, Scotland and Northern England. It was remarked at the time that Margaret Thatcher had destroyed more acreage of British industry than had Adolf Hitler. Misery continued throughout the Eighties as the coal industry and its dependent trade disappeared and the rump of heavy engineering and shipbuilding was cleared in 1991.

After 1992, the physical economy resumed an uneasy stability and some areas expanded. The luxury durables sector had largely weathered the storm and in addition a somewhat antithetical duopoly of health-related and arms-related industries had emerged to dominate manufacturing revenues.

Between 1995 and 2002 UK industrial production fell by 0.1% compared with an aggregate increase of 18% for the OECD industrial nations, and 14.3% for the EU. Germany and France increased factory production by 16.5% and 16.4% respectively. Surprisingly, Japan showed a fall of 4.8% in this period. But in 2002 alone British production dropped 4%.

After the War, the British pharmaceutical industry emerged from a century of struggle in the face of US and German oligopolies. In 1987-90 milliards (thousands of millions) of pounds Sterling worth of research investment yielded British pharma firms a two-to-one patent ratio vis-à-vis competitor nations, America excluded. By 1995 British medicinal drug exports were worth six milliard pounds, second only to North Sea Oil, and the British medical drug trade surplus with the rest of the World was two milliards Sterling. Seventy-five thousand Britons worked in pharmaceutical factories and a further quarter of a million were indirectly employed, though an unknown large number of these were employed overseas.

The British are notoriously coy about defence-related installations and employment but arms and aerospace are thought to be the principal remaining manufactures. This is possibly reflected in the fact that Hampshire and Lancashire are now the UK's leading factory counties (respectively 88000 hands or 13.1% of county employment; and 76100 for 16.2%). Hampshire includes the Solent Conurbation of naval-related industrialisation and Lancashire the Ribbleside fighter-plane industry and several semi-governmental nuclear establishments. In 2005 the UK aerospace industry (which has a significant civil component) had a turnover of £22.7 milliard, the largest aerospace industry in the World, the US excepted. A further £6.5 milliard was earned from UK aerospace manufactures in other lands. The net contribution to the British trade balance was a positive £2.3 milliard. Direct UK employment is 124000, with a further 152000 in ancillary goods and services.

Around the end of the Eighties a revival in the British finance sector coincided with the Canary Wharf development in London's East End. That development was itself a reuse of dockland made redundant when the Port of London collapsed in 1980, as did the ports of Liverpool and Hull at around the same time. Some allege that British banking and investment finance, including international stock and commodities dealing, has now regained the World supremacy lost to New York during The First World War. According to one contemporary American assessment, London is the top financial center of the Earth. The London Stock Exchange is the World's largest foreign exchange market with a daily turnover rate of $504 billion dollars, which is more then New York and Tokyo combined. It is said to control over 80% of Europe's capital assets and 20% of the world's investment fund assets.

The only British finance department to suffer a recent decline is insurance. Many of the problems of insurance reflect the disappearance of the ships and factories that constituted its staple basis, and increasing reliance upon the retail sector, where high premiums and payout defaults have eroded trade relative to foreign providers. The Refuge left its old headquarters in Central Manchester for cheaper suburban premises at Wilmslow, following many such firms in a provincial diaspora. The old Refuge Building on Oxford Street is now a conference hotel for the likes of foreign tourists and home-based examiners' conventions. Lloyd's of London suffered a severe crisis in the period 1988 to 1994 that bankrupted many of its "names" (unlimited liability investors).

Meanwhile cargo handling containerised, and much of UK sea-borne trade now passes through the port of Felixstowe in Suffolk, which handles 35% of UK container cargo, although other significant container ports exist at Southampton, Tilbury, Thamesport (Grain) and Liverpool. Container handlings rose form 2.753 million units in 1988 to 4.467 million in 1999.

The collapse of extensive basic industries has led to a return of the kinds of intractable structural unemployment that bedevilled the Britain of the 1930's. The Governments of the last twenty-five years have, however, been reluctant to acknowledge the scale of the problem, probably because remedial options are limited whilst experience has shown that any widespread discussion of employment or labor issues is electorally disastrous.

As in the Thirties the clerical and semi-skilled classes have been especially hard-hit, though a novel feature of modern unemployment is its more even presence at all socio-educational levels.

In 2008 formal registered unemployment by JSA-claiming job seekers is approximately 754600, with a further 895400 registered job seekers not claiming contributory dole. But in addition some three million are temporarily "incapacitated" (not registered invalids) and in receipt of the appropriate benefit whilst a few thousand are on short-term employer-funded sick leave. It is claimed that whilst the actual National Health Service (NHS) costs £100 milliard per annum, an equal figure is expended in support of the absent sick. Taken together these health-related costs account for some 20% of the British GNP. In addition to this four and a half million of effective unemployed there are probably an equal number of submerged jobless including single parents and miscellaneous inactives (excluding pensioners), on and off State benefits. So there are about nine million *de facto* unemployed for an "at work" population of 29.4 million, or about 23.4%. The number of "asylum seekers" and other foreign migrants who are unemployed in Britain is not known. In December 2007 the British Government admitted to 7.92 million economically-inactive persons of working age of whom 2.26 million were housewives or househusbands. This official figure is 21.2% of the labor force. Amongst the over-fifties unemployment is much higher, probably over thirty percent.

Partially to address issues of structural unemployment, the incoming government of 1997 determined to expand the public sector, especially in health and education. In a regime of low income tax and declining fiscal revenues from other sources this expenditure would be financed by State borrowing.

Clearly many of the unemployed or marginally in work were not professionally qualified for traditional medical or teaching rôles, but ancillary or clerical positions, often part-time, could be created to absorb large numbers.

By September 2007 total public sector employment had reached 5.770 million, about 20% of the labor force. 435000 State schoolteachers were almost outnumbered by 306000 internal school support staff. In early 2008 the Government decided to enforce pay-parity between the sexes in Local Government employment. Remarkable anomalies "came to light". In one Black Country primary school for 4 to 11-year-olds the headmaster protested that he had immediately to conjure £165000 from a miniscule annual budget, whereupon scrutiny discovered that in a school of 450 students the 15 teachers were helped by 45 support staff. Other council services were creatively overmanned, and the NHS was no different.

National Health Service figures are difficult to obtain, but in the case of Northern Ireland a Parliamentary question elicited that whilst in March 2001 the province had 41526.81 WTE (Whole Time Equivalent) units of staff, five years later the figure was 50418.97, a rise of 21.4%. If the latter figure is extrapolated to the UK on a populational *pro-rata* basis, then the whole NHS employs the equivalent of 1753900 full-time workers. Previously, from 1998 to 2004, Birmingham University College Hospitals (UHB) staff rose from 4787 persons to 6550, a rise of 36.82%. I should emphasise that the vast majority of these are not clinicians: 55% of UHB staff have either no qualifications, or only GCSE or A-level standard certification.

In Birmingham as a whole, in Britain's leading industrial city, 25% of labor was employed in the public sector (other than the NHS), well over 100000 people.

One estimate is that UK public sector employment grew by a net 860000 jobs between 1997 and 2006, with a forecast for an additional 360000 in the years 2007 to 2009. Of that estimated 1220000 only some 331000 are "front line workers" (e.g. doctors, nurses, teachers, policemen), some 27%. The rest are "managerial" or ancillary workers. This contrasts with a 481000-job private sector growth between 1997 and 2004. In the same interval the claimant count fell by 787000.

In England 20% of workers are in the public sector, about 23% in Wales and 25% in Scotland. In Northern Ireland 30% of the workforce is in the public sector.

Overall, the NHS and education together account for 60% of State employment, contrasted with 40% in 1983.

Meanwhile, revenue-generating employment has continued to fall. In a third spasm of de-industrialisation around the year 2003 "Staffordshire Work" and other luxury consumer durable manufactures were decimated. The former battleship-maker Vickers sold its Rolls-Royce car subsidiary to German interests, but production was resumed at new premises in Sussex. Two-hundred-year-old potter Royal Doulton closed its Nile Street (Stoke) factory and outsourced all further production to the Far East, as largely did other ceramics firms, except Royal Worcester which favored Portuguese manufacture. The UK's last toymaker, teddy bear producer Merrythought closed its doors, but re-opened to make a handful of collectors' bears. Stafford luxury shoemaker Lotus (established 1759) had already left the town by 1998. By 1994 the entire Leek silk industry had disappeared, as had by 2001 the major part of the Stourbridge table crystal manufacture: All World-famous brands.

Novel occupations have emerged, or revived.

By 1999, 647000 worked in the arts outwith education, accounting for 2.4% of employment, more than British agriculture. Respectable export earnings were collectively achieved, including some taken from tourists visiting London's West End Theatreland. One third of Britain's cultural workers are London-based, and the South-East as a whole contains the majority of them. Recent employment growth rates are variously estimated as 70% amongst librarians, 40% amongst curators and 300% for musicians. Sixty-five percent of arts workers are male except amongst librarians and archivists, who are 70% female. Fifty-three percent of cultural workers are graduates whereas 24% of those employed in the general UK economy have degrees.

In other sectors of the UK's quaternary "knowledge economy" estimates of growth and decline are bedevilled by definitional problems, both as regards what is a "knowledge industry", and within a knowledge industry what is a "knowledge worker". Controversially, many formulations include such as call-center operatives whom many regard as at best semi-skilled. An indubitable component is British higher education (universities and teaching technical institutes) that has witnessed dramatic commercial growth in the last thirty years and now contributes £5.5 milliard to Britain's annual foreign exchange earnings. But printing and publishing, classified as manufacture because a physical product is produced, accounts for about 20% of UK generated value-added even today, only slightly less than the lead sector, food processing. Today (17th March 2008) the American firm News International opened the World's largest printing press at Broxbourne in Hertfordshire. Equipped with twelve gigantic color printing machines it covers an area of 1.1 million square feet and cost £110 million. The establishment will produce the three major News International newspaper titles, The Times and The Sun dailies, and The Sunday Times. These newspapers were, before the 1980's, made at Printing House Square off Fleet Street in the very center of London. When the London Docks closed the company moved its presses to cheaper and more accessible derelict ground at Wapping in the East End. Simultaneous computerisation enabled journalists to commit copy direct to forme, an innovation that disemployed an entire class of London print artisans. Now land values and access issues have prompted a move to a far suburb. The British writing industry is still the most important in the World, excluding, as we usually must, the American. Dizzy growth rates for the UK knowledge industries are sometimes canvassed, but in the case of Computer Services it is from a very low base: In this case £18.3 milliard in 1999 after 138.7% growth from 1994, but still very impressive, though much depends upon imported technology. Home-grown software offshore business rose form £3 milliard in 2000 to £8.7 milliard in 2007.

So much for the grand conspectus.

Now let me paint you a picture.

Malvern is a genteel Georgian spa town of 28749 souls, sleeping below the looming mass of The Worcestershire Beacon (1395 feet), a small mountain visible from most hilltops in Central England, and whose solicitous brow ensures the little conurbation never suffers a sunset or even a chill Welsh wind.

From the top of The Worcestershire Beacon a toposcope indicates the peaks visible in the clearest weather: The Harboro Rocks of The White Peak, 74.4 miles North; The Wrekin a mere forty miles; Snowdon the summit of Wales, 98.75 miles West and, right across The Mercian Plain, Ivinghoe Beacon in The Chilterns 75.8 miles South-East.

Falling through Pre-Cambrian diorites, tonalites and granites Malvern Water is famous for containing "nothing at all" and for many decades was bottled and exported by Schweppes. This famous mixer maker was founded at Bristol, England in 1783 and is another of those epicene organisations that is not quite sure whether it is American or British. It now appears to be an arm of the equally ambidextrous Coca-Cola Corporation.

Along the windswept ridge between the Beacon and his brother, The Herefordshire Beacon, strode chemist and greatest of England's lonely composers Sir Edward Elgar as he dreamt of Gerontius and formulated his great requiem to our fallen, the Cello Concerto in E Minor. As the first flakes of that silenced autumn fell aloft he may have surveyed with pride the ghostly green glow of the twinkling lights below. Malvern is one of only two remaining British towns with a handful of gas lamps in whole streets. Malvern's remaining 109 grace the Priory Churchyard and three or four hill-skirt streets where they are presumably appreciated by Malvern's many specters who, however, are so numerous they would be obliged to share. Certainly those two literary luminaries CS Lewis and JRR Tolkein approved the gas lamps when the lanterns lit the snow along their walks together. Perhaps all were charmed alike by the whistle of the Hereford train as it dove through a high tunnel to emerge at Colwall where Piers Plowman turned the sod for Langland in the shadowed dawn of English letters. Malvern is a little less jealous of the original red penny-post pillar-boxes of the 1840's for of these she arrogates only four of the six surviving examples.

East from the Worcestershire Beacon's summit the little conurbation of Malvern is laid out as if in an aerial photograph. Its great public school Malvern College founded in 1865 has 539 students, and numbers amongst its old boys Jeremy Paxman, Aleister Crowley, Francis Aston, Denholm Elliott and CS Lewis. It is famous for a stained glass clerestory that honors its boys who fell in The Great War. Fees are up to £22000 per annum, but are a fraction of that for day-boys. One hundred are employed. Malvern Girls' College is a separate school that occupies EW Elmslie's Imperial Hotel that was completed in August 1862 at a cost of £18000. It remains one of the largest buildings in the town, a token of Malvern's mid-Victorian heyday as a great spa resort.

Malvern is very Mercian and literary.

Besides its municipal theater it has, since 1999, boasted The Theatre of Little Convenience, the smallest in the World. Founded by Mr Dennis Neale in a derelict Victorian gentlemen's public lavatory it presents an eclectic repertoire of drama, opera and recital. But it has something of a specialism in puppetry, for which it has international renown.

Possibly the largest employer in Malvern is QinetiQ (pronounce it "kinetic"), a shadowy "defence technology" company that started as The Telecommunication Research Establishment when, in 1940, the Government partly retreated to Malvern because it was expected that London and the South-East would fall under Nazi occupation. The TRE occupied the Malvern College buildings and still occupies its land. Also in 1940 John Randall and Henry Boot came from Birmingham University, bringing with them their cavity magnetron. This is a quantum-physical resonant centimetric microwave generation device, key to the development of scanning radar. The device is also the driving element of microwave cookers. After the War the TRE transmuted into The Royal Radar Establishment.

Today, as QinetiQ, the Malvern outfit is one of the largest arms research concerns on Earth, confessedly employing some 11400. QinetiQ (Co.Ltd.?, LLC?, plc?) is yet another of these promiscuously interpenetrated Anglo-American organisations, especially, but not exclusively, in the weapons sector. Whilst still under British MoD control it purchased several American defence technology companies. During the privatisation of this firm in 2001 the British public was excluded from share purchase arrangements, but the company was already 33% owned by the US Carlyle Group, and as of 2008 the ownership and control of QinetiQ, and its activities, are unclear.

The health technology sector is represented by two laboratory glassware specialist manufacturers.

Forty-year-old Malvern Instruments has since 1970 especially concerned itself with particle size analysis instrumentation, with rheological devices, and with nebulisers for medical and agricultural applications. It too has partially acquired technology through company acquisition.

In Pickersleigh Avenue is "what now remains" (their words, not mine) of the great Chance Brothers glass works of Smethwick. A very small factory produces microscope slides for medical practice, precision bore glass tubing and hypodermic syringes. The firm demerged from Pilkington's at the end of the twentieth century and once again functions as an independent entity.

Next door to Chance is the slightly more extensive works of The Morgan Motor Company, the largest British car-maker. Founded in 1909 it specialises in hand-built retro-styled sports cars. For these it has long waiting lists, currently about eighteen months, down from ten years. A family firm, Morgan employs 163 and output 640 cars in 2007.

CANADA
The Canada Tower at Poplar

Location: The Canada Tower, One Canada Square, Canary Wharf,
                       Poplar, London
Date of Photograph: pm 14 September 2004
OS Grid Reference: TQ375803
Co-ordinates: 51:30:19N 0:01:08W
Elevation: 11.3 meters

This is The Canada Tower, now usually called One Canada Square, but widely known as The Canary Wharf Tower or even simply Canary Wharf after its geographical location. Riparian London is reclaimed swampland underlain by a mobile Eocene clay and is not economically suitable for the erection of tall buildings.

The Canada Tower, however, has a squat aspect ratio and very deep foundations, and at 235 meters or 771 feet the tallest habitable building in The British Isles. It accommodates commercial premises on fifty stories and is Europe's second tallest building. There is no observation platform and access to the structure is controlled, due to Britain's vulnerability to terrorist attack.

The Isles of Dogs is a swampy peninsula in a broad meander loop of the tidal River Thames, about five kilometers East of the notional center of The City of London around The Guildhall. For many centuries it was a sodden and malarial place, avoided for habitation and perhaps apocryphally the place Henry VIII kenneled his dogs. In any event, the modern Canary Wharf is no pun as sometimes thought: The name dates from as recently as the 1920's when banana boats from the Canary Islands started to dock there.

Around the end of the eighteenth century, West India merchant Robert Milligan was dismayed at his losses to theft and delay when ships reached London. Besides general indiscipline and incompetence, the delays were caused by congestion upon land and water, and the fact that twice a day moored shipping was grounded by the tide. Milligan combined with George Hibbert and other influential traders to promote a West India Dock Company that would construct a walled wet dock in the Isle of Dogs area.

The enabling West India Dock Act 1799 was passed and construction of the two Northern Docks commenced the next year.

William Jessop, assisted by consulting engineer John Rennie, completed these, the first wet docks in London, by 27th August 1802, when they were opened by William Pitt the Younger and his Lord Chancellor, Lord Loughborough.

The docks comprised a thirty acre Import Dock, the North Dock, and a 24 acre Export, or Middle Dock. Because the docks unbridged an isthmus, ship and lighter traffic could be marshaled systematically across the complex to minimise congestion. A complex of warehouses was built at the Import Dock from which ships would process to the Export Dock to load with return cargos.

Much later, in the 1860's, a larger South Dock was added to the complex, and it became the case that the Isle of Dogs, a true island since 1800, also became almost more water than land.

During the 1960's and 1970's British shipping and trade declined dramatically and the Port of London, including the West India Docks, was virtually abandoned. Ships had in any case become too large to approach the city through the shallows and had to dock at more Easterly wharfages such as Tilbury, Felixstowe or Sheerness. Furthermore, the containerisation of handling meant that less congested rail and road access was necessary, and this could be arranged at these relatively more rural places.

Commerce and industry in London's East End failed, and unemployment and outmigration ensued.

The West India Docks were officially closed in 1980.

Around that time the British Government sought to regenerate The East End but was partly frustrated by its own ideological commitment to laissez-faire. Nevertheless, the Canadian firm Olympia and York were commissioned to develop a grandiose scheme of US-style skyscraper precincts around Canary Wharf on the isthmus part of the old West India Docks. The water acreage was to be retained as an amenity feature.

Unfortunately, the project bankrupted Olympia and York, but by the late Eighties the outline had been laid and commercial tenants from further West in London, and indeed Worldwide, took leases.

Argentine architect César Pelli was asked to design a skyscraper similar to an existing Olympia and York edifice in New York, and by 1987 he had commenced construction of The Canada Tower.

The structure is in the form of an approximate square prism surmounted by a pyramid and is faced in stainless steel panels and flush plate glass. It contains 4388 internal steps, 32 passenger lifts, 2 cargo lifts and 2 firemen's lifts. The lobby is 36 feet high, paneled in Italian marble. The basement contains a shopping mall and a rapid transit interchange.

The Canada Tower was constructed in four years despite a four-month builders' strike and opened to tenants in 1991. None of the tenants occupy Floor 13: That is for air-conditioning equipment only.

There are currently 28 tenants including The Trinity Mirror newspaper group, The Bank of New York, KPMG, Coutts and Company (the Royal bankers), The Swiss Stock Exchange, and several international trade associations including those for sugar, grains and health products.

City Pride

Postscript 29 May 2022

The Shard by Renzo Piano at (1016 ft or 309.6 meters) is now the tallest habitable building in London. The Shard is currently the tallest European skyscraper west of Warsaw.

HOLLYLOD
Flats in Oakeshott Avenue at Highgate

Location:	Oakeshott Avenue, Holly Lodge Estate, Highgate, London, England, UK
Date of Photograph:	am 12 October 2006
OS Grid Reference:	TQ285868
Co-ordinates:	51:33:58N: 0:08:50W
Elevation:	88.1 meters

In 1798 Sir Henry Tempest built a villa on Highgate Rise overlooking London, spread out on the alluvial plain to the South. It was this house that was to become Holly Lodge, and it stood in a big park that constituted one of the largest tracts of undeveloped land in Middlesex. In 1815, the royal banker, Thomas Coutts acquired the villa and purchased the adjacent lots. When Coutts wife, Harriet Mellon died in 1837, she left this extensive, and now potentially-valuable, property to her husband's grand-daughter, the socialite Angela Burdett.

Between 1849 and 1906, Holly Lodge was used for lavish private festivals that royalty and statesmen attended, but when Angela Burdett-Coutts died, her husband placed the whole estate on the market. Perhaps surprisingly, it failed to sell as a unity, so in 1907 it was re-offered in several lots, but again there was no buyer interest. Finally, in

1922 fragments of the estate were sold, and in 1923 the central element known as "The Holly Lodge Estate" was purchased by The London Garden Suburbs Limited for £45000. The actual lodge villa was demolished and high-density development commenced.

    Women and girls had always worked in the mining and manufactures of Britain, but invariably near to the home where fathers, husbands and brothers could guard their virtue. Accordingly, an important exception to female employment was the transport sector, broadly defined, including the London specialties of banking, insurance and brokerage work. Around the time of Victoria's death, however, the status of commercial clerical work declined and wages stagnated. The male mobility and mortality of The First World War accelerated changes in employment, and women who had entered the labor market stayed in it, and began to drift to big cities to look for office or light industrial work.

    Nevertheless, many women of the type who sought City work were not at ease with the concept of shared lodgings with male strangers, and accordingly the Lady Workers' Homes Limited acquired the estate to cater to their wants. So instead of houses as originally intended, it was decided to build blocks of bed-sitting room apartments with shared lavatories, and with kitchens and meal rooms in centralised communal facilities.

    The first bedsit block was Langbourne Mansions with 88 units, quickly followed by blocks on Makepeace and Oakeshott Avenues with respective totals of 269 rooms and 408 flats.

    The communities were gated, and the dining centers also had reading rooms, theatres and tennis courts. Whilst the streets were tarmacadamed they were narrow, and access for motor vehicles was inconvenient. No garages were provided. Male tenants were not permitted and male callers discouraged.

    Each block is four or five stories in a uniform Tudorbeathan idiom with gabled and balconied South facades intervisible with the city center four miles away. The rear and side elevations are in a plain style.

    By the early 1960's the privately-landlorded blocks were in disrepair and in 1964 The Metropolitan Borough of St Pancras (now The London Borough of Camden) assumed a 150-year lease on the entire estate, and recently the policy of only placing women on the estate has been allowed to lapse. New regulations dictate that tenants must have private bathrooms and kitchens, and in 2004 alterations were put in hand to extend all bed-sitting rooms in this way, with a corresponding decrease in occupational densities. The central dining and leisure facility was closed in the 1950's and later replaced by Camden Council with further flats.

    Together with the Modernist development at Roehampton, Holly Lodge is arguably the most salubrious of the UK's notorious council estates.

HOPEX
The Hop and Malt Exchange at Southwark

Location: Southwark Street, Southwark, London SE1, England
Date of Photograph: pm 13 September 2007
OS Grid Reference: TQ325801
Co-ordinates: 51:30:18N: 0:05:29W
Elevation: 6 meters

The hop is a climbing vine-like plant that can be used as a traditional preservative in beer. It imparts a distinctive bitter taste, the essential flavoring of English "bitter" beers, traditionally drunk at room temperature. Hops were introduced to England from the Netherlands, possibly around the Seventeenth-Century.

Hops are grown in Herefordshire and Kent, but it is the latter source that supplied the brewers of Southwark and of wider London, and that was offered for auction upon the floor of The Hop Exchange. Kentish hops were harvested by seasonal London labor and brought to Southwark by river or later by rail to London Bridge.

The Hop and Malt Exchange was built to the design of RH Moore with extensive skylights to illuminate the trading floor and stories of internal balconies for the bidders. Behind the balconies are traders' offices. The cast iron balcony rails are decorated by courses of the arms of The County of Kent, a white horse rampant upon a gules shield. The splendid Southwark Street porch has an external tympanum with a fine sculpted relief illustrating hop-pickers at work.

Many similar commodity exchanges once graced London, but most have fallen to war, fire or re-development. The Hop Exchange was itself severely damaged by fire in 1918, necessitating the removal of the upper two stories.

Since the demolition of The Coal Exchange in the 1960's, and the successive modernizations of the Stock and Metal Exchanges, The Hop Exchange has been the only survivor of the metropolis's old-fashioned outcry floors.

MERRY
The Merrythought Teddy Bear Factory at Ironbridge

Location:	The Merrythought Company Limited, Dale End, The Wharfage, Ironbridge, Shropshire, England, UK
Date of Photograph:	am 16 November 2007
OS Grid Reference:	SJ666037
Co-ordinates:	52:37:48N 2:29:38W
Elevation:	42.7 meters

      Coalbrookdale is usually thought of as the Birthplace of Industry, but here it shows an industry habitually associated with the nonage of man.

      The Ironbridge Gorge is crowded with industrial monuments that in the eighteenth century based themselves on the valley's then seemingly infinite resources of coal, ironstone, fireclay and bitumen. It is a United Nations World Heritage Site.

      In 1894 the German toymaker Sussenguth Brothers presented a stuffed toy bear in their catalog. Three years later, their competitor Steiff showed its "Roly-Poly" bear at a Leipzig trade fair, and by 1899 Margarete Steiff had patents for twenty-three of her soft toy designs including several ursine themes.

In 1902 American satirist Clifford Berryman published, in the Washington Post, a cartoon of noted huntsman Theodore Roosevelt refusing to shoot a bear cub. The cartoon was syndicated worldwide and the US Commander-in-Chief was indelibly associated with a little bear. The "Teddy Bear" was born, and by November Morris Michtom had sold the first in his Brooklyn shop.

The next year Steiff exported three thousand 55PB bears to the USA, and they and their American competitors dominated the craze before The Great War.

In 1919, the Armistice brought slump to the enormous and workmanlike British textile industry. Notwithstanding, WG Holmes and GH Laxton opened a small mill in Yorkshire to spin imported mohair. They purchased Dyson Hall and Company Limited of Huddersfield and expanded vertically into weaving mohair plush.

To provide an outlet for their mohair plush they made a further vertical move into soft toy manufacture, and in September 1930 teddy bear maker Merrythought Limited was founded. Holmes and Laxton set it up in a temporary factory with a workforce of twenty, including managers enticed from Birmingham rival Chad Valley.

In February 1931 Merrythought leased an 1898 foundry complex from The Coalbrookdale Company. This premises was of course at Ironbridge, to which Merrythought moved.

Another key worker from Chad Valley was the deaf mute artist Florence Attwood who presented thirty-two toy designs for the 1930 season, and the first teddy in 1931. She prepared a range of soft toy designs for Merrythought until her death in 1949.

By 1932, over two hundred were employed at Dale End and the works was electrified. After three more years Merrythought was the largest soft toy maker in the United Kingdom.

In September 1939 the Merrythought factory was requisitioned by The Admiralty. Teddy production was banished to extempore works in nearby Wellington. The Dale End factory's situation in a wooded defile made aerial bombing difficult. The Ironbridge complex was given over to secret map-making and plywood storage. Later, The Royal Navy used Dale End to make uniform badges, helmet linings, gas mask bags, specialist ammunition bags and a diversity of war goods made form gabardine and velour.

In March 1946, toy production resumed at the Dale End site. Nylon and Draylon entered the fabric and new machinery was installed. In 1955 a compressed-air actuated stuffing machine was imported from the US and worked in parallel with hand stuffing. During this era of post-war expansion the foundry buildings were renovated and design and commercial offices, as well as a showroom, erected on site. The next year Merrythought purchased the freehold from The Coalbrookdale Company.

Throughout the Sixties and Seventies, however, British consumer manufactures suffered a dramatic decline in the face of foreign competition. Many such industries were based upon a pre-scientific handicraft tradition and were aimed squarely at achieving a product life of decades, if not centuries, in a market where unit cost was no desideratum.

In its latter years, Merrythought boasted that it was the last British toymaker and that no two of its examples were identical. An American or Japanese maker would of course have regarded the latter diagnostic of process misconfiguration. In 1988 Merrythought opened a teddy bear retail outlet in an old shop premises beside the works gate.

On 27th November 2006 Merrythought should have been at its busiest point of the year. Fifty-six year old engineer Oliver Holmes, grandson of the founder, called his forty-eight remaining workers together. He thanked his staff for their talent and loyalty. He remarked that it was impossible for Merrythought to compete with foreign goods made at "significantly lower" manufacturing and overhead costs. The workers were told that they would not get their redundancy money until after Christmas.

The next day television news reported the closure and interviewed some of Merrythought's tearful former employees before the factory gate. Later a journalist explained that it cost in one week to run the Telford workshops what it cost in one year to run a Chinese teddy bear factory. He added that Merrythought toys start at £40 whereas you could buy an imported teddy for a fiver.

On 14th December 2006 Merrythought Toys Limited was placed into Creditors' Voluntary Liquidation. Some of its major creditors, the employees, were however in a difficult position because the principal saleable asset, the designs' patents and copyrights, were the property of the holding company, Merrythought Limited, which was not in liquidation.

Collectors worldwide "ran on" toyshops and cleared the shelves of remaining Merrythought product.

On 24th January 2007 the Merrythought Toys Limited residual body, Smudged Limited, sold its stock, assets and work-in-progress to Merrythought Limited and within five months a 2007 Merrythought catalog was published. Limited production for the collectors' market resumed at Dale End.

The British bear had been reprieved.

He would now set you back between £47 and £295.

A Sad Teddy In the Window of the Merrythought Shop

PARKLANE
The Old Cleveland Petrol Station at Fallings Park

Location: The Old Cleveland Petrol Station, Park Lane, Fallings Park, Wednesbury, Staffordshire, England, UK
Date of Photograph: pm 20 November 1999
OS Grid Reference: SO989968
Co-ordinates: 52:34:10N 2:01:03W
Elevation: 115 meters

Cleveland Petrol was named for Cleveland, the district in the North Riding of Yorkshire, and not as is sometimes thought, Cleveland Ohio.

Cleveland was taken over by Esso, the European avatar of Standard Oil, sometime during the 1930's. The brand specialised in alcoholic gasoline mixtures exemplified by its "Discol" offering, and various types of benzolated gasoline.

The latter made a brief re-appearance on the British market as loaded high-compression petrol was phased-out during the Nineties, but was itself rapidly withdrawn due to its known carcinogenic effects.

Cleveland earned something of a reputation for the high quality of its gratis road maps given to customers at its filling stations: These are now expensive collectors' items.

In 1972 Esso decided to withdraw the Cleveland brand and its specialist fuels and by 1974 stocks were exhausted.

In the late Eighties' and Nineties I frequently passed the Park Lane filling station and noticed its gradual disintegration. When I last passed in August 2007 the pumps had been cleared, but the gallows sign remained, minus its Swan lamp holders, and in a barely-legible condition.

REFUGE
The Old Refuge Assurance Building at Manchester

Location: Oxford Street, Manchester, Lancashire, England, UK
Date of Photograph: 28 May 2005
OS Grid Reference: SJ841975
Co-ordinates: 53:28:27N 2:14:26W
Elevation: 39.6 meters

The Refuge Assurance Company, now part of The Royal London Group, was founded by James Procter and other Manchester businessmen in 1835. Although it is now principally a provider of private pensions, much of the Refuge's original income would have come from the fire insurance of readily-combustible, but then ubiquitous, cotton mills and warehouses.

Since 1987 The Refuge has occupied purpose-built offices at Wilmslow.

The pictured interior is of the foyer of the Refuge Building in central Manchester, built for the insurance firm and occupied by them from 1891 to 1987. This foyer area was, however, moribund by 1972. When I passed it as an undergraduate I was most impressed and intrigued by the massive and very closed iron gates that sealed a silent Victorian cobbled courtyard in which shrubs grew from the stones.

The now-renovated Italianate edifice is of structural pressed red brick and Doulton terracotta with lavish interiors of Burmantoft faience and glazed brick. Building work extended from 1891 to 1895. There is a copper-domed tower on the corner of Oxford and Whitworth Streets and the main Oxford Street frontage is graced by a 217-feet copper-domed terracotta clock tower, one of the icons of Manchester and now seen nationally on television weather glimpses from the city. Under the clock tower is a large ornamental portico of polished gray granite. The main building is by Quaker architect Alfred Waterhouse (1830-1905). He was a Liverpudlian but had the good sense to become an Owen's alumnus. This architect's most celebrated structure is The British Museum of Natural History at Kensington: The same as starred in "One of our Dinosaurs is Missing". The clock tower was added in 1910-12 by Alfred's son Paul. Further co-ordinated extensions were ranged along Whitworth Street by Stanley Birkett in 1932.

The structure is Listed Grade Two Star.

Whilst basically Cisalpine the architecture reflects Alfred Waterhouse's eclectic Late Victorian style as reflected in the "Gothic" museum and other prestige buildings such as The (London) University College Hospital, The National Liberal Club and the striking Victoria University ("Owen's") complex half a mile South along Manchester's Oxford Street. Waterhouse Senior designed numerous other university buildings across England.

The interior of The Refuge is, if anything, even more breathtaking than the façade, glittering with stained-glass, faience and iron and would have left on unforgettable impression in the ghostly green glow of Welsbach lamps. There is a marvellous marble and bronze staircase fit for The Vatican.

In 1996 Richard Newman adapted the premises for Meridien Palace Hotels Limited, who run the building as the four-star Palace Hotel, allegedly the most expensive in Manchester.

The refurbishment cost £7 million and included a partitioning into 257 en-suite guest rooms together with numerous bars and conference rooms as well as an 810-seat restaurant open plan to the main first-floor Tempus Bar. There is air-conditioning in 60 guest rooms (according to the staff) and 257 (according to Meridien Hotels).

As a hotel the Palace has enjoyed mixed reviews. My room was large and very clean but overlooked the debris-strewn trickle in the concrete ditch that passes as the River Medlock. The breakfast was of good quality and of all you could physically consume. The Palace is however widely despised, largely it seems because the aircon and the service both conform to the traditional Mancunian standards. Some foreign guests also find the drunkenness and lawlessness of the adjacent streets disconcerting.

The pictured scene looking Southwards into the new Oxford Street foyer is accessible to non-residents as it is on the way to the main Tempus Bar, the dining area and the lavatories. Extended explorations would require arrangement with Meridien Palace Limited.

STAFFA
The Ruined Storm Refuge on Staffa

Location:	The "Wordsworth Hotel" Ruined Storm Refuge, Staffa, Inner Hebrides, Argyllshire, Scotland, UK
Date of Photograph:	pm 27 July 2006
OS Grid Reference:	NM324354
Co-ordinates:	56:26:09N 6:20:31W
Elevation:	26.2 meters

      The Norse name of Staffa, *Stafi Øy,* or stave island, reflects the fact that it is surrounded by almost impenetrable palisades of thirty-meter high basalt columns that rise sheer from the sea.
      Before the age of the helicopter this made access always difficult, frequently dangerous and often impossible.
      In the eighteenth century subsistence pasturage was managed by a handful of residents who made a precarious living from sheep and black cattle. By 1798 the island was abandoned.

After its "discovery" in 1772 the dramatic island became a major destination for scientific and aesthetic researchers, the wealthy fashionable, and the more existential kind of tourist.

The Napoleonic Wars denied The Continent to leisured travellers and they turned their attention to British watering-places and edifices of culture. By 1810 Staffa was attracting hundreds of well-to-do visitors every year.

In the age of sail, Staffa landings were very difficult and not always feasible in wild Atlantic waters where high seas and storms were usual. With the advent of the paddle steamer, timely departures were much more certain, but safe returns even more problematical. A stage was reached at which insurance was either prohibitive or impossible and steamer masters would not hazard their vessels if heavy weather looked probable.

Therefore, the likelihood was that visitors might be stranded for days at a time on a shelterless island.

Accordingly, sometime around 1825, Ranald MacDonald installed a shelter in the Western central dell of the plateau at about twenty-five meters above the sea. He dug a small well nearby and the dangerous feral black cattle were cleared. The bothy was a drystone rectangular structure built of basalt column fragments. Around the periphery MacDonald built a tall earthen berm to dissipate the energy of wind and water that raged over the cliff brink during hurricanes. Ironically, the chasm that opens before this "Wordsworth Hotel" had the Gaelic name Port an Fhasgaidh, or Sheltered Harbor! I have seen a rubber dinghy drawn up there in the best weather, but it is otherwise inaccessible.

There is an 1830 pastel drawing by Pancoucke that depicts the Staffa Plateau with the refuge shown centrally as a whitewashed hut with two Gothic windows facing the observer. (Pancoucke was a major Parisian bookseller known to have been active in the production of scientific prints). The hut is apparently roofless but otherwise appears new and it is difficult to say if you are looking at a dilapidation of an old structure, or, as I surmise, a structure in the process of completion. The only other published depiction is a 1922 photograph of MacBrayne workmen (possibly landed to repair the Clamshell Cave ladder) who had rigged a tarpaulin roof over part of the then ruin as a storm shelter. At the other end of the ruin a drystone Gothic arch, precariously spanning, has been partially blocked with rubble. This window vanished altogether sometime in the twentieth century.

The refuge enjoyed the services of a resident concierge for some of the season, but neither he nor it were always appreciated. Gentlemen were reluctant to write of "arrangements" or other logistical incidentals to their travels, unless of course they had been entertained by a social superior. Nevertheless, they and others usually arrived in foul temper and failed to enjoy saturated and lousy bedding benighted beneath the roar of the ocean and whistling winds.

As steamers became larger and more seaworthy, landings became less frequent, but those landings and boardings as were made were less problematical.

Within thirty or forty years the "Wordsworth Hotel" had been abandoned.

By the twentieth century, landings were made only in the best weather of the summer, and from attendant steamers. After the withdrawal of MacBrayne circuits in 1974, small boats resumed landings in favorable conditions, any rescues *in extremis* being effected by helicopter.

CHAPTER FOURTEEN

Art and Landscape

The British have a traditional aversion to representational art that possibly pre-dates The Reformation. It is only in the last sixty years that it has become acceptable to display sculpture or mural art in outdoor places, under qualified circumstances. Vandalism, and in the case of bronze or steel, mercenary theft, are widespread and unresolved problems of public art display, at least on Great Britain. On the other hand, advertising has always been welcome, and is often an object of connoisseurship.

After The Second World War the British attitude to public art softened. Before the War only statues or war memorials were allowed in civil spaces, but the Modernist School led by Henry Moore, Barbara Hepworth and Ben Nicolson began tentatively to introduce non-representational carvings, at first to private property.

As a rule, the acceptance of art increases the further West you go in The British Isles. Anything exposed in London or Kent will excite controversy and probably be removed by official fiat. Travel toward the Celtic West and sculpture in parks and the grounds of official buildings gradually increases, but is never common until you cross the sea into The Republic where you suddenly find representational bronzes everywhere. By the time you reach Kerry or Clare, wayside sculpture is ubiquitous, usually of a devotional character, or of splendid wild fauna, though some superb Famine-related studies are also accessible.

Back in Britain the Welsh and the Cornish were the first to leave wayside art that has come down to us. It was usually commemorative of departed rulers, and bears eroded inscriptions in Latin (or occasionally Ogham). The design as well as the epigraphy owe much to Roman archetypes remembered by the Dark Age upper classes. Translations of the nearly illegible inscriptions in elided Latin are always objects of antiquarian controversy.

The evocatively-named Slaughterbridge Stone in Cornwall is about nine feet long and now lies decumbently not far from where it was erected around 540AD. Its Latin and Ogham epigraphy definitely commemorate one Latinus (**LATINI HIC JACET**) who is possibly the son of Arthur the Great (**FILIUS MAGNI ARTURI**) or maybe son of Macarius (**FILIUS MACARI**).

Also in Eastern Cornwall is the even more famous Tristan Stone, also early sixth century . This erect sub-obelisk on a circular base is *in situ* just North West of Fowey. The Latin inscription gives "Drustanus lies here, son of Cunomorus". Some identify Drustanus with Isolde's lover Tristan, and Cunomorus with King Mark of Cornwall, central figures of Arthurian legend as celebrated by Malory, Wagner, *et al*.

Amongst several wayside Dark Age pillars in Wales in Eliseg's Pillar, near Llangollen in the North. It is an erect eight feet high stone cylinder surmounted by crude carved volutes suggestive of an Ionic capital. The epigraphy is now illegible in the field but this late example is known to have been erected by King Cyngen of Powys before 854AD. The pillar is thought to commemorate the ascendancy of the Powismen over the English.

During the Middle Ages numerous stone wayside crosses were erected and some of these, for instance in chartered marketplaces, were elaborate semi-habitable shelters. Besides their devotional service most of the simpler column crosses served as way markers and turn points, and the stumps of these frequently survive beside ancient upland routes, for example on Dartmoor and in The Peak District. A virtually intact example restored in 1926 is the Butter Cross, that survives on an obsolete pack route near Cheddleton (SJ989523).

The most celebrated of the medieval crosses are the twelve elaborate freestone shrines erected at the command of Edward I in 1291. They mark the spots where the coffin of his queen Eleanor of Castile nightly rested upon its procession to London. Only three of the original Eleanor Crosses survive, at Geddington and Hardingstone in Northamptonshire, and at Waltham Cross in Hertfordshire.

Iconoclasts between 1536 and 1660 destroyed many of the more accessible crosses of England and Scotland, as well as church shrines.

During the long period from The Reformation to The Second World War almost all public art was secular and aristocratic. Neo-classicising columns were erected in towns or private parks, and heroic statues might be set atop or nearer vulgar study, whilst semi-habitable landscape follies of all kinds proliferated. Shugborough Park contains many such self-congratulatory structures, and the exquisite Lanthorn of Diogenes rests well within this tradition.

After the Napoleonic Wars a fashion revived a very ancient tradition. Iron Age artists carved votary horses and other animals into the turf of Southern chalk scarps so that they would show white for miles, especially in twilight. A variation on that theme survives near Cerne Abbas in Dorset where an ithyphallic Hercules graces a chalk hillside. He is thought to be Roman, but may be as late as seventeenth century. The nineteenth century revivals were primmer: Regimental badges or military horsemen whose mounts somehow lacked the fluid spirituality of their ancient ancestors.

Funereal monumentality continued throughout, and some great aesthetic and technical achievements were made in Victorian cemetery memorials and in a minority of the cenotaphs to the dead of The Great War. In 1886 Mr B Beebee unveiled a civic statue to the late Anglican nun Dorothy Pattison at Walsall. Foundress of The Walsall Hospital she was the first common female so to be honored and she marked the watershed to a more egalitarian world. Slowly the seed of a British vernacular art revival diffidently broke to light.

During Victorian times a fashion evolved for the creation of urban municipal parks throughout the British Empire and both local councils and individual wealthy dignitaries would commission functional but highly-ornamented cast-iron sculptures for permanent installation. The first planned park of this kind was opened at Birkenhead in 1847. Gardener and glasshouse designer Joseph Paxton, who four years later would build the 1851 Great Exhibition's Crystal Palace, designed this. Glasgow rapidly became the best park-endowed major city in the anglophone world, possibly because its tenement tradition denied gardens to individual households.

Park fitments included fountains, urinals, drinking-fountains, seating benches, bandstands, conservatories and shelters. From the outset public parks were regarded as amenities mainly for women and children. Uniformed male attendants were provided and drinking and prostitution discouraged. In 1849 William MacFarlane founded his Saracen Foundry in Saracen Lane in Central Glasgow, virtually next door to the then site of Glasgow University. As his business expanded it moved in 1872 to the Northern suburb of Possilpark, where the entire economy came to depend upon ornamental castings by William MacFarlane and Company Limited, and later a companion foundry firm, A&J Main Limited. The Saracen Foundry was demolished in 1967, and Main subsequently closed.

A rare British gable-end mural in Saracen Street depicts the eight-acre Saracen Foundry with its glass dome and crested chimneys, together with a foundry man and a selection of characteristic Saracen products. The mural was painted anonymously in 1990, but is unfortunately already in a poor state. Modern synthetic paints lack the resilience of the old, now-illegal, lead-based paints and are especially vulnerable in Britain's humid climate, where the brick or ashlar substratum is itself persistently damp. Notwithstanding, a number of recent gable-end murals currently exist in Scotland and Western Britain and a handful of more permanent wall mosaics have been professionally fitted to existing outdoor walls in the English West Country.

The Second World War and its various propaganda agencies brought a vast epidemic of public art in the form of films, posters, paintings and photographs. Though these are ephemeral forms their effect was to rehabilitate art as a respectable object of Protestant middle-class endeavor and to habituate the public to "high art" (as opposed to advertising) in their environment.

Modernist sculptors and Jacob Epstein enjoyed a heyday as they were worked hard to help restore the nation's blitzed wastelands with a contribution of humane objects. Epstein installed his 1935 image of Christ, "*Ecce Homo*" in the ruins of old Coventry Cathedral. By the time Sir Basil Spence had in 1962 completed his masterpiece, the new cathedral attached to the ruins, Epstein had affixed his great bronzes "St Michael's Victory over the Devil" at its entrance.

In 1951 Sir William Keswick set out to assemble the World's first post-Classical collection of sculpture in a natural setting. He elected to use his land at Glenkiln near Dumfries, a sheltered and secluded valley with scattered copses, above an attractive municipal reservoir. Here he scattered various representational and abstract figure sculptures by Moore, Rodin and Epstein, mostly in bronze and mostly of a devotional character. Highlights include Rodin's "John the Baptist" and Epstein's "Visitation", both Gospel bronzes, and Moore's "King and Queen". Gatherment was active between 1951 and 1976.

During the 1980's Ms Diane Gorvin created a number of civic bronze and concrete statues or less figurative sculptures. These frequently feature animals such as the bronze geese at Barnard's Wharf, in the former Surrey Docks at London. Another notable Gorvin work is the atmospheric "Bo Peep and her Sheep" in Birchwood Forest Park at

Warrington. A robed and spectrally-patinated bronze Bo Peep is followed at a distance by the concrete rugosity of her faithful attendant. Not far away, in the grounds of "haunted" Bewsey Old Hall may be studied the further Gorvin works "White Lady Ghost" and "Sun and Moon Bronzes".

In 1992 The Cass Foundation was endowed to commission and promote monumental sculpture. Its twenty-six acre natural woodland park at Goodwood displays a rotating presentation of around seventy works by fifty artists at all stages of their careers. The Cass Foundation commission between twelve and fifteen great sculptures every year, finding the artists' fabrication costs which it recoups with a small commission when the works are sold.

A phenomenon of the last twenty years has been the career of Mr Anthony Gormley, a monumental figurative sculptor whose slightly bleak outdoor statues are usually in finned sheet steel. "Iron: Man" (1993) is installed in Birmingham's Victoria Square, but his world-renowned works are the massive "Angel of the North" at Gateshead (1998) and the very evocative platoon of seaward-gazing intertidal giants at Crosby Sands. Called "Another Place" this major landscape group was installed in 1997. It may be moved to further suitable settings. Controversial at the times of their appearances, these vast creations are beginning to win public acceptance.

British mural art is always representational, often an eclectic pastiche, and usually epitomises local traditions, industries and landmarks. Several, such as at Mallaig, Leamington Spa and Kippax have marine or sea-fishing themes. At Cockenzie a large paint mural by Mr Andrew Crummy celebrates the local colliery and herring fishery industries against a backdrop of the town's power station turbines. At the opposite end of Britain, a wonderful cartouched mosaic at Shirley in Southampton entitled "Strawberry Fields" depicts strawberry growers at their varied tasks.

Splendid Liskeard murals by Mr David Whittley and dated 1998 depict the impact of The Industrial Revolution on the East Cornish town. Finely executed scenes crowded of labor and expectation accompany a locomotive's arrival against a background of smoking mine engine houses. In the same town wistful mural mosaics grace the local Co-op supermarket. In one a Celtic wayside cross fronts a rolling pastoral landscape, and in another an ancient dolmen shares a hillside with an engine house.

DARKLANT
The Lanthorn of Demosthenes at Shugborough

Location:	Shugborough Estate, near Great Haywood, Staffordshire, England, UK
Date of Photograph:	17 April 2005
OS Grid Reference:	SJ984219
Co-ordinates:	52:47:41N 2:01:25W
Elevation:	86.6 meters

This is The Lanthorn of Demosthenes, sometimes called "The Dark Lantern". It is a garden ornament.

It is modelled on the Choragic Monument of Lysicrates near the Athenian Acropolis. Lysicrates was a choragus (theatrical chorus impresario) and the original commemorates the first prize he won for a play produced in 335 or 334BC.

The original is a Corinthian drum on a square podium with a frieze illustrating the Dionysian Rites. The prize was a bronze tripod that surmounted the drum.

The imitation at Shugborough originally cradled a Wedgwood bowl but this was removed together with its supporting tripod. These elements were replaced in the 1960's with fiberglass copies. A member of the collection of eighteenth century follies in the policies of Shugborough Hall, The Lanthorn of Demosthenes was designed by James "Athenian" Stuart, and was the last of the Shugborough structures he contributed. It was installed in 1771 under the patronage of Thomas Anson, Earl of Lichfield.

The Lanthorn originally graced the side of the Stafford to Rugeley public road but that was realigned to the South in 1804.

For the classical background supplied, I am indebted to Richard R at Castrovalva.

DONNA
The Tree of Birds in the Donna Cooper Memorial Garden

Location:	The Donna Cooper Memorial Garden, Goscote, Walsall, Staffordshire, England, UK
Date of Photograph:	am 2 November 2007
OS Grid Reference:	SK016026
Co-ordinates:	52:37:17N 1:58:38W
Elevation:	133.5 meters

On 6th January 1993 a stolen car driven by 17-year-old Goscote thief Carl Sherwood knocked down and killed 13-year-old Donna Cooper.

Sherwood was on bail for another car theft the previous day. He and his accomplice were charged with manslaughter and on 7th October, at Stafford Crown Court, Sherwood was sent down for seven years.

Donna was a budding artist and just before she died completed an owl design that is now the emblem of her Memorial Garden.

Shortly afterward, several local, national and European agencies came together to, in a small but impressive manner, do something to ameliorate the dire blight of Goscote.

Donna's parents led the efforts. They were supported by Walsall "Metropolitan" Borough Council (the local government), Groundwork Black Country, English Partnerships, the European Regional Development Fund, The Millennium Commission, and ad-hoc groups from the local community, including schoolchildren.

The collaborators selected the dank little valley of the Clock Mill Brook, between Goscote and its Eastern neighbor Pelsall as the site of the new Donna Cooper Memorial Garden.

Gujarati artist Ms Anuradha Patel specialises in ceramics and in traditional floral pierced work in coated galvanized steel. In 1997 she was commissioned to create the garden's metal arch, and also The Tree of Birds, set upon a rose-bedecked mound amidst four small circular earthworks. The metal fabrications were undertaken by West Midlands Gates and Trailers.

The galvanized steel tree is 2.34 meters high and its sheet metal birds turn in the wind.

It is hoped that the garden will become a focus for creative community events and artwork installations. Progress is, however, very slow, and in 2007 the two hundred by twenty-five meter garden is mainly a dog walkers' resource.

The Clock Mill Brook, really no more than an overgrown ditch, is said to be a rare contemporary habitat for the delightful water vole. Before entering the garden I had seen a buzzard cruising over the adjacent pastures, and as I left the garden's entrance a timid and tiny creature darted into the grass verge and disappeared, appropriately in the general direction of Mouse Hill! On another occasion I passed the time of day with a young but surprisingly large water shrew (*Neomys fodiens*) on the metalled track beside the brook.

After decades of dereliction and decay the notorious Council slums of Blakenall Heath and Goscote are beginning to turn around. Unemployment and illiteracy remain intractable, but crime is beginning to decline, and the physical environment has been greatly enhanced. Crime-ridden tower blocks are being replaced by low-rise flats, shopping streets rehabilitated and derelict houses renovated. Across Walsall the 2007 national Smoking Ban has yielded an unanticipated benefit: The widespread closure of its numerous taverns and drinking clubs.

DUNSEATH
The Wesley Memorial at West Bromwich

Location:	High Street, West Bromwich, Sandwell, Staffordshire, Mercia, England, UK
Date of Photograph:	pm 23 November 2007
OS Grid Reference:	SP004911
Co-ordinates:	52:31:07N 1:59:39W
Elevation:	163.4 meters

This commemorates the ministry of the Methodist evangelical John Wesley (1703-1791) who with his brother Charles frequently visited the Black Country to preach. Their receptions were, however, mixed, and they were frequently confronted by riots.

Chris Dunseath was born in Northern Ireland in 1949. He studied at Yeovil School of Art, Cheltenham College of Art and The Slade. Mr Dunseath has held numerous fellowships and exhibits widely in England and the USA.

He usually presents abstract sculptures in a variety of traditional media. This work often elaborates themes suggested by theoretical physics. Mr Dunseath's public work is however representational; cast in bronze and mostly of a spiritual character. His Black Country commissions include other work for Sandwell MBC and a series of works at the Richardson Brothers Waterfront Development in Brierley Hill.

As aforenoted, both John and Charles Wesley visited The Black Country but John was especially active in the district and preached forty-five times from the horseblock in The High Bullen of Wednesbury as well as on numerous occasions across West Bromwich, Darlaston and Walsall. He was confronted by violent mobs in all four townships and local authorities refused assistance. When John first spoke at Wednesbury on 23rd October 1743 there was a serious disturbance. Wednesbury crowds were agitated by the local Anglican priest and could be particularly volatile but many there became his converts and protectors, and the town became a local center for the new sect. John was unable to get a hearing in Walsall but in 1743 preached from Fishley Rock, an erratic boulder in a lonely spot by a byway on the Northern boundary of Walsall Foreign. Fishley Rock is now a protected monument but was sadly broken in half some years ago, probably by a reversing truck.

Mementoes of John Wesley's Wednesbury visits, including a piece of cast-iron that a rioter threw at him, and the actual horseblock from which he spoke are preserved at the Wednesbury Wesleyan Church in Spring Head.

John last preached to the people of Wednesbury on 22nd March 1790 when he was 87 years old.

The plaque beneath the bronze reads:-

*This sculpture by Chris Dunseath, is dedicated
to John Wesley preacher and religious reformer,
who preached many times in the 18th century,
in what is now The Borough of Sandwell,
including the nearby Oak House.
His Biblical teaching resulted in a revival of
The Christian Church and the founding of
The Methodist Movement.*

*The Hand and Cross is a symbolic representation
of the Message being accepted by The People.
The steps refer to the Medieval horseblock
from which Wesley preached. The horseblock
is currently sited beside the Wesley Chapel
at Springhead in Wednesbury.*

*The sculpture was unveiled on 23rd October 1989
by Councillor R Davis, Leader of
Sandwell Metropolitan Borough Council.*

The church spire is that of St Michael and All Angels, West Bromwich.

GRETNA
The Lovers Sculpture at Gretna Green

Location: "The Lovers", The Old Smithy Courtyard, Gretna Green, Dumfriesshire, Scotland, UK
Date of Photograph: pm 29 July 2006
OS Grid Reference: NY321684
Co-ordinates: 55:00:21N: 3:03:44W
Elevation: 39 meters

      On 11th May 1745 the Pragmatic Army, an Anglo-Austrian coalition led somewhat aptly by The Duke of Cumberland confronted the French at Fontenoy by the River Schelt. Though pessimistic about his chances, by the end of the day the French marshal had won the battle, and 1237 British dead lay on the field.
      Little regarded at the time was the lifeless body of Captain John Campbell, a minor aristocrat from Dumbartonshire.
      On 9 December 1725 he had contracted an irregular marriage with Jean Campbell at Roseneath in Scotland (probably Rosneath in Argyll). They had had three children, of whom one survived.
      An irregular marriage, or "common law marriage" in the old, correct sense, was quite valid, in both Scots and English legal codes. It was only necessary that both consenting parties were at least seven years of age and of different sexes. Further, the officiator had to have two witnesses, but secret marriages were quite permissible as long as they were celebrated in a fit place and time as allowed by the 1604 Canon Acts.

When Mistress Campbell learned of her husband's death in war, she applied to the authorities to inherit his estate. A certain Mistress Kennedy, nee Magdalen Cochran, learned of this and applied to the authorities to herself inherit, on the grounds that she was John's lawful wife. Mistress Kennedy claimed to have contracted an irregular marriage with John Campbell on 3 January 1724 at Paisley Abbey. Naturally this claim initially met with cynicism, and when Magdalen went on to claim that John only married Jean because she was pregnant and John dare not offend her powerful uncle, The Duke of Argyll, the ribald doubts of magistrates only deepened. Jurists understandably remained incredulous that a woman would wait twenty-two years to requite her husband's vows.

But Magdalen produced a series of fifty letters of John's hand admitting their marriage and promising to leave Jean and join Magdalen at an opportune juncture. Further, there were reciprocal letters, urging John to quit Jean. Despite the fact that it was a criminal offence to try to seduce a married man, there was ambiguity about who was married to whom.

The case went to the Lords.

Their Lordships found in favor of Jean Campbell and her Roseneath marriage. It had to be presumed that Jean was ignorant of her bigamy, if that is what it was, and that Magdalen had sent her letters in good faith and sound law.

The Lords determined to pass a law that would forever prevent a similar scandal in Scotland, but as they were unable to modify Scots Law, it turned out that the new rules would mostly inconvenience the English!

In 1754 Lord Hardwicke introduced The Marriage Act, which was duly passed, but only applied to England and Wales. It stipulated that marriages must be public; that banns be published and potential objectors canvassed; that ordained Church of England vicars must officiate (except for Jews and Quakers who could select whichever celebrant they saw fit); that the male must be unmarried and at least 14 years of age and the spinster at least 12; and, crucially, that either party if under 21 years of age, must have their father's permission to marry. Any clergyman who saw fit to vary or abridge these articles would be awarded 14 years transportation, so that he might be branded and sent as a slave to some American plantation.

The scene was set for one hundred years of Gretna Green's golden age.

An indelible image springs to mind. Two teenagers gallop in pillion across the haunted marshes and spray-swept quicksand. Within a windborne shout's length a cursing gentleman and a posse of ruffian bailiffs race after them. But none dare shoot, whether for fear of striking the girl or the burly grasp of foreign constables, as all splash and flounder into the darkling fog of a boreal dusk, of whose precise nationality none are certain. The youngsters reach land, a tiny smithy and a pair of lime-washed hovels. The workman gathers two yokels, and the rite is uttered in the light of the guttering rushes. An irate and ruddy man bursts in alone, and blusters to null effect. The everlasting romance of Gretna Green, a hamlet a thousand meters within Scotland, is born.

A cheerful chaos reigned again.

In 1857, Lord Brougham brought in an act that stipulated that couples who married in Scotland must have lived there for at least 21 days which curtailed, but did not cease, English elopements. In 1977 the 21-day residency rule was abolished and replaced by a 14-day written notice to The Gretna Registry Office:- effectively the asking of banns. A by-product of this new protocol, perhaps unanticipated, was that Gretna marriage was internationalised. In 1994 Church of Scotland ministers were allowed to officiate "over the anvil" and in 2002 Registrars were allowed to leave their offices and conduct weddings "over the anvil" or in other places deemed to be of fitting dignity.

Today four thousand weddings are performed at Gretna Green every year, about 17% of all Scottish weddings, although of course the couples are drawn from nearly every country on Earth.

KNOCKER
The Knockerdown Inn at Carsington

Location: Knockerdown, near Carsington, Derbyshire, England, UK
Date of Photograph: 9 November 2006
OS Grid Reference: SK232519
Co-ordinates: 53:03:51N 1:39:13W
Elevation: 245.4 meters

The art and the usage of this gallows sign painting at the Knockerdown Tavern embody a complex pun.

Just North of Carsington, and perhaps a mile from the tavern, is Carsington Pasture, the largest unenclosed field in The White Peak. Caves on Carsington Pasture contain prehistoric and Roman inhumations, and even woolly rhinoceros remains, whilst the limestone is raddled with lead mine shafts and galleries dating from prehistory to The Second World War. Most of these remains are undocumented and clearly the pasture should not be walked without expert guidance. Immediately East of the pub the recent Carsington Reservoir had to be grouted for unmapped workings and is thought to occupy the site of the Roman lead-smelting town of *Lutudarum* where a cupel was sited, strangely in a province noted for the lack of silver in its lead. Carsington Pasture is on The King's Field.

The Knockerdown Inn is today a well-regarded family restaurant and day resort. The existing fabric dates back to the seventeenth century, and may have been patronised by travellers on the London to Manchester coach route via Hognaston. In any event, a hostelry would early have been established to serve thirsty miners.

With regard to the literalities of the toponym, "knockerdown" means an operative who uses the rapid and economical method of ore-hewing known as overhand stoping (pronounced "stoaping"). This involves braking ore from the ceiling, rather the floor, of the excavated void. A "down" is a Saxon term for a limestone hill, common in Southern England, but otherwise unknown on The White Peak. (If you decide to google "overhand stoping" take great care to use my exact spelling!!!).

The etymology of "knockerdown" is uncertain, but a "knocker" is a kind of goblin who inhabits mines and makes a tapping sound either to indicate rich ore seams or to warn of impending disasters. If offended, however, he can easily revert to stealing tools or playing other pranks. Today the classic knocker tends to be associated with Cornwall or the US, but mine sprites are known worldwide and pervade Germanic tradition down to Grimm and Wagner. The Germans call this fairy a "kobald" from which the element cobalt derives its name, and it is almost certainly via this route that the Anglo-Saxon tradition derives.

In less enlightened ages, people said that knockers were the ghosts of Jews, cursed by the Romans to labor in expiation of The Crucifixion of Christ. And they were pictured as neurasthenic little creatures with hooked noses and a distinctly dependent and vicarious status.

Our lad, however, seems far from this conception. Square-jawed and muscle-bound he seems to owe more to Knockerdown's Classical rather than its Saxon past, nude with but a stole to preserve his modesty, glowing with supernal power and ready for immediate and decisive action. With his tousled and determined blond visage he looks more like a young George W Bush rather than an old Paul Wolfowitz; only useful.

LLANEGGS
Egg Sculptures at the Llanelli National Wetland Centre

Location:	Llanelli National Wetland Centre division of the Waterfowl and Wetlands Trust at Llwynhendy, near Llanelli, Carmarthenshire, Wales, UK
Date of Photograph:	am 3 May 2002
OS Grid Reference:	about SS5398
Co-ordinates:	51:39:41N 4:06:56W
Elevation:	4.0 meters

  This 500-acre reserve is a sanctuary for resident and migratory waterfowl and other wetland fauna. It is accessible to the public on payment of a fee. Excavated from a salt marsh to the North of Burry Inlet the reserve is designated a Site of Special Scientific Interest, Special Protected Area and Ramsar Site.
  Observations and hides are provided, as are lavatory and restaurant arrangements, and townshoe walkways maintained.
  The sculptures, by Pamela, Lady Byrd, are crane eggs and indeed were laid by cranes that waddled to the site over duckboards using caterpillars.
  The swirling courses of red and purple stone represent the intestinal primogenesis of inchoate life in the primordial egg, and echoes an earlier design by Wren.

NELSON
The Late Mr Noel Nelson, Neighbourhood Street Warden

Location:	The Lincoln Court Basketball Ground, Bethune Road, Stoke Newington, London N16, England, UK
Date of Photograph:	am 17 September 2007
OS Grid Reference:	TQ329876
Co-ordinates:	51:34:21N: 0:04:58W
Elevation:	24 meters

This spray-paint mural by Roger Jones accompanies others of recent British sportsmen and women which grace a set of movable steel shutters on the Western side of a small tarmacadamed basketball court.

The murals commemorate the life and work of Mr Noel Nelson (1966-2004), Stoke Newington resident, sportsman, and Neighbourhood Street Warden. The paintings and the court celebrate the short but unselfish life of Mr Nelson and his dedication to the people of his community and to their aspirations and welfare.

In 2003 Noel Nelson was Commended in the annual Personal Achievement Award category of The Home Office Crime Reduction Agency for his services to the elderly, the youth, and the vulnerable of his neighborhood.

The eight annual Neighbourhood Warden Achievement Awards continued and in 2005 the Personal Award was re-named The Noel Nelson Personal Achievement Award in Nelson's honor. The 2005 accolade was won by Kwami Agbo of The Clapton Street Crime Wardens, London.

I happened to chance upon the scene as I passed by whilst researching the vernacular history of my country.

Mrs Roz Simons, of the Bethune Road Community, explained to me how distressed the man's friends and neighbors had been by his sudden death from a heart attack whilst on a visit to Jamaica. She confided that the small plot of land, its macadam and its fencing was all that they could afford to remember their friend, together with the spray cans they placed in the hands of Mr Jones.

The result is a masterpiece.

PERROTT
Perrott's Folly in Ladywood

Location:	Waterworks Road, Ladywood, Birmingham, Warwickshire, England, UK
Date of Photograph:	12 February 2000
OS Grid Reference:	SP045863
Co-ordinates:	52:28:28N 1:55:52W
Elevation:	159.1 meters

Perrott's Folly is a 96 feet high Gothic brick tower of octagonal section. It is one of the oldest surviving structures in Birmingham, having been built by John Perrott in 1758. It is Listed Grade Two Star.

Its design purpose is uncertain but it was probably intended for use as an astronomical observatory. Other towers built at this period had a diversity of motivations: Social prestige, provision of employment or even conscious structural experimentation.

From 1881 to 1979 the tower was a meteorological observatory, which from 1966 was run by the Geography Department of Birmingham University.

In the background of the picture, and on the immediate Eastern shore of Rotton Park Reservoir, can be seen the Waterworks Tower.

Rotton Park Reservoir (now usually called Edgbaston Reservoir) was originally a roach pond and springs upon a lordly estate but was engineered into the current larger lagoon by the great Scottish civil engineer Thomas Telford between the years 1825 and 1829. Its principal water supply is not the pre-existing springs but another higher-level reservoir at Tipton. Rotton Park Reservoir's function is to feed the Birmingham and Wolverhampton Levels Navigation.

JRR Tolkein, a Birmingham man, was possibly inspired to write The Two Towers, the second book of his Lord of the Rings trilogy by Perrott's Folly and The Waterworks Tower. Surviving sketches of his appear to identify those two towers respectively with Orthanc and Minas Morgul.

Ladywood today is a dangerous place to walk around, especially with a camera. Directly after taking the photograph I was attacked by a gang of stone throwing youths. Fortunately, they missed their marks, and I confronted them with the slightly intimidating posture I can affect, whereupon they backed away.

Not content with Niagara, on 6th December 1924, Blondin gave his "last and farewell performance" by crossing Rotton Park Reservoir on a tight wire. My Late Mother was born in Monument Retreat, not half a mile away, and would have been two and a half at the time. If she ever witnessed this feat, or even knew of it, I never heard her or either of her parents mention the spectacle.

QMSUITE
The Queen Mary Suite at Dudley Zoo

Location:	The Queen Mary Suite, Dudley Zoological Garden. Castle Hill, Dudley, Staffordshire, England, UK
Date of Photograph:	am 24 July 2007
OS Grid Reference:	SO947908
Co-ordinates:	52:30:58N: 2:04:46W
Elevation:	217 meters

Berthold Lubetkin was a major constructivist modernist architect of the first half of the twentieth-century, who was born in Tiflis, trained in Moscow and Petrograd, and lived through the 1917 Revolution there. It is highly probable that he was a personal friend of Stalin, who of course was a young seminarian living under his natural name, and a fellow Georgian.

In any event, Lubetkin emigrated to France where he set up his Tecton design partnership. During the Twenties the Soviet Government commissioned him to design the USSR Pavilion at the Bordeaux Exposition and invited him to compete for a design for the new Palace of the Soviets in Moscow, intended to be an enormous neo-classical skyscraper, the largest building in the World.

Lubetkin's submission was not successful, but he moved on to Britain where he was commissioned to design art deco flats in North London and health centres for Labour councils. After WWII, the new Labour Government commissioned him to design a statue of Lenin for erection in the UK, as well as Peterlee New Town and several other Modernist grands-projet (excuse my French).

In c1933 The Zoological Society of London commissioned Lubetkin to re-model their outstation at Whipsnade, and later to install a Penguin Pool and other structures at Regents Park Zoo.

In 1935 Dudley Council invited him to build an entirely new zoo on the Castle Hill at Dudley, which was opened in 1937. Engineered by Ove Arup it featured many flying balconies of steel reinforced concrete, for both human and animal access, as well as many art deco amenities.

The 70-year-old structures are now spalling badly and are ill-suited to modern concepts of animal welfare. Some of the accommodations are distressing for the animals, especially those native to hotter climes: And by that condition distressing for the more sensitive of the visitors. However, the park includes 7 Grade Two buildings and 5 Grade Two Star by Lubetkin as well as the castle antiquities, and though the DMBC has withdrawn its financial support for ethical reasons, DZG continues to generate revenue and the park remains the most extensive art deco relic in the Midlands.

Though dilapidated, the restaurant is in continuous use when the Zoo is open: 10-5 daily. The actual terrace is not used, and there has been obvious land slippage on this very steep and geologically incompetent site. Normal visitor access to the eatery is through the South doors and it is possible that the Eastern side that I visited had been untrodden for several years (judging by the moss).

Lubetkin presumably intended this to be a smoking terrace giving views of the surrounding bustle and industry, on the rare days when the wind cleared the smog.

All the art deco buildings at Dudley are dilapidated and would have vanished 50 years ago, but for the Listings: Several were demolished in the Sixties.

STONESIS
Stones Island Sculptures at Carsington Water

Location:	Stones Island, Carsington Water, near Wirksworth, Derbyshire, England, UK
Date of Photograph:	9 November 2006
OS Grid Reference:	SK243514
Co-ordinates:	53:03:34N 1:38:16W
Elevation:	201.8 meters

This is taken within the sculpture group at Stones Island, a peninsula within Carsington Water.

After a decade of construction beset with ground difficulties the Carsington Reservoir was filled during 1991, and the little peninsula of Stones Island, connected to Great Britain by a narrow isthmus, formed on its Western edge.

In 1992 Severn-Trent Water commissioned Lewis Knight to install an arrangement of frustal monoliths suggestive perhaps of some jungle-girt Toltec observatory. The sculptures, of Derbyshire gritstone, vary from 1.7 to 4 meters in height, and weigh up to 7.6 tonnes.

Holes are bored through some of the pillars and can be peered-through to descry various landscape features. With this end in mind certain of the holes are set at a height at which small children may use them.

TOMBSTON
The Tombstone Holding Yard of Walsh and Company

Location: Bloxwich High Street, Staffordshire, England, UK
Date of Photograph: am 4 October 2007
OS Grid Reference: SK001015
Co-ordinates: 52:36:42N 1:59:58W
Elevation: 157 meters

      This was the work yard of Bloxwich monumental masons Walsh and Company who earned a certain local notoriety over the "Black Diana" fiasco of 2000. Around 1995 they moved to new premises, an old tool factory in Park Street about half-a-mile North. The yard became an open waste space littered with some expensive-looking pieces of cut and polished stone.
      About 2003, the galvanized iron fence was erected and finished stones parked within. I do not know why. The scene forms a tableau of some mortuary mirth on the walk to Walsall.

VISITATI
Epstein's Visitation at Glenkiln

Location: Glenkiln, Dumfriesshire, Scotland, UK
Date of Photograph: pm 3 April 1999
OS Grid Reference: NX842769
Co-ordinates: 55:04:02N 3:50:00W
Elevation: 221.6 meters

This is a 1926 bronze cast of the "Visitation" by the American-born twentieth-century sculptor Sir Jacob Epstein. It is sited on a brae above Glenkiln.

Epstein specialised in major Christian and allegorical figures in bronze or stone, but was controversial during his lifetime for the frequent frontal nudity in his art.

The precative figure celebrates the Visitation of The Mother of Christ to her cousin Elizabeth to announce that she, Mary, is pregnant (Luke 1:39-56).

Further copies may be seen at Tate Britain, and at Baltimore (Maryland) and Washington DC.

CHAPTER FIFTEEN

Defence and Decline

Defence and Decline

In some preceding pages we have been privileged to remember the courage, intellect and altruism of a few heroes of the past, to glimpse their sites of action, and to ponder whither their works lead. The sailors, soldiers and airmen are of their number. Gratitude is not enough, for I am acutely conscious that without their sacrifice I could not write my love for my country, or attempt, however ineptly, to raise the esteem in which it is held.

The great Naval victories and defeats of Britain and all its overseas endeavors are of course well beyond the scope of this book, as are most castles and other aristocratic facilities.

We shall rather consider the places the common people would have known, and the modest redoubts that reflected their fears.

Little is known of our Stone Age and even Bronze Age peoples. None of their records, if any, have descended to us. The former laid out massive stone circles and avenues that appear to have been planned upon astronomical or mathematical principles, but are of unknown purpose. Signally lacking from that heritage is any structure or earthwork of defensive value. Perhaps they lived an Arcadian peace, or like Mongols embraced a mobile and offensive strategy.

It was possibly as late as Periclean times (say 500BC) that the first considerable defensive relics that remain were built. These take the form of promontory forts distinguished by a berm and sulcus across the necks of headlands, or of hill forts circuited by such. These forts are usually at or near the coast, as were most of Britain's defensive structures until 1940, because it was not until The Second World War that the British expected to fight a deep penetration into their homeland.

There are exceptions. The mountainous margins with Wales and Scotland (variously defined) were always labile and violent and in those Marcher regions two thousand years of small forts and small castles abound. And, like Picardy, the landscape presents some striking omissions as well as inclusions. In the center of England, near the village of Alrewas is the confluence of three rivers navigable to early craft. In many countries this would now be the site of a great city, but today, and for at least a thousand years, it is empty pasturage. It reminds us that enemies have penetrated to the heart of England in the past, when the very capital of Mercia, Repton, was sacked by the Vikings, and York taken for their own.

Sometime in the British Iron Age and possibly in response to the Rise of Rome, or maybe the migration of displaced persons, strategic fortification became general. In addition, and spasmodically, enclosed masonry refuge paddocks have tentatively been identified. Even in the far North of Scotland elaborate round tower houses of worked stone ringed the coasts, designed so that animals and provisions could be gathered into an enclosed courtyard whilst people manned the walls. The stumps of most of these brochs survive, except in Shetland where they are essentially complete.

When the Romans occupied Britannia the hill and promontory forts fell into disuse. The Romans built non-defensive but walled cities on the plain, with reinforced military frontiers on what is now the Welsh Border, as well as along The Great Whin Sill and the Forth-Clyde isthmus. As they themselves came under attack from sea-borne raiders in the fourth century AD, the Romans built massively-walled redoubts from The Wash to Portchester. Like most of these coastal strongpoints throughout history they seemed to function as enclosures of temporary refuge rather than permanently-manned military works. Major remains of these Saxon Shore forts can be seen at Brough (Suffolk) , Richborough (Kent) and Portchester (Hampshire).

When Rome left permanent defences were neglected and various Germanic and Norse invaders infiltrated the whole archipelago.

The Normans who arrived in 1066 revived the use of ashlar and constructed military castles at various strategic locations, focusing upon the debatable land at the Welsh or Scottish Borders, and the penetrable estuaries of the South and East of England. Whittington is typical of the little castles that were almost everywhere along the border with Wales, then a group of hostile independent countries. But it is important to remember, as can be detected from their architecture, that Norman castles were intended to subdue rather than protect.

During the fifteenth centuries the collapse of Byzantium and the Ottoman advance into Eastern Europe and The Maghreb produced a distinctive problem. Central control over North Africa weakened quickly and encouraged by the disarray of the European Reformation the Muslim potentates of Tunis, Algiers and Morocco turned pirate. Starting in 1587 they raided the Christian coasts of The Mediterranean as well as Christian commerce by using slave-powered galleys. But by the end of the century, European renegades joined their number bringing their own sail, and the technology to build further sailing ships capable of extended tours in The Atlantic. Ranging as far as Iceland, they raided the South-Western coast of Britain and Ireland for slaves.

On 20th June 1631, enjoying the pilotage of a traitor, the Flemish renegade Murad Rais (possibly Dutch renegade Jan Janzoon van Haarlem) out of Algiers sacked the County Cork coastal village of Baltimore, abducting 108. Only two of these captives saw Ireland again. Most subsequent settlement moved further inland to Skibbereen. During the summer of 1625, several coastal villages in Devon, Cornwall and Dorset, as well as Ireland, were depopulated. It is probably in this era that many refuge castles, such as Oxwich, saw their fullest development.

During the early seventeenth century 20000 Europeans were taken to the slave markets of Algiers alone, and between 1530 and 1780, one and a quarter million Europeans were enslaved in Islamic North Africa.

Some wealthy captives were ransomed, and communities and entire governments succumbed to blackmail under threat of raid. European disunity enfeebled effective response, but in 1655 a counter-raid upon Tunis by The Royal Navy under Robert Blake gave the pirates a severe set-back. Barbary pirates and slavers continued, however, to plague the South-West, and between 1627 and 1632 and possibly again in 1645 Arabs occupied Lundy Island in the Bristol Channel threatening to stifle the English American trade. Lundy was relieved by the time of Cromwell.

As the Royal Navy strengthened during The Commonwealth and the reign of Charles II it was able to meet more punishment upon the Barbary slavers and pirates generally. Sir Cloudesley Shovell destroyed four Barbary sail at Tripoli in 1674. Several Anglo-Dutch reprisals were organised and in 1682 and again in 1683 the French bombarded Algiers. Raids upon Britain and The North diminished.

At the close of the Napoleonic Wars, Anglo-Dutch strategists determined to make an end of European slavery in North Africa. Lord Exmouth and Admiral Van de Capellen sacked Algiers, and the Algerines and Tunisians were forced to liberate three thousand. At the Congress of Aix-le-Chapelle in 1818, Europe agreed to concert against the Barbary pirates, and in 1830 France occupied North-West Africa, ending the terror of the Arab slavers forever.

As slaving and piracy diminished, coastal settlement once again became viable and fishing, shipbuilding and other coastal trade increased, to be supplemented in the sunnier lands by salt-panning. The European remained, however, a threat unto himself.

At the end of the eighteenth century the threat of French invasion inspired the building of sturdy Martello gun towers along the shoreline of South-East England.

One hundred and three of these circular towers were built in brick, with walls thirteen feet thick. Thirty feet high, they mounted a cannon with a 360-degree arc of fire, and along vulnerable stretches were built closely enough to have continuous coastline in range. Seventy-four were built in Kent and Sussex, and 29 in Essex and Suffolk. They fired no shot in anger. Nine remain in their original state and a further 45 as ruins or converted to housing.

In the 1850's another Napoleon, Napoleon III built the French Navy to parity with the British, and threatened to invade. The 1859 Royal Commission on Defence recommended the construction of immense brick or ashlar redoubts at the approaches to principal Naval dockyards. These would be permanently garrisoned and mount long-range rifled cannon to cover all quarters. The largest overlook the major bases of Portsmouth and Plymouth, but there is a complex of some ten of these Palmerston Forts at Milford Haven, some occupying whole islands. The Fort Road fortlet that guards the South-West of Pembroke Dock is by far the smallest. Once again, it was a false alarm and no Palmerston Fort ever fired in anger. After a century of dereliction the forts are being rehabilitated as museums, hotels or housing.

Coastal fortifications were revamped during The First World War, but the next great building-generative emergency was The Second World War.

For the fourth time in one hundred and fifty years there was fear of imminent invasion, but for the first time in a thousand the British expected to fight not merely upon the coast but also in their interior.

Because the Nazi enemy had the technology and the organisation to occupy hundreds of miles of hostile territory within days of outset, fortifications and other military facilities were built suddenly and throughout the UK, even in remote highland areas. Reinforced gun emplacements were built within weeks at such unlikely places as The Lothbeg Sands in Sutherland, where they were still numerous in 1968, and at Burrow Head overlooking the Northern Irish Sea. The western coast was reinforced with airfields in case the Irish accommodated a Nazi assault from that quarter. "Secret" factories, camps and airfields appeared literally wherever terrain allowed, and tiny concrete bunkers for three or four gunners were installed at every vaguely strategic juncture, even at remote road bridges like that over the River Dye in the Scottish Highlands. At what is now The National Memorial Arboretum near Alrewas a good specimen can be visited *in situ* beside the River Tame (navigable by the desperate) and another is seen on the distance covering the Birmingham to Derby railway as it crosses the river.

In May 1940, the FW3 Agency of The War Office convened to define pillbox designs. Of these mini-bunkers, six basic concrete designs were approved. As you might expect there are local variations, especially in the substitution of mortared granite ashlar for concrete. A seventh type was specialised for Hotchkiss gunners. Type 24, of which 1787 are recorded. It was the commonest design and was a sub-hexagonal form 14 feet long, and with walls 12 to 50 inches thick. Type 22, a regular hexagon had six-foot sides with walls 12 to 40 inches thick. There are 1209 documented Type 22's.

Because of their sturdy construction and obscure locations these "hardened field defences", ubiquitous in my boyhood, frequently survive. The weather and road improvements are, however, taking their toll.

The British took it for granted that, with invincible France occupied in weeks, they would presently find the Nazi in the streets of Swadlincote and on the braes of Breadalbane.

Like the Serbs and the Japanese they planned an immolative Gotterdamurung for their inviolable motherland.

As the War developed, and to the great surprise of all, the German did indeed visit these places, but as a tame and often amenable prisoner. Again, prisoner-of-war camps appeared almost literally anywhere, though the few in The Scottish Highlands or in remote Northumbria were usually reserved for SS personnel or card-carrying National Socialists. The ordinary prisoner might find himself anywhere from a commandeered Liberal Club building to a rural stately home or a purpose-built camp. From two camps in 1939 there were 600 prison camps in Britain by 1945. On Cannock Chase the Hippodamian foundations of what appeared to be a prison camp were visible as late as the nineteen-eighties.

Shadow factories and "secret" facilities also abound, though like the camps these are succumbing to dereliction and re-development. Others continue in overt or covert use.

Twenty years ago I visited a large factory in Mercia to conduct an academic examination for some of their employees. I parked my car at the West Gate and passed the guardhouse on foot. A smiling guard accosted me and for five minutes boasted of the tanks (armored gun vehicles) that they made. He dilated upon the technical nature of the plate steel they used, "the best in the World". A few weeks later I returned for a similar duty, but this time I parked at the South Gate. A different unsmiling guard closely scrutinised my credentials and interrogated me about my exact provenance and work schedule. I casually asked "What do you make here then?" He replied "Plastic telephone boxes, Sir". I made the obvious repost.

Another activity that demanded heavy concrete works, and whose vestiges accordingly tend to survive was the post-war rocket development effort. By the 1970's independent rocketry was being phased-out, laving vestiges at remote forested locations such as Spadeadam (Cumberland), and on The Isle of Wight and elsewhere.

Also shrouded in mystery, but slowly being pieced into history, are the British nuclear, biological and chemical weapons efforts of the twentieth century. Recently a large and partially-derelict chemical ammunition plant has "come to light" at Rhydymwym in an obscure but rail-accessible corner of North Wales. Parts have been photographed by antiquarians, whilst others have been able to provide pictures of the Avonmouth site (now cleared) where the evil contents were allegedly made.

The prosaic vestiges of desperate defence are almost as common as Britain's regular industrial sites, disused and active, and provide a vast and largely unexplored resource for the archaeologist and vernacular historian. Most documentation has been deliberately destroyed or "lost to history", but equally the sites are inherently durable enough to survive for study, and as the Internet expands and old men remember, and young men delve, more "comes to light" almost weekly.

CHARTLEY
Chartley Castle in Staffordshire

Location:	Chartley, near Hixon, Staffordshire, England, UK
Date of Photograph:	18 October 2002
OS Grid Reference:	SK010285
Co-ordinates:	52.85399°N: 1.98659°W
Elevation:	118.9 meters

This is a distant view of the remains of Chartley Castle from the A518 road to the East.

Chartley Castle is strategically sited in a valley controlling passage from the Trent-Dove waterways to the North and East and The Severn Basin to the South-West.

It was started around 900AD as a timber structure, almost certainly to pre-empt Viking excursions to West Mercia. After the Conquest a large motte and bailey were dug into shape and in 1220 Ranulph de Blondeville, 4th Earl of Chester, built a magnificent edifice of mortared stone with a circular keep defended by a curtain wall. This outer work incorporated two half-towers which still stand in a ruinous, but impressive, state. There remain also fragments of the curtain wall, a twin-towered gatehouse and an angled tower. This motte-and-bailey castle, Chartley I, passed by marriage to the Ferrers estate.

Sometime around 1485, Chartley II, a moated manor house was built 300 meters West of Chartley I, and this is the premises thought to have accommodated Mary Stuart, Queen of Scots, when she was the prisoner of Shrewsbury. Chartley I was abandoned and Leland described it as a ruin in 1545. Chartley II, a half-timbered house, was burnt down in 1781, and replaced. But the replacement also burnt in 1847.

A much larger unmoated building 500 meters West of Chartley I, was called Chartley Castle Farm, but has recently been re-designated Chartley Castle (III), and is a bed-and-breakfast hotel. It contains a chair cover and a set of curtains said to have been made at Chartley II by The Queen of Scots. (In the days when it was not *infra dig* to use your hands).

Chartley is indelibly associated with secret messages, early cryptographic science and Renaissance espionage.

As is of course true of all such affairs the details are unclear and remain controversial. Around the start of 1586 English Government fears of Catholic restoration intensified and new laws were introduced to provide for the execution of anyone who might benefit from, as opposed actively to perpetrate, the placing of Mary Stuart upon the Throne of England. It seems that Elizabeth's spymaster, Sir Francis Walsingham, orchestrated or at least manipulated a plot that would implicate Mary herself, and so pave the way for her personally to be killed.

Local Catholic gentry, principally Anthony Babington, aged 25, an infatuate of Mary, and John Ballard, Jesuit, were suitably framed.

A covert line of communication was developed between Chartley and double-agent Gilbert Gifford. Enciphered letters to and from Mary were smuggled concealed within the bungs of beer barrels.

Intercepted decrypts from Mary adverted to her supporters in France, whilst replies from Babington included treasonable remarks about his non-allegiance to Elizabeth. The mathematics of the coded messages is of some considerable historical interest in itself, involving early use of inferential statistics, including frequency analyses.

In an encrypt sent to Chartley in July 1586, Babington proposed to Mary that Elizabeth be assassinated, that Spain should invade England, and that the Protestant ministers Burghley and Walsingham should be killed.

Walsingham then arrested Babington when Babington applied for a passport to go to Spain. Babington's six co-conspirators were quickly identified, probably by torture, and they were arrested on 15th August 1586. A total of fourteen men were convicted of treason and sentenced to be hanged, drawn, and quartered. This was an obscene and horrific method of slow killing reserved for low-born male traitors. The first group of seven, including Babington and Ballard, were killed on 20th September. It is said that the weeping and screaming of the tortured men was such that Elizabeth ordered that the second batch of seven be allowed to die in the noose before being butchered.

The Queen of Scots was taken to another prison at Fotheringhay. Elizabeth Tudor signed her cousin's death warrant and on 8th February 1587 Mary Stuart was beheaded there. So inept was the deed that the Scotswoman was alive at the third blow, the second having sliced off the top of her cranium.

It is difficult to associate the romantic and pastoral, if somnolent, Staffordshire dell of today with those lurid and baleful events.

In 1603, Elizabeth died childless; Mary's son James, "The Wisest Fool in Christendom", ascended the English Throne, and The United Kingdom of Great Britain was born.

CHASERID
A First World War Rifle Range Butt on Cannock Chase

Location:	Penkridge Bank, Cannock Chase, near Rugeley, Staffordshire, England, UK
Date of Photograph:	am 11 January 2006
OS Grid Reference:	SJ994186
Co-ordinates:	52:45:55N 2:00:34W
Elevation:	187.1 meters

      Cannock Chase is an Area of Outstanding Natural Beauty in Southern Staffordshire. It is a dry sandy plateau of about forty square miles, deeply dissected and rising to between six and seven hundred feet. It is comprised of incompetent Permo-Triassic sands and conglomerates overlying Coal Measures, which latter were intensively worked for coal between 1298 and 1993. The plateau itself was crowded with small mines during the nineteenth century. It obviously goes without saying that the Chase is intensively haunted.

      At the time of writing in 2007 the Eastern part of the Chase is quarried for constructional sands and aggregates but the preponderant part is Forestry Commission (i.e. Forest Enterprises) plantations of Scots pine and exotic softwoods. The North-West part is occupied by native oakwood, once coppiced for local iron industries. There are several scientific nature reserves but most of the Chase is freely accessible with due caution for false ground. In warm weather care should be taken not to tread upon European Vipers (*Vipera berus*), Britain's only dangerous snake, which is ubiquitous on Cannock Chase. Deer abound on this former Medieval hunting range, and giant squirrels and other unusual wildlife are sometimes glimpsed.

During the First World War, and again in the Second, Cannock Chase was given over to intensive military use.

In the First World War there were two major Army training camps and a large military hospital as well as other large installations served by a special railway, the Tacaroo Line, and other complex infrastructures. JRR Tolkein, author of The Lord of the Rings, trained on the Chase before embarking for The Western Front. It is said that his encampments upon the Plains of Mordor were suggested by his familiarity with the then bleak and bare wastes of Cannock Chase. It is also alleged that the Manichean iconography of the plot is a grim satire of The First World War and its bloody but pointless evolutions.

The New Zealanders were based at Brockton, the Northern camp, and buried their regimental dog "Frieda" there, and also graced the waste with a scale model of their battlefield in France. The dog's grave is maintained but the model is lost beneath encroaching scrub.

In the Second World War large prison camps were built, as well as RAF training camps. There is a Commonwealth War Cemetery at the South-West margin of Cannock Chase. After the War it was decided to consolidate all German war graves in the UK in a compound near the Commonwealth Cemetery. The German War Cemetery is officially territory of the German Republic but may be entered without formality. There is a resident custodian who is apparently blasé about the reputation of his domain as one of the most haunted spots in England.

There are two major rifle butts at Penkridge Bank. The taller World War Two Eastern berm; and the older, lower, but longer World War One butt seen in the photograph. Little is known about this latter sand bank but it is expertly built, showing little sign of slumping or ablation even after ninety years. It may owe something to its surrounding shelter of tall Scots pines. It shows no impact damage or embedments. Its material seems to have been scooped out of the immediately adjacent sandy surface of the heathland.

There is still a small Territorial Army camp about a kilometer South of the pictured ridge, but all other military buildings have been demolished. A World War One dormitory hut that was originally on the Chase but moved elsewhere in Staffordshire has been re-erected at the Cannock Chase Visitor Centre as a museum. A unique training trench has been re-discovered on the Chase, but its location is undivulged.

FAULD
The Fauld Crater near Hanbury

Location:	Fauld, near Hanbury, Staffordshire, England, UK
Date of Photograph:	pm 26 October 2004
OS Grid Reference:	SK182277
Co-ordinates:	52:50:46N 1:43:57W
Elevation:	126.5 meters

The explosion crater at Fauld is about a half-a-mile East of Hanbury. At this location a steep escarpment overlooks the floodplain of the meandering River Dove to the North. The escarpment comprises thick deposits of Mercian Mudstone of Triassic age. This is a resistant, impermeable rock that leads to sodden, heavy soils on the Needwood Forest plateau above. Interbedded in the mudstone are two thick but discontinuous strata of hydrous calcium sulfate (gypsum) that reverts to an anhydrous form called anhydrite at depth. The better quality of the gypsum is massive and translucent and has for centuries been used by the Mercians as a marble substitute (alabaster) in the production of interior ornaments and sepulchres, and it was the finest grade of this material that was mined at Fauld for many centuries. In 1960 Fauld provided Princess Margaret's bridal bath.

At Fauld the mines were worked on a pillar-and-stall principle that extracted only three-quarters of the stone. Unlike coal measures, the mudstone is sufficiently competent to hold its void upon abandonment, and this fact commended the Fauld levels to use as a secret and bomb-proof repository. The production of gypsum for builders' plaster continued in part of Fauld Mine when the RAF commandeered the disused parts in 1937. The RAF stored a stockpile of 40000 tons of bombs in the workings throughout the Second World War.

At 1111 on 27th November 1944 the Fauld Mine exploded. The exact circumstances are of course unclear, but it is semi-officially claimed that the accident was due to the inept removal of a damaged bomb exploder returned to the arsenal from deployment. 3670 tons of HE bombs were said to have been present at the time, and 4000 tons of unexploded ordnance is alleged to remain: Needless to add, the mathematics is suspect.

It is the largest accidental blast in history, the second largest to have occurred in Europe, and the fourth largest of World War Two, exceeded only by the confessedly fission blasts above Trinity Sands, Hiroshima and Nagasaki. Seismographs as far away as Casablanca variously registered the detonation as being between 4.5 and 5.7 kilotons. Upper Castle Hayes Farm, its livestock and six human inhabitants vaporised. The Cock Inn, Hanbury was demolished at a distance of half-a-mile and buildings in Hanbury Village a mile away badly damaged by falling rock, some of which landed six miles away. The shock was felt in Birmingham and heard at London and Weston-super-Mare, which is 190 kilometers away. Chimney pots were blown off in Burton-upon-Trent, where two church steeples were cracked and one of them had to be demolished. The explosion and its mushroom cloud were seen forty miles away. The destruction of a small dam destroyed the local plaster factory killing thirty-three inside. Over a million tons of rock became airborne and gypsum dust carpeted a wide area of pasture ten centimeters deep. Individual clasts weighed up to one ton. It was possible to walk the dust noiselessly. The resulting crater had a diameter of 250 meters and a depth of 100 meters, (though the onsite notice claims 400 feet depth and three-quarters of a mile of length).

The ammunition dump employed a number of British airmen and also former Italian prisoners-of-war who had volunteered to remain after the Italian armistice of 1943. About fifty of these men and women died, including six Italians. The semi-official death toll is seventy-six. Many more were of course permanently disabled.

The moving memorials at Hanbury Church include a modest stone plaque inscribed in Italian set up about 1992: Clearly a mother's bequest to her long-dead son. At the site itself is a large block of Italian white biotite granite inscribed with the names of the known dead and given by Novara Munitions Depot on behalf of The People of Italy. It was dedicated in 1990.

It would appear that the Fauld Disaster resulted from the accidental detonation of a small atom bomb. It is similar to a slightly larger blast that occurred, also in rock tunnels, on the German island of Heligoland when it was under British Army control in 1946. Significantly, the human population had been evacuated a few days previously. The British did not admit to the possession of nuclear weapons until 1957.

GUNTOWER
The South-Western (Fort Road) Gun Tower at Pembroke Dock

Location:	Fort Road, Pembroke Dock, Pembrokeshire, Wales, UK
Date of Photograph:	13 April 1992
OS Grid Reference:	SM955036
Co-ordinates:	51:41:38N 4:57:36W
Elevation:	2.1 meters

This gun tower is at the Western (seaward) end of Fort Road.

In 1814 Royal Naval development operations were transferred from Milford on the North shore of the Milford Haven ria, to Paterchurch on the South. A large semi-secret shipyard was constructed and the evolving settlement renamed Pembroke Dock.

Whilst some routine heavy warships were to be built the yard was intended to specialise in experimental designs, especially those involving iron construction or steam propulsion. To protect specialised materials from the weather and assist security a number of cast-iron framed hangars were constructed over the slips, in addition to the traditional wooden covers still to be seen at Chatham. The cast-iron sheds were designed by Fox Henderson and built in 1844 for £15480. In 1851, Fox Henderson used the technology developed at Pembroke Dock to build the Crystal Palace.

In 1826, HMS Erebus was built for diplomat and explorer Sir John Franklin, former Governor of Van Dieman's Land (Tasmania), and himself a senior Naval officer. Erebus had central heating, both sail and steam screw propulsion, and was ice strengthened. The ship and its commander disappeared in the Canadian Arctic sometime in the 1840's.

The first warship principally-reliant upon steam was launched at Pembroke Dock in 1834, but it was in 1837 that HMS Gorgon the first successful steam build appeared.

During the 1840's concerns grew about the resurgence of French sea power and over the course of the next twenty years an extensive complex of shore forts were built to protect Southern naval harbors. They were probably misconceived, but were rendered feasible by the new Armstrong rifled-cannon technology, which could project explosive shells accurately over a range of miles.

The family of forts at Milford Haven numbered fourteen of diverse size and design, built on washed ledges or cliff tops. Their total cost exceeded one million pounds.

The Fort Road fortlet is one of a pair actually at Pembroke Dock and was designed to rake the West wall of the dockyard with 12-pounder or 32-pounder shot and shrapnel in the event of an attempted storming.

At the turn of the century, Pembroke Dock proved inadequate to the building of new classes of "Dreadnaught" battleships and the downscaling that began in the 1870's continued. The static forts were de-manned in 1904. The Washington Naval Treaty of 1926 subjected the Royal Navy size and strength to strict US Government controls and RN developments at Pembroke Dock ceased. Subsequently, and until the postwar era, Pembroke Dock was an RAF seaplane base.

Pembroke Dock today is a pleasant but sleepy Welsh town of ten thousand with an Irish ferry and some light engineering. The Fort Road Gun Tower (sometimes incorrectly called a "Martello" tower) is being converted into a private dwelling whilst the other Pembroke Dock tower on the Northern flank is now a museum.

MERCJEEP
Captured Argentine Vehicle in Cosford RAF Museum

Location:	The Royal Air Force Museum, RAF Cosford, Albrighton, Shropshire. Mercia, England, UK
Date of Photograph:	23 December 2003
OS Grid Reference:	SJ785052
Co-ordinates:	52:38:41N 2:19:04W
Elevation:	85 meters

This is a Mercedes-Benz G-Wagen G290 general purpose light military car equipped with a 2.3-liter petrol engine.
I will let the museum's exhibit notice explain the drip pan:-

This jeep was captured by Gurkhas during the Falklands campaign in June 1982 and given to no 18 Squadron.
It had a 30mm cannon hole in the bonnet.
It was brought to the UK by sea and then moved by Chinook helicopter to RAF Gutersloh in Germany.

Here the shell hole was repaired, it was given British Forces Germany licence plates and used as a squadron transport and hire vehicle, still in its Argentinean paint scheme.

A neighbouring squadron hijacked the jeep and returned it with a new tiger stripe paint scheme. This was not to the liking of 18 Squadron, who repainted the jeep in black and red, the squadron colours.

When a new gearbox part was needed it transpired that the Jeep was unpaid for and Mercedes requested the vehicle back. As spoils of war it was not available for return. Mercedes refused to supply parts and spares had to be obtained elsewhere.

When 18 Squadron returned to England, the jeep proved impossible to register with the DVLA as it had no importation documents. It had always been the intention to donate the jeep to the RAF Museum and it was moved to Cosford, again by Chinook, on 14 June 2001.

OXCASTLE
Oxwich Castle on the Gower Peninsula

Location:	Oxwich Castle at Oxwich, Glamorganshire, Wales, UK
Date of Photograph:	am 2 May 2002
OS Grid Reference:	SS497862
Co-ordinates:	51:33:18N 4:10:06W
Elevation:	69.5 meters

The site has been fortified from at least the Middle Ages, but the parts that remain visible are essentially sixteenth-century.

They constitute a large, lightly-fortified Tudor manor house that may have been built as a tower-of-refuge from Arab slavers who raided the South-Western coasts of Britain and Ireland in the sixteenth and seventeenth centuries. Lundy Island, thirty-eight miles sailing to the South-West was occupied by Barbary pirates in 1627-1632.

Oxwich Castle is arranged around a courtyard whose gatehouse bears the arms of Sir Rice Mansel, whose family had held Oxwich since 1459. Three self-contained ranges, one of a tenement-like character, were erected some time prior to 1578 by Sir Rice and improved by his son, Sir Edward. The oldest, two-story Southern range may be as early as 1520, and it is this that is still occupied. By 1632, the Mansels had moved to Margam and leased Oxwich to a tenant. In 1947 the South range constituted a farmhouse, and in that year Lady Apsley rescued it from demolition and gave it to the State.

In 2002 Oxwich Castle was still a working farm but under the care of Cadw, with regular openings to the public. (Cadw is the Welsh national monuments administration).

WHITTING
Whittington Castle Gatehouse in Shropshire

Location:	Whittington, Shropshire, England, UK
Date of Photograph:	pm 23 April 2004
OS Grid Reference:	SJ326310
Co-ordinates:	52:32:25N 3:00:10W
Elevation:	90.8 meters

This scene has changed somewhat since the picture was taken in the Spring of 2004. The castle precinct includes a partially-moated gatehouse with a functional cottage as seen, together with a larger moated ruin surrounding a courtyard, hard to the South. The whole assemblage is set within a broad circular sulcus. The castle complex covers twelve acres and is of Norman origin.

This gatehouse is haunted by the wraiths of small children who are sometimes seen peeping from its windows, and Whittington Castle pays even greater homage to fashionable cupidity as another of the temporary stopovers of The Holy Grail.

As a Marcher castle, Whittington was unusual in not being within a meander loop, atop a crag, or otherwise exploiting obvious natural defences. But it had an even better natural defence against Medieval assault: It was set within a marsh. In the days before helicopters and other aviation, forts and towns within marshes were almost impregnable since they could not be stormed on foot, upon horseback, or even by boat. Like almost all English marshes this has long succumbed to agricultural improvements.

There was a wooden stronghold built by the Mercian King Offa as part of his March defences before William Peverel built the Norman motte and bailey structure of stone.

The Normans probably commenced with a twelfth century tower keep rebuilt in 1222. The gatehouse was likely added by Sir Faulke Fitzwarin in the earliest years of the thirteenth century, and originally accommodated a drawbridge for the wide moat. A stone bearing his arms is set above the gateway. The arms of Sir Richard Whittington, he who turned thrice Lord Mayor of London, is very similar, leading to speculation that the boy with the cat hailed from this little town. The surviving cottage pictured behind the gatehouse is Elizabethan.

William Peverel had no male heir so his eldest daughter Mollet inherited the stronghold. Frenchman Warin de Metz won her hand in a tournament and the Fitzwarin family held the castle until 1420.

Sir Faulke Fitzwarin was proscribed by King John and may be one of the legendary heroes whose exploits contributed to the formation of Robin Hood lore.

After the time of the Fitzwarins, England's *de facto* union with Wales led to a rapid decline for Whittington and the rest of the Marcher strongpoints. Since 1420 the castle has had a succession of owners of whom only the Fitzalans, Earls of Arundel, were aristocrats. Notwithstanding its untitled ownership, Whittington came out for the King during the English Civil War, and was taken by Parliament in 1643, after which the fortress was almost certainly slighted with powder.

The grounds are now a favorite spot with picnicers, especially those who like my Wife and I break a journey to or from North Wales. The Whittington Castle Trust has taken out a 99-year lease on the precinct from its owners, Mrs A Hamilton-Hill and The Lady Newborough. Since the photograph was taken the Trust has spent £1.5 million on repair and restoration, inclusive of £950000 from The Heritage Lottery Fund. This has led to renewal of the cottage and gatehouse surfaces, and the demolition of the curtain wall at (0.25,0.25). That wall has been replaced by a wooden tearoom with large glass windows facing the pathway.

Conclusion

What can we conclude from our short and very eclectic survey?

On the Wikipedia it says that Great Britain is an island bounded by 17820 kilometers of coastline. About twenty years ago a mathematical fashion for the fractal came and went. Researchers pointed out that an indented natural boundary like a shoreline has no knowable length, but is sensibly infinite. When you say it is 17820 kilometers it is because you smoothed out the little corrugations of caverns and covelets; when you include those you have a longer length, but now have to consider rocks and boulders; count them in and you must now account for the pebbles at the water's margin; and so in infinite regress until you try to measure things so little that they are not sure where they are, and change their minds if you look.

Britain is like a Klein Bottle. Pushing the envelope, its periphery is at the center of civilisation, infinitely continuous, self-referential and intestinal, finitely infinite, an endless existential narrative, the surface and the essence of things.

No one knows the beginning of Britain, and its end is also unknown. In between is something like a Sierpinsky Gasket, infinitely porous yet describable in outline. Every delving, every enquiry, every experiment or act of scholarship from the probing of a nucleus to the consultation of a timetable adds a new fragment of color to the glittering mosaic of its infinite reticule. But if a pattern appears then it is emergent and local. When, in spite of that, we stand back, between the dark interstices we behold, like a Newton or a Rutherford in other worlds, a firmament of glory.

In 1798 the Surrey clergyman Thomas Malthus published "An Essay on the Principle of Population". His underlying thesis was that generational breeding expanded a population geometrically through time, whilst the production of necessary resources expanded only arithmetically. Therefore a time would inevitably succeed when the numbers of people outstripped supply and "miseries" such as war, plague and famine would supersede and cut the population catastrophically. Malthus could point to such calamities from The Bible to The Black Death to bear out his argument, but after much travel and enquiry he discovered that some communities and some whole countries had evolved social stratagems that enabled them to sidestep such disasters.

The Norwegians had the remarkable trick of enforcing military service for all males less than about thirty, which, in the presence of female chastity, removed them from the breeding pool. The Scots had the even more interesting device of diverting a proportion of their cereal harvest to inessential alcohol distillation: In parlous times they could cut into that margin to make bread. The Turks arbitrarily confiscated excess wealth wherever it arose, thus stifling ambition of any kind, including begetting.

By Malthus' time the Irish poor had come to subsist upon a single crop of beguiling utility, the potato, and they reserved none of it for making vodka. When in 1845 to 1852 pestilence struck the potato, three of Ireland's nine million died and another three million emigrated. Sadly, Malthus' dismal science was vindicated. And it has taken that tragic land one and a half hundred years to sow the seeds of recovery.

When I read Malthus' book I found it impossible to tell if he had perceived that his own place and time had chosen, by accident for sure, yet another apocalypse-cheating stratagem: Industrialisation.

A revolution in agriculture and importation kept famine at bay, whilst the mightiest Navy held war at arm's length, away from the population. Engineering, drainage and vaccination suppressed epidemic.

The four horsemen were banished, at least for a time, and the British population stormed past its crisis level of six million, past the organic bearing capacity of the land at eleven million to forty million in 1905 to sixty million in 2005.

At the end of the old millennium British industry and shipping suddenly vanished. Most of what remained was sold to foreign interests and credit replaced production as the source of the sustentation of the people.

At the beginning of 2008 the Governor of The Bank of England said that his countrymen needed to replace property inflation and other credit sources with production and export.

Further revolutions await.

UNDERSTANDING PICTURE CO-ORDINATES

In some of the place sections, features of interest within the pictures are located from the text in terms of relative Cartesian co-ordinates in which we imagine that, for the picture in question, the height is 1.0 vertical units and the length 1.0 horizontal units

Because the photographs are not squares this naturally implies that the two units have differing absolute physical length, but this does not matter for our purpose.

The locations on the pictures are specified as (0.hh,0.vv) where hh and vv are respectively decimal fractions of the relevant dimension.

We need to imagine the horizontal split into ten equal strips (perhaps with eleven equally-spaced green lines?), and the vertical also so split. Lets say with eleven equally-spaced imaginary blue lines. If we had time we could even realise this imaginary scheme with a physical graticule on acetate sheet or tracing paper, but this is not really worthwhile once we get the hang of the technique.

We then use the quoted fractions further to refine the displacements along the vertical and the horizontal, and project lines from those points on the axes: Where the projected lines meet is the object referred to.

For example, look at this panorama of Stonehaven.

We want to locate three features quickly and unambiguously: The Tolbooth, The Belfry of The Old Town House, and the Steeple of The Market Hall.

The appropriate co-ordinates are as follows:-

The Tolbooth	(0.983,0.50)
The Belfry	(0.573,0.57)
The Steeple	(0.29,0.66)

Strictly, the leading zeros before the point are redundant, but I always include them for clarity.

Here is the original, full-contrast picture of the town for clarity:-

Now look at our locational scheme:-

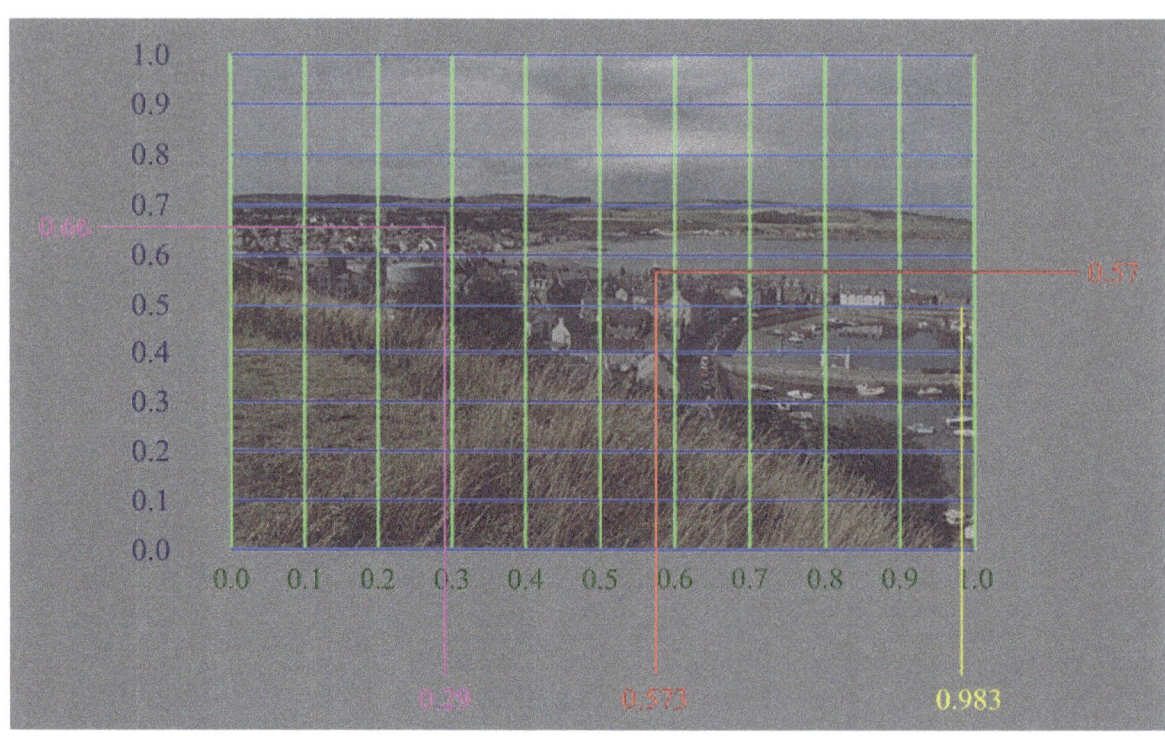

I have not bothered to quote the vertical co-ordinate of the red sandstone Tolbooth on the quayside, because it coincides with the horizontal 0.5 line for half-way up the vertical. But the yellow x-coordinate is given as 0.983. On my pictures the third significant digit is really superfluous and is only included here for clarity.

Similarly, the red lines locate the Belfry of the Old Town House as picture co-ordinate (0.573, 0.57). Horizontal (x) co-ordinates always come first.

Finally, (0.29, 0.66) locates the Steeple on the Market Hall.

You can of course use such co-ordinates to locate any feature on a rectangular picture

British Units of Measurement

During the late twentieth century the old Imperial measures current in Britain for centuries gradually fell into disuse. The French Metric System had been used in scientific work almost since its inception but by 1970 the Metric System, and in particular the SI convention, began spreading to engineering and general use.

By 2008, the Imperial measures were retained together with Metric in the labelling of pre-packaged groceries (that were themselves in Metric containers); and in distances upon road signs. In the Irish Republic, older black-and-white road signs are labelled in miles, and the new green ones in kilometers.

American Customary units differ slightly in size from their UK counterparts.

Length, Distance and Depth

One Inch is legally defined as 2.54 centimeters exactly.

There are 12 inches in a foot; 3 feet in a yard; 2 yards in a fathom; and 1760 yards in a mile. Furthermore a Chain is 22 yards and a Furlong 220 yards. Accordingly there are 8 Furlongs in one mile.

One Statute (land) mile is 1609.344 meters.

At sea, a Cable is 185.2 meters. There are 10 Cables in A Nautical Mile that is about 6076.1155 feet or 1.852 kilometers exactly.

Occasionally, historical documents will refer to a measure called an ell or similar, especially in reference to cloth. One ell is 45 inches or 1.143 meters.

Area

The traditional British land area measure is the Acre that can be of any shape but may be thought of as a rectangle of one Chain times one Furlong, or 4840 square yards.

This equals 4046.856422 square meters or about 0.4047 hectares.

Prior to 1824 a Scottish Acre was about 1.3 English Acres of 4850 square yards.

Weight

Technically, Imperial measures are of mass gravimetrically assessed.

Basically, a Pound (weight) is 453.59237 grams which is of course 0.45359237 kilograms. A pound contains 16 Ounces.

There are 2240 pounds in a Long Ton (confusingly, this is identical to the Shortweight Ton), the usual measure of industrial goods. There are 2000 (American) pounds in a Short Ton.

Accordingly, one Long ton is 1.0160469088 Metric tonnes.

In the measure of refined precious metals one sometimes encounters the Troy Ounce: It is 31.1034768 grams. Concentrated ore from The King's Field was usually quoted in Dishes. A Wirksworth Dish is 65 pounds or roughly 29.48 kilograms.

Volume

A Pint is 568.261 milliliters. There are 8 Pints in an (Imperial) Gallon. Accordingly, a gallon is 4.54609 liters. Wine and beer were measured in hogsheads. A wine hogshead was 52.5 gallons and a beer hogshead 54 gallons.

Bulk fish was measured in Cran, originally a Scottish measure. One cran is 37.5 gallons or 170.5 liters.

Currency

The English currency is the Pound Sterling. Before decimalisation, which took place on 15 February 1971, there were 2 Farthings in a Halfpenny; 2 Halfpennies in a Penny; 12 pence (pennies) in a Shilling; 5 shillings in a Crown; and 4 Crowns in a Pound. By the mid twentieth century amounts were written in the format £nn:ss:ddf, where n are pounds s are shillings, d are pence, and f is a fraction of a penny.

A different notational convention applied to small amounts of cash. One third of a pound is six shillings and eight pence written in the format ss/ddf[d], to render 8/6d. Eight and sixpence halfpenny was 8/6½. But ten shillings was written 10/-, or three shillings 3/-. Eleven pence three farthings was noted as 11¾d.

In Medieval times one Noble was six shillings and eight pence (6/8d) or one third of a pound. A Guinea was one pound and one shilling, or in modern notation £1.05. The Guinea declined after the introduction of paper currency (circa 1910) and fell out of use upon decimalisation. Both the Guinea and the Noble were denominated as gold coins at various times. When gold was removed from circulation during the early twentieth century, only the Sovereign and Half Sovereign (worth respectively one pound and ten shillings) were legal tender.

In Scotland, the Scots Pound was latterly equivalent to one shilling and eight pence English; thus a Scots Shilling was one English penny. One Merk was two-thirds of a Pound Scots. A bawbee was one Scots halfpenny or one twenty-fourth of a penny English: About £0.000173611 or $US0.0000842772. It is difficult to understand the utility of such small denominations until one remembers that in Feudal Europe there was limited cash payment and a restricted range of purchasable goods and services. The Scots Pound was abolished in 1707, when under the terms of The Act of Union twelve were redeemable for every Pound Sterling.

LIST OF WEBSITE REFERENCES

Abbreviations

       wiki/   Prefix with http://en.wikipedia.org/

Unless shown with the Prefix http:
prefix all other forms with http://www.

ABEREIDD
    pembrokeshirevirtualmuseum.co.uk/main_menu/trad_and_industry/train…
    pembrokeshire-onlline.co.uk/geolmap.htm

ABHD
    thehorndanceofabbotsbromley.co.uk/id3.html
    wiki/Abbots_Bromley_Horn_Dance

AMBUACH
    travelpublishing.co.uk/CountyIntros/InnerHebridesIntro.htm
    british-history.ac.uk/report.aspx?compid=45302&strquery=Staffa#s67
    geo.ed.ac.uk/scotgaz/features/featurefirst1557.html
    scotland.com/reserves/staffa-nature-reserve/
    wiki/Staffa
    fullbooks.com/The-Student-s-Elements-of-Geology10.html
    mull-historical-members.co.uk/members-area/geology/lava_flows_and_dykes.htm
    volcano.und.edu/vwdocs/vw_hyperexchange/col_joint.html

BIRASSAY
    theassayoffice.co.uk/hallmarking_history.html

BELPERWR
    belpernorthmill.org/AboutTheMill.asp
    derwentvalleymills.org/04_his/print/his_001h.htm

BISHOPSC
    scit.wlv.ac.uk/~jphb/shropshire/BishopsCastle.html

BMW
    birmingham.gov.uk
    wiki/Boulton_Watt_and_Murdoch

BRATCH
    dynamike.net/thebratch/tech.htm

BRIDESTN
    english-nature.org.uk/citation/citation_photo/1002268.pdf
    visitnorthyorkshiremoors.co.uk/content.php?nID=561
    english-nature.org.uk/citation/citation_photo/1002268.pdf
    visitnorthyorkshiremoors.co.uk/content.php?nID=561
    http://links.jstor.org/sici?sici=1478-4017(1956)1%3A22%3C55%3ATFATBI%3E2.0.CO%3B2-2
    horne28.freeserve.co.uk/eybib88.htm
    ravilious.net/kate/publications/Rockwatch.html
    http://encyclopedia.jrank.org/COM_COR/CORALLIAN_Fr_Corallun_.html
    mysteriousbritain.co.uk/gods&goddesses/celtic/brigid.html

BRIGBALG
    wiki/Brig_o'_Balgownie
    geo.ed.ac.uk/scotgaz/features/featurefirst1488.html

BUTTERLY
    wiki/Benjamin_Outram
    wiki/Butterley_Company
    butterleyengineering.com/structures/structures2.htm
    butterleyengineering.com/cranes/cranes.htm
    ampleforth.org.uk/OANews/html/StPancrasStation.html
    http://en.allexperts.com/e/b/bu/butterley_company.htm

CALMAC
    shipsofcalmac.co.uk/cmbhistory.asp
    shipsofcalmac.co.uk/history_timeline.asp

CHANCE
    wiki/Chance_Brothers
    chanceglass.co.uk/?p=history
    search.revolutionaryplayers.org.uk/engine/resource/exhibition/standard/default.asp?resource=4439
    wiki/Hyperradiant_Fresnel_lens
    british-history.ac.uk/report.aspx?compid=36177

CHARLCOT
    smr.herefordshire.gov.uk/hsmr/db.php?smr_no=6374

CHARTLEY
    wiki/Chartley_Castle
    homepage.mac.com/phillipdavis/English%20sites/3316.html
    genuki.org.uk/big/eng/STS/ChartleyHolme/index.htnl
    wiki/Babington_Plot

COLESCH
: british-history.ac.uk/report.asps?compid=42654
coleshillparishchurch.org.uk/homedir/concise.htm
wiki/Coleshill_Warwickshire

DARKLANT
: search.staffspasttrack.org.uk/engine/resource/exhibition/standard/…
search.staffspasttrack.org.uk/engine/resource/default.asp?resource=2799
flickr.com/castrovalva/279123228/

DAVY
: Encyclopaedia Britannica (textual CDROM edition 1999)
bbc.co.uk/dna/h2g2/A25568445
wiki/Humphry_Davy

DITHERIN
: search.revolutionaryplayers.org.uk/engine/resource/exhibition/standard/…

DONNA
: pmsa.cch.kcl.ac.uk/BM/WMwaBLvh004.htm
wiki/Pelsall

DOROTHEA
: llechicymru.info/IHistindRev.english.htm
penmorfa.com/slate/beamengine.html

DUNSEATH
: rbs.org.uk/cgibin/rbs_gallery.cgi?userid=102&letter=D&imageid=1&display=info
axisweb.org/seCVPG.aspx?ARTISTID=5746
somersetartweek.org.uk/artist.cfm?id=32&CFID=19044812&CFTOKEN=70345492

ECTON
: search.digitalhandsworth.org.uk/engine/resource/default.asp?theme=239…

FAULD
: geolsoc.org.uk/template.cfm?name=EMRG2003
carolyn.topmum.net/tutbury/fauld/fauldcrater.htm

FORTINGA
: rampantscotland.com/know/blkknow_fortingall.htm
sacredconnections.co.uk/holyland/fortingallyew.htm

FROG
    wiki/Common_Frog

GEESE
    http://daviswiki.org/Canada_Geese
    rspb.org.uk/wildlife/birdguide/name/c/canadagoose/
    wiki/Canada_Goose

GEEVOR
    geevor.com/more/history/History%20index.htm
    cornishlight.co.uk/cornish-tin-mine.htm
    wiki/Geevor_Tin_Mine
    mindat.org/loc-1296.html

GOATS
    cast.org.uk/clatteringshaws.htm
    uksponsorship.com/a614.htm
    geocities.com/magicgoatman/feralgoat.html

GOONWIND
    yes2wind.com/noflash_details.php?Region=Devon+and+Cornwall&Site…

GRETNA
    wiki/Gretna_Green
    wiki/Marriage_Act%2C_1753

GUNTOWER
    pembroke-dock.co.uk/History%202006%20Mod/h_army_4.htm
    pembrokeshiremaritimeexperience.org.uk/pembrokeshiremaritimeheritage…

HAKIN
    geograph.org.uk/photo/369379
    http//brynjones.members.beeb.net/wastronhist/welshastronobs.html

HARVESTR
    news.bbc.co.uk/1/hi/scotland/603558.stm
    maib.gov.uk

HELVETIA
    welcometogower.co.uk/2007/08/helvetia.html
    explore-gower.co.uk/Content/pa=showpage/pid=21.html

HEYSHAM
dti.gov.uk/energy/sources/nuclear/technology/generation/page17922.html
newsvote.bbc.co.uk/mpapps/pagetools/print/news.bbc.co.uk/1/hi/uk_politics/vot
…
djclark.com/2000/days/nuclear/info.htm
wiki/Heysham_Power_Station
wiki/Heysham_Stage_2_Nuclear_Power_Station
wiki/Magnox
ministry-of-information.co.uk/blog1/0502/190205-21.htm

HOLLYLOD
wiki/Holly_Lodge_Estate

HOLOPRIS
wiki/Holloway_Prison
richard.clark32.btinternet.co.uk/holloway.html

HOPEX
venuereseervations.co.uk/hopexchange.htm
southwark.gov.uk/DiscovreSouthwark/BluePlaquesSection/Nominees2004/thehopexchange.html
victorianlondon.org/gl/queenslondon60.htm

HORSELEY
bcn-society.co.uk/bp170_junctions.php
walsall.gov.uk/print/index/view_the_statutory_list_of_buildings.htm
pelsall-history.co.uk/iron%20works.html
steamindex.com/manlocos/manulist.htm
practicalmachinist.com/cgi-bin/ubbcgi/ultimatebb.cgi?ubb=print_topic;f=11;t=004110
bcn-society.co.uk/bp173_Worsey.php
http://presidentschoice.imeche.org.uk/NR/rdonlyres/506556DE-A65E-43C3-A249-FC5A701F6C79/196/PCHO_PRES_1997_112_003_01.pdf
laws.sandwell.gov.uk/ccm/content/sandwelldirect/leisuredirect/history/historyofsandwell.en;jsessionid=bQ7KxV0iZef_
genuki.org.uk/big/eng/STS/Tipton/index.html#Occupations
wiki/Engine_Arm
wiki/Horseley_Ironworks
wiki/Aaron_Manby
abebooks.de/search/sortby/3/an/Allen+/tn/+Horseley+Tipton
countrybookshop.co.uk/books/index.phtml?whatfor=1901522903

IMACHAR
  minersoc.org/pages/Archive-MM/Volume_42/42-321-141.pdf
  arranmuseum.co.uk/the_cambrian.htm

IONA
  argyle-bute.gov.uk/localplans/Local_plan%20568.pdf
  ftp://ftp.royalmail.com/Downloads/public/ctf/po/Proposed_area_plan_Greater_Glasgow.pdf
  scotland.org.uk/guide/Isle_of_Iona
  undiscoveredscotland.co.uk/iona/iona/index.html
  wiki/Iona

JCB
  jcb.co.uk/aboutjcb/welcome.aspx
  virtualtourist.com/travel/Europe/United_Kingdom/Uttoxeter-303674/Off_the_Beaten_Path-Uttoxeter-BR-1.html#2
  wiki/J._C._Bamford
  wiki/Rocester

KILCOBBN
  wiki/William_Hillary
  rnli.org.uk/rnli_near_you/southwest/stations/TheLizardCornwall/history
  lizard-lifeboat.co.uk/pages/shouts-2006/Latest-news-2006.htm

KIRKMAID
  rcahms.gov.uk/pls/portal/newcanmore.details_gis?inumlink=61095
  mull-of-galloway.co.uk/history/myths_legends.html

KIRKPAT
  eioba.com/a30949/the_difference_between_cast_and_malleable_iron
  experianbi.co.uk/downloads/sample_reports/Market_Research_CR_Download.xls
  kirkpatrick.co.uk

KNOCKER
  wiki/Knockers
  mysteriousbritain.co.uk/folklore/english_folk/knockers.html

LAUNER
  launer.com

LEEKMILL
    exploringthepotteries.org.uk/Nof_website1/local_history_static_exhibition…
    british-history.ac.uk/report.asp/compid=22910
    boydell.co.uk/97227864.HTM
    seacrh.staffspasttrack.org.uk/engine/resource/default.asp?resource=5247
    wiki/Reform_Act_1832

LETOCETM
    roman-britain.org/places/letocetum.htm

LIONSALT
    (unknown source)

LLANEGGS
    http://wwt.org.uk/centre/120/national_wetland_centre_wales.html
    aboutbritain.com/WWTLlanelli.htm

LONGDON
    wiki/Shrewsbury_Canal
    http:/en.structurae.de/structures/data/index.cfm?ID=s0002274

MAGPIE
    cressbrook.co.uk/visits/magpie.php
    peak-experience.org.uk/tourism/explore-the-guides/peak-experience-guid…

MAYNARD
    cadburyschweppes.com/EN/Brands/History/factsheet.htm?id=%7b4EF2FBB1-D097-46D2-A1FC-33051C8F0C8C%7d

MELCHURCH
    cpat.demon.co.uk/projects/longer/churches/montgom/19470.htm

MELINNA
    greatorme.org.uk/melangell.html
    bbc.co.uk/wales/mid/sites/walks/pages/pererindod_melangell.shtml

MENAI
    anglesey-history.co.uk/places/bridges/
    princeton.edu/~civ102/labs/menai_article.pdf
    prosciectmenai.co.uk/telfordeng.html
    steamindex.com/backtrak/bt12.htm
    wiki/Menai_Bridge
    wiki/Menai_Suspension_Bridge
    worldwideschool.org/library/books/hst/biography/

TheLifeofThomasTelford/chap18.html

MERRY
theteddybearmuseum.com/teddy-facts.htm
teddybear.org/e_gesch.htm
cymruted.com/html/merrythought.html
shropshirestar.com/2006/11/teddy-bear-firm-closes/
merrythought.co.uk/press.htm
http://news.bbc.co.uk/1/hi/england/shropshire/6202537.stm
merrythought.co.uk/press.htm
teddybears.co.uk/bear_essentials_548?-
session=teddybears_usr:42F942AA1af47189D6RlG1B05100

MULLHORN
nlb.org.uk/ourlights/history/mullofgalloway,htm
taighsolais.com/mull_of_galloway_archives.htm

NEWFOUND
wiki/James_Foster_(ironmaster)
wiki/John_Urpeth_Rastrick
wiki/Stourbridge_Lion
iarecordings.org/bradmth.html

OXCASTLE
castlewales.com/oxwich

PARKLANE
ianbyrne.free-online.co.uk/clevelan.htm

PEACEPAG
wiki/Peace_Pagoda
chezpaul.org.uk//buddhism/uk/talaka.htm
chezpaul.org.uk/buddhism/uk/news/talaka98.htm

PELSALL
pmsa.cch.kcl.ac.uk/BM/WMwaPEvh002.htm

PENTRICH
pentrich.org.uk/html/site.map.html
wiki/Pentrich

PERROTT
birminghamuk.com/wikipedia/perrotts.html
digital-ladywood.org.uk/timeline17-18c.asp

digital-ladywood.org.uk/timeline19c.asp
search.digital-ladywood.org.uk/engine/resource/exhibition/sequential/…

POLITI
glias.org.uk/news/201news.html#J

PORTBILL
trinityhouse.co.uk/interactive/gallery/portland_bill.html

PRIESTLY
search.revolutionaryplayers.org.uk/content/files/121/115/360.txt

QUEENSF
geo.ed.ac.uk/scotgaz/towns/townfirst294.html
queensferryhistorygroup.org.uk
undiscoveredscotland.co.uk/queensferry/southqueensferry/index.html
wiki/South_Queensferry

RAGWORT
bio.bris.ac.uk/research/plantrepro/oxford_ragwort.html

RECORDE
Encyclopaedia Britannica (textual CDROM edition 1999)
wiki/Robert_Recorde
http://www-groups.dcs.st-and.ac.uk/~history/Biographies/Recorde.html

REFUGE
wiki/Refuge_Assurance
wiki/Refuge_Assurance_Building
wiki/Burmantofts_Pottery
wiki/Alfred_Waterhouse
wiki/Paul_Waterhouse
lookingatbuildings.org.uk/default.asp?Document=3.T.7&Image=105&gst=…
travel.yahoo.com/p-hotel-353159-action-describe-le_meridien_palace-l…

REPTON
reptonvillage.org.uk/history_group/history_group_homepage.htm
repton.org.uk/mainlist.html?pgi=head.hist
reptonvillage.org.uk/history_group/gas_works.htm
reptonvillage.org.uk/history_group/repton_early_history.htm

ROYALCOL
http://phys.strath.ac.uk/public/history/photos.php
wiki/University_Of_Strathclyde

wiki/John_H._D._Anderson

SCHIEHAL
sacredconnections.co.uk/holyland/fortingallyew.htm

SEAL
wiki/Grey_Seal
bbc.co.uk/wales/mid/sites/wildlife/pages/grey_seal.shtml
arkive.org/species/ARK/mammals/Halichoerus_grypus/
whalewatchwestcork.com/seals-ireland.html
renew.freeuk.com/newholl/seals.html

SHOTDAWN
shotatdawn.org.uk/page43.html
shotatdawn.org.uk/page24.html

SKOMER
rosemoor.com/IPFiles/Nationalpark/skomer.html

SNAIL
wiki/Helix_aspersa

SPIDER
wiki/Giant_House_Spider

STONESIS
geograph.org.uk/photo/17864
derbyshire-peakdistrict.co.uk/carsingtonwater.htm

STONHVN
mearns.org.uk/stonehaven/romans.htm
mearns.org.uk/stonehaven/county.htm
mearns.org.uk/stonehaven/history.htm
mearns.org.uk/stonehaven/fishing.htm
mearns.org.uk/stonehaven/thomson.htm
scottishgeology.com/outandabout/classic_sites/locations/stonehaven.html

TANKER
http://shropshiremines.org.uk/tankerville/tankhist.htm

THIRSTHO
peakwalk.org.uk/deepdale.asp
themodernantiquarian.com/site/5192/thirst_house.html
peakdistrictview.com/?page=place&placeid=798

capra.group.shef.ac.uk/1/nmid.html#Thirst%20House%20Cave
youandyesterday.co.uk/articles/Deepdale:_A_HOB_Story
capra.group.shef.ac.uk/7/743Research.pdf
wiki/Carboniferous_limestone
thepeakdistrict.info/fast/html/peak_district_geology.html

TONGLAND
wiki/Tongland
wiki/Galloway_Hydro_Electric_Scheme

TREVIT
Encyclopaedia Britannica (textual CDROM edition 1999)
wiki/Richard_Trevithick

UCL
wiki/University_College_London

WERBURGH
wiki/Werburgh

WHITPRIO
undiscoveredscotland.co.uk/whithorn/whithornpriory/index.html

WHITTING
btinternet.com/~whittington.castle

WIGGIN
oldhallclub.co.uk/jjw1.htm
oldhallclub.co.uk/jjw2.htm
carpathian.co.uk/welcome.asp

WIGTOWN
josephrwalker.com/Rutherford.htm
wiki/Wigtown

WIGTOWNCH
guide.visitscotland.com/vs/guide/…
dumfriesmuseum.demon.co.uk/wigtowncross.html

WITHERIN
wiki/Digitalis
wiki/William_Withering

WROXETER
roman-britain.org/places/viroconium.htm

List of Book References

ALBION
    Title: Early Bristol Paddle Steamer Shipwrecks
    Author: George Harries
    Publisher: Merrivale
    Edition: First
    Date: 1993
    Town: St David's
    New ISBN: ISBN 978-0951520734
    Pages   80
    Price: £6.99

ECTON
    Title: The Copper and Lead Mines of Ecton Hill, Staffordshire
    Author: JA Robey and L Porter
    Publisher: Moorland Publishing
    Date: August 1972
    Town: Ashbourne
    Old ISBN: ISBN 0-903485-01-X
    New ISBN: ISBN 978-0903485012
    Pages: 92
    Price: £7.25

GEEVOR
    Title: Cornish Mines
    Author: Roger Burt
    Publisher: University of Exeter Press
    Date: June 1987
    Town: Exeter
    New ISBN: ISBN 978-0859892872
    Pages: 220
    Price: £15.19

    Title: Cornish Mining
    Author: Bryan Earl
    Publisher: Cornish Hillside Publications
    Edition: Second
    Date: July 1994
    Town: St Austell
    New ISBN: ISBN 978-0951941935
    Pages: 121
    Price: £9.98

GOODLUCK, MAGPIE

Title:	Derbyshire Mineral Statistics
Author:	Roger Burt
Publisher:	University of Exeter Press
Date:	September 1981
Town:	Exeter
New ISBN:	ISBN 978-0950762401
Pages:	141
Price:	£4.49

Title:	Lead Mining in the Peak District
Author:	TD Ford and JH Rieuwerts (Eds)
Publisher:	Peak District National Park Authority
Edition:	Fourth
Date:	May 2000
Town:	Matlock Bath and Ashbourne
Old ISBN:	ISBN 0-901-522-15-6
New ISBN:	ISBN 978-0907543602
Pages:	207
Price:	£9.95

GOONWIND

Title:	Where to Visit Wind Farms (Wind Energy Fact Sheet 10a)
Author:	Department of Trade and Industry
Date:	2001
Town:	London
Price:	£0.00

Title:	Wind Farms of the UK
Author:	Paul Hannah
Publisher:	British Wind Energy Association
Town:	London
Price:	£0.00

HARVESTR

Title:	The Loss of Solway Harvester
Author:	Marine Accident Investigation Branch
Publisher:	Department of Trade and Industry
Date:	July 2003
Town:	London
Price:	£0.00

HORSELEY

Title:	History of Horseley, Tipton, A: Two Centuries of Engineering Progress
Author:	JS Allen
Publisher:	Landmark Publishing Ltd
Edition:	First
Date:	June 2000
Town:	Ashbourne
New ISBN:	ISBN 9781901522907
Pages:	176
Price:	£25.26

INTRO

Title:	The Population of Britain in the 1990s
Author:	T Champion, C Wong, A Rooke, D Dorling, M Coomes, C Brunsdon
Publisher:	Oxford University Press
Date:	October 1996
Town:	Oxford
Old ISBN:	ISBN 0-19-874175-8
New ISBN:	ISBN 978-0198741756
Pages:	155
Price:	£5.00

KIRKPAT, LAUNER

Title:	Made in Britain
Author:	James Fielding
Publisher:	Summersdale Publishers Limited
Date:	1 October 2007
Town:	Chichester
Old ISBN:	ISBN 1-84024-605-7
New ISBN:	ISBN 978-1840246056
Pages:	256
Price:	£6.59

NEWFOUND

Title:	Foster and Rastrick Foundry Public Consultation (leaflet)
Author:	West Midlands Historic Buildings Trust
Town:	Stourbridge
Pages:	2
Price:	£0.00

RECORDE

    Title: A History of Mathematics
    Author: Carl B Boyer
    Publisher: John Wiley and Sons
    Edition: International
    Date: 1968
    Town: New York
    Old ISBN: ISBN 0-471-09373-4
    New ISBN: ISBN 978-0471093732
    Pages: 717
    Price: £8.99

    Quotation from the "Whetstone of Witte" (1557) is on Page 297

SEAL

    Title: Fauna Britannica
    Author: Duff Hart-Davis
    Publisher: Weidenfeld Nicolson Illustrated
    Date: August 2002
    Town: London
    New ISBN: ISBN 978-0297825326
    Pages: 416
    Price: £19.99

    Title: Grey Seals
    Author: HR Hewer
    Publisher: The Sunday Times
    Date: 1962
    Town: London
    Pages: 25
    Price: 3s:6d

STAFFA

    Title: Staffa
    Author: Alastair De Watteville
    Publisher: Romsey Fine Art
    Date: July 1993
    Town: Romsey
    New ISBN: ISBN 978-0952151708
    Pages: 44
    Price: £5.95

TANKER
- Title: The Mines of Shropshire and Montgomeryshire with Cheshire and Staffordshire
- Author: R Burt, P Waite and R Burnley (Eds)
- Publisher: University of Exeter Press
- Date: September 1990
- Town: Exeter
- Old ISBN: ISBN 0-85989-343-X
- New ISBN: ISBN 978-0859893435
- Pages: 144
- Price: £8.40

List of Journal References

FAULD
- Paper: The Explosion Crater at Fauld
- Author: Tony Waltham
- Journal: Mercian Geologist
- Year: 2001
- Volume: 15
- Part: 2
- Pages: 123-125

POLITI
- Paper: Politi Turkish Delight Works
- Author: Richard Graham
- Journal: Greater London IA Society (Notes and News)
- Year: 37469

SCHIEHAL
- Paper: An Account of Observations made on the Mountain Schehallien for finding its Attraction
- Author: Nevil Maskelyne
- Journal: The Philosophical Transactions of The Royal Society
- Year: 1775
- Volume: 65
- Pages: 500-542

www.ingramcontent.com/pod-product-compliance
Lightning Source LLC
Chambersburg PA
CBHW050806220426
43209CB00088BA/1676